Victorian Theatricals

Sara Hudston is a writer and freelance journalist. She was born in 1968 and educated at St John's College, Oxford, where she gained a first in English. She has also published *Islomania*, a book about the fascination of islands. She lives in Dorset and is working on a novel.

VICTORIAN THEATRICALS

From menageries to melodrama

SARA HUDSTON

Methuen

Published by Methuen 2000

1 3 5 7 9 10 6 4 2

First published in 2000 by Methuen Publishing Ltd
215 Vauxhall Bridge Road, London SW1V 1EJ

Methuen Publishing Limited Reg. No. 3543167

A CIP catalogue record for this book
is available from the British Library

ISBN 0 413 74460 4

Typeset by Deltatype Ltd, Birkenhead, Merseyside
Printed and bound in Great Britain by
Creative Print and Design (Wales), Ebbw Vale

Contents

Introduction

Henry James found the London theatres of the late 1870s to be expensive and mediocre. Picking over what he regarded as a decayed institution, he formed 'the impression that the theatre in England is a social luxury and not an artistic necessity'. In a series of articles between 1877 and 1881 he criticised English actors, theatres and plays for the smallness of their capacities and ambitions. The audience too was attacked for being 'well-dressed, tranquil, motionless, it suggests domestic virtue and comfortable homes; . . . it looks as if it had come to the play in its own carriage, after a dinner of beef and pudding'. He complained that the audience members 'are much more naif than Parisian spectators – at least as regards being amused. They cry with much less facility, but they laugh more freely and heartily.' This laughter was distinguished by 'its deep-lunged jollity and its individual guffaws'.

What were these supposedly unintellectual, hearty, complacent audiences paying so much to see in those five years between 1877 and 1881? Three words – Gilbert and Sullivan – are still guaranteed to make the cultured groan. These were the years when Gilbert and Sullivan's first full-length comic operas burst upon the public. *The Sorcerer* premiered in 1877, followed by *HMS Pinafore* in 1878, *The Pirates of Penzance* in 1879 and *Patience* in 1881. When the public had enough of opera, there were always the romantic, drawing-room comedies of T.W. Robertson undergoing continuous revivals at the Prince of Wales and the Haymarket. In 1877 a new playwright, Arthur Wing Pinero, launched his prolific career with *£200 a Year* at the Globe. Though Pinero would later produce serious drama, his early work was sentimental farce. For the more serious-minded there were Henry Irving's productions of Shakespeare at the Lyceum, starting in 1878 with *Hamlet*.

From the picture that emerges so far, readers would be tempted to sympathise with Henry James. Silly, lightweight rubbish from Gilbert and Sullivan, piffling comedy from Robertson which was already old hat for its time, flim-flam from Pinero, or earnest, reverently 'realistic' productions of Shakespeare – the choice sums up the dire state of the Victorian theatre, blind to its faults and desperately in need of new artistic impetus. In 1880 Ibsen's *Pillars of Society* was not considered worthy of a full performance and was given a morning reading only at the Gaiety. It wasn't until the 1890s that the influence of Ibsen, Shaw and Wilde cleared the stage of its mid-Victorian lumber and revitalised the theatre's intellectual content, or so the theory goes. No wonder then that professionals nowadays seldom perform truly Victorian theatrical works, leaving them to amateur dramatic and operatic societies. Gilbert and Sullivan are unmentionable in cultured operatic circles and the plays which are revived tend to be Wilde's brittle 1890s comedies.

In the 1890s English theatre transformed itself, and in doing so it discarded many of its uniquely Victorian qualities. The purpose of this volume is to explore these lost qualities and to try to capture some of the character of Victorian theatre before it metamorphosed. For this reason, this edition of plays and extracts deliberately ignores the genius of Wilde and Shaw and stops at 1895, the year Henry Irving was knighted, Wilde sent to prison and the theatre became almost respectable. Drama might have become 'better' in the 1890s, that is more attractive to modern tastes, but something died in the process, something lively and curious, something peculiarly representative of a particular period in history.

This selection also omits the music hall, a decision that deserves explanation. Music halls were a distinct phenomenon that grew out of the rough entertainments laid on in taverns. They flourished from 1852 onwards and reached their apogee at the turn of the century, a period that lies beyond the chronological scope of this volume. There is a second reason for leaving them out. Mention Victorian theatre today and most people think only of the music hall. Readers have, understandably, rather lost sight of the breadth of Victorian popular entertainment. *Victorian Theatricals* is an attempt to bring some of the less well known aspects of the theatre back into the general public view.

Victorian theatre was anything but dull. Henry James criticised the reputable theatres but the raffish end of society, including Edward, the Prince of Wales, and the Duke of Cambridge, was also to be seen at the music halls where it was entertained with saucy songs and dances. And then there was pantomime and extravaganza, melodrama and burlesque, the ballet, plays starring horses or dogs, plays featuring human freaks, penny theatres – attended mostly by children – where the theatrical equivalents of video nasties were staged, all blood and murder. There was theatre performed in the tents and booths of travelling fairs where yokels could wonder at learned pigs or watch a re-enactment of *Turpin's Ride to York*. And there were menageries and beast shows displaying the riches of the British Empire. Theatre was not just a middle class or aristocratic cultural institution to be visited in a carriage for a few hours of an evening, it was a truly popular entertainment for all classes, urban and rural, an aspect of life which penetrated even the sacred domestic interior of respectable Victorian homes in the shape of amateur theatricals.

The only other literary art form to achieve comparable influence during the period was the novel. Unlike the theatre, the nineteenth-century novel was both popular and highly regarded, and has continued to be so. Intellectually, the century was dominated by the novel, and works by Dickens, Thackeray, Eliot and Hardy articulated and defined important social changes and ideas. This, after all, was a century of change, one which saw massive social, industrial and technological upheavals. The Industrial Revolution turned a country with a largely rural population into one where most people lived in cities. Work changed, transport changed, lives changed. Gaslight and, by the end of the period, electricity, ended the almost total reliance on natural light; railways and steamships opened up continents and bridged oceans. Between 1800 and 1900 the population of London alone quadrupled. Social unrest, especially during the years of Chartism in the 1830s and 1840s, raised the threat of public disorder, and keeping the peace at large gatherings such as boxing matches, fairs and public executions became problematic. Many of these irrepressible public events were theatrical in the most immediate sense, according perfectly with the dictionary definition of being extravagantly histrionic, stagy and calculated for display. More than this, their noisy reality often borrowed the tricks of the stage to attract attention. The theatre in its turn used reality in the shape of genuine props – objects that had been used in the real events depicted on stage – and increasingly convincing effects to validate its fantastical fancies.

Novels, however, were distanced from such vulgar immediacy. They were for reading quietly, isolated in the tranquillity of a parlour; they could be closed and put neatly away so that their elegant covers served to furnish the room. While nineteenth-century novelists enjoyed occupying the intellectual high ground, the best of them were also deeply envious of the theatre's protean capacity. Successful stage adaptations were written of Dickens' and Hardy's works, but not in general by Dickens or by Hardy, and often to the annoyance of the original authors. It was the lesser novelists who were the better dramatists. The flow of ideas and plots between novels and the stage was usually uni-directional, the equivalent of books and films nowadays. Occasionally the flow was channelled the other way and a successful play would be written up as a novel, as with Charles Reade and Tom Taylor's *Masks and Faces* (1852) which Reade turned into *Peg Woffington*, but this was hack-work done for money, not art. By the 1880s, theatre had been firmly relegated to the category of entertainment rather than literature, and by 1887 many agreed with the American critic William Winter that the theatre presented 'a complete avalanche of trash'.

In 1892 the divide between literature (as represented by the novel) and drama had become so distinct that the critic William Archer wrote a piece in the *Fortnightly Review* blaming novelists for the breach and urging a reunion. The *Pall Mall Gazette* entered the fray and asked leading novelists of the day to comment. Thomas Hardy took the bait and replied in a letter mixing evasion with crossness at the public taste, published on 31 August 1892. In Hardy's view, novels were by far the best means of bringing ideas before the public because:

> in general, the novel affords more scope for getting nearer to the heart and meaning of things than does the play as nowadays conditioned, when parts have to be moulded to actors, not actors to parts; when managers will not risk a truly original play; when scenes have to be arranged in a constrained and arbitrary fashion to suit the exigencies of scene-building, although spectators are absolutely indifferent to order and succession, provided they can have before them a developing

thread of interest. The reason of this arbitrary arrangement would seem to be that the presentation of human passions is subordinated to the presentation of mountains, cities, clothes, furniture, plate, jewels and other real and sham-real appurtenances, to the neglect of the principle that the material stage should be a conventional or figurative arena, in which accessories are kept down to the plane of mere suggestions of time or place so as not to interfere with the high-relief of the actions and emotions.

Hardy was writing on the cusp of theatrical change. His views were in tune with those of the modernisers and his criticisms hit at the heart of the Victorian theatre, where plays were often extravagantly staged with the intention of provoking sensation rather than thought. In answer to the question of whether he had ever wanted to write plays himself, Hardy added: 'Have occasionally had a desire to produce a play, and have, in fact, written the skeletons of several. Have no such desire in any special sense just now.' This defensively casual reply conceals 30 years of frustrated dramatic ambitions.

Less than a year after Hardy's letter to the *Pall Mall Gazette*, he was writing one play and sketching the scenario of another. One of these premiered in June 1893 as *The Three Wayfarers*. It flopped. Hardy's efforts to infiltrate the theatre preceded his career as a novelist, beginning in the 1860s when he was in his early twenties and living in London. During this time he attended the theatre frequently, going mostly to Shakespeare. In a bizarre attempt to learn more about the theatrical business he actually appeared on stage (for one night only) in a minor part in an 1866 production of *Ali-Baba and the Forty Thieves* at Covent Garden. His love of circuses and shows lasted all his life, and he attended two public hangings. He was friendly with Henry Irving and knew Mrs Patrick Campbell. But despite all his research, and his theatrical contacts, Hardy never managed to write a truly successful play or adaptation of his novels. Others had no difficulty: in 1882 there was a sharp exchange of letters with Pinero, whom Hardy accused of plagiarising *Far from the Madding Crowd* in his play *The Squire*.

Dickens too found the stage frustrating and fascinating. In his case its influence went far beyond the colourful sketches of theatrical life he wrote for *Nicholas Nickleby* and *Great Expectations*. He gave famously theatrical public readings from his works, and these events may be seen as an attempt to connect the private, interior world of the novel with the public dynamism of the theatre. Dickens enjoyed acting and, in accordance with middle-class taste, had a private theatre erected in his London home for the amusement of his friends and family. The first performances of some of Wilkie Collins' plays were staged here, the irony being that Collins had managed to do what Dickens could not and write popular novels as well as some well-received plays. He adapted his novel *The Woman in White* for the stage in 1871 and collaborated with Dickens on *No Thoroughfare* (1867). Dickens did not lack adaptors willing to convert his work for the theatre, and a huge number of adaptations were produced, many done by dramatists Edward Stirling and W.T. Moncrieff. There is evidence that Dickens collaborated with his most favoured dramatists passing them copies of his latest works in advance of their serialisation, partly as a defence against those hacks who would rush out their own versions. It was common for novels to be plagiarised for the stage, and Dickens attacked just such unauthorised adaptors in *Nicholas Nickleby*.

Dickens' relationship to the stage was more than show-off enthusiasm. It's easy to see why the chaotic world of the Victorian theatre appealed to him – its diversity of characters, its appetite for the grotesque, its overblown sentimentality, its excess energy, could all be described as typically Dickensian. This, however, is looking at the situation with hindsight. It may be more accurate to say that the most Dickensian aspects of Dickens' writing have theatrical origins. When it came to writing directly about the theatre, there was really nothing he could say that went beyond amusing reportage because every exaggeration, every ludicrous distortion could be matched in reality. Dickens was capable of creating superbly dramatic moments and unforgettable characters in his novels, but was somehow defeated by the stage.

Because the theatre had no literary reputation to keep up it was free to explore the devious backways of the Victorian mind. Although fashions came and went and presentations changed to suit the popular taste, the public's underlying appetite stayed the same. Audiences of all classes wanted to be diverted. Rich or poor, educated or ignorant, they wanted something odd, something new and startling. This was not solely a desire for sensation in itself but a symptom of a real hunger for knowledge that was part of the Victorian character in a scientific era that sent explorers out across the globe to expand the limits of human knowledge and increase the borders of the British Empire. The theatre had no time for the leisurely considerations of the novel, instead it grabbed at whatever was most immediately interesting, with an almost complete lack of artistic discrimination, to feed the appetites of its audience. Henry James was mistaken; in its most Victorian incarnation the theatre was a social necessity and not an artistic luxury.

Further Reading

Michael Booth, *English Plays of The Nineteenth Century* (5 vols, Oxford University Press, 1969–1976). Five volumes of plays with useful prefaces and some contemporary Victorian criticism.

Michael Booth, *Theatre in the Victorian Age* (Cambridge University Press, 1991).

Michael Booth (ed.), *The Revels History of Drama in English, vol. VI 1750–1880, vol. VII 1880 to present* (Methuen, 1975–83).

Henry James, *The Scenic Art, Notes on Acting And The Drama 1872–1901*, edited by Allan Wade (Rutgers University Press, 1948).

Michael Millgate, *Thomas Hardy, a biography* (Oxford University Press, 1982).

Allardyce Nicoll, *A History of English Drama*, vol. IV 1800–1850, vol. V 1850–1900 (Cambridge University Press, 1955).

George Rowell, *The Victorian Theatre: A Survey* (Oxford University Press, 1956).

George Rowell (ed.), *Victorian Dramatic Criticism* (Methuen, 1971). Selection of essays.

Adrienne Scullion (ed.), *Female Playwrights of the Nineteenth Century* (J. M. Dent, 1996). Redresses the balance slightly for women writers.

THEATRICAL BEHAVIOUR

1   MANSFIELD PARK

When Henry James moved from Paris to London in 1876 he entered a society possessed by theatrical mania. 'Plays and actors are perpetually talked about, private theatricals are incessant,' he grumbled.

> If you go to an evening party, nothing is more probable than that all of a sudden a young lady or a young gentleman will jump up and strike an attitude and begin to recite a poem or speech. Every pretext for this sort of exhibition is ardently cultivated and the London world is apparently filled with stage-struck young persons whose relatives are holding them back from a dramatic career.

James blamed this urban phenomenon on the countryside. Theatrical diversions flourished in drawing rooms across England and it was all because of the 'prevalence of country life, the existence of an enormous class of people who have nothing in the world to do'. Unimpressed by the general standard of performance both amateur and professional, James castigated professional actors for affecting the manner of gentlemanly amateurs. 'Clever people on the London stage today aim at a line of effect in which their being "amateurs" is almost a positive advantage. Small, realistic comedy is their chosen field.' He was appalled by the 'infantile' rubbish presented at fashionable theatres such as The Prince of Wales:

> The Prince of Wales is a little theatre, and the pieces produced there dealt mainly in little things – presupposing a great many chairs and tables, carpets, curtains, and knick knacks, and an audience placed close to the stage. They might, for the most part, have been written by a cleverish visitor at a country house, and acted in the drawing room by his fellow inmates.

Country drawing rooms imprisoning house parties of minor aristocracy, footling people with too much time on their hands and too little talent, unable to see the world beyond their own comfortable, domestic existence; these are James' targets rather than the rumbustious and diverse theatre of Victorian London. He couldn't leave this aspect of English life alone and wrote about it repeatedly, exhibiting simultaneous attraction and repulsion of the milieu he found himself penetrating in real life. As an American citizen, James was sensitive to his status as civilised outsider. His short story, *The Siege of London* (1883), about an American adventuress forcing herself into English society, explores his ambivalent position and is a fine piece of Jamesian oscillation, teetering between sympathy and condemnation. But James' journalistic remarks about the theatre amount to more than cultivated expatriate disgruntlement. Here he has identified a mode of behaviour, a cultural impulse, which permeated the leisure hours of educated society throughout the nineteenth century.

James' scorn for the little world of country house theatricals could be applied much earlier than the 1880s. In *Mansfield Park* (1814), Jane Austen, working at one of her famously miniaturised slices of life, invents exactly the kind of theatre and actors James would have despised. Her production of *Lovers' Vows* displays what Edmund Bertram deplores as 'the raw efforts of those who have not been bred to the trade, – a set of gentlemen and ladies, who have all the disadvantages of education and decorum to struggle through'. The plot at this point in the novel is simple; the two sons and two daughters of a baronet decide to amuse themselves in the absence of their father by putting on a play. Four friends make up the numbers: the Crawfords, a lively sister and brother staying nearby; Yates, a rather fast young man who is friendly with the baronet's eldest son; and Rushworth, a rich fool who is engaged to the baronet's eldest daughter Maria. There is also a timid cousin called Fanny Price who lives at Mansfield but refuses to take part in the play on grounds of propriety. She is the heroine.

The Mansfield Park theatricals have always posed a problem for readers and critics. It's well known that Austen herself took part in amateur plays and enjoyed going to the theatre, yet here similar revels are treated with moral disapproval so strong that it warps the characterisation of the good characters and makes them appear prissy. Readers caught in the novel's imaginative world find it difficult to sympathise with Fanny's feeble refusal to act, or to understand her nebulous fear of 'impropriety'. Despite valid thematic reasons for her conduct, reasons which are perfectly acceptable and straightforward on a mechanistic level, and a number of convincing arguments from critics which draw out hidden historical and political meanings, the honest reader is left feeling annoyed with Fanny. Why shouldn't Edmund propose to Miss Crawford and why shouldn't Maria chuck the dimwit Rushworth for the brilliant Henry? Why won't shy Fanny loosen up? The only answer provided by the narrator is that the Crawfords are superficial, morally suspect and don't have enough respect for religion. This will not do, especially as the narrator has a great deal of fun taking sly pokes at her characters' delusions. What is this terrible, corrupting power exercised by the theatre?

There may be a specific personal memory behind Austen's portrayal of the Mansfield theatricals. In *Jane Austen, A Family Record*, her descendents recount how Austen's cousin Eliza de Feuillide tried to get Phylly Walter to join a theatrical party held one Christmas at Austen's childhood home of Steventon. In a letter to Phylly written in December 1787, Eliza invites her to stay 'provided you could bring yourself to act, for My Aunt Austen declares "She has not room for any *idle young* people."' The letter admonishes: 'I will only allow myself to take notice of the strong reluctance You express to what You call *appearing in Publick*. I assure You our performance is to be by no means a publick one, since only a selected party of Friends will be present.' The inference is that Phylly refused to act for nebulous reasons of propriety and publicity, very like Fanny. Mrs Austen's brisk intolerance of idleness could almost be one of Mrs Norris's pointed criticisms of Fanny's inactivity. Coercion, unease, notions of decorum; all the things that trouble the Mansfield theatricals are hinted at in this letter. Austen turned 12 that December and had a minor part in the play. She would have been in the midst of everything and the right age to hear what went on without anybody taking much notice of her.

Whatever the social currents eddying around the Steventon party, the Mansfield theatricals sail straight into dangerous water. The production is guilty of committing an appalling crime, the worst thing that can happen in an Austen novel; the infliction of emotional pain and social disharmony. The house party fissures into individual-istic units, wrong pairings sure to bring further unhappiness both personal and social. What acting there is takes place off stage on a personal level when the characters pretend that their fictional roles are mere make-believe, hiding the fact that the rehearsals grant liberty for their true behaviour. Maria gets to embrace Henry Crawford even though she's engaged to another man, thus hurting Rushworth, and Edmund is allowed to propose to Mary Crawford even though he shouldn't because good little Fanny loves him.

Why does this happen? Edmund is initially opposed to the play; what makes him change his mind about acting? It is as if his conscience falls victim to the theatricals which intoxicate in a world where absolute sobriety is the ideal. This is true in both a literal and a metaphorical sense. Clear-headedness is the perfected state towards which all Austen heroines are propelled. Although wine is served at meals, and wine and water taken at bedtime, no-one ever gets drunk. People suffer instead from a variety of metaphorical intoxications from giddy silliness to pompous somnolence which makes them say and do risible things. The Mansfield theatricals inebriate the house guests, causing them to be emotionally demonstrative and impairing their judgement. In this feverish atmosphere the characters forget how they should behave. When Tom Bertram later seeks to excuse the episode to his father he blames Yates for bringing 'the infection' from another house. Only Fanny has kept her head, but what a trembling, anxious figure she cuts posed against the confident disorder of the theatre.

Fanny's trepidation should be treated seriously. Her beliefs are purely secular, adhering to conservative notions of propriety and decorum which value the group above the individual, yet here and throughout the novel her stance has a religious implication. This after all was intended to be a novel 'about ordination'. Fanny is posed against the evil of social calamity and the odds are she will be overwhelmed. With the theatricals, later on when the party visits Rushworth's house and lose touch with each other in the Wilderness – and later still when Henry Crawford tries to ensnare her – she is like Daniel in the lions' den; her weakness and purity threatened by evil vitality. The growing evangelical movement promoted passive femininity as a godly ideal and, by the Victorian era, Fanny's brand of anxious belief would have passed as a standard feminine virtue. The Victorians, however, made the conflict between purity and violation more sensational. Half a century after *Mansfield Park* was published Gerard Manley Hopkins took the fantasy to its extreme in *The Wreck of the Deutschland*, posing drowning nuns against ravening elemental forces to imagine the metaphorical meeting between 'Christ's lily and beast of the waste wood'.

'Beast' has a rather more ironical tone when applied to the libertine Henry Crawford. He is an insincere, shape-shifting flirt who excels at acting; an unstable character whose attention wanders. He preens and sparkles before the ladies; he is, in short, dangerously theatrical and great fun. Even Fanny enjoys his acting. Regency readers would have recognised his particular pattern of degeneracy. Private theatricals enjoyed a revival of interest at the end of the eighteenth century and theatres were constructed at several grand country houses including Chatsworth in Derbyshire, Wynnstay in Denbighshire and Wargrave in Berkshire. As the nineteenth century began, the new evangelical movement lost no time in condemning the stage and was keen to press home what the critic and scholar Marilyn Butler calls 'the link between upper-class immorality and its rage for private theatricals'.

In the nineteenth century the theatre exercised a power nowadays ceded to cinema and TV. The stage provided thrills and explanations, it indulged the pleasure-seeker and it gave comfort by offering emotion-based interpretations of human relations. In doing this it articulated desires which could seem wicked and drew on an unrefined energy which the high-minded found threatening. It suggested a fluidity of roles and characters for the most trivial of reasons – entertainment. It was naughty and spicy; the objection to the Mansfield play *Lovers' Vows* is that it is about sexual romance. The theatre was not to be taken seriously and certainly not copied in real life; that was the job of the novel. When the novel used the theatre it was usually as a means to express moral disapproval.

★

from MANSFIELD PARK
Jane Austen

CHAPTER XVIII

Everything was now in a regular train; theatre, actors, actresses, and dresses, were all getting forward: but though no other great impediments arose, Fanny found, before many days were past, that it was not all uninterrupted enjoyment to the party themselves, and that she had not to witness the continuance of such unanimity and delight, as had been almost too much for her at first. Everybody began to have their vexation. Edmund had many. Entirely against *his* judgment, a scene painter arrived from town, and was at work, much to the increase of the expenses, and what was worse, of the eclat of their proceedings; and his brother, instead of being really guided by him as to the privacy of the representation, was giving an invitation to every family who came in his way. Tom himself began to fret over the scene painter's slow progress, and to feel the miseries of waiting. He had learned his part – all his parts – for he took every trifling one that could be united with the Butler, and began to be impatient to be acting; and every day thus unemployed, was tending to increase his sense of the insignificance of all his parts together, and make him more ready to regret that some other play had not been chosen.

Fanny, being always a very courteous listener, and often the only listener at hand, came in for the complaints and distresses of most of them. *She* knew that Mr Yates was in general thought to rant dreadfully, that Mr Yates was disappointed in Henry Crawford, that Tom Bertram spoke so quick he would be unintelligible, that Mrs Grant spoilt everything by laughing, that Edmund was behind-hand with his part, and that it was misery to have any thing to do with Mr Rushworth, who was wanting a prompter through every speech. She knew, also, that poor Mr Rushworth could seldom get anybody to rehearse with him; *his* complaint came before her as well as the rest; and so decided to her eye was her cousin Maria's avoidance of him, and so needlessly often the rehearsal of the first scene between her and Mr Crawford, that she had soon all the terror of other complaints from *him*. – So far from being all satisfied and all enjoying, she found everybody requiring something they had not, and giving occasion of discontent to the others. – Everybody had a part either too long or too short; – nobody would attend as they ought, nobody would remember on which side they were to come in – nobody but the complainer would observe any directions.

Fanny believed herself to derive much innocent enjoyment from the play as any of them; – Henry Crawford acted well, and it was a pleasure to *her* to creep into the theatre, and attend the rehearsal of the first act – in spite of the feelings it excited in some speeches for Maria. – Maria she also thought acted well – too well; – and after the first rehearsal or two, Fanny began to be their only audience – and sometimes as prompter, sometimes as spectator – was often very useful. – As far as she could judge, Mr Crawford was considerably the best actor of all; he had more confidence than Edmund, more judgment than Tom, more talent and taste than Mr Yates. – She did not like him as a man, but she must admit him to be the best actor, and on this point there were not many who differed from her. Mr Yates, indeed, exclaimed against his tameness and insipidity – and the day came at last, when Mr Rushworth turned to her with a black look, and said – 'Do you think there is any thing so very fine in all this? For the life and soul of me, I cannot admire him; – and between ourselves, to see such an undersized, little, mean-looking man, set up for a fine actor, is very ridiculous in my opinion.'

From this moment there was a return of his former jealousy, which Maria, from increasing hopes of Crawford, was at little pains to remove; and the chances of Mr Rushworth's ever attaining to the knowledge of his two and forty speeches became much less. As to his ever making any thing *tolerable* of them, nobody had the smallest idea of that except his mother – *She*, indeed, regretted that his part was not more considerable, and deferred coming over to Mansfield till they were forward enough in their rehearsal to comprehend all his scenes, but the others aspired at nothing beyond his remembering the catchword, and the first line of his speech, and being able to follow the prompter through the rest. Fanny, in her pity and kind-heartedness, was at great pains to teach him how to learn, giving him all the helps and directions in her power, trying to make an artificial memory for him, and learning every word of his part herself, but without his being much the forwarder.

Many uncomfortable, anxious, apprehensive feelings she certainly had; but with all these, and other claims on her time and attention, she was as far from finding herself without employment or utility amongst them, as without a companion in uneasiness; quite as far from having no demand on her leisure as on her compassion. The gloom of her first anticipation was proved to have been unfounded. She was occasionally useful to all; she was perhaps as much at peace as any.

There was a great deal of needle-work to be done moreover, in which her help was wanted; and that Mrs Norris thought her quite as well off as the rest, was evident by the manner in which she claimed it: 'Come Fanny,' she cried, 'these are fine times for you, but you must not be always walking from one room to the other and doing the lookings on, at your ease, in this way, – I want you here. – I have been slaving myself till I can hardly stand, to contrive Mr Rushworth's cloak without sending for any more satin; and now I think you may give me your help in putting it together. – There are but three seams, you may do them in a trice. – It would be lucky for me if I had nothing but the executive part to do. – *You* are best off, I can tell you; but if nobody did more than *you*, we should not get on very fast.'

Fanny took the work very quietly, without attempting any defence; but her kinder aunt Bertram observed on her behalf,

'One cannot wonder, sister, that Fanny *should* be delighted; it is all new to her, you know, – you and I used to be very fond of a play ourselves – and so am I still; – and as soon as I am a little more at leisure, *I* mean to look in at their rehearsals too. What is the play about, Fanny, you have never told me?'

'Oh! sister, pray do not ask her now; for Fanny is not one of those who can talk and work at the same time. – It is about Lovers' Vows.'

'I believe,' said Fanny to her aunt Bertram, 'there will be three acts rehearsed to-morrow evening, and that will give you an opportunity of seeing all the actors at once.'

'You had better stay till the curtain is hung,' interposed Mrs Norris – 'the curtain will be hung in a day or two, – there is very little sense in a play without a curtain – and I am much mistaken if you do not find it draw up into very handsome festoons.'

Lady Bertram seemed quite resigned to waiting. – Fanny did not share her aunt's composure; she thought of the morrow a great deal, – for if the three acts were rehearsed, Edmund and Miss Crawford would then be acting together for the first time; – the third act would bring a scene between them which interested her most particularly, and which she was longing and dreading to see how they would perform. The whole subject of it was love – a marriage of love was to be described by the gentleman, and very little short of a declaration of love be made by the lady.

She had read, and read the scene again with many painful, many wondering emotions, and looked forward to their representation of it as a circumstance almost too interesting. She did not *believe* they had yet rehearsed it, even in private.

The morrow came, the plan for the evening continued, and Fanny's consideration of it did not become less agitated. She worked very diligently under her aunt's directions, but her diligence and her silence concealed a very absent, anxious mind; and about noon she made her escape with her work to the East room, that she might have no concern in another, and, as she deemed it, most unnecessary rehearsal of the first act, which Henry Crawford was just proposing, desirous at once of having her time to herself, and of avoiding the sight of Mr Rushworth. A glimpse, as she passed through the hall, of the two ladies walking up from the parsonage, made no change in her wish of retreat, and she worked and meditated in the East room, undisturbed, for a quarter of an hour, when a gentle tap at the door was followed by the entrance of Miss Crawford.

'Am I right? – Yes; this is the East room. My dear Miss Price, I beg your pardon, but I have made my way to you on purpose to entreat your help.'

Fanny, quite surprised, endeavoured to show herself mistress of the room by her civilities, and looked at the bright bars of her empty grate with concern.

'Thank you – I am quite warm, very warm. Allow me to stay here a little while, and do have the goodness to hear me my third act. I have brought my book, and if you would but rehearse it with me, I should be *so* obliged! I came here today intending to rehearse it with Edmund – by ourselves – against the evening, but he is not in the way; and if he *were*, I do not think I could go through it with *him*, till I have hardened myself a little, for really there *is* a speech or two – You will be so good, won't you?'

Fanny was most civil in her assurances, though she could not give them in a very steady voice.

'Have you ever happened to look at the part I mean?' continued Miss Crawford, opening her book. 'Here it is. I did not think much of it at first – but, upon my word – . There, look at *that* speech, and *that*, and *that*. How am I ever to look him in the face and say such things? Could you do it? But then he is your cousin, which makes all the difference. You must rehearse it with me, that I may fancy *you* him, and get on by degrees. You *have* a look of *his* sometimes.'

'Have I? – I will do my best with the greatest readiness – but I must *read* the part, for I can *say* very little of it.'

'*None* of it, I suppose. You are to have the book of course. Now for it. We must have two chairs at hand for you to bring forward to the front of the stage. There – very good school-room chairs, not made for a theatre, I dare say; much more fitted for little girls to sit and kick their feet against when they are learning a lesson. What would your governess and your uncle say to see them used for such a purpose? Could Sir Thomas look in upon us just now, he would bless himself, for we are rehearsing all over the house. Yates is storming away in the dining room. I heard him as I came up stairs, and the theatre is engaged of course by those indefatigable rehearsers, Agatha and Frederick. If *they* are not perfect, I *shall* be surprised. By the bye, I looked in upon them five minutes ago, and it happened to be exactly at one of the times when they were trying *not* to embrace, and Mr Rushworth was with me. I thought he began to look a little queer, so I turned it off as well as

I could, by whispering to him, "We shall have an excellent Agatha, there is something so *maternal* in her manner, so completely *maternal* in her voice and countenance." Was not that well done of me? He brightened up directly. Now for my soliloquy.'

She began, and Fanny joined in with all the modest feeling which the idea of representing Edmund was so strongly calculated to inspire; but with looks and voice so truly feminine, as to be no very good picture of a man. With such an Anhalt, however, Miss Crawford had courage enough, and they had got through half the scene, when a tap at the door brought a pause, and the entrance of Edmund the next moment, suspended it all.

Surprise, consciousness, and pleasure, appeared in each of the three on this unexpected meeting; and as Edmund was come on the very same business that had brought Miss Crawford, consciousness and pleasure were likely to be more than momentary in *them*. He too had his book, and was seeking Fanny, to ask her to rehearse with him, and help him to prepare for the evening, without knowing Miss Crawford to be in the house; and great was the joy and animation of being thus thrown together – of comparing schemes – and sympathising in praise of Fanny's kind offices.

She could not equal them in their warmth. *Her* spirits sank under the glow of theirs, and she felt herself becoming too nearly nothing to both, to have any comfort in having been sought by either. They must now rehearse together. Edmund proposed, urged, entreated it – till the lady, not very unwilling at first, could refuse no longer – and Fanny was wanted only to prompt and observe them. She was invested, indeed, with the office of judge and critic, and earnestly desired to exercise it and tell them all their faults; but from doing so every feeling within her shrank, she could not, would not, dared not attempt it; had she been otherwise qualified for criticism, her conscience must have restrained her from venturing at disapprobation. She believed herself to feel too much of it in the aggregate for honesty or safety in particulars. To prompt them must be enough for her; and it was sometimes *more* than enough; for she could not always pay attention to the book. In watching them she forgot herself; and agitated by the increasing spirit of Edmund's manner, had once closed the page and turned away exactly as he wanted help. It was imputed to very reasonable weariness, and she was thanked and pitied; but she deserved their pity, more than she hoped they would ever surmise. At last the scene was over, and Fanny forced herself to add her praise to the compliments each was giving the other; and when again alone and able to recall the whole, she was inclined to believe their performance would, indeed, have such nature and feeling in it, as must ensure their credit, and make it a very suffering exhibition to herself. Whatever might be its effect, however, she must stand the brunt of it again that very day.

The first regular rehearsal of the three first acts was certainly to take place in the evening; Mrs Grant and the Crawfords were engaged to return for that purpose as soon as they could after dinner; and every one concerned was looking forward with eagerness. There seemed a general diffusion of cheerfulness on the occasion; Tom was enjoying such an advance towards the end, Edmund was in spirits from the morning's rehearsal, and little vexations seemed everywhere smoothed away. All were alert and impatient; the ladies moved soon, the gentlemen soon followed them, and with the exception of Lady Bertram, Mrs Norris, and Julia, everybody was in the theatre at an early hour, and having lighted it up as well as its unfinished state admitted, were waiting only the arrival of Mrs Grant and the Crawfords to begin.

They did not wait long for the Crawfords, but there was no Mrs Grant. She could not come. Dr Grant, professing an indisposition, for which he had little credit with his fair sister-in-law, could not spare his wife.

'Dr Grant is ill,' said she, with mock solemnity. 'He has been ill ever since; he did not eat any of the pheasant to day. He fancied it tough – sent away his plate – and has been suffering ever since.'

Here was disappointment! Mrs Grant's non-attendance was sad indeed. Her pleasant manners and cheerful conformity made her always valuable amongst them – but *now* she was absolutely necessary. They could not act, they could not rehearse with any satisfaction without her. The comfort of the whole evening was destroyed. What was to be done? Tom, as Cottager, was in despair. After a pause of perplexity, some eyes began to be turned towards Fanny, and a voice or two, to say, 'If Miss Price would be so good as to *read* the part.' She was immediately surrounded by supplications, everybody asked it, even Edmund said, 'Do Fanny, if it is not *very* disagreeable to you.'

But Fanny still hung back. She could not endure the idea of it. Why was not Miss Crawford to be applied to as well? Or why had not she rather gone to her own room, as she had felt to be safest, instead of attending the rehearsal at all? She had known it would irritate and distress her – she had known it her duty to keep away. She was properly punished.

'You have only to *read* the part,' said Henry Crawford, with renewed entreaty.

'And I do believe she can say every word of it,' added Maria, 'for she could put Mrs Grant right the other day in twenty places. Fanny, I am sure you know the part.'

Fanny could not say she did *not* – and as they all persevered – as Edmund repeated his wish, and with a look of even fond dependence on her good nature, she must yield. She would do her best. Everybody was satisfied – and she was left to the tremors of a most palpitating heart, while the others prepared to begin.

They *did* begin – and being too much engaged in their own noise, to be struck by an unusual noise in the other part of the house, had proceeded some way, when the door of the room was thrown open, and Julia appearing at it, with a face all aghast, exclaimed, 'My father is come! He is in the hall at this moment.'

2 VANITY FAIR

The Victorians' liking for outlandish clothes went beyond their excessive fashions; waist-crushing corsets, men's wing collars and the bustle. Henry Cyril Paget, 5th Marquis of Anglesey (1875–1905) was a notoriously decadent poseur whose love of dressing up and prancing about in costume earned him the nickname of 'The Dancing Marquess'. Paget converted the chapel at his home of Plas Newydd into a theatre where he staged lavish productions with himself in the lead role. Photographs from the 1890s show him looking like a bizarre flash-forward to a 1960s rock god. His end-of-century capers appear totally alien to the moral agonising of *Mansfield Park*, but there is a traceable line of descent. In his book *The Naughty Nineties*, Angus Wilson made a case for Regency raffishness having survived Victorian disapproval to emerge revived in the 1890s. Wilson argued: 'The aristocratic rake and his middle-class hangers-on continued their way of life right through the Victorian age only truly to come to the surface again in the nineties. They can be glimpsed again and again in the novels of Thackeray and Dickens.' Wilson's conception of the Regency as a brutal time of fist fights and whoring is a truth which Jane Austen elides in her sketches of young men with fast gigs and easy manners. Austen's fictional world is so restrained because the reality was often so coarse. She had only to hint at an impropriety to remind her readers of the full-blooded truth.

Private theatricals could be shamelessly titillating. One particularly saucy form of entertainment began in Georgian times as a private aristocratic amusement and spread downwards in the Victorian era to become a popular feature of disreputable theatres, music halls and taverns. 'Poses plastiques' or tableaux vivants were introduced to England in their most pretentious form by Lady Emma Hamilton (1761–1815), lover of Admiral Lord Nelson. Within the confines of various drawing rooms, Emma Hamilton would assume the attire and poses of famous statues and pictures, usually lightly clad. The best 24 of these were drawn and published in a volume of engravings by the satirical cartoonist Frederick Rehberg. In a savage cartoon of 1791 entitled 'Lady H . . . Poses', the caricaturist Thomas Rowland-son suggested that her modelling was little more than a sex show. In the same year that the Steventon theatricals agitated Phylly Water's conscience, Goethe witnessed one of Hamilton's remarkable dis-plays. He recorded the experience in *Italian Journey* (published 1816–17). In a letter from Naples dated 16 March 1787 he described Emma as:

> an English girl of twenty with a beautiful face and perfect figure. He [Sir William Hamilton] has had a Greek costume made for her which becomes her extremely. Dressed in this, she lets down her hair and, with a few shawls, gives so much variety to her poses, gestures, expressions, etc., that the spectator can hardly believe his eyes. He sees what thousands of artists would have liked to express realized before him in movements and surprising transformations – standing, kneel-ing, sitting, reclining, serious, sad, playful, ecstatic, contrite, alluring, threatening, anxious, one pose follows another without a break. She knows how to arrange the folds of her veil to match each mood, and has a hundred ways of turning it into a head-dress. The old knight idolizes her and is enthusiastic about everything she does.

Goethe was wrong in his estimation of Emma Hamilton's age – she was nearer 30 than 20. His mistake testifies to the success of her art. She still beguiled 13 years later at the age of nearly 40 when she posed, eight months pregnant, at a Christmas party held in Fonthill Abbey. Her appearance at William Beckford's ill-fated Gothic folly on 23 December 1800 made a suitably theatrical opening to the new century. Hamilton, who was accompanied by both her aged husband and by Nelson, the father of her unborn child, chose a classical theme for her performance. In a piece of outrageous bad taste she represented the loyal wife Agrippina presenting the ashes of her murdered husband to the people of Rome. No one seems to have minded the irony and *The Gentleman's Magazine* reported that she drew tears of compassion from the company.

Hamilton's rise in society from obscure nurserymaid to titled lady and companion to England's hero was facilitated by her theatrical gifts. In her teens she acted in amateur theatricals staged by her employers and for a time she was the chief attraction at London's notorious Temple of Health, a brothel disguised as a pseudo-scientific health spa whose central stage was the magneto-electric Celestial Bed. For £50 a night, childless couples could make love on a mattress stuffed with hair from the tails of English stallions, and after coition the bed would tilt 'to aid conception'. Both Hamilton's spectacular rise and her remarkable performance at Fonthill find their literary paradigm in Becky Sharp of Thackeray's *Vanity Fair*. Written and published in monthly numbers between January 1847 and July 1848, *Vanity Fair* is a historical novel set in the Georgian/Regency period. It is also a novel about shameless social ambition on a scale which makes even Austen's most marriage-hungry characters seem like genteel underachievers. Becky Sharp, the daughter of a none too reputable French dancer, insinuates herself into society by acting a part; she is perhaps the greatest actress in English fiction and it is her bravura performance which animates the novel.

Vanity Fair is explicitly theatrical in theme and effect. The very title alludes to the jostling, variegated spectacle of theatre in its oldest and most popular form. Thackeray's 1848 preface 'Before the Curtain' sets out his stall.

> There is a great quantity of eating and drinking, making love and jilting, laughing and the contrary, smoking, cheating, fighting, dancing, and fiddling: there are bullies pushing about, bucks ogling the women, knaves picking pockets, policemen on the look-out, quacks (*other* quacks, plague take them!) bawling in front of their booths, and yokels looking up at the tinselled dancers and poor rouged tumblers, while the light-fingered folk are operating on their pockets behind.

None of this is particularly original. Thackeray's rather self-mocking preface echoes Wordsworth's picture of Bartholomew Fair in Book VIII of *The Prelude* (1805).

> All freaks of Nature, all Promethean thoughts
> Of man; his dulness, madness, and their feats,
> All jumbled up together to make up
> This Parliament of Monsters. Tents and Booths
> Meanwhile, as if the whole were one vast Mill,

Are vomiting, receiving, on all sides,
Men, Women, three-years' Children, Babes in arms.

Oh, blank confusion! and a type not false
Of what the mighty City is itself . . .

It is fitting that the pinnacle of Becky's social triumph is an
evening of charades, which she arranges and performs with the
greatest *élan*. Becky's life has been a series of calculated impersona-
tions, and the charades offer an ironic commentary on her
performance so far. Like Emma Hamilton at Fonthill, she gets away
with murder – literally in this case since she chooses to portray the
husband-killing Clytemnestra. Thackeray is of course making a
moral point. It is a measure of the vanity and corruption of high
society that it chooses to indulge in such self-aggrandising activities.
In contrast to *Mansfield Park*, nobody in this novel seems at all
concerned with the possible impropriety of proceedings.

Is the theatricalism of *Vanity Fair* anything more than a handy,
somewhat obvious fictional trope? In his preface, Thackeray casts
himself as a puppet-master, manipulating his show for the goggling
masses, and sells the novel on the promise of entertainment. In
effect, he makes a bargain with the reader; I provide colourful life
and in return you submit to my authority as narrator, otherwise you
could be lost and misled. This relationship works well until the
question of Becky's sexual conduct becomes too pressing and
Thackeray ticks off the reader for wanting to see behind the curtain,
or as he puts it, below the waterline and glimpse his siren's 'hideous
tail'. He hints at, but refuses to tell, what she's actually been doing
with her gentlemen friends. This is his show and the audience will
see only what he chooses to display.

★

from VANITY FAIR
William Makepeace Thackeray

from CHAPTER 51
In which a charade is acted which may or may not puzzle the reader

At the time whereof we are writing, though the Great George was on the throne and ladies wore *gigots* and large combs like tortoise-shell shovels in their hair, instead of the simple sleeves and lovely wreaths which are actually in fashion, the manners of the very polite world were not, I take it, essentially different from those of the present day: and their amusements pretty similar. To us, from outside gazing over the policemen's shoulders at the bewildering beauties as they pass into Court or ball, they may seem beings of unearthly splendour, and in the enjoyment of an exquisite happiness by us unattainable. It is to console some of these dissatisfied beings, that we are narrating our dear Becky's struggles, and triumphs, and disappointments, of all of which, indeed, as is the case with all persons of merit, she had her share.

At this time the amiable amusement of acting charades had come among us from France: and were considerably in vogue in this country, enabling the many ladies amongst us who had beauty to display their charms, and the fewer number who had cleverness, to exhibit their wit. My Lord Steyne was incited by Becky, who perhaps believed herself endowed with both the above qualifications, to give an entertainment at Gaunt House, which should include some of these little dramas – and we must take leave to introduce the reader to this brilliant *réunion*, and, with a melancholy welcome too, for it will be among the very last of the fashionable entertainments to which it will be our fortune to conduct him.

A portion of that splendid room, the picture-gallery of Gaunt House, was arranged as the charade theatre. It had been so used when George III was king; and a picture of the Marquis of Gaunt is still extant, with his hair in powder and a pink ribbon, in a Roman shape, as it was called, enacting the part of Cato in Mr Addison's tragedy of that name, performed before their Royal Highnesses the Prince of Wales, the Bishop of Osnaburgh, and Prince William Henry, then children like the actor. One or two of the old properties were drawn out of the garrets, where they had lain ever since, and furbished up anew for the present festivities.

Young Bedwin Sands, then an elegant dandy and Eastern traveller, was manager of the revels. An Eastern traveller was somebody in those days, and the adventurous Bedwin, who had published his quarto, and passed some months under the tents in the desert, was a personage of no small importance. – In his volume there were several pictures of Sands in various oriental costumes; and he travelled about with a black attendant of most unprepossessing appearance, just like another Brian de Bois Guilbert. Bedwin, his costumes, and black man, were hailed at Gaunt House as very valuable acquisitions.

He led off the first charade. A Turkish officer with an immense plume of feathers (the Janizzaries were supposed to be still in existence, and the tarboosh had not as yet displaced the ancient and majestic head-dress of the true believers) was seen couched on a divan, and making believe to puff at a narghilé, in which, however, for the sake of the ladies, only a fragrant pastille was allowed to smoke. The Turkish dignitary yawns and expresses signs of weariness and idleness. He claps his hands and Mesrour the Nubian appears, with bare arms, bangles, yataghans, and every eastern ornament – gaunt, tall, and hideous. He makes a salaam before my lord the Aga.

A thrill of terror and delight runs through the assembly. The ladies whisper to one another. The black slave was given to Bedwin Sands by an Egyptian Pasha in exchange for three dozen of Maraschino. He has sown up ever so many odalisques in sacks and tilted them into the Nile.

'Bid the slave-merchant enter,' says the Turkish voluptuary, with a wave of his hand. Mesrour conducts the slave-merchant into my lord's presence: he brings a veiled female with him. He removes her veil. A thrill of applause bursts through the house. It is Mrs Winkworth (she was a Miss Absolom) with the beautiful eyes and hair. She is in a gorgeous oriental costume; the black braided locks are twined with unnumerable jewels; her dress is covered over with gold piastres. The odious Mahometan expresses himself charmed by her beauty. She falls down on her knees, and entreats him to restore her to the mountains where she was born, and where her Circassian lover is still deploring the absence of his Zuleikah. No entreaties will move the obdurate Hassan. He laughs at the notion of the Circassian bridegroom. Zuleikah covers her face with her hands, and drops down in an attitude of the most beautiful despair. There seems to be no hope for her, when – when the Kislar Aga appears.

The Kislar Aga brings a letter from the Sultan. Hassan receives and places on his head the dread firman. A ghastly terror seizes him, while on the negro's face (it is Mesrour again in another costume) appears a ghastly joy. 'Mercy! mercy!' cries the Pasha; while the Kislar Aga, grinning horribly, pulls out – *a bow-string*.

The curtain draws just as he is going to use that awful weapon. Hassan from within bawls out, 'First two syllables' – and Mrs Rawdon Crawley, who is going to act in the charade, comes forward and compliments Mrs Winkworth on the admirable taste and beauty of her costume.

The second part of the charade takes place. It is still an eastern scene. Hassan, in another dress, is in an attitude by Zuleikah, who is perfectly reconciled to him. The Kislar Aga has become a peaceful black slave. It is sunrise on the desert, and the Turks turn their heads eastward and bow to the sand. As there are no dromedaries at hand, the band facetiously plays the 'The Camels are coming.' An enormous Egyptian head figures in the scene. It is a musical one, – and, to the surprise of the oriental travellers, sings a comic song, composed by Mr Wagg. The eastern voyagers go off dancing, like Papageno and the Moorish King, in the Magie Flute. 'Last two syllables' roars the head.

The last act opens. It is a Grecian tent this time. A tall and stalwart man reposes in a couch there. Above him hang his helmet and shield. There is no need for them now. Ilium is down. Iphigenia is slain. Cassandra is a prisoner in his outer halls. The king of men (it is Colonel Crawley, who, indeed, has no notion about the sack of Ilium or the conquest of Cassandra), the anax andrôn is asleep in his chamber at Argos. A lamp casts the broad shadow of the sleeping warrior flickering on the wall – the sword and shield of Troy glitter in its light. The band plays the awful music of Don Juan, before the statue enters.

Ægisthus steals in pale and on tiptoe. What is that ghastly face looking out balefully after him from behind the arras? He raises his dagger to strike the sleeper, who turns in his bed, and opens his broad chest as if for the blow. He cannot strike the noble slumbering chieftain. Clytemnestra glides swiftly into the room like an apparition – her arms are bare and white, – her tawny hair floats down her shoulders, – her face is deadly pale, – and her eyes are lighted up with a smile so ghastly, that people quake as they look at her.

A tremor ran through the room. 'Good God!' somebody said, 'it's Mrs Rawdon Crawley.'

Scornfully she snatches the dagger out of Ægisthus's hand, and advances to the bed. You see it shining over her head in the glimmer of the lamp, and – and the lamp goes out, with a groan, and all is dark.

The darkness and the scene frightened people. Rebecca performed the part so well, and with such ghastly truth, that the spectators were all dumb, until, with a burst, all the lamps of the hall blazed out again, when everybody began to shout applause. 'Brava! brava!' old Steyne's strident voice was heard roaring over all the rest. 'By —, she'd do it too,' he said between his teeth. The performers were called by the whole house, which sounded with cries of 'Manager! Clytemnestra!' Agamemnon could not be got to show in his classical tunic, but stood in the background with

Ægisthus and others of the performers of the little play. Mr Bedwin Sands led on Zuleikah and Clytemnestra. A great personage insisted upon being presented to the charming Clytemnestra. 'Heigh ha? Run him through the body. Marry somebody else, hay?' was the apposite remark made by his Royal Highness.

'Mrs Rawdon Crawley was quite killing in the part,' said Lord Steyne. Becky laughed; gay, and saucy looking, and swept the prettiest little curtsey ever seen.

Servants brought in salvers covered with numerous cool dainties, and the performers disappeared, to get ready for the second charade-tableau.

The three syllables of this charade were to be depicted in pantomime, and the performance took place in the following wise:–

First syllable. Colonel Rawdon Crawley, C.B., with a slouched hat and staff, a great coat, and a lantern borrowed from the stable, passed across the stage bawling out, as if warning the inhabitants of the hour. In the lower window are seen two bagmen playing apparently at the game of cribbage, over which they yawn much. To them enters one looking like Boots, (the Honourable G. Ringwood,) which character the young gentleman performed to perfection, and divests them of their lowering covering; and presently Chambermaid (the Right Honourable Lord Southdown) with two candlesticks, and a warming-pan. She ascends to the upper apartment, and warms the bed. She uses the warming-pan as a weapon wherewith she wards off the attention of the bagmen. She exits. They put on their night-caps, and pull down the blinds. Boots comes out and closes the shutters of the ground-floor chamber. You hear him bolting and chaining the door within. All the lights go out. The music plays Dormez, dormez chers Amours. A voice from behind the curtain says, 'First syllable.'

Second syllable. The lamps are lighted up all of a sudden. The music plays the old air from John of Paris, Ah quel plaisir d'être en voyage. It is the same scene. Between the first and second floors of the house represented, you behold a sign on which the Steyne arms are painted. All the bells are ringing all over the house. In the lower apartment you see a man with a long slip of paper presenting it to another, who shakes his fist, threatens and vows that it is monstrous. 'Ostler, bring round my gig,' cries another at the door. He chucks Chambermaid (the Right Honourable Lord Southdown) under the chin; she seems to deplore his absence, as Calypso did that of that other eminent traveller Ulysses. Boots (the Honourable G. Ringwood) passes with a wooden box, containing silver flagons, and cries 'Pots' with such exquisite humour and naturalness, that the whole house rings with applause, and a bouquet is thrown to him. Crack, crack, crack, go the whips. Landlord, chambermaid, waiter rush to the door; but just as some distinguished guest is arriving, the curtains close, and the invisible theatrical manager cries out 'Second syllable.'

'I think it must be: "Hotel," ' says Captain Grigg of the Life Guards; there is a general laugh at the Captain's cleverness. He is not very far from the mark.

While the third syllable is in preparation, the band begins a nautical medley – All in the Downs, Cease Rude Boreas, Rule Britannia, In the Bay of Biscay O – some maritime event is about to take place. A bell is heard ringing as the curtain draws aside. 'Now, gents, for the shore!' a voice exclaims. People take leave of each other. They point anxiously as if towards the clouds, which are represented by a dark curtain, and they nod their heads in fear. Lady Squeams (the Right Honourable Lord Southdown), her lap-dog, her bags, reticules, and husband sit down, and cling hold of some ropes. It is evidently a ship.

The Captain (Colonel Crawley, C.B.), with a cocked hat and a telescope, comes in, holding his hat on his head, and looks out; his coat tails fly about as if in the wind. When he leaves go of his hat to use his telescope, his hat flies off, with immense applause. It is blowing fresh. The music rises and whistles louder and louder; the mariners go across the stage staggering, as if the ship was in severe motion. The Steward (the Honourable G. Ringwood) passes reeling by, holding six basins. He puts one rapidly by Lord Squeams – Lady Squeams giving a pinch to her dog, which begins to howl piteously, puts her pocket-handkerchief to her face and rushes away as for the cabin. The music rises up to the wildest pitch of stormy excitement, and the third syllable is concluded.

There was a little ballet, Le Rossignol, in which Montessu and Noblet used to be famous in those days, and which Mr Wagg transferred to the English stage as an opera, putting his verse, of which he was a skilful writer, to the pretty airs of the ballet. It was dressed in old French costume, and little Lord Southdown now appeared admirably attired in the disguise of an old woman hobbling about the stage with a faultless crooked stick.

Trills of melody were heard behind the scenes, and gurgling from a sweet pasteboard cottage covered with roses and trellis work. 'Philomèle, Philomèle,' cries the old woman, and Philomèle comes out.

More applause – it is Mrs Rawdon Crawley in powder and patches, the most *ravissante* little Marquise in the world.

She comes in laughing, humming, and frisks about the stage with all the innocence of theatrical youth – she makes a curtsey. Mamma says 'Why, child, you are always laughing and singing,' and away she goes, with –

THE ROSE UPON MY BALCONY

The rose upon my balcony the morning air perfuming.
Was leafless all the winter time and pining for the spring;
You ask me why her breath is sweet and why her cheek is blooming
It is because the sun is out and birds begin to sing.

The nightingale, whose melody is through the greenwood ringing,
Was silent when the boughs were bare and winds were blowing keen:
And if, Mamma, you ask of me the reason of his singing;
It is because the sun is out and all the leaves are green.

Thus each performs his part, Mamma, the birds have found their voices,
The blowing rose a flush, Mamma, her bonny cheek to dye;
And there's sunshine in my heart, Mamma, which wakens and rejoices,
And so I sing and blush, Mamma, and that's the reason why.

During the intervals of the stanzas of this ditty, the good-natured personage addressed as mamma by the singer, and whose large whiskers appeared under her cap, seemed very anxious to exhibit her maternal affection by embracing the innocent creature who performed the daughter's part. Every caress was received with loud acclamations of laughter by the sympathising audience. At its conclusion (while the music was performing a symphony as if ever so many birds were warbling) the whole house was unanimous for an *encore*: and applause and bouquets without end were showered upon the NIGHTINGALE of the evening. Lord Steyne's voice of applause was loudest of all. Becky, the nightingale, took the flowers which he threw to her, and pressed them to her heart with the air of a consummate comedian. Lord Steyne was frantic with delight. His guests' enthusiasm harmonised with his own. Where was the beautiful black-eyed Houri whose appearance in the first charade had caused such delight. She was twice as handsome as Becky, but the brilliancy of the latter had quite eclipsed her. All voices were for her. Stephens, Caradori, Ronzi de Begnis, people compared her to one or the other, and agreed with good reason, very likely, that had she been an actress none on the stage could have surpassed her. She had reached her culmination: her voice rose trilling and bright over the storm of applause: and soared as high and joyful as her triumph. There was a ball after the dramatic entertainments, and everybody pressed round as the great point of attraction of the evening. The Royal Personage declared with an oath, that she was perfection, and engaged her again and again in conversation. Little Becky's soul swelled with pride and delight at these honours; she saw fortune, fame, fashion before her. Lord Steyne was her slave; followed her everywhere, and scarcely spoke to any one in the room beside; and paid her the most marked compliments and attention. She still appeared in her Marquise costume, and danced a minuet with Monsieur de Truffigny, Monseieur Le Duc de la Jabotière's attaché; and the Duke, who had all the traditions of the ancient court, pronounced that Madame Crawley was worthy to have been a pupil of Vestris, or to have figured at Versailles. Only a feeling of dignity, the gout, and the strongest sense of duty and personal sacrifice, prevented his Excellency from dancing with her himself; and he declared in public, that a lady who could talk and dance like Mrs Rawdon, was fit to be ambassadress at any court in Europe. He was only consoled when he heard that she was half a Frenchwoman by birth. 'None but a compatriot,' his Excellency declared, 'could have performed that majestic dance in such a way.'

Then she figured in a waltz with Monsieur de Klingenspohr, the Prince of Peterwaradin's cousin and attaché. The delighted Prince, having less *retenue* than his French diplomatic colleague, insisted upon taking a turn with the charming creature, and twirled round the ball-room with her, scattering the diamond out of his boot-tassels and hussar jacket until his highness was fairly out of breath. Papoosh Pasha himself would have liked to dance with her if that amusement had been the custom of his country. The company made a circle round her, and applauded as wildly as if she had been a Noblet or a Taglioni. Everybody was in ecstasy; and Becky too, you may be sure. She passed by Lady Stunnington with a look of scorn. She patronised Lady Gaunt and her astonished and mortified sister-in-law – she *écraséd* all rival charmers. As for poor Mrs Winkworth, and her long hair and great eyes, which had made such an effect at the commencement of the evening; where was she now? Nowhere in the race. She might tear her long hair and cry her great eyes out; but there was not a person to heed or to deplore the discomfiture.

The greatest triumph of all was at supper time. She was placed at the grand exclusive table with his Royal Highness the exalted personage before-mentioned, and the rest of the great guests. She was served on gold plate. She might have had pearls melted into her champagne if she liked – another Cleopatra; and the potentate of Peterwaradin would have given half the brilliants off his jacket for a kind of glance from those dazzling eyes. Jabotière wrote home about her to his government. The ladies at the other tables who supped off mere silver, and marked Lord Steyne's constant attention to her, vowed it was a monstrous infatuation, a gross insult to ladies of rank. If sarcasm could have killed, Lady Stunnington would have slain her on the spot.

Rawdon Crawley was scared at these triumphs. They seemed to separate his wife farther than ever from him somehow. He thought with a feeling very like pain how immeasurably she was his superior.

When the hour of departure came, a crowd of young men followed her to her carriage, for which the people without bawled, the cry being caught up by the link-men who were stationed outside the tall gates of Gaunt House, congratulating each person, who issued from the gate and hoping his Lordship had enjoyed this noble party.

Mrs Rawdon Crawley's carriage, coming up to the gate after due shouting, rattled into the illuminated court-yard, and drove up to the covered way. Rawdon put his wife into the carriage, which drove off. Mr Wenham had proposed to him to walk home, and offered the Colonel the refreshment of a cigar.

They lighted their cigars by the lamp of one of the many link-boys outside, and Rawdon walked on with his friend Wenham. Two persons separated from the crowd and followed the two gentlemen; and when they had walked down Gaunt Square a few score of paces, one of the men came up, and touching Rawdon on the shoulder, said, 'Beg your pardon, Colonel, I vish to speak to you most particular.' The gentleman's acquaintance gave a loud whistle as the latter spoke, at which signal a cab came clattering up from those stationed at the gate of Gaunt House – and the aide-de-camp ran round and placed himself in front of Colonel Crawley.

That gallant officer at once knew what had befallen him. He was in the hands of the bailiffs. He started back, falling against the man who had first touched him.

'We're three on us – it's no use bolting,' the man behind said.

'It's you, Moss, is it?' said the Colonel, who appeared to know his interlocutor. 'How much is it?'

'Only a small thing,' whispered Mr Moss, of Cursitor Street, Chancery Lane, and assistant officer to the Sheriff of Middlesex – 'One hundred and sixty-six, six and eightpence, at the suit of Mr Nathan.'

'Lend me a hundred, Wenham, for God's sake,' poor Rawdon said – 'I've got seventy at home.'

'I've not got ten pounds in the world,' said poor Mr Wenham – 'Good night, my dear fellow.'

'Good night,' said Rawdon ruefully. And Wenham walked away – and Rawdon Crawley finished his cigar as the cab drove under Temple Bar.

3 ACTING PROVERBS

Drawing-room theatricals soon became standard home entertainment for the respectable middle classes and charades came to be regarded as tame, even somewhat passé. In 1858 Routledge published a new volume of playlets intended for home production. *Acting Proverbs; or, Drawing Room Theatricals* were part of the Cheap Literature series and appeared alongside the stirring novels of Captain Marryat and James Fenimore Cooper. The series incorporated The Useful Library, whose titles included *Things Worth Knowing, Home Book of Household Economy, Lives of Good Servants* and *Rats, with Anecdotes*. This was literature with a practical purpose to instruct as it entertained. The preface to *Acting Proverbs* is worth quoting in full.

It is our pleasing office to present a new friend to the public, under the name of *Acting Proverbs* – a name soon destined, we trust, to be associated with mirth and amusement in many drawing-room circles, and around many hearths. *Acting Charades*, which are members of the same family, have long been deservedly popular, and have agreeably beguiled many a long evening at the genial season of Christmas. But *Acting Proverbs* constitute a fresh, though kindred pastime, and besides the merit of novelty, possess advantages of their own. It is no easy matter to select a good word for charades, which shall not have been already hackneyed by previous use; in consequence of which, a great deal of repetition necessarily takes place, and the enigma is often known to half the audience before the first syllable is played out. *Acting Proverbs* are free from these drawbacks: they are familiar to us all, from the youngest to the oldest; they are full of homely truth, of wholesome application, and of racy humour. An 'acting proverb' is not circumscribed by adherence to syllables, takes a wide range, and will furnish novel employment for the divining powers of a friendly audience. Those proverbs which the author has selected are all well known, and thoroughly English. They have been illustrated with care, to elucidate a healthy moral along with such food for mirth and merriment as they may contain. Each piece is expressly intended for the drawing-room, for a drawing-room audience, drawing-room scenes and drawing-room performers. The curtain is now raised, the overture at an end, and the *débutante* is presented to the public. It is time for the manager to make his bow, and retire, hoping that the new friend he has just introduced may, before long, become a household word, associated with mirth and gaiety, around the Christmas fireside.

Here is a Victorian Christmas with all the Dickensian trimmings, a warmly domestic, eminently respectable occasion totally unlike the fantastic, aristocratic Christmas entertainment at Fonthill. Homely truths and healthy morals with a wholesome application are wrapped up in good, clean English fun. The jolly heartiness of this neutralises any danger that the so-called 'racy humour' will be anything more than extremely mild. Of the eight playlets in the pamphlet, none contains anything more than the traditional naughtiness of the seaside postcard. They display an over-the-top silliness, a facetious playfulness which serves to emphasise that they are a game to be played by the rules and not to be taken seriously in real life. The Victorians loved parlour games, which exercised their ingenuity and wit in much the same way that the Elizabethans enjoyed conceits and stratagems and we, perhaps, relish crosswords and quiz shows. *Acting Proverbs* was part of a distinct genre which also included *The Amateur's Handbook and Guide to Home or Drawing Room Theatricals* (1856) by William Sorrell, which included advice on staging theatricals in the special setting of a country house, and was reprinted numerous times in the 1860s and 70s, plus Charles Harrison's *Theatricals and Tableaux Vivants for Amateurs* (1882).

The content of *Acting Proverbs* gives clues as to its market. The preface makes it clear that this is intended as a holiday entertainment, perhaps for people who had less leisure time than those they aped. Although the proverbs might have been acted by 'those with nothing in the world to do' as Henry James called them, the content is more likely to appeal to the actively virtuous middle classes. Taken as a whole the playlets promote conservative social morals. They teach respect for one's betters (particularly royalty), distrust of shady lower-class characters, and the value of thrift, honesty and loyal service. The proverbs themselves share similar themes of prudency. 'All is not gold that glitters', 'Penny wise and pound foolish', 'Small beginnings make great ends', 'Honesty is the best policy'. If they were all performed back to back an audience might guess the unifying coda to be 'virtue is its own reward'. The one chosen for reproduction here is 'A bird in the hand is worth two in the bush'. Set in the time of the English Civil War, this proverb requires historical costume colourful enough to match the melodramatic 'olde English' deployed so magnificently by the playwright. 'With the aid of a few swords, &c, and a little care and taste, the tableau can be rendered effective enough' advises the author. The Victorians took an earnest interest in the past and the professional stage made sincere attempts to recreate historical periods. 'A bird in the hand' demonstrates a more relaxed mood and the Victorian enjoyment of striking attitudes for its own sake.

It's not clear who was the author of *Acting Proverbs*. No name appears on the cover or title pages, although a series list inside the back cover has the name Harwood beside the title. The proverbs are well written and pacy enough to be the hack-work of an established journalist or dramatist, produced to order to provide some cash. It is to be hoped that he was paid reasonably well for such an entertaining work.

★

from ACTING PROVERBS: OR, DRAWING ROOM THEATRICALS

PROVERB III
A bird in the hand is worth two in the bush

Characters
KING CHARLES II
OLIVER CROMWELL
CORPORAL JAHALEEL KILLJOY
LADY MAURICE
EDITH MAURICE
LOUISA – *Edith's Maid*
SOLDIERS

SCENE I – *Chamber of Dais, in Maurice Hall.*
LADY MAURICE, EDITH.

LADY M: What noise is that without? A strange voice! O, Edith, what can it be?

EDITH: Do not be alarmed, dearest mother. I will go and see if anything new has occured. (*Rises, and goes towards the door.*)

LADY M: I am very silly to tremble at shadows as I do, but is not our situation full of peril and of misery? My husband an exile, Roundhead soldiers quartered in my house, our friends proscribed, our king a hunted fugitive, ever since that fatal – fatal day at Worcester! (*Weeps.*)

EDITH (*returns*): Nay, mother, dear mother, do not give way thus. Let us put our faith in Providence, and hope for brighter prospects. Yet I too must weep, when I think of my own dear, dear murdered Frank. (*Sobs.*)

LADY M: Take comfort, darling child. You said well – we will trust in Providence for happier days. Frank Eustace, I feel assured, escaped the slaughter of that sad battle, and has not yet been heard of, though a price was offered for his head.

EDITH: But if yet alive, what chance of escape has he? The cruel fanatics scour the country like bloodhounds on the track of a wounded deer. General Cromwell –

LADY M: Name not the regicide and rebel! But what do I say? is he not under our very roof – our most unwelcome guest?

Enter LOUISA.

LOUISA: Please, my Lady, and Mistress Edith, there's a poor young man outside.

LADY M: Relieve his wants, my good girl. Bid the butler give him food and drink, and let him rest awhile in the kitchen, if he chooses. Thank Heaven, though the master of Maurice Hall is in banishment, we need not yet drive the poor from our doors fasting.

LOUISA: But this isn't like a common young man, please your La'ship's goodness.

EDITH: Some one in disguise. Perhaps one of our persecuted friends. Is it – can it be Frank?

LOUISA: No, Mistress Edith, it's none of Master Frank. It's quite another sort of a parsonage.

LADY M: A parsonage! You mean a parson, I suppose? Admit the reverend gentleman at once.

LOUISA (*laughs*): Beg your La'ship's pardon; but la! he's not much like a parson, for sure. He's a right down saucy one, with *such* merry eyes, and a tongue like a bird in a hedge. He's so pert, I threatened to box his ears for him, and I would, too, only I was afraid the Roundhead soldiers might hear the slap.

LADY M: The soldiers! have they returned already?

LOUISA: That have they, my Lady; and the kitchen's full of the redcoat knaves, drinking ale and munching beef and white bread, for good barley loaves won't serve them. Set them up, quotha! And there's the Corporal, too. I can't abide that Corporal Jahaleel Killjoy.

EDITH: But this poor young man, mother: he must be one of our proscribed cavaliers, and if so, we must not let him fall into Cromwell's hands.

LOUISA: Old Noll's come back, too. I saw him ride into the stable-yard.

Enter KING CHARLES II, *disguised as a woodcutter's lad.*

KING C: Zounds, fair ladies, I ask you a thousand pardons for my country bluffness; but 'tis almost time to drop masquerading. You may guess, perhaps, who I am.

LADY M: A saucy varlet, it should seem. You are somewhat over bold, friend, for your station. Louisa, take him to the kitchen, and –

KING C: Give up the calf to the butchers, eh, Madam? Zoons! mine may be a calf's head, but, such as it is, I prefer to keep it on my shoulders.

EDITH: Mother, this disguise does not cheat me. This – this stranger is not what he seems.

KING C: Pretty young lady, I seem what I am – the most unfortunate youngster in the kingdom.

LADY M: This is no fit season for jesting. What art thou?

KING C: A young man.

LADY M (*impatiently*): That is easy to be seen. What further?

KING C: *The* Young Man.

LADY M: He presumes upon our patience. Fellow, what is thy name?

KING C: That depends upon which name you choose to bestow upon me. Those who wear steeple-crowned hats and sad-coloured raiment, they who snuffle texts over their ale, and sing psalms through the nose, call me the Young Man.

EDITH: I was right; I was right. To your knees, mother, and pray for his sacred life! Oh, Louisa, be secret, if you love me.

LADY M: Has anxiety crazed you, daughter? or what mummer's jest is going on?

KING C: Never kneel for a graceless loon like me, my dear sweet Mistress Edith, if that is your name. I am too fresh from the three-hour sermons of my Scottish preachers not to know the unworthiness of Charles Stuart.

LADY M: His Sacred Majesty!

LOUISA (*falls on her knees*): The King! Oh, and only to think how narrowly I missed boxing his Majesty's ears!

KING C: I should not have been the first of English Kings who received a box on the ear. And as for 'Majesty' and 'sacred,' why, zoons! my Lady Maurice, I have just the majesty of a woodcutter's boy, and I doubt if I should be held sacred where those crop-eared curs in the kitchen to discover in me the heir of three kingdoms.

LOUISA: Does your Majesty? – can your Majesty? –

KING C: My Majesty *does* some strange things, and *can* do others.

LOUISA: Can your Majesty – forgive that box on the ear I so nearly gave you?

KING C: I deserved it richly, in return for the kiss which I – but your ladyship looks distressed. Let me go as I came. I would not bring danger on your roof. (*Turns and walks towards door.*)

LADY M (*rushes forward*): No, no, my liege! though all others are traitors or faint of heart, you shall not lack shelter or assistance while one stone of the house of Jasper Maurice stands on another.

KING C: Noble Sir Jasper! you may well be proud of such a wife!

EDITH: What! your Majesty knows my father?

KING C: Aye, fair mistress, and never had monarch a truer servant. I know Frank Eustace, too. Aha! you blush.

EDITH: Your Majesty – But, pardon my boldness. Is – is Master Eustace well?

KING C: I trust he is. He was, three days since, when I left Boscobel. And he is waiting, I trust, with Wilmot, at the Ferry, and has provided horses, thanks to which I may reach the coast, and a fishing-smack, and so escape.

One stoup of wine, a cantle of a pasty, a slice of beef, a manchet of bread –
anything, pretty maid (*to* LOUISA), and I shall be ready for the road.

LADY M: Run to the pantry, girl. Be quick and discreet.

LOUISA: Yes, my Lady. Did your Majesty –

LADY M: How can you prate so? Quick, silly wench!

KING C: Nay, none so hungry am I but I can answer a question. What is
it, my lass?

LOUISA: Did your Majesty know Job Twackington?

KING C: An honest, loyal lad, for all his Roundhead name! Yes, he is
with his master, Frank Eustace, and the horses, at the Ferry.

LOUISA: O, Gemini! what a man for setting folks at ease your Majesty is!

Exit LOUISA.

LADY M: How my heart bleeds to see my King – pardon me, sire – in
such a guise.

KING C: A very good guise, if it prove a *dis*guise. But what's this?

Re-enter LOUISA.

LOUISA: Oh, we're all undone. Murder! fire! mur–der!

LADY M: Hold your foolish tongue. The soldiers will hear you.

EDITH: Pray be quiet, Louisa, and tell us calmly what has occurred.

LOUISA: 'Tain't what's occurred, Mistress Edith; it's what's going to
occur. It's murder, and robbery, and rigid–side!

LADY M: Regicide! how?

LOUISA: As I went out to get the pastry and the wine, I met –

Enter CROMWELL.

EDITH: Whom did you meet?

LOUISA: I met ugly Old Noll, with his red nose –

CROMWELL: Ugly Old Noll is infinitely obliged to you, maiden.

LOUISA (*screams*): Oh!

KING C: Cromwell! the regicide!

CROMWELL: Ha, lad! what dost thou say?

KING C (*laughs vacantly*): I said I'd seen thee with thy Ironsides, and so I
have.

CROMWELL: Thou, stupid oaf? And where wert thou when an unworthy
potsherd led on the soldiers of Zion?

KING C: I wur at Worcester Foight; I wur.

CROMWELL: Thou, clodpate! How came such a clown into a battle?

KING C: A bottle! Oh, the bottle o' cider thou mean'st. Fearmer Hodge
gave it me, he did. How didst 'ee know I *had* a bottle?

CROMWELL: Tush, fool! Dame Maurice, I must burden your hospitality
yet for awhile. I pray you let me have something to eat, and a tankard of

wine, or even a poor horn of ale, if wine be not at hand. There is not in all our Elect Army a plainer soldier than I am.

LOUISA (*aside*): That's true enough, for an uglier old fright – (*aloud*) Did you speak, Sir? – oh, I mean my Lord.

CROMWELL: Cozen me not with vain titles, maiden, for I am no lord nor knight, but downright Oliver Cromwell, though men do call me Lord-General, and I have been snatched like a brand from the burning.

LADY M: Go, and be quick, girl. Bring the Lord-General the refreshments he requires.

Exit LOUISA.

LADY M: You have been riding, Sir?

CROMWELL: Yea, and with a goodly company, and on a righteous errand. Truly the blood of the malignants is a sweet savour, and a rich thanks-offering, and we will smite them hip and thigh, and Amalek shall not again cry 'boot and saddle,' neither shall the men of Moab which be in Scotland gird on armour for the young man, even Charles Stuart –

KING C (*aside*): How the rebel blows his own trumpet!

CROMWELL: What! come forward, and repeat thy words. I heard thee speak of a trumpet.

KING C: I asked if th' trumpeter-lad of thy regiment was dead, or no, that's all. He used to play pipe and tabor at the Leather Bottle, he did. I'fackins, he'd ha' made thee dance and caper to hear 'un.

CROMWELL: Hold thy prate, knavish fool, or foolish knave. The Lord-General of England makes foes dance with cannon-shot and push of pike; to promote the dancing of such as thou he has the strappado and wooden horse. Interrupt me no more.

EDITH: Pray, my Lord, be clement to the poor fellow. 'Tis a simple lad, whose idle talk my father was used to encourage.

Enter LOUISA, *with refreshments.*

CROMWELL: Truly, the viands have a pleasant savour. I will eat. Hum – here is ale, and here is wine. We are weak, miserable things of clay. Are there no strong waters?

LOUISA: Water, your Worship!

CROMWELL: Worship not me, foolish wench. I spoke of the waters of Geneva or of Nantz.

LOUISA: Oh, brandy! – to be sure, my Lord.

Exit.

CROMWELL *sits down to table.*

KING C: That I should stand by, hungry and athirst, while this canting Puritan eats his meal!

CROMWELL: Thou hast a hungry look, boy. Sit, and share this meat with me, an' ye will. I am not proud. I am a plain man. I say, I am a plain man. I am lower than the lowliest. Why should I, plain Oliver, scorn to sit at meat with such as thou? I ask thee why?

KING C: I doan't know why 'ee should. (*Eats*) This is the proimest o' beef, and the bread's as white as Nell's teeth.

CROMWELL (*rises*): Who is Nell?

KING C: Nell's th' miller's daughter, ye know.

CROMWELL: Thou sayest 'I know.' I know nought of her.

KING C (*aside*): Nor I, as I am an honest man.

    Enter CORPORAL JAHALEEL KILLJOY, *with soldiers.*

CROMWELL: Is there news abroad, friend Killjoy?

CORPORAL: Yea and indeed, Lord-General! for, lo! Habakkuk Strive-with-sin hath come in, hot and hungry, with his horse overridden and foundered.

CROMWELL: A grievous fault! Brother Habakkuk shall taste of the strappado. Yet stay − peradventure he brought news weighty enow to excuse him.

CORPORAL: Of a truth, Lord-General. The Young Man hath eluded the Elect. He hath escaped from them who sought to bind and to slay.

LOUISA: O, how lucky! − I mean, what a pity!

CORPORAL: He climbed into a tree, so that our soldiers saw him not, and the very bloodhounds were at fault. Then he descended, like unto a timid hart −

LOUISA: More like a squirrel, *I* should think.

CROMWELL: Maiden, keep in order that tongue of thine. Proceed, Corporal Jahaleel.

CORPORAL: And sought a shelter among the tents of the wicked, even the huts of certain woodcutters −

CROMWELL (*suspiciously*): Woodcutters? ha!

EDITH: There are many in the forest.

LADY M: Especially some miles off.

CROMWELL: Perhaps I need not seek so far for tidings. Boy, stand forth.

KING C: Can't ye let me finish my dinner? Zooks! I can tell 'ee, I don't get meat every day.

CROMWELL: Stand up; let me see your face. So. Now tell me, did'st ever see the young man Charles?

KING C (*laughs*): What queer things thou dost ask o' me! like play-acting, faith! Ever seen Charles? − every day, man.

CROMWELL: Thou seest Charles daily, sayest thou?

EDITH: What imprudence.

KING C: Aye, man, to be sure, and feels 'un too, sometimes, just as when he broke my head with his cudgel, just acause I said, ye know –

CROMWELL: Silence, babbling idiot!

CORPORAL: Of a verity, brother Habakkuk brought other tidings in his wallet. Wilmot, that man of Belial, whom the Young Man hath gilded over with the vain title of Earl of Rochester, hath been espied, along with another most desperate malignant, the profane Francis Eustace –

EDITH: Frank!

LADY M: Hush, my child.

CROMWELL: Proceed, Jahaleel Killjoy.

CORPORAL: These men of wrath have been espied by a trusty cobbler, one who dwelleth among the tents of Kedar.

CROMWELL: Never mind Kedar just now. Whither bent they their steps?

CORPORAL: Towards the south, leading with them a spare horse, even a pacing palfrey.

CROMWELL: For the Young Man, no doubt. Ho! Ironsides, girth and saddle! We will spur to the Ferry.

KING C: I must be off. Oddsfish! matters grow serious.

EDITH: Hush! – pray hush! It is too late.

CROMWELL: A most unbeseeming oath, youth, and one better suited to the mouth of a debauched cavalier than that of such an oaf as thee. I fear thou hast kept evil company.

CORPORAL: So please ye, Lord-General, this young hewer of wood is not, to my thinking, such a fool as he looks.

KING C: Malapert crop-ear! (*Strikes him.*)

CROMWELL: Ha! that is no peasant's voice. What have we here?

CORPORAL (*draws*): A malignant son of Moab, whom I will smite with the edge and with the point, for buffeting a Corporal of Salem.

EDITH: For shame! Lord-General, do not permit murder.

LOUISA (*screams*): Mur—der! mur—der! O, how I wish Job Twackington was here with his quarter-staff.

CROMWELL: Corporal Jahaleel, put up thy sword promptly. Soldiers, lay hold upon this clown! Varlet, thou canst not now deceive me. Art thou not the servant of some young courtier of the Stuart's?

KING C: If I be a servant, I never get a penny of wages, Measter, and that's sartain.

CROMWELL: Gibes cannot serve thy purpose. Soldiers, search him. (*Soldiers discover a picture*) Ho! a picture! a miniature! Ha! let me see it.

KING C: Look at it, if thou be'est not ashamed.

CROMWELL: It is the man Charles – the executed tyrant's very likeness.

The cipher, C. R., in jewels! Boy, answer or die – where lurks he who gave you this?

KING C: Anan?

CROMWELL: I brook no trifling. Answer, where is the Moabitish stripling? where is Charles Stuart?

EDITH (*aside*): O, Louisa, you have a ready wit. Do something, risk something, but save the King.

LOUISA: If I could! but I'll try, anyway.

Exit.

KING C (*in his natural voice*): I will no longer affect rustic simplicity. But this much I *will* say, I'll never betray King Charles to you. I might as well be hanged at once, as do it.

CROMWELL (*sternly*): And hanged shalt thou be! Ho! without! Noose me a halter speedily. The old oak in the court-yard will serve for a gibbet.

LADY M (*kneels*): O, spare him, Lord-General, for your glory's sake! Stain not your name –

CROMWELL: Peace, Madam. One more chance, boy, remains. Wilt win life and reward, or die like a dog?

KING C: I ask but one favour at your hands – let me die a soldier's death.

CROMWELL: So bold! Nay, then thou shalt.

EDITH: Mercy!

Re-enter CORPORAL JAHALEEL.

CORPORAL: The noose is dangling over a bough, even a bough of the oak tree that grows at hand.

CROMWELL: He shall have a soldier's fate. Corporal Jahaleel, bid your men load their carbines.

LADY M ⎫
EDITH ⎭ Mercy! mercy! my Lord-General.

KING C: Plead not, sweet ladies. It is useless, and hope is past. Better to end thus, than on a scaffold before Whitehall.

Re-enter LOUISA, *running.*

LOUISA: O, la! please your noble Worship's honour.

CROMWELL: Worship me no worship. What seekest thou?

LOUISA: Are there not five thousand pounds to be given to whoever catches King Charles?

CROMWELL: The Man, thou meanest? Yea! maiden.

LOUISA: Then I'll earn it, please, Sir.

EDITH: O, you wicked girl!

LADY M: Traitress, hush! for shame's sake.

LOUISA: Not I, my Lady. But please, General, shall I have the reward?

CROMWELL: Yea! if thou denouncest the troubler of Israel.

LOUISA (*pouting*): Then this was how it was, General – I was in the orchard, getting pippins off the tree that was grafted just seven years ago, by the Dutch –

CROMWELL: Tush! tell me of *him*.

LOUISA: Of *him?* Oh, of the Dutch gardener, your Lordship means. Well, I will as well as I can, though I was quite a child when he came with his great steeple-hat and his great trunk hose, and he talked –

CROMWELL: Insufferable! Girl, trifle not! Where is the young Stuart?

LOUISA: And so, up at the top o' the hill, I saw three men, leading horses along by the bridle, and they had all long hair in nice curling love-locks, and embroidered coats all over mud, and –

CROMWELL: Sayest thou so, and I yet dally here? Ho! to horse! Ironsides, to horse!

LOUISA: Bless us, General, don't go to go a horseback, for it's all among the shrubs, and bushes, and fences, and trees, where you'll be forced to go a-foot, and they're a-foot, and you'll catch him nicely.

CROMWELL: Then hasten, Jahaleel Killjoy; out with ye, soldiers of Zion! Take sword and carbine! take, knock down, and bind! I myself will lead ye. Lose not a precious moment.

JAHALEEL: And this Midianite?

CROMWELL: Let the poor knave alone. We have other prey. A ram caught by the horns! Victory! even the victory of Zion!

Exit CROMWELL, *with his sword drawn.*

CORPORAL: I would fain have hung up yonder malignant; but – five thousand pounds! Forward, Jabez and Jeremiah! we will all be captains and colonels of horse.

Exeunt CORPORAL *and* SOLDIERS.

LOUISA: Now, you Majesty! please your Majesty to look alive!

KING C: That I am alive, or look alive, I owe to you, my good girl.

LOUISA: General Cromwell's horse stands saddled in the yard. The soldiers are all gone.

KING C: And in an hour I shall reach the Ferry and my friends. Farewell, kind Lady Maurice – nay, you must let me kiss your hand, in token that when I get my own, your husband shall be a peer of England.

EDITH: My prayers and thoughts will follow your Majesty.

KING C: But won't poor Frank be jealous? Nay, never blush! The day that sees Charles king, shall see Frank Eustace a baronet. And for you, my pretty preserver, I shall not forget you, nor honest Job What's-his-name –

LOUISA: Twackington, please your Majesty.

KING C: Once more, thanks! and farewell!

Exit.

LOUISA: Won't old Noll be pleased when he finds out that the King's ridden off on his own horse? Ha! ha! ha! I shall die of laughing!

4 THE SORROWS OF SATAN

Henry Cyril Paget, The Dancing Marquess, would have been an ideal guest at the Devil's pageant in Marie Corelli's *The Sorrows of Satan* (1895). He would have enjoyed taking part in the sensational tableaux vivants and perhaps offered one or two tips to improve their impact. Afterwards he could have mingled with the distinguished guests, many of whom would no doubt have been known to him.

Up until 1894 novels were first published in three volumes. Most of these editions were bought by the circulating libraries and lent out. Many readers waited to buy their copy until the cheap edition came out a few months later. In June 1894 the major circulating libraries announced that from 1895 they would pay less for new novels and that they would expect publishers to wait a year before issuing cheap editions. Publishers retaliated by issuing new novels straight off in cheap one-volume editions. Popular authors who could sell a lot of books did well and became known as bestsellers – of which Corelli was the first. Like most bestsellers, *The Sorrows of Satan* stole themes and effects from more literary works and reprocessed them with a suitable amount of contemporary moral comment. Corelli's mass audience evidently required a lot of moral comment, less, one feels, for improving reasons than to enable its vicarious enjoyment of the vices so thoroughly investigated by the author. Corelli was a bit of a drama queen herself. Born Mary Mackay in 1855, she wrote her first novel, *A Romance of Two Worlds*, when she was 30. Her books were derided by the critics but loved by the public, who lapped up her incredible plots and loopy theories about personal electricity. Without Corelli there would have been no *Thelma and Louise* or, indeed, no Mavis Wilton in *Coronation Street*, for it was Corelli who invented and popularised the Christian names Thelma and Mavis. Corelli cultivated a romantic lifestyle which mirrored the extravagant world of her books, buying a house in Stratford-upon-Avon and sailing a Venetian gondola up the river. She set herself up as an authority on Shakespeare, exposing herself to further ridicule. At the height of her popularity her books sold 100,000 copies a year.

The Sorrows of Satan is an angry book, written partly as an attack on the literary critics who slated Corelli's work. The first edition carries an abrupt 'Special Notice' informing readers that 'no copies of this book are sent out for review'. Members of the press would have to buy their own. Unfortunately, Corelli proceeds to ruin her credibility with a laughable portrait of a saintly lady novelist who treats her ignorant reviewers with Christian forebearance. During the course of the book Corelli blasts away at a bewildering assemblage of pet hates, but one of her main targets is the corrupting New Woman fiction which she castigates for contaminating women's minds and morals. One of the tableaux vivants, 'Seeds of Corruption', features a fashionable young girl surrounded by novels of a ' "sexual" type'. Corelli believed in the power of fiction to shape lives and she presents the tableaux to her reader in the same spirit that the Devil presents them to his fictional audience. There is no game here, no word to be guessed; these are 'true pictures' with a transparent meaning. Corelli relishes the make-believe imaginative process of inventing them and piles on her pious lessons.

The tableaux vivants and the gala that follows are vividly visualised. Corelli's florid and sensational language, 'flashings of ice and fire', expends its full descriptive power on the scene. Satan, with all his presumed technical resources, uses standard 1890s pantomime effects. His fairy figures bear wands reminiscent of those used on the stage, with electric lights stuck to the ends, and the frequent bursts of coloured fire copy the coloured limelight used in the theatre to simulate flames. Unlike *Mansfield Park* or *Vanity Fair*, the theatricality is all on the surface and there is no attempt to frame the episode within a genuinely dramatic structure. While the first volume of *Mansfield Park* closes as if it were a play, with the company frozen by Julia's announcement 'My father is come!', and Becky Sharp's triumph concludes with the quieter disaster of Rawdon being caught by the bailiffs, Corelli deflates the energy of her chapter by ending with a low-key chat between Lucio – as Satan – and her hero Geoffrey Tempest. Readers still dazzled by the previous brilliant spectacle are likely to skim through this bit, their imaginative retinas blinded by the afterglow of what came before.

The Sorrows of Satan was published in the year of the Oscar Wilde trials. Wilde was one of the few literary figures to have praised Corelli's earlier novels, perhaps recognising a similar taste in literary sentimentality that overrode his famous comment 'there is no such thing as a moral or an immoral book. Books are well written or badly written. That is all.' Corelli was luckier than Wilde in one respect; being a woman she could live for years with her devoted companion Bertha Vyver without the public raising an eyebrow.

Wilde had served a year in prison and *The Sorrows of Satan* had sold thousands of copies by the time the Prince of Wales' horse Persimmon won the Derby. This was one of those great popular moments which captivated the public imagination. Derby Day was a theatrical event in itself and one which drew massive crowds from all classes to the downs outside Epsom. Corelli acknowledged its importance in *The Sorrows of Satan* when she had the Devil arrange for Geoffrey's horse to win the race. 'If you win the Derby you will be a really famous man,' he advises. Of course the Prince of Wales was already famous but Persimmon's victory in 1896 brought publicity of a new and exciting kind. The event was caught on film and shown on bioscope at the Empire music hall in Leicester Square. This jerky, indistinct moment of sporting glory was the first public screening of moving pictures and its consequence cannot be underrated. Corelli's sensationally cinematic descriptions, appealing to the inner eye, were already reaching forward to a new age of story-telling where they could achieve visible expression. Although the Victorian theatre was splendidly visual and grew increasingly lavish in its attempts to delight the eye, it was capable of presenting a view from one perspective alone. Cinema could dodge about and give one person the sightlines of many, like a novel. One of cinema's major effects was to erase the insufferable vulgarity associated with appearing 'in Publick' and being looked at by the masses. In our own age, the urge to appear on television is so strong that people not only welcome cameras at moments of personal tragedy, they are prepared to fake emotions and situations merely to appear on TV. We are no longer afraid, as our ancestors were, that acting is a version of lying; for us it is an expression of hidden truth. This is the belief that police detectives play on when they stage televised press conferences for murder suspects who refuse to confess. They hope that the strain of appearing in public and keeping up the act of innocence will make the murderer crack.

The three novelists featured in this section do a similar thing to police detectives, prodding their suspects to reveal themselves. Austen and Thackeray expose their characters' true natures through their theatrical behaviour, while Corelli simplifies the situation by openly offering her characters (and her readers) a dramatic picture of themselves in the hope that they will own up. The happy escapism of *Acting Proverbs* operates in reverse to reinforce accepted values of class and morality by giving the participants the opportunity to act out eschatological truths.

*

from THE SORROWS OF SATAN
Marie Corelli

from CHAPTER XXIV

Just as the sun began to sink, several little pages came out of the house, and with low salutations, distributed among the guests daintily embossed and painted programmes of the 'Tableaux Vivants,' prepared for their diversion in the extemporized bijou theatre. Numbers of people rose at once from their chairs on the lawn, eager for this new spectacle, and began to scramble along and hustle one another in that effective style of 'high-breeding' so frequently exhibited at Her Majesty's Drawing-Rooms. I, with Sibyl, hastily preceded the impatient, pushing crowd, for I wished to find a good seat for my beautiful betrothed before the room became full to over-flowing. There proved however, to be plenty of accommodation for everybody, – what space there was seemed capable of limitless expansion, and all the spectators were comfortably placed without difficulty. Soon we were all studying our programmes with considerable interest, for the titles of the 'Tableaux' were somewhat original and mystifying. They were eight in number, and were respectively headed – 'Society,' – 'Bravery: Ancient and Modern,' – 'A Lost Angel,' – 'The Autocrat,' – 'A Corner of Hell,' – 'Seeds of Corruption,' – 'His Latest Purchase,' – and 'Faith and Materialism.' It was in the theatre that everyone became at last conscious of the weirdly beautiful character of the music that had been surging round them all day. Seated under one roof in more or less enforced silence and attention, the vague and frivolous throng grew hushed and passive, – the 'society' smirk passed off certain faces that were as trained to grin as their tongues were trained to lie, – the dreadful giggle of the unwedded man-hunter was no longer heard, – and soon the most exaggerated fashion-plate of a woman forgot to rustle her gown. The passionate vibrations of a violoncello, superbly played to a double harp accompaniment, throbbed on the stillness with a beseeching depth of sound, – and people listened, I saw, almost breathlessly, entranced, as it were, against their wills, and staring as though they were hypnotized, in front of them at the gold curtain with its familiar motto –

'All the world's a stage
And all the men and women merely players.'

Before we had time to applaud the violoncello solo however, the music changed, – and the mirthful voices of violins and flutes rang out in a waltz of the giddiest and sweetest tune. At the same instant a silvery bell tinkled, and the curtain parted noiselessly in twain, disclosing the first tableau – 'Society.' An exquisite female figure, arrayed in evening dress of the richest and most extravagant design, stood before us, her hair crowned with diamonds, and her bosom blazing with the same lustrous gems. Her head was slightly raised, – her lips were parted in a languid smile, – in one hand she held up-lifted a glass of foaming champagne, – her gold-slippered foot trod on an hour-glass. Behind her, catching convulsively at the folds of her train, crouched another woman in rags, pinched and wretched, with starvation depicted in her face, – a dead child lay near. And, overshadowing this group, were two Supernatural shapes, – one in scarlet, the other in black, – vast and almost beyond the stature of humanity, – the scarlet figure represented Anarchy, and its blood-red fingers were advanced to clutch the diamond crown from 'Society's' brow, – the sable-robed form was Death, and even as we looked, it slowly raised its steely dart in act to strike! The effect was weird and wonderful, – and the grim lesson the picture conveyed, was startling enough to make a very visible impression. No one spoke, – no one applauded, – but people moved restlessly and fidgetted on their seats, – and there was an audible sigh of relief as the curtain closed. Opening again, it displayed the second tableau – 'Bravery – Ancient and Modern.' This was in two scenes; – the first one depicted a nobleman of Elizabeth's time, with rapier drawn, his foot on the prostate body of a coarse ruffian who had evidently, from the grouping, insulted a woman whose slight figure was discerned shrinking timidly away from the contest. This was 'Ancient Bravery,' – and it changed rapidly to 'Modern,' showing us an enervated, narrow-shouldered, pallid dandy in opera-coat and hat, smoking a cigarette and languidly appealing to a bulky policeman to protect him from another young noodle of his own class, similarly attired, who was represented as sneaking round a corner in abject terror. We all recognised the force of the application, and were in a much better humour with this pictured satire than we had been at the lesson of 'Society.' Next followed 'A Lost Angel,' in which was shown a great hall in the palace of a king, where there were numbers of brilliantly attired people, all grouped in various attitudes, and evidently completely absorbed in their own concerns, so much so as to be entirely unconscious of the fact that in their very midst, stood a wondrous Angel, clad in dazzling white, with a halo round her fair hair, and a glory, as of the sunset, on her own half drooping wings. Her eyes were wistful, – her face was pensive and expectant; she seemed to say, 'Will the world ever know that I am here?' Somehow, – as the curtain slowly closed again, amid loud applause, for the picture was extraordinarily beautiful, I thought of Mavis Clare, and sighed. Sibyl looked up at me.

'Why do you sigh?' she said – 'It is a lovely fancy, – but the symbol is wasted in the present audience, – no one with education believes in angels now-a-days.'

'True!' I assented; yet there was a heaviness at my heart, for her words reminded me of what I would rather have forgotten, – namely her own admitted lack of all religious faith. 'The Autocrat,' was the next tableau, and represented an Emperor enthroned. At his footstool knelt a piteous crowd of the starving and oppressed, holding up their lean hands to him, clasped in anguished petition, but he looked away from them as though he saw them not. His head was turned to listen to the side-whisper of one who seemed, by the courtly bend and flattering smile, to be his adviser and confidant, – yet that very confidant held secreted behind his back, a drawn dagger, ready to strike his sovereign to the heart. 'Russia!' whispered one or two of the company, as the scene was obscured; but the scarcely-breathed suggestion quickly passed into a murmur of amazement and awe as the curtain parted again to disclose 'A Corner of Hell.' This tableau was indeed original, and quite unlike what might have been imagined as the conventional treatment of such a subject. What we saw was a black and hollow cavern, glittering alternately with the flashings of ice and fire, – huge icicles drooped from above, and pale flames leaped stealthily into view from below, and within the dark embrasure, the shadowy form of a man was seated, counting out gold, or what seemed to be gold. Yet as coin after coin slipped through his ghostly fingers, each one was seen to change to fire, – and the lesson thus pictured was easily read. The lost soul had made its own torture, and was still

at work intensifying and increasing its own fiery agony. Much as this scene
was admired for its Rembrandt effect of light and shade, I, personally, was
glad when it was curtained from view; there was something in the dreadful
face of the doomed sinner that reminded me forcibly and unpleasantly of
those ghastly Three I had seen in my horrid vision on the night of Viscount
Lynton's suicide. 'Seeds of Corruption' was the next picture, and showed us
a young and beautiful girl in her early teens, lying on a luxurious couch *en
deshabille*, with a novel in her hand, of which the title was plainly seen by all;
– a novel well-known to every-one present, and the work of a much-
praised living author. Round her, on the floor, and cast carelessly on a chair
at her side, were other novels of the same 'sexual' type, – all their titles
turned towards us, and the names of their authors equally made manifest.

'What a daring idea!' said a lady in the seat immediately behind me – 'I
wonder if any of those authors are present!'

'If they are they won't mind!' replied the man next to her with a
smothered laugh – 'Those sort of writers would merely take it as a first-class
advertisement!'

Sibyl looked at the tableau with a pale green face and wistful eyes.

'That is a *true* picture!' she said under her breath – 'Geoffrey, it is painfully
true!'

I made no answer, – I thought I knew to what she alluded; but alas! – I
did not know how deeply the 'seeds of corruption' had been sown in her
own nature, or what a harvest they would bring forth. The curtain closed, –
to open again almost immediately on 'His Latest Purchase.' Here we were
shown the interior of a luxurious modern drawing-room, where about eight
or ten men were assembled, in fashionable evening-dress. They had
evidently just risen from a card-table, – and one of them, a dissipated
looking brute, with a wicked smile of mingled satire and triumph on his face
was pointing to his 'purchase,' – a beautiful woman. She was clad in
glistening white like a bride, – but she was bound, as prisoners are bound, to
an upright column, on which the grinning head of a marble Silenus leered
above her. Her hands were tied tightly together, – with chains of diamonds;
her waist was bound, – with thick ropes of pearls; – a wide collar of rubies
encircled her throat; – and from bosom to feet she was netted about and
tied, – with strings of gold and gems. Her head was flung back defiantly
with an assumption of pride and scorn, – her eyes alone expressed shame,
self-contempt, and despair at her bondage. The man who owned this white
slave was represented, by his attitude, as cataloguing and appraising her
'points' for the approval and applause of his comrades, whose faces variously
and powerfully expressed the differing emotions of lust, cruelty, envy,

callousness, derision, and selfishness, more admirably than the most gifted painter could imagine.

'A capital type of most fashionable marriages!' I heard some-one say.

'Rather!' another voice replied – 'The orthodox "happy couple" to the life!'

I glanced at Sibyl. She looked pale, – but smiled as she met my questioning eyes. A sense of consolation crept warmly about my heart as I remembered that now, she had, as she told me 'learnt to love,' – and that therefore her marriage with me was no longer a question of material advantage alone. She was not my 'purchase,' – she was my love, my saint, my queen! – or so I chose to think, in my foolishness and vanity!

The last tableau of all was now to come, – 'Faith and Materialism,' and it proved to be the most startling of the series. The auditorium was gradually darkened, – and the dividing curtain disclosed a ravishingly beautiful scene by the sea-shore. A full moon cast its tranquil glory over the smooth waters, and, – rising on rainbow-wings from earth towards the skies, one of the loveliest creatures ever dreamed of by poet or painter, floated angel-like upwards, her hands holding a cluster of lilies clasped to her breast, – her lustrous eyes full of divine joy, hope, and love. Exquisite music was heard, – soft voices sang in the distance a chorale of rejoicing; – heaven and earth, sea and air, – all seemed to support the aspiring Spirit as she soared higher and higher, in ever-deepening rapture, when, – as we all watched that aerial flying form with a sense of the keenest delight and satisfaction, – a sudden crash of thunder sounded, – the scene grew dark, – and there was a distant roaring of angry waters. The light of the moon was eclipsed, – the music ceased; a faint lurid glow of red shone at first dimly, then more vividly, – and 'Materialism' declared itself, – a human skeleton, bleached white and grinning ghastly mirth upon us all! While we yet looked, the skeleton itself dropped to pieces, – and one long twining worm lifted its slimy length from the wreck of bones, another working its way through the eye-holes of the skull. Murmurs of genuine horror were heard in the auditorium, – people on all sides rose from their seats, – one man in particular, a distinguished professor of sciences, pushed past me to get out, muttering crossly – 'This may be very amusing to some of you, but to me, it is disgusting!'

'Like your own theories, my dear Professor!' said a rich laughing voice, as Lucio met him on his way, and the bijou theatre was again flooded with cheerful light – 'They are amusing to some, and disgusting to others! — Pardon me! – I speak of course in jest! But I designed that tableau specially in your honour!'

'Oh, you did, did you?' growled the Professor – 'Well, I didn't appreciate it.'

'Yet you should have done, for it is quite scientifically correct,' – declared Lucio laughing still. 'Faith, – with the wings, whom you saw joyously flying towards an impossible Heaven, is *not* scientifically correct, – have you not told us so? – but the skeleton and the worms were quite of your *cult!* No materialist can deny the correctness of that "complexion to which we all must come at last." Positively, some of the ladies look quite pale! How droll it is, that while everybody (to be fashionable, and in favour with the press) must accept Materialism as the only creed, they should invariably become affrighted, or let us say offended, at the natural end of the body, as completed by material agencies!'

'Well, it was not a pleasant subject, that last tableau,' – said Lord Elton, as he came out of the theatre with Diana Chesney hanging confidingly on his arm – 'You cannot say it was festal!'

'It was, – for the worms!' replied Lucio gaily – 'Come, Miss Chesney, – and you Tempest, come along with Lady Sibyl, – let us go out in the grounds again, and see my will-o'-the-wisps lighting up.'

Fresh curiosity was excited by this remark; the people quickly threw off the gruesome and tragic impression made by the strange 'tableaux' just witnessed, – and poured out of the house into the gardens chattering and laughing more noisily than ever. It was just dusk, – and as we reached the open lawn we saw an extraordinary number of small boys, clad in brown, running about with will-o'-the-wisp lanterns. Their movements were swift and perfectly noiseless, – they leaped, jumped and twirled like little gnomes over flowerbeds, under shrubberies, and along the edges of paths and terraces, many of them climbing trees with the rapidity and agility of monkeys, and wherever they went they left behind them a trail of brilliant light. Soon, by their efforts, all the grounds were illuminated with a magnificence that could not have been equalled even by the historic fêtes at Versailles, – tall oaks and cedars were transformed to pyramids of fire-blossoms, – every branch was loaded with coloured lamps in the shape of stars, – rockets hissed up into the clear space showering down bouquets, wreaths and ribbons of flame, – lines of red and azure ran glowingly along the grass-borders, and amid the enthusiastic applause of the assembled spectators, eight huge fire-fountains of all colours sprang up in various corners of the garden, while an enormous golden balloon, dazzlingly luminous, ascended slowly into the air and remained poised above us, sending from its glittering car hundreds of gem-like birds and butterflies on fiery wings, that circled round and round for a moment and then vanished. While we were yet loudly clapping the splendid effect of this sky spectacle, a troop of beautiful girl-dancers in white came running across the grass, waving long silvery wands that were tipped with electric stars, and to the sound of strange tinkling music, seemingly played in the distance on glass bells, they commenced a fantastic dance of the wildest yet most graceful character. Every shade of opaline colour fell upon their swaying figures from some invisible agency as they tripped and whirled, – and each time they waved their wands, ribbons and flags of fire were unrolled and tossed high in air where they gyrated for a long time like moving hieroglyphs. The scene was now so startling, so fairy-like and wonderful, that we were well-nigh struck speechless with astonishment, – too fascinated and absorbed even to applaud, we had no conception how time went, or how rapidly the night descended, – till all at once without the least warning, an appalling crash of thunder burst immediately above our heads, and a jagged fork of lightning tore the luminous fire-balloon to shreds. Two or three women began to scream, – whereupon Lucio advanced from the throng of spectators and stood in full view of all, holding up his hand.

'Stage thunder, I assure you!' he said playfully, in a clear somewhat scornful voice – 'It comes and goes at my bidding. Quite a part of the game, believe me! – these sort of things are only toys for children. Again – again, ye petty elements!' he cried, laughing, and lifting his handsome face and flashing eyes to the dark heavens – 'Roar your best and loudest! – roar, I say!'

Such a terrific boom and clatter answered him as baffled all description, – it was as if a mountain of rock had fallen into ruins, – but having been assured that the deafening noise was 'stage thunder' merely, the spectators were no longer alarmed, and many of them expressed their opinion that it was 'wonderfully well done.' After this, there gradually appeared against the sky a broad blaze of red light like the reflection of some great prairie fire, – it streamed apparently upward from the ground, bathing us all where we stood, in its blood-like glow. The white-robed dancing-girls waltzed on and on, their arms entwined, their lovely faces irradiated by the lurid flame, while above them now flew creatures with black wings, bats and owls, and great night-moths, that flapped and fluttered about for all the world as if they were truly alive and not mere 'stage properties.' Another flash of lightning, – and one more booming thud of thunder, – – and lo! – the undisturbed and fragrant night was about us, clear, dewy and calm, – the young moon smiled pensively in a cloudless heaven, – all the dancing-girls had vanished, – the crimson glow had changed to a pure silvery radiance, and an array of pretty pages in eighteenth century costumes of pale pink and blue, stood before us with lighted flaming torches, making a long triumphal avenue, down which Lucio invited us to pass.

'On, on fair ladies and gallant gentlemen!' he cried – This extemporized path of light leads, – not to Heaven – no! that were far too dull an ending! – but to supper! On! – follow your leader!'

Every eye was turned on his fine figure and striking countenance, as with one hand he beckoned the guests, – between the double line of lit torches he stood, – a picture for a painter, with those dark eyes of his alit with such strange mirth as could not be defined, and the sweet, half-cruel, wonderfully attractive smile playing upon his lips; – and with one accord the whole company trooped pell-mell after him, shouting their applause and delight. Who could resist him! – not one in that assemblage at least; – there are few 'saints' in society! As I went with the rest, I felt as though I were in some gorgeous dream, – my senses were all in a whirl, – I was giddy with excitement and could not stop to think, or to analyse the emotions by which I was governed. Had I possessed the force or the will to pause and consider, I might possibly have come to the conclusion that there was something altogether beyond the ordinary power of man displayed in the successive wonders of this brilliant 'gala,' – but I was, like all the rest of society, bent merely on the pleasure of the moment, regardless of how it was procured, what it cost me, or how it affected others. How many I see and know to-day among the worshippers of fashion and frivolity who are acting precisely as I acted then! Indifferent to the welfare of everyone save themselves, grudging every penny that is not spent on their own advantage or amusement, and too callous to even listen to the sorrows or difficulties or joys of others when these do not in some way, near or remote, touch their own interests, they waste their time day after day in selfish trifling, wilfully blind and unconscious to the fact that they are building up their own fate in the future, – that future which will prove all the more a terrible Reality in proportion to the extent of our presumption in daring to doubt its truth.

More than four hundred guests sat down to supper in the largest pavilion, – a supper served in the most costly manner and furnished with luxuries that represented the utmost pitch of extravagance. I ate and drank, with Sibyl at my side, hardly knowing what I said or did in the whirling excitement of the hour, – the opening of champagne-bottles, the clink of glasses, the clatter of plates, the loud hum of talk interspersed with monkey-like squeals or goat-like whinnies of laughter, over-ridden at intervals by the blare of trumpet-music and drums, – all these sounds were as so much noise of rushing waters in my ears, – and I often found myself growing abstracted and in a manner confused by the din. I did not say much to Sibyl, – one cannot very well whisper sentimental nothings to the ear of one's betrothed when she is eating ortolans and truffles. Presently, amid all the hubbub, a deep bell struck twelve times, and Lucio stood up at the end of one of the long tables, a full glass of foaming champagne in his hand –

'Ladies and gentlemen!'

There was a sudden silence.

'Ladies and gentlemen!' he repeated, his brilliant eyes flashing derisively, I thought, over the whole well-fed company, 'Midnight has struck and the best of friends must part! But before we do so, let us not forget that we have met here to wish all happiness to our host, Mr Geoffrey Tempest and his bride-elect, the Lady Sibyl Elton.' Here there was vociferous applause. 'It is said' – continued Lucio, 'by the makers of dull maxims, that "Fortune never comes with both hands full" – but in this case the adage is proved false and put to shame, – for our friend has not only secured the pleasures of wealth, but the treasures of love and beauty combined. Limitless cash is good, but limitless love is better, and both these choice gifts have been bestowed on the betrothed pair whom to-day we honour. I will ask you to give them a hearty round of cheering, – and then it must be good-night indeed, though not farewell, – for with the toast of the bride and bridegroom-elect, I shall also drink to the time, – not far distant perhaps, – when I shall see some of you, if not all of you again, and enjoy even more of your charming company than I have done to-day!'

He ceased amid a perfect hurricane of applause, – and then everyone rose and turned towards the table where I sat with Sibyl, and naming our names aloud, drank wine, the men joining in hearty shouts of 'Hip, hip, hip hurrah!' Yet, – as I bowed repeatedly in response to the storm of cheering, and while Sibyl smiled and bent her graceful head to right and left, my heart sank suddenly with a sense of fear. Was it my fancy – or did I hear peals of wild laughter circling round the brilliant pavilion and echoing away, far away into distance? I listened, glass in hand. 'Hip, hip, hip hurrah!' shouted my guests with gusto. 'Ha – ha –! ha – ha!' seemed shrieked and yelled in my ears from the outer air. Struggling against this delusion, I got up and returned thanks for myself and my future bride in a few brief words which were received with fresh salvos of applause, – and then we all became aware that Lucio had sprung up again in his place, and was standing high above us all, with one foot on the table and the other on the chair, confronting us with a fresh glass of wine in his hand, filled to the brim. What a face he had at that moment! – what a smile!

'The parting cup, my friends!' he exclaimed – 'To our next merry meeting!'

With plaudits and laughter the guests eagerly and noisily responded, – and as they drank, the pavilion was flooded by a deep crimson illumination as of fire. Every face looked blood-red! – every jewel on every woman flashed like a living flame! – for one brief instant only, – then it was gone, and there followed a general stampede of the company, – everybody hurrying as fast as they could into the carriages that waited in long lines to take them to the station, the last two 'special' trains to London being at one a.m. and one thirty. I bade Sibyl and her father a hurried good-night, – Diana Chesney went in the same carriage with them, full of ecstatic thanks and praise to me for the splendours of the day which she described in her own fashion as 'knowing how to do it, –' and then the departing crowd of vehicles began to thunder down the avenue. As they went an arch of light suddenly spanned Willowsmere Court from end to end of its red gables, blazing with all the colours of the rainbow, in the middle of which appeared letters of pale blue and gold, forming what I had hitherto considered as a funereal device,

'Sic transit gloria mundi! Vale!'

Further Reading

William and Richard Arthur Austen-Leigh, revised by Deirdre Le Faye, *Jane Austen, A Family Record* (British Library, 1989).

Marilyn Butler, *Jane Austen and the War of Ideas* (Oxford University Press, 1975).

R.W. Chapman, *Jane Austen, Facts and Problems* (Oxford University Press, 1948).

Dan Cruickshank, 'Ghost of Christmas Past' in *The Guardian* (22 December 1997). Includes account of Emma Hamilton's Fonthill presentation.

Goethe, *Italian Journey*, translated by W.H. Auden and Elizabeth Mayer (Collins, 1962).

Edgar Johnson, *Charles Dickens: His Tragedy and Triumph*, 2 vols, (Simon and Schuster, 1952). Standard scholarly biography.

Anthony J. Lambert, *Victorian and Edwardian Country-House Life* (B.T. Batsford, 1981). Contains picture of Cyril Paget.

Brian Masters, *Now Barrabas was a Rotter: The Extraordinary Life of Marie Corelli* (Hamish Hamilton, 1978).

Teresa Ranson, *The Mysterious Miss Marie Corelli, Queen of Victorian Bestsellers* (Sutton Publishing, 1999).

George Rowell, *Queen Victoria Goes to the Theatre* (P. Elek, 1978).

David Spring, 'Evangelists and Private Theatricals', *Victorian Studies*, VI (1962–3), p 263.

Tony Tanner, Introduction to *Mansfield Park* (Penguin Books, 1966). Still one of the best pieces about *Mansfield Park*.

Walter Thornbury, *Haunted London*, (Chatto and Windus, 1880). History of London from a Victorian perspective with an account of the Temple of Health and the Coal Hole Tavern.

Angus Wilson, *The Naughty Nineties* (Eyre Methuen, 1976).

FUN & FREAKS

5 NICHOLAS NICKLEBY

Sensation seekers visting the Egyptian Hall in Piccadilly in August 1846 came to see The Wild Man of the Prairies, a savage, hairy man-animal who rattled the bars of his cage, gibbered and tore at lumps of raw meat. A story circulated that one day, to the audience's terror and delight, a member of the crowd stepped up to the bars and greeted the Wild Man by his Christian name. Showing no fear, the gentleman entered the beast's cage and, in attempting to shake hands, he pulled off a large chunk of its black, gorilla-like fur. The audience howled as the Wild Man was revealed to be a dwarf circus star, whose ability to jump ten feet in the air with the help of his disproportionately long and powerful arms had earned him the stage name of The Gnome Fly. The crowd had been tricked; promised the missing link between humanity and the apes it been fobbed off with nothing more than a common freak.

The freak's real name was Harvey Leech and he was born in Westchester County, New York, in 1804. His soubriquet was adopted from a play he starred in at the Bowery Theatre in New York in 1840. Called *Tale of Enchantment; or, The Gnome Fly*, it featured Leech as a gnome, a baboon and a bluebottle fly. In 1843 Leech came to London and took the lead in a stage play written specially for him, *The Son of the Desert and the Demon Changeling*, at the Olympic Theatre. Leech was one of many individuals whose physical idiosyncrasies fitted them for theatrical careers. In the disreputable and chaotic world of the nineteenth century, popular theatre managers made a good living by exploiting the curiosity of thrill-seeking audiences. People whose physical characteristics differed from the average were always a reliable draw and canny impresarios were adept at putting a spin on their novelties. Leech's metamorphosis into The Wild Man may have been arranged and promoted by the famous American showman T.P. Barnum.

The term 'freak', when applied to curiosities exhibited for show, is Victorian in origin, a contraction of the phrase 'freak of nature', meaning an abnormal individual. The phrase implies monstrosity and encapsulates an uneasy belief that freaks were not fully human, but some weird mix of man and other, possibly animal. Managers such as Barnum fostered the notion that their charges were exceptional and playbills always stress the exhibits' unique, abnormal or non-human qualities. It was all the better if the proceedings could steal a dash of pseudo-respectability by advertising claims of 'scientific' inquiry. Contemporary accounts of meetings with freaks burst with amazement in the best traditions of amateur scientific observation to find that the subjects have normal, commonplace likes and dislikes. When the theatrical manager Charles Mathews met the diminutive Sicilian Fairy, a nine-year-old the size of a toddler, whose skeleton is still on public display at the Hunterian Museum in London, he was astonished that she drank tea and walked about the room just like any other child. Bearded women, Siamese twins and tribal people from foreign countries were theatrical mainstays throughout the century. Novelty might be said to be measured by the extent to which the object on stage deviated from the audience's narrow pattern of white, Christian humanity. The comparison fascinated and reassured those on the right side of the footlights but often led to depression and even death for the performers. Harvey Leech died six months after being unmasked and at least one account suggests that he expired from sheer humiliation. The irony was that in playing the Wild Man, Leech was simply being honest; taking public curiosity to its logical extreme and acting out what the public believed to be his true inner nature.

If non-human attributes had the potential to enthral audiences then it was logical to consider some animals marvellous. Britain had a tradition of performing animals which spilled out beyond the confines of actual theatre buildings into travelling fairs, agricultural shows and even yards or back rooms at inns. By the beginning of the century learned pigs who could spell, read and play cards, dancing bears and sagacious horses had all made an impression on the impressionable. A newer development was the exhibition of gigantic animals who were famous merely for being huge. Improvements in agriculture and the breeding of better stock focused on the production of vast beasts whose preposterous proportions were celebrated by artists and created a new genre of painting – the farm animal portrait. Often naive in style, these pictures glory in every misplaced and extraneous roll of fat. The animals themselves became stars and were exhibited at fairs and shows. In 1802 more than 2,000 copies were made of an oil painting of the most famous, the Durham Ox, who travelled around the country in a wagon and whose stately image also graced china carving dishes. The Ox weighed 272 stone and stood five feet and six inches tall at the shoulder. There is no doubt that the display of these animals was theatrical in a popular sense and that it catered to the same appetites as human freak shows. Both animal and human oddities were displayed dead as well as alive: humans were often mummified or preserved in formaldehyde, dissected into parts, or boiled down to skeletons, while the carcasses of celebrated beasts were hung up for display in markets and butchers, exposed to the public for the last time before fashionable ladies bought cuts for the dinner table. In her excellent book, *The Animal Estate*, Harriet Ritvo asserts that the exhibition of these meats 'was more theatrical than scientific'.

The two worlds of animal and human display converge most neatly in the life of the artist John Vine of Colchester. Vine was born without arms and as a child he was exhibited in a caravan as a curiosity. He had a talent for drawing and toured the agricultural fairs, executing small pictures for his rustic audience. When he returned to live in Colchester in c. 1830, aged about 22, he lived at first in his caravan and set himself up as a portrait painter, specialising in the animals he had once been exhibited alongside. Many of Vine's pictures survive and their unsentimental charm and vigour mark them out as among the best of their kind.

That Vine should have started in the business so young is not at all surprising, indeed his youth must have been a positive advantage. During the Georgian/Regency period there was a craze for child performers. Edmund Kean first appeared on stage in 1801 billed as Master Carey, the Pupil of Nature. Although Kean went on to better things, his early fame was eclipsed by William Henry West Betty, the original Infant Roscius. Betty was followed by a series of child prodigies in the 1800s. One of them, Miss Mudie, The Theatrical Phenomenon, achieved the distinction of being too ridiculous for popular taste. She was a dwarf, and when she made her debut at Covent Garden the poor eight-year-old was hissed off the stage. By the time Charles Dickens was writing *Nicholas Nickleby* in 1838–39, precocious children were a common feature of the theatre and Miss Crummles, The Infant Phenomenon, was an instantly recognisable type.

Dickens' portrait of the Crummles family is a valuable, and largely accurate, picture of a small theatrical troupe working a provincial circuit. Even the classically Dickensian exaggerations, the Fairy Porcupine or Crummles' concern to use his working pump and tubs in a production, have counterparts in theatre record. Dickens was writing about a world which was naturally even more Dickensian than his own imaginary inventions.

Nicholas Nickleby was originally published in monthly instalments, and at least 25 stage adaptations were produced while the novel was still in progress. It can be argued that the theatrical versions, produced concurrently with the novel, melded audiences and readers and went some way to breaking down the distinctions between the novel as an interior experience and the theatre as an extrovert and public entertainment. Perhaps readers settling down to the latest instalment 'heard' and 'saw' the characters in ways influenced by stage versions they may have seen. It is certainly the case that Dickens' enthusiasm for theatrical methods is evident in his talent for voicing his characters, both on paper and in the flesh. Even if readers didn't attend the theatre, it is likely that many experienced Dickens' novels being read out loud. Dickens' legendary performances at public readings sharpened an established popular taste, prompting other writers to embark on reading tours around the country. At a simple, domestic level we know that family readings around the fireside were an idealised aspect of Victorian life. In these sanitised circumstances theatrical impulses could be indulged safely and might even have a healthy effect in warding off the onanistic pleasures of reading alone.

Why were Dickens' public readings so much more successful than his forays into playwriting? On the surface, Dickens' work seems to show that the imaginary worlds of the nineteenth-century popular novel and the theatre were intertwined in terms of voice, technique and subject. Closer examination reveals that they remained discrete. Although the instincts and sympathy of nineteenth-century culture as a whole were intrinsically theatrical, the barriers between reputable literature and disreputable play acting remained firmly marked. The popularity of public readings illustrates this division, irrespective of whether the performer was the novelist in a public hall or the paterfamilias in front of the drawing-room fire. The critic Deborah Vlock believes that the appetite for such readings would suggest 'that a significant portion of the population sought a sanitised alternative to the dubious conventional theatre. Public readings represented a legitimation of performance, drawing it closer to the more "serious", the purer, literary genres; such modified performance privileged text and voice but rejected the extravagances, the baroque complexities of detail, typical of standard theatrical entertainment.'

★

from THE LIFE AND ADVENTURES OF NICHOLAS NICKLEBY
Charles Dickens

CHAPTER XXIII
Treats of the company of Mr Vincent Crummles, and of his affairs, domestic and theatrical

As Mr Crummles had a strange four-legged animal in the inn stables; which he called a pony, and a vehicle of unknown design, on which he bestowed the appellation of a four-wheeled phaeton, Nicholas proceeded on his journey next morning with greater ease than he had expected: the manager and himself occupying the front seat: and the Master Crummleses and Smike being packed together behind, in company with a wicker basket defended from wet by a stout oilskin, in which were the broad-swords, pistols, pigtails, nautical costumes, and other professional necessaries of the aforesaid young gentlemen.

The pony took his time upon the road, and – possibly in consequence of his theatrical education – evinced, every now and then, a strong inclination to lie down. However, Mr Vincent Crummles kept him up pretty well, by jerking the rein, and plying the whip; and when these means failed, and the animal came to a stand, the elder Master Crummles got out and kicked him.

By dint of these encouragements, he was persuaded to move from time to time, and they jogged on (as Mr Crummles truly observed) very comfortably for all parties.

'He's a good pony at bottom,' said Mr Crummles, turning to Nicholas.

He might have been at bottom, but he certainly was not at top, seeing that his coat was of the roughest and most ill-favoured kind. So, Nicholas merely observed that he shouldn't wonder if he was.

'Many and many is the circuit this pony has gone,' said Mr Crummles, flicking him skilfully on the eyelid for old acquaintance' sake. 'He is quite one of us. His mother was on the stage.'

'Was she?' rejoined Nicholas.

'She ate apple-pie at a circus for upwards of fourteen years,' said the manager; 'fired pistols, and went to bed in a nightcap; and, in short, took the low comedy entirely. His father was a dancer.'

'Was he at all distinguished?'

'Not very,' said the manager. 'He was rather a low sort of pony. The fact is, he had been originally jobbed out by the day, and he never quite got over his old habits. He was clever in melodrama too, but too broad – too broad. When the mother died, he took the port-wine business.'

'The port-wine business!' cried Nicholas.

'Drinking port-wine with the clown,' said the manager; 'but he was greedy, and one night bit off the bowl of the glass, and choked himself, so his vulgarity was the death of him at last.'

The descendant of this ill-starred animal requiring increased attention from Mr Crummles as he progressed in his day's work, that gentleman had very little time for conversation. Nicholas was thus left at leisure to entertain himself with his own thoughts, until they arrived at the drawbridge at Portsmouth, when Mr Crummles pulled up.

'We'll get down here,' said the manager, 'and the boys will take him round to the stable, and call at my lodgings with the luggage. You had better let yours be taken there, for the present.'

Thanking Mr Vincent Crummles for his obliging offer, Nicholas jumped out, and, giving Smike his arm, accompanied the manager up High Street on their way to the theatre; feeling nervous and uncomfortable enough at the prospect of an immediate introduction to a scene so new to him.

They passed a great many bills, pasted against the walls and displayed in windows, wherein the names of Mr Vincent Crummles, Mrs Vincent Crummles, Master Crummles, Master P. Crummles, and Miss Crummles, were printed in very large letters, and everything else in very small ones; and, turning at length into an entry, in which was a strong smell of orange-peel and lamp-oil, with an under-current of sawdust, groped their way through a dark passage, and, descending a step or two, threaded a little maze of canvas screens and paint pots, and emerged upon the stage of the Portsmouth Theatre.

'Here we are,' said Mr Crummles.

It was not very light, but Nicholas found himself close to the first entrance on the prompt side, among bare walls, dusty scenes, mildewed clouds, heavily daubed draperies, and dirty floors. He looked about him; ceiling, pit, boxes, gallery, orchestra, fittings, and decorations of every kind, – all looked coarse, cold, gloomy, and wretched.

'Is this a theatre?' whispered Smike, in amazement; 'I thought it was a blaze of light and finery.'

'Why, so it is,' replied Nicholas, hardly less surprised; 'but not by day, Smike – not by day.'

The manager's voice recalled him from a more careful inspection of the building, to the opposite side of the proscenium, where, at a small mahogany table with rickety legs and of an oblong shape, sat a stout, portly female, apparently between forty and fifty, in a tarnished silk cloak, with her bonnet dangling by the strings in her hand, and her hair (of which she had a great quantity) braided in a large festoon over each temple.

'Mr Johnson,' said the manager (for Nicholas had given the name which Newman Noggs had bestowed upon him in his conversation with Mrs Kenwigs), 'let me introduce Mrs Vincent Crummles.'

'I am glad to see you, sir,' said Mrs Vincent Crummles, in a sepulchral voice. 'I am very glad to see you, and still more happy to hail you as a promising member of our corps.'

The lady shook Nicholas by the hand as she addressed him in these terms; he saw it was a large one, but had not expected quite such an iron grip as that with which she honoured him.

'And this,' said the lady, crossing to Smike, as tragic actresses cross when they obey a stage direction, 'and this is the other. You too, are welcome, sir.'

'He'll do, I think, my dear?' said the manager, taking a pinch of snuff.

'He is admirable,' replied the lady. 'An acquisition, indeed.'

As Mrs Vincent Crummles recrossed back to the table, there bounded on to the stage from some mysterious inlet, a little girl in a dirty white frock with tucks up to the knees, short trousers, sandaled shoes, white spencer, pink gauze bonnet, green veil and curl-papers; who turned a pirouette, cut twice in the air, turned another pirouette, then, looking off at the opposite wing, shrieked, bounded forward to within six inches of the footlights, and fell into a beautiful attitude of terror, as a shabby gentleman in an old pair of buff slippers came in at one powerful slide, and chattering his teeth, fiercely brandished a walking-stick.

'They are going through the Indian Savage and the Maiden,' said Mrs Crummles.

'Oh!' said the manager, 'the little ballet interlude. Very good, go on. A little this way, if you please, Mr Johnson. That'll do. Now!'

The manager clapped his hands as a signal to proceed, and the Savage, becoming ferocious, made a slide towards the maiden; but the maiden avoided him in six twirls, and came down, at the end of the last one, upon the very points of her toes. This seemed to make some impression upon the savage; for, after a little more ferocity and chasing of the maiden into corners, he began to relent, and stroked his face several times with his right thumb and four fingers, thereby intimating that he was struck with admiration of the maiden's beauty. Acting upon the impulse of this passion, he (the savage) began to hit himself severe thumps in the chest, and to exhibit other indications of being desperately in love, which being rather a prosy proceeding, was very likely the cause of the maiden's falling asleep; whether it was or no, asleep she did fall, sound as a church, on a sloping bank, and the savage perceiving it, leant his left ear on his left hand, and nodded sideways, to intimate to all whom it might concern that she *was* asleep, and no shamming. Being left to himself, the savage had a dance, all alone. Just as he left off, the maiden woke up, rubbed her eyes, got off the bank, and had a dance all alone too – such a dance that the savage looked on in ecstacy all the while, and when it was done, plucked from a neighbouring tree some botanical curiosity, resembling a small pickled cabbage, and offered it to the maiden, who at first wouldn't have it, but on the savage shedding tears relented. Then the savage jumped for joy; then the maiden jumped for rapture at the sweet smell of the pickled cabbage. Then the savage and the maiden danced violently together, and, finally, the savage dropped down on one knee, and the maiden stood on one leg upon his other knee; thus concluding the ballet, and leaving the spectators in a state of pleasing uncertainty, whether she would ultimately marry the savage, or return to her friends.

'Very well indeed,' said Mr Crummles; 'bravo!'

'Bravo!' cried Nicholas, resolved to make the best of everything. 'Beautiful!'

'This, sir,' said Mr Vincent Crummles, bringing the maiden forward, 'This is the infant phenomenon – Miss Ninetta Crummles.'

'Your daughter!' inquired Nicholas.

'My daughter – my daughter,' replied Mr Vincent Crummles; 'the idol of every place we go into, sir. We have had complimentary letters about the girl, sir, from the nobility and gentry of almost every town in England.'

'I am not surprised at that,' said Nicholas; 'she must be quite a natural genius.'

'Quite a — !' Mr Crummles stopped; language was not powerful enough to describe the infant phenomenon. 'I'll tell you what, sir,' he said; 'the talent of this child is not to be imagined. She must be seen, sir – seen – to be ever so faintly appreciated. There; go to your mother, my dear.'

'May I ask how old she is?' inquired Nicholas.

'You may, sir,' replied Mr Crummles, looking steadily in his questioner's face, as some men do when they have doubts about being implicitly believed in what they are going to say. 'She is ten years of age, sir.'

'Not more!'

'Not a day.'

'Dear me!' said Nicholas, 'it's extraordinary.'

It was; for the infant phenomenon, though of short stature, had a comparatively aged countenance, and had moreover been precisely the same age – not perhaps to the full extent of the memory of the oldest inhabitant, but certainly for five good years. But she had been kept up late every night, and put upon an unlimited allowance of gin-and-water from infancy, to prevent her growing tall, and perhaps this system of training had produced in the infant phenomenon these additional phenomena.

While this short dialogue was going on, the gentleman who had enacted the savage, came up, with his walking-shoes on his feet, and his slippers in his hand, to within a few paces, as if desirous to join in the conversation. Deeming this a good opportunity he put in his word.

'Talent there, sir!' said the savage, nodding towards Miss Crummles. Nicholas assented.

'Ah!' said the actor, setting his teeth together, and drawing in his breath with a hissing sound, 'she oughtn't to be in the provinces, she oughtn't.'

'What do you mean?' asked the manager.

'I mean to say,' replied the other, warmly, 'that she is too good for country boards, and that she ought to be in one of the large houses in London, or nowhere; and I tell you more, without mincing the matter, that if it wasn't for envy and jealousy in some quarter that you know of, she would be. Perhaps you'll introduce me here, Mr Crummles.'

'Mr Folair,' said the manager, presenting him to Nicholas.

'Happy to know you, sir.' Mr Folair touched the brim of his hat with his forefinger, and then shook hands. 'A recruit, sir, I understand?'

'An unworthy one,' replied Nicholas.

'Did you ever see such a set-out as that?' whispered the actor, drawing him away, as Crummles left them to speak to his wife.

'As what?'

Mr Folair made a funny face from his pantomime collection, and pointed over his shoulder.

'You don't mean the infant phenomenon?'

'Infant humbug, sir,' replied Mr Folair. 'There isn't a female child of common sharpness in a charity school, that couldn't do better than that. She may thank her stars she was born a manager's daughter.'

'You seem to take it to heart,' observed Nicholas, with a smile.

'Yes, by Jove, and well I may,' said Mr Folair, drawing his arm through his, and walking him up and down the stage. 'Isn't it enough to make a man crusty to see that little sprawler put up in the best business every night, and actually keeping money out of the house, by being forced down the people's throats, while other people are passed over? Isn't it extraordinary to see a man's confounded family conceit blinding him, even to his own interest? Why I *know* of fifteen and sixpence that came to Southampton one night last month, to see me dance the Highland Fling; and what's the consequence? I've never been put up in it since – never once – while the "infant phenomenon" has been grinning through artificial flowers at five people and a baby in the pit, and two boys in the gallery, every night.'

'If I may judge from what I have seen of you,' said Nicholas, 'you must be a valuable member of the company.'

'Oh!' replied Mr Folair, beating his slippers together, to knock the dust out; 'I *can* come it pretty well – nobody better, perhaps, in my own line – but having such business as one gets here, is like putting lead on one's feet instead of chalk, and dancing in fetters without the credit of it. Holloa, old fellow, how are you?'

The gentleman addressed in these latter words, was a dark-complexioned man, inclining indeed to sallow, with long thick black hair, and very evident indications (although he was close shaved) of a stiff beard, and whiskers of the same deep shade. His age did not appear to exceed thirty, though many at first sight would have considered him much older, as his face was long, and very pale, from the constant application of stage paint. He wore a checked shirt, an old green coat with new gilt buttons, a neckerchief of broad red and green stripes, and full blue trousers; he carried, too, a common ash walking-stick, apparently more for show than use, as he flourished it about, with the hooked end downwards, except when he raised it for a few seconds, and throwing himself into a fencing attitude, made a pass or two at the side-scenes, or at any other object, animate or inanimate, that chanced to afford him a pretty good mark at the moment.

'Well, Tommy,' said this gentleman, making a thrust at his friend, who parried it dexterously with his slipper, 'what's the news!'

'A new appearance, that's all,' replied Mr Folair, looking at Nicholas.

'Do the honours, Tommy, do the honours,' said the other gentleman, tapping him reproachfully on the crown of the hat with his stick.

'This is Mr Lenville, who does our first tragedy, Mr Johnson,' said the pantomimist.

'Except when old bricks and mortar takes it into his head to do it himself, you should add Tommy,' remarked Mr Lenville. 'You know who bricks and mortar is, I suppose, sir?'

'I do not, indeed,' replied Nicholas.

'We call Crummles that, because his style of acting is rather in the heavy and ponderous way,' said Mr Lenville. 'I mustn't be cracking jokes though, for I've got a part of twelve lengths here, which I must be up in tomorrow night, and I haven't had time to look at it yet; I'm a confounded quick study, that's one comfort.'

Consoling himself with this reflection, Mr Lenville drew from his coat-pocket a greasy and crumpled manuscript, and, having made another pass at his friend, proceeded to walk to and fro, conning it to himself and indulging occasionally in such appropriate action as his imagination and the text suggested.

A pretty general muster of the company had by this time taken place; for beside Mr Lenville and his friend Tommy, there were present, a slim young gentleman with weak eyes, who played the low-spirited lovers and sang tenor songs, and who had come arm-in-arm with the comic countryman – a man with a turned-up nose, large mouth, broad face, and staring eyes. Making himself very amiable to the infant phenomenon, was an inebriated elderly gentleman in the last depths of shabbiness who played the calm and virtuous old men; and paying especial court to Mrs Crummles was another elderly gentleman, a shade more respectable, who played the irascible old men – those funny fellows who have nephews in the army, and perpetually run about with thick sticks to compel them to marry heiresses. Besides these, there was a roving-looking person in a rough great-coat, who strode up and down in front of the lamps, flourishing a dress cane, and rattling away, in an undertone, with great vivacity for the amusement of an ideal audience. He was not quite so young as he had been, and his figure was rather running to seed; but there was an air of exaggerated gentility about him, which bespoke the hero of swaggering comedy. There was, also, a little group of three or four young men, with lantern jaws and thick eyebrows, who were conversing in one corner; but they seemed to be of secondary importance, and laughed and talked together without attracting any attention.

The ladies were gathered in a little knot by themselves round the rickety table before mentioned. There was Miss Snevellicci – who could do anything, from a medley dance to Lady Macbeth, and also always played some part in blue silk knee-smalls at her benefit – glancing, from the depths of her coal-scuttle straw bonnet, at Nicholas, and affecting to be absorbed in the recital of a diverting story to her friend Miss Ledrook, who had brought her work, and was making up a ruff in the most natural manner possible. There was Miss Belvawney – who seldom aspired to speaking parts, and usually went on as a page in white silk hose, to stand with one leg bent, and contemplate the audience, or to go in and out after Mr Crummles in stately tragedy – twisting up the ringlets of the beautiful Miss Bravassa, who had once had her likeness taken 'in character' by an engraver's apprentice, whereof impressions were hung up for sale in the pastry-cook's window, and the greengrocer's, and at the circulating library, and the box-office, whenever the announce bills came out for her annual night. There was Mrs Lenville, in a very limp bonnet and veil, decidedly in that way in which she would wish to be if she truly loved Mr Lenville; there was Miss Gazingi, with an imitation ermine boa tied in a loose knot round her neck, flogging Mr Crummles, junior, with both ends, in fun. Lastly, there was Mrs Grudden in a brown cloth pelisse and a beaver bonnet, who assisted Mrs Crummles in her domestic affairs, and took money at the doors, and dressed the ladies, and swept the house, and held the prompt book when everybody else was on for the last scene, and acted any kind of part on any emergency without ever learning it, and was put down in the bills under any name or names whatever, that occurred to Mr Crummles as looking well in print.

Mr Folair having obligingly confided these particulars to Nicholas, left him to mingle with his fellows; the work of personal introduction was completed by Mr Vincent Crummles, who publicly heralded the new actor as a prodigy of genius and learning.

'I beg your pardon,' said Miss Snevellicci, sidling towards Nicholas, 'but did you ever play at Canterbury?'

'I never did,' replied Nicholas.

'I recollect meeting a gentleman at Canterbury,' said Miss Snevellicci, 'only for a few moments, for I was leaving the company as he joined it, so like you that I felt almost certain it was the same.'

'I see you now, for the first time,' rejoined Nicholas with all due gallantry. 'I am sure I never saw you before; I couldn't have forgotten it.'

'Oh, I'm sure – it's very flattering of you to say so,' retorted Miss Snevellicci with a graceful bend. 'Now I look at you again, I see that the gentleman at Canterbury hadn't the same eyes as you – you'll think me very foolish for taking notice of such things, won't you?'

'Not at all,' said Nicholas. 'How can I feel otherwise than flattered by
your notice in any way?'

'Oh! you men are such vain creatures!' cried Miss Snevellicci. Whereupon, she became charmingly confused, and, pulling out her pocket
handkerchief from a faded pink silk reticule with a gilt clasp, called to Miss
Ledrook –

'Led, my dear,' said Miss Snevellicci.

'Well, what is the matter!' said Miss Ledrook.

'It's not the same.'

'Not the same what?'

'Canterbury – you know what I mean. Come here! I want to speak to
you.'

But Miss Ledrook wouldn't come to Miss Snevellicci, so Miss Snevellicci
was obliged to go to Miss Ledrook, which she did, in a skipping manner that
was quite fascinating; and Miss Ledrook evidently joked Miss Snevellicci
about being struck with Nicholas; for, after some playful whispering, Miss
Snevellicci hit Miss Ledrook very hard on the backs of her hands, and retired
up, in a state of pleasing confusion.

'Ladies and gentlemen,' said Mr Vincent Crummles, who had been
writing on a piece of paper, 'we'll call the Mortal Struggle to-morrow at ten;
everybody for the procession. Intrigue, and Ways and Means, you're all up
in, so we shall only want one rehearsal. Everybody at ten, if you please.'

'Everybody at ten,' repeated Mrs Grudden, looking about her.

'On Monday morning we shall read a new piece,' said Mr Crummles;
'the name's not known yet, but everybody will have a good part. Mr
Johnson will take care of that.'

'Hallo!' said Nicholas, starting, 'I —'

'On Monday morning,' repeated Mr Crummles, raising his voice, to
drown the unfortunate Mr Johnson's remonstrance; 'that'll do, ladies and
gentlemen.'

The ladies and gentlemen required no second notice to quit; and, in a few
minutes, the theatre was deserted, save by the Crummles' family, Nicholas,
and Smike.

'Upon my word,' said Nicholas, taking the manager aside, 'I don't think I
can be ready by Monday.'

'Pooh, pooh,' replied Mr Crummles.

'But really I can't,' returned Nicholas; 'my invention is not accustomed to
these demands, or possibly I might produce —'

'Invention! what the devil's that got to do with it!' cried the manager,
hastily.

'Everything, my dear sir.'

'Nothing, my dear sir,' retorted the manager, with evident impatience. 'Do you understand French?'

'Perfectly well.'

'Very good,' said the manager, opening the table-drawer, and giving a roll of paper from it to Nicholas. 'There! Just turn that into English, and put your name on the title-page. Damn me,' said Mr Crummles, angrily, 'If I haven't often said that I wouldn't have a man or woman in my company that wasn't master of the language, so that they might learn it from the original, and play it in English, and save all this trouble and expense.'

Nicholas smiled and pocketed the play.

'What are you going to do about your lodgings?' said Mr Crummles.

Nicholas could not help thinking that, for the first week, it would be an uncommon convenience to have a turn-up bedstead in the pit; but he merely remarked that he had not turned his thoughts that way.

'Come home with me then,' said Mr Crummles, 'and my boys shall go with you after dinner, and show you the most likely place.'

The offer was not to be refused; Nicholas and Mr Crummles gave Mrs Crummles an arm each, and walked up the street in stately array. Smike, the boys, and the phenomenon, went home by a shorter cut, and Mrs Grudden remained behind to take some cold Irish stew and a pint of porter in the box-office.

Mrs Crummles trod the pavement as if she were going to immediate execution with an animating consciousness of innocence, and that heroic fortitude which virtue alone inspires. Mr Crummles, on the other hand, assumed the look and gait of a hardened despot; but they both attracted some notice from many of the passers-by, and when they heard a whisper of 'Mr and Mrs Crummles!' or saw a little boy run back to stare them in the face, the severe expression of their countenances relaxed, for they felt it was popularity.

Mr Crummles lived in Saint Thomas's Street, at the house of one Bulph, a pilot, who sported a boat-green door, with window-frames of the same colour, and had the little finger of a drowned man on his parlour mantel-shelf, with other maritime and natural curiosities. He displayed also a brass knocker, a brass plate, and a brass bell-handle, all very bright and shining; and had a mast, with a vane on the top of it, in his back yard.

'You are welcome,' said Mrs Crummles, turning round to Nicholas when they reached the bow-windowed front room on the first floor.

Nicholas bowed his acknowledgments, and was unfeignedly glad to see the cloth laid.

'We have but a shoulder of mutton with onion sauce,' said Mrs

Crummles, in the same charnel-house voice; 'but such as our dinner is, we beg you to partake of it.'

'You are very good,' replied Nicholas, 'I shall do it ample justice.'

'Vincent,' said Mrs Crummles, 'what is the hour?'

'Five minutes past dinner-time,' said Mr Crummles.

Mrs Crummles rang the bell. 'Let the mutton and onion sauce appear.' The slave who attended upon Mr Bulph's lodgers, disappeared, and after a short interval re-appeared with the festive banquet. Nicholas and the infant phenomenon opposed each other at the pembroke-table, and Smike and the master Crummleses dined on the sofa bedstead.

'Are they very theatrical people here?' asked Nicholas.

'No,' replied Mr Crummles, shaking his head, 'far from it – far from it.'

'I pity them,' observed Mrs Crummles.

'So do I,' said Nicholas; 'if they have no relish for theatrical entertainments, properly conducted.'

'Then they have none, sir,' rejoined Mr Crummles. 'To the infant's benefit, last year, on which occasion she repeated three of her most popular characters, and also appeared in the Fairy Porcupine, as originally performed by her, there was a house of no more than four pound twelve.'

'Is it possible?' cried Nicholas.

'And two pound of that was trust, pa,' said the phenomenon.

'And two pound of that was trust,' repeated Mr Crummles. 'Mrs Crummles herself has played to mere handfuls.'

'But they are always a taking audience, Vincent,' said the manager's wife.

'Most audiences are, when they have good acting – real good acting – the regular thing,' replied Mr Crummles, forcibly.

'Do you give lessons, ma'am?' inquired Nicholas.

'I do,' said Mrs Crummles.

'There is no teaching here, I suppose?'

'There has been,' said Mrs Crummles. 'I have received pupils here. I imparted tuition to the daughter of a dealer in ships' provision; but it afterwards appeared that she was insane when she first came to me. It was very extraordinary that she should come, under such circumstances.'

Not feeling quite so sure of that, Nicholas thought it best to hold his peace.

'Let me see,' said the manager cogitating after dinner. 'Would you like some nice little part with the infant?'

'You are very good,' replied Nicholas hastily; 'but I think perhaps it would be better if I had somebody of my own size at first, in case I should turn out awkward. I should feel more at home, perhaps.'

'True,' said the manager. 'Perhaps you would. And you could play up to the infant, in time, you know.'

'Certainly,' replied Nicholas: devoutly hoping that it would be a very long time before he was honoured with this distinction.

'Then I'll tell you what we'll do,' said Mr Crummles. 'You shall study Romeo when you've done that piece – don't forget to throw the pump and tubs in by-the-bye – Juliet Miss Snevellicci, old Grudden the nurse. – Yes, that'll do very well. Rover too; – you might get up Rover while you were about it, and Cassio, and Jeremy Diddler. You can easily knock them off; one part helps the other so much. Here they are, cues and all.'

With these hasty general directions Mr Crummles thrust a number of little books into the faltering hands of Nicholas, and bidding his eldest son go with him and show where lodgings were to be had, shook him by the hand, and wished him good night.

There is no lack of comfortable furnished apartments in Portsmouth, and no difficulty in finding some that are proportionate to very slender finances; but the former were too good, and the latter too bad, and they went into so many houses, and came out unsuited, that Nicholas seriously began to think he should be obliged to ask permission to spend the night in the theatre, after all.

Eventually, however, they stumbled upon two small rooms up three pair of stairs, or rather two pair and a ladder, at a tobacconist's shop, on the Common Hard: a dirty street leading down to the dockyard. These Nicholas engaged, only too happy to have escaped any request for payment of a week's rent beforehand.

'There! Lay down our personal property, Smike,' he said, after showing young Crummles down stairs. 'We have fallen upon strange times, and Heaven only knows the end of them; but I am tired with the events of these three days, and will postpone reflection till to-morrow – if I can.'

6 FAR FROM THE MADDING CROWD

Vincent Crummles' shambling pony had a truly illustrious theatrical parentage. Its mother, who fired pistols and went to bed in a nightcap, probably worked for Andrew Ducrow at Astley's Royal Amphitheatre while the rather low-life father is more likely to have worked at the Surrey, better known for the canine stars of its melodramas. Here at the Surrey, wrote the Victorian historian Henry Barton Baker in 1889, 'pieces of the most degraded description were produced'. Astley's and the Surrey were both extraordinary places, somewhere between the theatre and the circus as we know it, which grew out of the restrictions imposed by the Licensing Act of 1737. Until the situation changed in 1843, only those theatres in possession of a Royal Patent were permitted to stage 'legitimate' plays, that is five-act tragedies and comedies with dialogue. In London this restricted performances of straightforward plays to the patent houses of Covent Garden, Drury Lane and the summer season at the Haymarket. However, minor theatres could be licensed to present musical and dancing entertainments and it was this loophole which fostered the development of some peculiarly illegitimate dramatic forms. As far as the nineteenth-century stage is concerned, hippodrama has a claim to being one of the first of these bastards.

'Cut the dialogue and come to the 'osses', was said to be Andrew Ducrow's favourite stage direction. Ducrow was a talented trick rider whose displays of horsemanship impressed all who saw him. In 1833 the visiting German Prince Hermann Pückler-Muskau watched Ducrow ride eight horses at once while dressed as a Chinese sorcerer, drive 12 at once while costumed as a Russian and then get into bed with a pony dressed as an old woman. He also performed *poses plastiques* on horseback, eliciting gasps of admiration from the spectators at his portrayals of famous statues. Other circus performers took the concept further and impersonated theatrical characters – James Cooke was famous for pantomiming Shakespearean heroes while balancing atop a cantering horse.

Astley's Amphitheatre, where Ducrow's feats were mostly performed, was rebuilt several times and each version shared the same curious double construction. There was a stage as usual with the orchestra below but a further performance space was provided by the sawdust ring occupying the central section of the auditorium. The horses generally appeared in the ring, although they might well be used on stage if the action so demanded. An engraving shows the interior of the fourth Astley's in about 1856, well after the Licensing Act was amended. The stage is occupied by actors playing *Richard III* while the ring is enlivened with seven horses performing diverting tricks apparently unconnected to the business above. This dual presentation would bewilder modern audiences used to a more reverential treatment of Shakespeare but by the standards of its time it was fairly tame. Shakespeare had to endure far more in other illegitimate theatres. Astley's rivals at the Royal Circus, later to become the Surrey, presented *Macbeth* as a ballet and the penny gaffs of the East End usually hacked the great tragedies down to a bare 20 minutes playing time. Astley's effectively invented its own genre, as Baker says, 'the drama of Astley's Amphitheatre was always peculiar to itself; its most salient features were noise, blood, thunder, and gunpowder; tyrant kings, and savage chiefs of the most ferocious types of theatrical humanity, and heroes of the most impossible bravery and virtue.'

Jane Austen went to Astley's and seems to have enjoyed it. In a letter written in August 1796 she says, 'we are to be at Astley's to night, which I am glad of.' Dickens made several references to Astley's and produced a brief account of its charms in 'Sketches of London', No. 11 (*Evening Chronicle*, 9 May 1835), although he was typically more interested in writing about a spectating family than the entertainment itself. The equestrian spectacles and horseback pantomimes at Astley's and the Surrey were so popular and profitable that the legitimate theatres soon began to leaven their bills with hippodrama and this type of entertainment became a common feature. By the time Surtees was writing his raffish sporting novels in the 1850s, actresses who took part in equestrian productions were a recognisable type, regarded as the fastest of a notoriously fast set. The most attractive character in *Mr Sponge's Sporting Tour* (1852) is the aptly named Lucy Glitters, introduced as 'the beautiful and tolerably virtuous Miss Glitters, of the Astley's Royal Amphitheatre'. Her friend Lady Scattercash is from the same stable, being:

late the lovely and elegant Miss Spangles of The Theatre Royal, Sadler's Wells. Sir Harry had married her before his windfall had made him a baronet, having, at the time, some intention of trying his luck on the stage, but he always declared that he never regretted his choice; on the contrary, he said, if he had gone among the 'duchesses', he could not have suited himself better. Lady Scattercash could ride – indeed she used to do scenes in the circle (two horses and a flag) – and she could drive, and smoke, and sing, and was possessed of many other accomplishments.

Horses were used in stage plays to add colour and effect, as in J.R. Planché's *Cortez, or the Conquest of Mexico* (1823) which employed 13 horses supplied by Ducrow and featured the trick rider himself playing an Indian riding for the first time. Equine actors might also take on roles in their own right, as in versions of *Richard III* which expanded the part of White Surrey, and their actions could be central to the plot, as in adaptations of Byron's poem *Mazeppa* where the hero (or heroine) is strapped to the back of a wild horse which gallops off into the mountains. The other use of horses was in spectacles such as re-enactments of the Battle of Waterloo, and in dramatisations of famous 'true' stories.

The most enduring and popular of these folk stories was Dick Turpin's legendary ride from London to York on his faithful steed Black Bess, which, played for the first time at Astley's in 1819, became a staple of travelling shows and survived in the circus until the 1920s. The same tale formed the basis of William Harrison Ainsworth's 1834 novel *Rookwood*. When Thomas Hardy wrote 'The Sheep Fair' episode in his 1874 novel *Far from the Madding Crowd* he drew upon his memory of a celebrated equestrian troupe that visited Dorchester in 1856 and which may well have performed this standard piece. A sheep fair is still held every year near Dorchester and, although the extraneous entertainment has withered, the main event – the sheep judging – is contested as hotly as ever. Local photographers make a decent day's wage taking pictures of the winning beasts; the modern equivalent of the Victorian animal portraitists.

Hardy's sheep fair is a theatrical event, a massive show to which everyone goes to see and be seen. The sheep are presented as exotic beasts in the long tradition of agricultural shows, where animals are expected to be strange and marvellous. The dramatic centrepiece – Sergeant Troy performing as Dick Turpin – is supposed to act as a foil to the real drama between Troy and Bathsheba, as Hardy explores the inevitable conflict between private and public selves caught up in this world of show. What actually happens is that, like Dickens before him, Hardy is more interested in the theatrical goings-on for their own sake, painting a lively picture of the entertainment and the reaction of the rustic audience. The details of Troy's performance are accurate; Black Bess leaping the toll gate and then later dying and being carried out of the tent on a shutter are all recorded features of real presentations.

★

from FAR FROM THE MADDING CROWD
Thomas Hardy

CHAPTER L
The sheep fair – Troy touches his wife's hand

Greenhill was the Nijni Novgorod of South Wessex; and the busiest, merriest, noisiest day of the whole statute number was the day of the sheep fair. This yearly gathering was upon the summit of a hill which retained in good preservation the remains of an ancient earthwork, consisting of a huge rampart and entrenchment of an oval form encircling the top of the hill, though somewhat broken down here and there. To each of the two chief openings on opposite sides a winding road ascended, and the level green space of ten or fifteen acres enclosed by the bank was the site of the fair. A few permanent erections dotted the spot, but the majority of visitors patronized canvas alone for resting and feeding under during the time of their sojourn here.

Shepherds who attended with their flocks from long distances started from home two or three days, or even a week, before the fair, driving their charges a few miles each day – not more than ten or twelve – and resting them at night in hired fields by the wayside at previously chosen points, where they fed, having fasted since morning. The shepherd of each flock marched behind, a bundle containing his kit for the week strapped upon his shoulders, and in his hand his crook, which he used as the staff of his pilgrimage. Several of the sheep would get worn and lame, and occasionally a lambing occurred on the road. To meet these contingencies, there was frequently provided, to accompany the flocks from the remoter points, a pony and waggon into which the weakly ones were taken for the remainder of the journey.

The Weatherbury Farms, however, were no such long distance from the hill, and those arrangements were not necessary in their case. But the large united flocks of Bathsheba and Farmer Boldwood formed a valuable and imposing multitude which demanded much attention, and on this account Gabriel, in addition to Boldwood's shepherd and Cain Ball, accompanied them along the way, through the decayed old town of Kingsbere, and upward to the plateau, – old George the dog of course behind them.

When the autumn sun slanted over Greenhill this morning and lighted the dewy flat upon its crest, nebulous clouds of dust were to be seen floating between the pairs of hedges which streaked the wide prospect around in all directions. These gradually converged upon the base of the hill, and the flocks became individually visible, climbing the serpentine ways which led to the top. Thus, in a slow procession, they entered the opening to which the roads tended, multitude after multitude, horned and hornless – blue flocks and red flocks, buff flocks and brown flocks, even green and salmon-tinted flocks, according to the fancy of the colourist and custom of the farm. Men were shouting, dogs were barking, with greatest animation, but the thronging travellers in so long a journey had grown nearly indifferent to such terrors, though they still bleated piteously at the unwontedness of their experiences, a tall shepherd rising here and there in the midst of them, like a gigantic idol amid a crowd of prostrate devotees.

The great mass of sheep in the fair consisted of South Downs and the old Wessex horned breeds; to the latter class Bathsheba's and Farmer Boldwood's mainly belonged. These filed in about nine o'clock, their vermiculated horns lopping gracefully on each side of their cheeks in geometrically perfect spirals, a small pink and white ear nestling under each horn. Before and behind came other varieties, perfect leopards as to the full rich substance of their coats, and only lacking the spots. There were also a few of the Oxfordshire breed, whose wool was beginning to curl like a child's flaxen hair, though surpassed in this respect by the effeminate Leicesters, which were in turn less curly than the Cotswolds. But the most picturesque by far was a small flock of Exmoors, which chanced to be there this year. Their pied faces and legs, dark and heavy horns, tresses of wool hanging round their swarthy foreheads, quite relieved the monotony of the flocks in that quarter.

All these bleating, panting, and weary thousands had entered and were penned before the morning had far advanced, the dog belonging to each flock being tied to the corner of the pen containing it. Alleys for pedestrians intersected the pens, which soon became crowded with buyers and sellers from far and near.

In another part of the hill an altogether different scene began to force itself upon the eye towards midday. A circular tent, of exceptional newness and size, was in course of erection here. As the day drew on, the flocks began to change hands, lightening the shepherds' responsibilities; and they turned their attention to this tent and inquired of a man at work there, whose soul seemed concentrated on tying a bothering knot in no time, what was going on.

'The Royal Hippodrome Performance of Turpin's Ride to York and the Death of Black Bess,' replied the man promptly, without turning his eyes or leaving off tying.

As soon as the tent was completed the band struck up highly stimulating harmonies, and the announcement was publicly made, Black Bess standing in a conspicuous position on the outside, as a living proof, if proof were wanted, of the truth of the oracular utterances from the stage over which the people were to enter. These were so convinced by such genuine appeals to heart and understanding both that they soon began to crowd in abundantly, among the foremost being visible Jan Coggan and Joseph Poorgrass, who were holiday keeping here to-day.

'That's the great ruffen pushing me!' screamed a woman in front of Jan over her shoulder at him when the rush was at its fiercest.

'How can I help pushing ye when the folk behind push me?' said Coggan, in a deprecating tone, turning his head towards the aforesaid folk as far as he could without turning his body, which was jammed as in a vice.

There was a silence; then the drums and trumpets again sent forth their echoing notes. The crowd was again ecstasied, and gave another lurch in which Coggan and Poorgrass were again thrust by those behind upon the women in front.

'O that helpless feymels should be at the mercy of such ruffens!' exclaimed one of these ladies again, as she swayed like a reed shaken by the wind.

'Now,' said Coggan, appealing in an earnest voice to the public at large as it stood clustered about his shoulder-blades, 'did ye ever hear such a onreasonable woman as that? Upon my carcase, neighbours, if I could only get out of this cheesewring, the damn women might eat the show for me!' 'Don't ye lose yer temper, Jan!' implored Joseph Poorgrass, in a whisper. 'They might get their men to murder us, for I think by the shine of their eyes that they be a sinful form of womankind.'

Jan held his tongue, as if he had no objection to be pacified to please a friend, and they gradually reached the foot of the ladder, Poorgrass being flattened like a jumping-jack, and the sixpence, for admission, which he had got ready half-an-hour earlier, having become so reeking hot in the tight squeeze of his excited hand that the woman in spangles, brazen rings set with glass diamonds, and with chalked face and shoulders, who took the money of him, hastily dropped it again from a fear that some trick had been played to burn her fingers. So they all entered, and the cloth of the tent, to the eyes of an observer on the outside, became bulged into innumerable pimples such as we observe on a sack of potatoes, caused by the various human heads, backs, and elbows at high pressure within.

At the rear of the large tent there were two small dressing-tents. One of these, allotted to the male performers, was partitioned into halves by a cloth; and in one of the divisions there was sitting on the grass, pulling on a pair of jack-boots, a young man whom we instantly recognize as Sergeant Troy.

Troy's appearance in this position may be briefly accounted for. The brig aboard which he was taken in Budmouth Roads was about to start on a voyage, though somewhat short of hands. Troy read the articles and joined, but before they sailed a boat was despatched across the bay to Lulwind Cove; as he had half expected, his cloths were gone. He ultimately worked his passage to the United States, where he made a precarious living in various towns as Professor of Gymnastics, Sword Exercise, Fencing, and Pugilism. A few months were sufficient to give him a distaste for this kind of life. There was a certain animal form of refinement in his nature; and however pleasant a strange condition might be whilst privations were easily warded off, it was disadvantageously coarse when money was short. There was ever present, too, the idea that he could claim a home and its comforts did he but choose to return to England and Weatherbury Farm. Whether Bathsheba thought him dead was a frequent subject of curious conjecture. To England he did return at last; but the fact of drawing nearer to Weatherbury abstracted its fascinations, and his intention to enter his old groove at that place became modified. It was with gloom he considered on landing at Liverpool that if he were to go home his reception would be of a kind very unpleasant to contemplate; for what Troy had in the way of emotion was an occasional fitful sentiment which sometimes caused him as much inconvenience as emotion of a strong and healthy kind. Bathsheba was not a woman to be made a fool of, or a woman to suffer in silence; and how could he endure existence with a spirited wife to whom at first entering he would be beholden for food and lodging? Moreover, it was not at all unlikely that his wife would fail at her farming, if she had not already done so; and he would then become liable for her maintenance: and what a life such a future of poverty with her would be, the spectre of Fanny constantly between them, harrowing his temper and embittering her words! Thus, for reasons touching on distaste, regret, and shame commingled, he put off his return from day to day, and would have decided to put it off altogether if he could have found anywhere else the ready-made establishment which existed for him there.

At this time – the July preceding the September in which we find him at Greenhill Fair – he fell in with a travelling circus which was performing in the outskirts of a northern town. Troy introduced himself to the manager by taming a restive horse of the troupe, hitting a suspended apple with a pistol-bullet fired from the animal's back when in full gallop, and other feats. For his merits in these – all more or less based upon his experiences as a dragoon-guardsman – Troy was taken into the company, and the play of Turpin was prepared with a view to his personation of the chief character. Troy was not greatly elated by the appreciative spirit in which he was undoubtedly treated, but he thought the engagement might afford him a few weeks for consideration. It was thus carelessly, and without having formed any definite plan for the future, that Troy found himself at Greenhill Fair with the rest of the company on this day.

And now the mild autumn sun got lower, and in front of the pavilion the following incident had taken place. Bathsheba – who was driven to the fair that day by her odd man Poorgrass – had, like every one else, read or heard the announcement that Mr Francis, the Great Cosmopolitan Equestrian and Roughrider, would enact the part of Turpin, and she was not yet too old and careworn to be without a little curiosity to see him. This particular show was by far the largest and grandest in the fair, a horde of little shows grouping themselves under its shade like chickens around a hen. The crowd had passed in, and Boldwood, who had been watching all the day for an opportunity of speaking to her, seeing her comparatively isolated, came up to her side.

'I hope the sheep have done well to-day, Mrs Troy?' he said nervously.

'O yes, thank you,' said Bathsheba, colour springing up in the centre of her cheeks. 'I was fortunate enough to sell them all just as we got upon the hill, so we hadn't to pen at all.'

'And now you are entirely at leisure?'

'Yes, except that I have to see one more dealer in two hours' time: otherwise I should be going home. I was looking at this large tent and the announcement. Have you ever seen the play of "Turpin's Ride to York"? Turpin was a real man, was he not?'

'O yes, perfectly true – all of it. Indeed, I think I've heard Jan Coggan say that a relation of his knew Tom King, Turpin's friend, quite well.'

'Coggan is rather given to strange stories connected with his relations, we must remember. I hope they can all be believed.'

'Yes, yes; we know Coggan. But Turpin is true enough. You have never seen it played, I suppose?'

'Never. I was not allowed to go into these places when I was young. Hark! What's that prancing? How they shout!'

'Black Bess just started off, I suppose. Am I right in supposing you would like to see the performance, Mrs Troy? Please excuse my mistake, if it is one; but if you would like to, I'll get a seat for you with pleasure.' Perceiving that she hesitated, he added, 'I myself shall not stay to see it: I've seen it before.'

Now Bathsheba did care a little to see the show, and had only withheld her feet from the ladder because she feared to go in alone. She had been hoping that Oak might appear, whose assistance in such cases was always accepted as an inalienable right, but Oak was nowhere to be seen; and hence it was that she said, 'Then if you will just look in first, to see if there's room, I think I will go in for a minute or two.'

And so a short time after this Bathsheba appeared in the tent with Boldwood at her elbow, who, taking her to a 'reserved' seat, again withdrew.

This feature consisted of one raised bench in a very conspicuous part of the circle, covered with red cloth, and floored with a piece of carpet, and Bathsheba immediately found, to her confusion, that she was the single reserved individual in the tent, the rest of the crowded spectators, one and all, standing on their legs on the borders of the arena, where they got twice as good a view of the performance for half the money. Hence as many eyes were turned upon her, enthroned alone in this place of honour, against a scarlet background, as upon the ponies and clown who were engaged in preliminary exploits in the centre, Turpin not having yet appeared. Once there, Bathsheba was forced to make the best of it and remain: she sat down, spreading her skirts with some dignity over the unoccupied space on each side of her, and giving a new and feminine aspect to the pavilion. In a few minutes she noticed the fat red nape of Coggan's neck among those standing just below her, and Joseph Poorgrass's saintly profile a little further on.

The interior was shadowy with a peculiar shade. The strange luminous semi-opacities of fine autumn afternoons and eves intensified into Rembrandt effects the few yellow sunbeams which came through holes and divisions in the canvas, and spirited like jets of gold-dust across the dusky blue atmosphere of haze pervading the tent, until they alighted on inner surfaces of cloth opposite, and shone like little lamps suspended there.

Troy, on peeping from his dressing-tent through a slit for a reconnoitre before entering, saw his unconscious wife on high before him as described, sitting as queen of the tournament. He started back in utter confusion, for although his disguise effectually concealed his personality, he instantly felt that she would be sure to recognize his voice. He had several times during the day thought of the possibility of some Weatherbury person or other appearing and recognizing him; but he had taken the risk carelessly. If they see me, let them, he had said. But here was Bathsheba in her own person; and the reality of the scene was so much intenser than any of his prefigurings that he felt he had not half enough considered the point.

She looked so charming and fair that his cool mood about Weatherbury people was changed. He had not expected her to exercise this power over him in the twinkling of an eye. Should he go on, and care nothing? He could not bring himself to do that. Beyond a politic wish to remain unknown, there suddenly arose in him now a sense of shame at the possibility that his attractive young wife, who already despised him, should despise him more by discovering him in so mean a condition after so long a time. He actually blushed at the thought, and was vexed beyond measure that his sentiments of dislike towards Weatherbury should have led him to dally about the country in this way.

But Troy was never more clever than when absolutely at his wits' end. He hastily thrust aside the curtain dividing his own little dressing space from that of the manager and proprietor, who now appeared as the individual called Tom King as far down as his waist, and as the aforesaid respectable manager thence to his toes.

'Here's the devil to pay!' said Troy.

'How's that?'

'Why, there's a blackguard creditor in the tent I don't want to see, who'll discover me and nab me as sure as Satan if I open my mouth. What's to be done?'

'You must appear now, I think.'

'I can't.'

'But the play must proceed.'

'Do you give out that Turpin has got a bad cold, and can't speak his part, but that he'll perform it just the same without speaking.'

The proprietor shook his head.

'Anyhow, play or no play, I won't open my mouth,' said Troy firmly. 'Very well, then let me see. I tell you how we'll manage,' said the other, who perhaps felt it would be extremely awkward to offend his leading man just at this time. 'I won't tell 'em anything about your keeping silence; go on with the piece and say nothing, doing what you can by a judicious wink now and then, and a few indomitable nods in the heroic places, you know. They'll never find out that the speeches are omitted.'

This seemed feasible enough, for Turpin's speeches were not many or long, the fascination of the piece lying entirely in the action; and accordingly the play began, and at the appointed time Black Bess leapt into the grassy circle amid the plaudits of the spectators. At the turnpike scene, where Bess and Turpin are hotly pursued at midnight by the officers, and the half-awake gatekeeper in his tasselled nightcap denies that any horseman has passed, Coggan uttered a broad-chested 'Well done!' which could be heard all over the fair above the bleating, and Poorgrass smiled delightedly with a nice sense of dramatic contrast between our hero, who coolly leaps the gate, and halting justice in the form of his enemies, who must needs pull up cumbersomely and wait to be let through. At the death of Tom King, he could not refrain from seizing Coggan by the hand, and whispering, with tears in his eyes, 'Of course, he's not really shot, Jan – only seemingly!' And when the last sad scene came on, and the body of the gallant and faithful Bess had to be carried out on a shutter by twelve volunteers from among the spectators, nothing could restrain Poorgrass from lending a hand, exclaiming, as he asked Jan to join him, "Twill be something to tell of at Warren's in future years, Jan, and hand down to our children.' For many a year in Weatherbury, Joseph told, with the air of a man who had had experiences in his time, that he touched with his own hand the hoof of Bess as she lay upon the board upon his shoulder. If, as some thinkers hold, immortality consists in being enshrined in others' memories, then did Black Bess become immortal that day if she never had done so before.

Meanwhile Troy had added a few touches to his ordinary make-up for the character, the more effectually to disguise himself, and though he had felt faint qualms on first entering, the metamorphosis effected by judiciously 'lining' his face with a wire rendered him safe from the eyes of Bathsheba and her men. Nevertheless, he was relieved when it was got through.

There was a second performance in the evening, and the tent was lighted up. Troy had taken his part very quietly this time, venturing to introduce a few speeches on occasion; and was just concluding it when, whilst standing at the edge of the circle contiguous to the first row of spectators, he observed within a yard of him the eye of a man darted keenly into his side features. Troy hastily shifted his position, after having recognized in the scrutineer the knavish bailiff Pennyways, his wife's sworn enemy, who still hung about the outskirts of Weatherbury.

At first Troy resolved to take no notice and abide by circumstances. That he had been recognized by this man was highly probable; yet there was room for a doubt. Then the great objection he had felt to allowing news of his proximity to precede him to Weatherbury in the event of his return, based on a feeling that knowledge of his present occupation would discredit him still further in his wife's eyes, returned in full force. Moreover, should he resolve not to return at all, a tale of his being alive and being in the neighbourhood would be awkward; and he was anxious to acquire a knowledge of his wife's temporal affairs before deciding which to do.

In this dilemma Troy at once went out to reconnoitre. It occurred to him that to find Pennyways, and make a friend of him if possible, would be a very wise act. He had put on a thick beard borrowed from the establishment, and in this he wandered about the fair-field. It was now almost dark, and respectable people were getting their carts and gigs ready to go home.

The largest refreshment booth in the fair was provided by an innkeeper from a neighbouring town. This was considered an unexceptional place for obtaining the necessary food and rest: Host Trencher (as he was jauntily called by the local newspaper) being a substantial man of high repute for catering through all the country round. The tent was divided into first and second-class compartments, and at the end of the first-class division was a yet further enclosure for the most exclusive, fenced off from the body of the tent by a luncheon-bar, behind which the host himself stood, bustling about in white apron and shirt-sleeves, and looking as if he had never lived anywhere but under canvas all his life. In these penetralia were chairs and a table, which, on candles being lighted, made quite a cozy and luxurious show, with an urn, plated tea and coffee pots, china teacups, and plum cakes.

Troy stood at the entrance to the booth, where a gipsy-woman was frying pancakes over a little fire of sticks and selling them at a penny a-piece, and looked over the heads of the people within. He could see nothing of Pennyways, but he soon discerned Bathsheba through an opening into the reserved space at the further end. Troy thereupon retreated, went round the tent into the darkness, and listened. He could hear Bathsheba's voice immediately inside the canvas; she was conversing with a man. A warmth overspread his face: surely she was not so unprincipled as to flirt in a fair! He wondered if, then, she reckoned upon his death as an absolute certainty. To get at the root of the matter, Troy took a penknife from his pocket and softly made two little cuts cross-wise in the cloth, which, by folding back the corners, left a hole the size of a wafer. Close to this he placed his face, withdrawing it again in a movement of surprise; for his eye had been within twelve inches of the top of Bathsheba's head. It was too near to be convenient. He made another hole a little to one side and lower down, in a shaded place beside her chair, from which it was easy and safe to survey her by looking horizontally.

Troy took in the scene completely now. She was leaning back, sipping a cup of tea that she held in her hand, and the owner of the male voice was Boldwood, who had apparently just brought the cup to her. Bathsheba, being in a negligent mood, leant so idly against the canvas that it was pressed to the shape of her shoulder, and she was, in fact, as good as in Troy's arms; and he was obliged to keep his breast carefully backward that she might not feel its warmth through the cloth as he gazed in.

Troy found unexpected chords of feeling to be stirred again within him as they had been stirred earlier in the day. She was handsome as ever, and she was his. It was some minutes before he could counteract his sudden wish to go in, and claim her. Then he thought how the proud girl who had always looked down upon him even whilst it was to love him, would hate him on discovering him to be a strolling player. Were he to make himself known, that chapter of his life must at all risks be kept for ever from her and from the Weatherbury people, or his name would be a byword throughout the parish. He would be nicknamed 'Turpin' as long as he lived. Assuredly before he could claim her these few past months of his existence must be entirely blotted out.

'Shall I get you another cup before you start, ma'am?' said Farmer Boldwood.

'Thank you,' said Bathsheba. 'But I must be going at once. It was great neglect in that man to keep me waiting here till so late. I should have gone two hours ago, if it had not been for him. I had no idea of coming in here; but there's nothing so refreshing as a cup of tea, though I should never have got one if you hadn't helped me.'

Troy scrutinized her cheek as lit by the candles, and watched each varying shade thereon, and the white shell-like sinuosities of her little ear. She took out her purse and was insisting to Boldwood on paying for her tea for herself, when at this moment Pennyways entered the tent. Troy trembled: here was his scheme for respectability endangered at once. He was about to leave his hole of espial, attempt to follow Pennyways, and find out if the ex-bailiff had recognized him, when he was arrested by the conversation, and found he was too late.

'Excuse me, ma'am,' said Pennyways; 'I've some private information for your ear alone.'

'I cannot hear it now,' she said coldly. That Bathsheba could not endure this man was evident; in fact, he was continually coming to her with some tale or other, by which he might creep into favour at the expense of persons maligned.

'I'll write it down,' said Pennyways confidently. He stooped over the table, pulled a leaf from a warped pocket-book, and wrote upon the paper, in a round hand –

'*Your husband is here. I've seen him. Who's the fool now?*'

This he folded small, and handed towards her, Bathsheba would not read it; she would not even put out her hand to take it. Pennyways, then, with a laugh of derision, tossed it into her lap, and, turning away, left her.

From the words and action of Pennyways, Troy, though he had not been able to see what the ex-bailiff wrote, had not a moment's doubt that the note referred to him. Nothing that he could think of could be done to check the exposure. 'Curse my luck!' he whispered, and added imprecations which rustled in the gloom like a pestilent wind. Meanwhile Boldwood said, taking up the note from her lap –

'Don't you wish to read it, Mrs Troy? If not, I'll destroy it.'

'Oh, well,' said Bathsheba carelessly, 'perhaps it is unjust not to read it; but I can guess what it is about. He wants me to recommend him, or it is to tell me of some little scandal or another connected with my work-people. He's always doing that.'

Bathsheba held the note in her right hand. Boldwood handed towards her a plate of cut bread-and-butter; when, in order to take a slice, she put the note into her left hand, where she was still holding the purse, and then allowed her hand to drop beside her close to the canvas. The moment had come for saving his game, and Troy impulsively felt that he would play the card. For yet another time he looked at the fair hand, and saw the pink finger-tips, and the blue veins of the wrist, encircled by a bracelet of coral chippings which she wore: how familiar it all was to him! Then, with the lightning action in which he was such an adept, he noiselessly slipped his hand under the bottom of the tent-cloth, which was far from being pinned tightly down, lifted it a little way, keeping his eye to the hole, snatched the note from her fingers, dropped the canvas, and ran away in the gloom towards the bank and ditch, smiling at the scream of astonishment which burst from her. Troy then slid down on the outside of the rampart, hastened round in the bottom of the entrenchment to a distance of a hundred yards, ascended again, and crossed boldly in a slow walk towards the front entrance of the tent. His object was now to get to Pennyways, and prevent a repetition of the announcement until such time as he should choose.

Troy reached the tent door, and standing among the groups there gathered, looked anxiously for Pennyways, evidently not wishing to make himself prominent by inquiring for him. One or two men were speaking of a daring attempt that had just been made to rob a young lady by lifting the canvas of the tent beside her. It was supposed that the rogue had imagined a slip of paper which she held in her hand to be a bank note, for he had seized it, and made off with it, leaving her purse behind. His chagrin and disappointment at discovering its worthlessness would be a good joke, it was said. However, the occurrence seemed to have become known to few, for it had not interrupted a fiddler, who had lately begun playing by the door of the tent, nor the four bowed old men with grim countenances and walking-sticks in hand, who were dancing 'Major Malley's Reel' to the tune. Behind these stood Pennyways. Troy glided up to him, beckoned, and whispered a few words; and with a mutual glance of concurrence the two men went into the night together.

7   AN EVENING AT A WHITECHAPEL GAFF

It is worth comparing Hardy's literary account, set as it is within the familiar landscape of the novel, with a piece of journalism describing a visit to a penny theatre – or gaff – in Whitechapel, which was published in the same year. James Greenwood writes about London life as if he is witnessing the rituals of a strange, uncivilised country, which in a sense he is. The mid-century onward was an era of social discovery when gentlemen of the press such as Henry Mayhew, George Augustus Sala and Charles Booth ventured into the unknown underworld of the urban poor and brought back reports which were eagerly read by the conscientious bourgeoisie. The following piece is taken from Greenwood's *The Wilds of London*, a title which makes London seem as untamed and exotically unexplored as the African or South American interior. Greenwood becomes an explorer in the true Victorian sense, measuring his normality against the otherness of the natives. There are several layers of strangeness here as the performance offers its own shabby attempt at foreign exotica.

Penny gaff presentations usually lasted an hour and were repeated several times to different audiences in the course of an evening. Spectators at these shows were mostly children, and social observers were appalled at the moral effect of such entertainment. In Henry Mayhew's words in *London Labour and the London Poor*,

> The audience is usually composed of children so young that these dens become the schoolrooms where the guiding morals of a life are picked up; and so precocious are the little things, that the girl of nine will, from constant attendance at such places, have learnt to understand the filthiest sayings, and laugh at them as loudly as the grown-up lads around her. What notions can the young female form of marriage and chastity, when the penny theatre rings with applause at the performance of a scene whose sole point turns upon the pantomimic

imitation of the unrestrained indulgence of the most corrupt appetites of our nature?

★

from THE WILDS OF LONDON
James Greenwood

An evening at a Whitechapel 'gaff'

Happening to pass that way in the morning, I was just in time to witness a gentleman belonging to the establishment (a lank, dirty-bearded gentleman he was, who smoked a dirty pipe, and wore the sleeves of his dirty shirt rolled above his dirty elbows) engaged in affixing to a great board that hung against the 'gaff' door an announcement of a new piece to be produced that evening.

It was an announcement calculated to arrest the attention of the passers-by, being inscribed in bold and flourishing red and blue letters on orange-coloured cardboard, and that it was the work of the gentleman who published it was evident from the fact that the face and hands and the sides of his trousers were smudged with the same brilliant colours. 'Astounding!' (in blue); 'Startling!!' (in red); 'Don't miss it!!!' (in red and blue artistically blended) were the head-lines of the placard, which further went on to inform the public that that evening 'your old favourites,' Mr and Mrs Douglas Fitzbruce, would appear, with the rest of the talented company, in a new and original equestrian spectacle entitled 'Gentleman Jack, or the Game of High Toby,' with real horses and a real carriage. By the time the person with the short pipe had finished up the placard, and had added a few additional touches by means of a small paint-brush to the most telling lines, several young men and women of the neighbourhood had congregated to spell and discuss its contents. Their criticism was highly favourable. They prognosticated that it would be a 'clippin'' piece, not only on account of the real horses, but because Mrs Douglas Fitzbruce was a 'reg'lar stunner' in the highwayman line. The majority of the critics vowed 'strike them blind' if they wouldn't come and see it, while the rest promised themselves the treat provided they could raise the ha'pence. As for me, I made up my mind on the spot.

'First performance at half-past six,' the bill stated, and, desirous of obtaining a front seat, I was at the 'gaff' door at least twenty minutes earlier. Not early enough, however. The 'pit' and 'box' passages leading to the inner doors were already densely thronged, and that by individuals who would not submit to elbowing. I did not attempt it. No one is so tenacious of his rights to recognition as a fellow-man as the budding costermonger aged fifteen or sixteen, and no one is readier to uphold his dignity than the female of his bosom, who, although a year or two younger, comes of a stock that will stand no nonsense. The mob pressing about the gaff were nearly all of the sort indicated; the exception being a few old men and a few children.

In a few minutes the doors were opened, and we were admitted – the box customers on payment of twopence, and the pit customers at the rate of a penny each. It was not a commodious building, nor particularly handsome, the only attempt at embellishment appearing at the stage end, where for the space of a few feet the plaster wall was covered with ordinary wall paper of a grape-vine pattern, and further ornamented by coloured and spangled portraits of Mrs Douglas Fitzbruce in her celebrated characters of 'Cupid' and 'Lady Godiva.' There were many copies of these portraits, and they were ticketed for sale – the former at sixpence, and the latter at nine-pence; though why the difference is hard to say, since in the matter of spangling, or, indeed, any other kind of covering, the cost of producing Lady Godiva must have been even less than that incurred in perfecting the print of the 'God of Love.' The stage itself was a mere platform of rough boards; the seats in the pit were of the same material. The boards that were the box seats, however, were planed, and, further to ensure the comfort of the gentility patronising that part of the theatre, there were written bills posted up to the effect that 'smoking and spitting was objected to on account of fire,' but as the audience treated this vague and contradictory notice with well-merited contempt, I was not sorry that I could advance no closer than the back seat of all.

The performance was commenced by a black man, – a brawny ruffian, naked to the waist, and with broad rings of red round his ankles and wrists, illustrative, as presently appeared, of his suffering from the chafing of the manacles he had worn in a state of slavery. It was a very long descriptive ballad, set to the not over lively tune of 'Mary Blane,' and the audience – who had possibly heard it on a few previous occasions – at the termination of the fifth verse expressed a desire that the singer should 'cut it short,' and on the oppressed negro taking no notice of the intimation, but beginning the sixth verse in all coolness, somebody threw a largish crust of bread at him, which narrowly missed his head, and somebody else threw a fish-bone with more certain aim, so that it was lodged in the unfortunate African's wool, and there instantly followed an explosion of mirth that by no means tended to solace the indignity cast on him. He glared to the right and the left of him, and, apparently marking the delinquent in the pit, jumped off the stage and rushed towards him. What then transpired, I cannot say, not being in a position to see, but after a minute of uproar, and cursing, and swearing, and yelling laughter, the black man scrambled on to the stage again with a good deal of the blacking rubbed off his face, and with his wool wig in his hand, exposing his proper short crop of carroty hair. 'Now looky' here!' exclaimed he, with a desperate, but not entirely successful, effort to delivery himself in a calm and impassionate manner, 'Looky' here, if you thinks by a-choking me off to get at the new piece a bit the sooner you're just wrong. When I've done a-singin' my song then the piece'll be ready and not a oat before, and the more you hinterrupts why the longer you'll be kept-a-waitin', that's all.' And having expressed these manly and British sentiments in genuine Whitechapel English, he readjusted his wig and became once more an afflicted African bewailing how

'Cruel massa stole him wife and lily piccaninny,'

and continued without further interruption till he had accomplished the eighth verse, and was about to commence the ninth when someone behind the scenes audibly whispered, 'Off, Ginger,' and off he went, and the star of the evening, Gentleman Jack, came in with a bound and a bow that elicited even a louder roar from the company than had greeted the lodgment of the fish-bone in Ginger's wool.

It was Mrs Douglas Fitzbruce fully equipped for the 'High Toby game.' She wore buckskin shorts, and boots of brilliant polish knee high and higher, and with spurs to them; her coat was of green velvet slashed with crimson, with a neat little breast pocket, from which peeped a cambric handkerchief; her raven curls hung about her shoulders, and on her head was a three-cornered hat, crimson edged with gold; under her arm she carried a riding whip, and in each hand a pistol of large size. By way of thanking her friends in the boxes and pit for their generous greeting (it is against the law for the actors to utter so much as a single word during the performance of a 'gaff' piece), she uttered a saucy laugh (she could not have been more than forty-five), and, cocking her firearms, 'let fly' at them point blank as it seemed; however, the whistling and stamping of feet that immediately ensued showed that nobody was wounded – indeed, that the audience rather enjoyed being shot at than otherwise.

Being debarred the use of speech, the bold highwayman was driven to the exercise of his vocal talent, in order to explain his own game in general, and the High Toby game in particular. The highwayman sang a song all about another highwayman, who, 'mounted on his mare, with his barkers at his belt,' boldly faced an old miller 'jogging home from market,' and appropriated his bag of gold after blowing his brains out. Also how the same thief and murderer was pursued by Bow Street runners – one a blue-eyed man. But the 'High Toby' boy, turning about in the saddle, took aim with his pistol at the runner and fired, and –

> 'His eyes of a colour a minute ago,
> Were now one of 'em *red* and the t'other one blue' –

a jocular result which the company assembled seemed keenly to appreciate. It terminated the song, and besides shouts of 'Hencore!' and stamping and whistling, there was a cry of 'Chuck 'em on!' followed by a casting of halfpence on to the stage. Not many, however; not more than amounted to sixpence; but the dashing highwayman seemed very grateful, and looked after the rolling coins with an avidity that showed how ill he could afford to forego the smallest of them.

Presently in rushed another highwayman, seedier than Gentleman Jack. This was Mr Douglas Fitzbruce, and, from his being pitted with small-pox, and having a slight squint in his right eye, I at once recognized in him the gentleman who had nailed up the outside poster in the morning. He came in for some applause, but chiefly from the female portion of the audience, the males appearing to entertain feelings of envy and jealousy against him as the lawful proprietor of the lady in the long boots.

The second highwayman, who was greeted as Tom King, seemed in a tremendous hurry about something. He slapped his breast energetically, and pointed repeatedly and determinedly in a certain direction; on which Gentleman Jack started violently and commenced to load his pistols to their muzzles with powder and ball, the other highwayman followed his example. Then Gentleman Jack straddled his legs and bobbed up and down, working his arms as though he held reins in his hands, as an intimation to the second highwayman that he wanted his horse; then, waving their hats in the most daring and gallant manner, they both rushed off.

After a lapse of about a minute a hurricane of applause welcomed the approaching sound of horse's hoofs, and presently appeared Gentleman Jack, with a bit of black crepe concealing the upper part of his features, on horseback. It was a remarkably docile horse, not to say a subdued one, and hung its big head down to its thick and heavy legs in a decidedly sleepy manner. Properly, I believe, he should have showed his high mettle by rearing and plunging a bit when Gentleman Jack spurred him, but though the bold rider sawed at its bit until the animal's toothless gums were visible, and spurred it until the rowels were completely clogged with the yielding hair of its flanks, it only wagged its tail languidly and snorted. Again was the sound of approaching hoofs heard, this time accompanied by the rumbling of wheels, and Gentleman Jack, rising in his stirrups, detected the sound and gave a low whistle, which was responded to, and Tom King promptly made his appearance with black crepe on his face, and a naked sword in one hand and a horse pistol in the other. Then the highwaymen clasped hands, and looked upwards, as though calling on the gods to witness the compact they had made to stick to each other till the death.

Now all was ready for the robbery, but it couldn't come off for some unknown reason. The rumbling of wheels had stopped suddenly, though the sound of hoofs had not, and there were heard as well strange muffled 'clucking' noises, as of men urging on a horse disinclined to move. This rather spoilt the scene, for the gentlemen of the audience having a practical knowledge of donkeys and horses, and of the obstinate fits that occasionally seize on those animals, instantly guessed the difficulty, and gleefully shouted suggestions as to the proper mode of treatment to be applied to the quadruped that was stopping the play. 'Hit him on the 'ock!' 'Twist the warmint's tail!' 'Shove him up behind!' Which – if either – of these suggestions was adopted I cannot say, but suddenly the vehicle that contained the highwaymen's booty bolted on to the stage, amid the uproarious plaudits of the spectators.

It was not a very magnificent turn-out, being nothing else indeed than an old street cab drawn by a vicious brother of the animal Gentleman Jack rode, and made to look slightly like a chariot by the driver's seat being set round with coloured chintz, hammercloth wise. A driver in a cocked hat sat on the box, and a footman with a cocked hat stood on the springs behind; but neither retained his place long, for from the saddle Gentleman Jack shot the coachman dead as a doornail, while Tom King, rushing on the footman with his naked sword, hacked him down in a twinkling, to the great delight of the young costermongers.

Then we came at the pith of the play. Loud shrieks were heard proceeding from the interior of the chariot, and simultaneously a gray-haired old man put his head out at one window and a lovely damsel put her head out at the other. The gray-haired old man clasped his hands, and the lovely damsel clasped her hands. With a gesture of joy, Gentleman Jack sprang from his horse, and, rushing to the carriage on the damsel side, flung open the door and caught the fair and fainting form that at that identical moment was tumbling out. Tom King rushed to the gray-haired side, and, flinging open the door, dragged out the old man, and, kneeling on his chest, pointed the naked sword at his throat and the muzzle of his pistol at his temple. At which stirring, though somewhat perplexing spectacle, the audience cheered more vociferously than ever, and 'chucked on' ninepence at the very least. The most inexplicable part of the business (to me, that is, though nobody else appeared so to regard it) was that the lovely damsel seemed well acquainted with Gentleman Jack, for as soon as that gallant had restored her to consciousness by the administration of kisses and something out of a bottle, she flung her arms round his neck with a cry that caused the gray-haired old man to wriggle visibly in spite of the threatening sword-blade and enormous weight pressing on him. Insignificant as the movement appeared to me, it was enough to furnish a clue to the keener perceptions of my fellow-occupants of the box.

'Now don't you twig, Ben?' remarked a young woman, with no bonnet and largish coral earrings, to her young man, who had just before expressed his inability 'to make 'eds or tails on it;' 'Now don't you twig? It's the old cove wots runnin' away with the gal wot Gentleman Jack used to keep the company of afore he took to High Toby. He's a takin' of her off to marry her or somethink, and Gentleman Jack is jest in time to prewent him.'

If this was not a strictly correct guess as to the state of the case, it was not far wrong, as the progress of the dumb-show drama proved. Rising from the prostrate old man, but still keeping the pistol pointed at his head, Tom King approached the chariot and hauled out a box labelled 'plate,' and several canvas bags, each branded '£5000.' As each bag was brought out the old man writhed and uttered a deep groan; but Tom's eyes glared on him, and he dare not rise. At last all the property was removed from the carriage and placed in a heap, and then Gentleman Jack led the beautiful damsel forward, her hand in his, and the pair stood by the money-bags and the plate-chest. The old man rolled his head from side to side and wrung his hands. Tom King whispered in his ear, and the old man shook his head fiercely and very decidedly. Evidently they wanted him to do something he had no mind to. The fair damsel went on her knees and clasped her hands, and Tom King glared and pressed the muzzle of his pistol to the old man's head. The old man was melted and shed tears. Seeing which, Tom King was melted too, and shed tears, as did Gentleman Jack and the damsel. Then the old man staggered to his feet, and, spreading his hands over the plate-box and the money-bags and Gentleman Jack and the damsel, as they knelt together with their hands lovingly locked, blessed the lot; and that was the end of the play.

8   THE ENCHANTED ISLE

The popular theatre's obsession with sensational 'true' stories may be broadly compared to modern television's and tabloid journalism's love of real-life drama. Then as now, crime was a favourite subject and melodramas such as *Sweeney Todd* and *Maria Martin, or The Murder in the Red Barn*, appeared in many versions and are still retained in popular culture today. The lurid nature of Victorian crime melodrama was advertised by such enjoyably sensationalist titles as *Poisoned Love*, *Bloodstained Jewels* and *The Horrible End of Emma Twinn*; clearly not light romantic comedies. Sensational effect rather than realistic reconstruction was the aim, though the use as stage props of actual objects associated, however peripherally, with the event lent it a desirable verisimilitude. Mr Crummles' working pump and tubs in *Nicholas Nickleby* mock an age where a notorious murder dramatised at the Surrey could trade on the fact that it featured the murderer's gig.

Much energy was spent translating real events into stunning fictionalised versions that were supported by increasingly real effects. Naval battles were re-enacted using exact-scale models of warships in huge tanks of water, developments in stage lighting enabled fires to be shown convincingly and one of the first uses for electricity in the 1890s was to illuminate fairy wands and crowns, making what was purely imaginary look real. This symbiosis of extreme realism and outlandish fantasy is one of the connecting strands of nineteenth-century drama and one of the main characteristics of Victorian theatricals as a whole. Audience tastes were at once serious and frivolous. While the theatre was loved for its otherness, there was a public insistence on the educational. This last requirement was not wholly bogus, being part of the Victorian hunger for knowledge, and wonder at the marvels of scientific discovery, hence the stress laid on the 'scientific' value of freakshows and performing animals. This appetite was readily exploited by the theatre which happily laced its spectacular and sensational titbits with the sharp relish of scholarly historical research, the sweets of mechanical ingenuity or the intoxicating claims of scientific progress.

The downright silliness of a lot of these entertainments is one facet of diverse and contradictory Victorian taste. It's wrong to see the people of this time as po-faced, serious and repressive. Humbug was a consistent target for satirists and one of the things the theatre did best was to laugh at sacred cultural cows. Shakespeare was no exception. At the same time as the nineteenth-century theatre reclaimed Shakespeare as a solemn cultural icon, it also mocked and deconstructed the same invention. Dickens attempted a satiric attack in his 1860–1 novel *Great Expectations* when he showed the erstwhile parish clerk Mr Wopsle playing Hamlet ludicrously badly. As before when dealing with the stage, the novelist's attempts are swallowed up by the greater Dickensian qualities of the real theatre which was more than capable of mangling Shakespeare even as it elevated him. Numerous Shakespeare travesties and burlesques were performed as well as more straightforwardly bad productions involving circus tricks and ballet dancers.

Victorians were avid improvers and increasing knowledge of the past put them, so they thought, in a position to correct Shakespeare. Managers and actors such as Charles Kean, William Macready, Samuel Phelps and Henry Irving considered they had the advantage in being able to stage Shakespearean plays in a manner beyond the bard's knowledge or resources. By the 1880s a vociferous debate had erupted over whether this massive, spectacular style was really suitable, but it nevertheless dominated productions for most of the century.

Victorian Shakespeare is an enormous subject, beyond the scope of this book, but no survey of the popular theatre would be complete without a short extract from one of the better burlesques, *The Enchanted Isle* (1848), by William and Robert Brough. A single scene is sufficient to get the measure of this entertainment with its ludicrous rhymes and constant punning. The brothers Brough came from a theatrical family. Robert (1828–1860) was a foreign correspondent, illustrator, poet, essayist and translator who also wrote an autobiographical novel. William (1826–1870) also turned his hand to numerous literary trades but wrote more for the theatre than Robert. *The Enchanted Isle* was their first dramatic collaboration.

★

from THE ENCHANTED ISLE
OR 'RAISING THE WIND' ON THE MOST
APPROVED PRINCIPLES:
Robert Barnabas Brough & William Brough

A DRAMA WITHOUT THE SMALLEST CLAIM TO LEGITIMACY,
CONSISTENCY, PROBABILITY, OR ANYTHING ELSE BUT
ABSURDITY; IN WHICH WILL BE FOUND MUCH THAT IS
UNACCOUNTABLY COINCIDENT WITH SHAKESPEARE'S
'TEMPEST'

Dramatis Personæ

ALONZO, *one of the numerous instances now-a-days of a monarch all abroad and quite at sea*

FERDINAND, *his son, a fast man thrown loose upon the waves*

GONZALO, *a minister in a queer state with many hankerings after the Home Department*

PROSPERO, *a Wizard of the North, South, East and West Winds, an exiled monarch, who, in his adverses of fortune, is blessed with excellent spirits*

ARIEL, *a magic page from Shakespeare's magic volume*

CALIBAN, *a smart, active lad, wanted (by* PROSPERO*) to make himself generally useful, but by no means inclined to do so, an hereditary bondsman, who, in his determination to be free, takes the most fearful liberties*

MIRANDA, *the original Miss Robinson Crusoe –* PROSPERO'*s pet and* FERDINAND'*s passion*

COURTIERS, *without a Court to shelter in*

LORDS, *doomed to short Commons*

EASA DI BACCASTOPPA, *Captain of the 'Naples Direct' steamer, first seen on the paddle-box, but subsequently discovered in the wrong box*

SMUTTIFACIO, *a Neapolitan stoker, very badly off in the commodity of Naples soap*

FAIRIES, *whom in consequence of the disturbed state of the times, it has been found necessary to swear in as special constables whose names are neither here nor there, but who will be found here, there, and everywhere*

SCENE IV

Before PROSPERO'*s Cell, a combination of a Cave and a modern Dwelling, being a rock,* L., *with a street door and a window let into it. On the door a plate, with 'Sig. Prospero'. A board,* R., *on which is pasted a poster, with 'Blaze of Triumph!! Positively the last week of Sig. Prospero the celebrated Wizard of the Isle!! who is about to Break his Staff and Drown his Book!!!' A Landscape and Sea View in the back.*

Enter MIRANDA *from door,* L.

MIRANDA: Now he may come as soon as e'er he pleases.
I think this style — as fast men say — 'the cheese' is. (*Looking at her dress.*)
I wonder who he is, and what he's like,
And if his fancy I may chance to strike.
But where's that Caliban! He's never near
When wanted. Caliban, where are you?

    CALIBAN (*within* R.):   Here!

MIRANDA: Come here, slave!

    Enter CALIBAN, R. *with a Wellington boot on one arm and a brush in his hand.*

CALIBAN: Slave! Come, drop that sort of bother;
Just let me ax, 'Ain't I a man and a brother?'

    MIRANDA: The airs that servants give themselves just now,
They are the 'Greatest Plague in Life', I vow.
Don't answer me, but work, you gaping swine;
Polish those boots, or else there'll be a shine.
Then come to me. (*Exit by door,* L.)

    CALIBAN: There, now; her dander's riz —
It's jolly hard upon a cove, it is.
List to my story; when it meets your ears
I'm sure the *Boxes* will be all in *tears*,
And in the *gentle pit* each *gent'll pity* me.
I'm plain, straightforward, honest, every *bit* o' me;
And though in polished articles I deal,
'A round unvarnished tale' I will reveal.

SONG

    TUNE — '*George Barnwell, good and pious*'.

Sons of freedom, hear my story,
  Pity and protect the slave,
Of my wrongs and inventory
  I'll just tip you in a stave.

Tiddle ol, &c.

(*Brushes the boot to the chorus*)

From morn till night I work like winkin',
 Yet I'm kicked and cuffed about,
With scarce half time for grub or drinkin',
 And they never lets me have a Sunday out.

Tiddle ol, &c.

And if jaw to the gov'nor I gives vent to,
 He calls up his spirits in a trice,
Who grip, squeeze, bite, sting, and torment — oh!
 Such friends at a *pinch* are by no means nice.

Tiddle ol, &c.

But I'll not stand it longer, that I'll not,
I'll strike at once, now that my *mettle's* hot.
Ha, here he comes! Now soon I'll make things better;
'Hereditary Bondsmen', hem! Et cetera.

(*Folds his arms and looks dignified.*)

  Enter PROSPERO. L.

PROSPERO: Well, sir, why don't you work?
CALIBAN (*giving the boot a single rub*): Ay, there's the rub.
PROSPERO: What, mutinous! out, vile, rebellious cub!
CALIBAN (*with sudden vigour*): Oh! who's afraid? Blow you and your boots
together. (*Throws boot down.*)
My soul's above your paltry upper leather.
PROSPERO (*aside*): That's democratic, and by no means moral!
(*To* CALIBAN.) Pick up that boot, unless you'd pick a quarrel.
You'd best not raise a breeze.
  CALIBAN: Oh! blow your breezes,
The love of liberty upon me seizes;
My bosom's filled with freedom's pure emotions,
And on the 'Rights of Labour' I've strong notions.
PROSPERO: You want work, then?
  CALIBAN: No — up for my rights I'll stick;
I've long enough been driven — now I'll kick.

SONG

TUNE — '*When the Heart of a Man*'.

When the back of a donkey's oppress'd with wares,
Which weigh rather more than is strength well bears,
 Instead of submitting he stoutly — stoutly

Plucks up a spirit and shows some airs.
Stripes are administer'd – kicks also,
But his stout ribs no emotion show.

Press him,
Caress him,
Try kicking
Or licking,

The more he is wollop'd the more he won't go.
PROSPERO: This sort of thing at once I'd better crush,
I'll stand no more – pick up that boot, then brush.

(Pointing off with staff)

CALIBAN: Never – I swear.
PROSPERO: Oh, very good; we'll see, sir.

Taps his wand on the stage, FAIRY SPECIALS *appear from all parts, and commence laying on to* CALIBAN *with their staves, chasing him round the stage.*

CALIBAN (*picks up the boot*): Oh, no, sir – don't sir – please, sir. 'Twasn't me, sir! (*Runs off, followed by* FAIRIES.)
PROSPERO: Thus disaffection should be timely checked.
Now for the Prince, whom shortly I expect;
He little thinks, in his perambulations,
How soon he'll drop upon some blood relations,
Nor that he stands on matrimony's edge;
For at his *uncle's* he must leave a *pledge* –
His heart; Miranda from his breast must pick it,
And on it lend her own – ay, that's the ticket.
I have a plan their passion to ensure –
All sorts of trouble I'll make him endure;
And on their intercourse I'll lay restriction,
So that they'll fall in love from contradiction.

MIRANDA (*from door* L.): Pa!
PROSPERO: Yes, dear!
MIRANDA: Come, and put some tidy things on.
PROSPERO: Well, look me out a collar, one with strings on.

(Exit by door, L.)

Railway music; a bell and steam whistle. A FAIRY SPECIAL *rises through trap,* C. *with a flag, and holds it out as Railway policemen do. A noise of an approaching Train is heard. Shortly after enter a fairy Locomotive,* R. *with* ARIEL *and a* SPECIAL *as engineer and stoker, attached to a car, in which sits* FERDINAND, *attended by* FAIRY SPECIALS. *Train stops at* C. ARIEL *and* FERDINAND *get out.*

ARIEL: Now then, sir, for the Wizard Cavern Station;
Your ticket, please – this is your destination.

(Jumps into train.)

FERDINAND (looking round amazed): Nay, pray explain – just say why here
you bring me.

(Train drives off, L.)

Gone, like the baseless fabric of a thing' me!
The train has vanished into sheer vacuity,
That engine shows the greatest ingenuity.
The very line's gone. Oh, it's clear as day
That line was but a 'Pencilling by the way';
And something's rubbed it out; or 'tis perhaps
One of those airy atmospheric chaps.   (Sees the door.)
But ho! What's here? 'A local habitation?'
Ay, 'and a name'. Now for some explanation.

(Reads the bill.)

'Um! 'Blaze of triumph!' That's a flaming placard;
I'll knock, and boldly; yes, egad, I'll whack hard

(He knocks.)

PROSPERO comes out suddenly followed by MIRANDA.

PROSPERO (fiercely): 'Who am dat a knocking at de door?'
FERDINAND: It's me!
PROSPERO: And pray, sir what may your intentions be?
FERDINAND: Pity the sorrows of a poor young man,
Whom fairy sprites have brought unto your door,
Who wishes you to give him – if you can,
A simple explanation – nothing more.
MIRANDA (aside): 'Tis he, I know, with Cupid's darts I'm struck.
FERDINAND (seeing MIRANDA): Good Heavens! What a captivating duck!
PROSPERO (aside): They're smitten. (Aloud and sternly.) For the questions
you have put,
I've but one answer, which is simply 'Cut!'

(Motioning his wand.)

FERDINAND (astonished): Cut?
MIRANDA: Cut?
PROSPERO: Yes, cut!
MIRANDA: Well really, Pa', I call
That cut the most unkindest cut of all.
PROSPERO: Silence, bold minx! Now, once for all, sir – hook it!
This is no inn – was it for such you took it?
FERDINAND: An inn your house by me was never thought to be,

Tho' I confess I really think it *ought* to be.
It might accommodation find at least
For man, since it accommodates a beast.
MIRANDA: Pa' I'm ashamed of you. (*Crosses to* R. *To* FERDINAND.) Sir,
don't suppose
That rudeness such as that my father shows
Runs in the family. I've none of it,
I don't take after him.
FERDINAND: You don't, a bit.
All I can say is — if from him you came,
'Deny thy father and refuse thy name',
And in return please to accept of me.   (*Opens his arms.*)
MIRANDA: I like the barter, most amazingly.
                                   (*About to rush into his arms.*)
PROSPERO (*stopping her*): Back, forward puss! egad, 'twas time to stop her;
Advances such as these are most improper.
FERDINAND: Our passion's sudden, but the style's not new,
We're 'Romeo and Juliet' number two.
Maiden, I swear —
PROSPERO: Pooh, pooh! Your vows are *hollow* as
Drums. And besides, we don't allow no followers,
Save men whose minds are honorably bent —
Not such as you — a trickster and a gent.
FERDINAND (*drawing his sword à la De Mauprat in 'Richelieu'*): Gent!
Zounds — Sir Conjuror!
PROSPERO: Ho, my angry child!
You've drawn your sword — you'd best have drawn it mild.
      (*Waves his wand.* FERDINAND *is transfixed and unable to move.*)
FERDINAND: Holloa! What's this? Quite powerless I'm grown;
From a real *brick* I'm changed into a *stone*.
I don't half like it — it quite spoils one's pleasure;
This is a most unfair Coercive Measure.
Come, please to set me free, old fellow, will you?
And 'pon my word, I'll promise not to kill you.
PROSPERO: You plead in vain; no, there take up your dwelling,
A fatal column of my magic spelling.
MIRANDA: You can't be such a brute, Pa', surely no;
I'll be his bail, if you will let him go.
FERDINAND: Thou art my *bale* of precious goods the rarest,
Within my heart locked up, and safely ware'us'd.
How I'd embrace thee, were I only free!

MIRANDA: 'More free than welcome' you could never be.

PROSPERO (*Aside*): All right! – I've changed my mind another way;
I'll punish you; therefore be free, I say.

FERDINAND *goes through pantomime expressive of being free.*

FERDINAND: As the first sign of liberty I seize
The freedom of the *press*, or rather squeeze.

(*Embraces* MIRANDA.)

PROSPERO: Phew! Here's an open armed and public meeting.
Egad! It's time that the RAPPEL was beating.

Knocks his wand on the stage as policemen do. The sound is answered, and FAIRY SPECIALS *flock in from all parts and group around.*

(*To* FERDINAND *and* MIRANDA.) Now then, disperse.

FERDINAND: Divide us if you can.
I s'pose you call yourself a loyal man.
And here you're getting up an agitation,
Our union to repeal by separation.

MIRANDA: Though as in Parliament, on every side
They stun our ears and cry 'Divide, divide',
Yet we'll not part.

PROSPERO: You won't?

FERDINAND: No!

PROSPERO: Then, of course.
The law's authority I must enforce.
Tear them asunder! (*The* SPECIALS *pull them apart.*) Now, my loving pair,
I'll teach you both my mighty power to dare.
(*To* MIRANDA.) You, miss, I sentence, ere the moon is full,
To work six ottomans in Berlin wool.
(*Turning to* FERDINAND.) And as for him, who'd 'steal what isn't his'n,'
(*Indicating* MIRANDA.)
Now that he's 'cotched', of course 'he goes to pris'n'.
Off with him – let him have some bread – nought richer;
His bed some straw; his only friend a pitcher.

SONG – PROSPERO *and* CHORUS

TUNE – '*Nix my Dolly*'.

In a box of the stone-jug all forlorn,
Whose walls your efforts will treat with scorn,
                    To break away,
All covered with irons, you'll have to lay,
Which will put a stop to your capers gay,

Fixed, my jolly pal, there you'll stay,
Fixed, my jolly pal, there you'll stay.

Exit into house. FAIRIES *march to music of the chorus, one detachment taking* MIRANDA *off by the door,* L., *the others taking* FERDINAND *off,* R.

9 JASON IN COLCHIS

Extravaganzas were another distinct variety of entertainment designed to amuse and divert. Related to burletta, pantomime and older forms of masque, these were witty and glamorous with a strong element of burlesque. James Robinson Planché (1795–1880) was the emperor of the extravaganza. Planché's long and prolific career produced a typically nineteenth-century mixture of light foolery underpinned with serious scholarly research. He specialised in the fantastic, fitting his material to the prevailing fashion. One of his earliest pieces, *The Vampire; or, The Bride of the Isles* (1820) traded on the mania for Gothic melodrama and invented a particular stage effect, known ever after as the vampire trap, which enabled actors apparently to disappear. *Cortez* deployed Ducrow's 'osses while the Drury Lane melodrama, *The Brigand*, (1829) took three fashionable paintings of Italian bandits and represented them on stage as living pictures. In the 1830s Planché created his first extravaganzas, modelling them on spectacular French forms of entertainment. During the 1840s, 50s and 60s he became known for his fairy extravaganzas and his work was a major influence on W. S. Gilbert. The libretto of Gilbert's *Thespis, or The Gods Grown Old* (1871) clearly owes a debt to Planché's treatment of classical subjects and Baron Factotum, the Great-Grand-Lord-High-Everything in Planché's pantomime *The Sleeping Beauty in the Wood* (1840) is a forerunner of Pooh-Bah in *The Mikado*. Planché and Gilbert knew each other well, though in the end it was Gilbert who saw Planché off when he attended his funeral.

Jason in Colchis is the first part of a two-part classical extravaganza, *The Golden Fleece*, written for Madame Vestus after she moved to the Theatre Royal in the Haymarket and was first performed there in 1845. Fairbrother's edition of the same year lays considerable stress on the learning and research which went into the production, but the facetious tone deliberately mocks its own pomposity in a classic piece of heavy Victorian wit. Planché was taking a rise out of his own considerable reputation as an antiquarian. He was besotted with the past and an acknowledged expert on historical costume. In his *Recollections* of 1872 he inveighs against inaccurate stage costumes, proudly citing his own authentic medieval costumes and props for Charles Kean's 1823 production of King John at Covent Garden as the first attempt to costume Shakespeare correctly.

Planché's obsession with getting it right according to the best and newest authorities was perfectly in line with public sympathies. The string of major archaeological discoveries throughout the century, beginning in 1816 when the Elgin Marbles went on show at the British Museum and progressing through Layard and Rawlinson's discoveries in Assyria between 1845 and 1855, Pompei, Ephesus, and Schliemann's Troy and Mycenae in the 1860s and 70s, made ancient cultures part of the popular imagination. In *Victorian Spectacular Theatre*, Professor Michael Booth writes that, 'antiquarian and archaeological investigation was part of the realistic movement and the general absorption in history'. In theory at least the theatre could be a living lesson in history, instructive as well as gorgeous.

Jason in Colchis doesn't live up to these lofty aims, in fact it pokes fun at them, though it does demand an audience familiar with the classics. *Jason* is a parody, written for an educated, well-dressed, theatre-going public in search of light entertainment. With its numerous misquotations from Shakespeare, dense allusions to classical myth and silly, witty rhymes and excruciating puns, it is clearly very different from the low melodramas of the penny theatres, though equally fitted to its intended audience's tastes and serving the same appetite for diverting spectacle.

The second half, *Medea in Corinth*, which is essentially the same as *Jason*, has been omitted. It is worth noting, however, that just as *Jason* ends with thunder and lightning, the palace sinking and the Argo under sail, so *Medea* concludes with the palace sinking again (the Victorian stage never underused exciting effects) and Medea carried off in a chariot drawn by two fiery dragons. Planché was renowned for his spectacular effects and transformations; in his 1849 extravaganza *The Island of Jewels*, a palm tree metamorphosised into a crowd of fairies clutching a coronet of jewels.

Jason in Colchis is a fine example of the Victorians' liking for silly songs and jokes. Gilbert's comic operas appealed to this taste, as did the ruder, cruder music of the halls which evolved in the second half of the century. Music hall had its beginnings in the song and supper rooms at taverns such as Evans in Covent Garden and the Coal Hole in the Strand. Here in these 'low' surroundings customers ate and drank while enjoying a form of cabaret with ballad singers, acrobats and dancing girls. Salacious extracts from notorious divorce trials were sometimes staged and the whole was presided over by a chairman. The format of these occasions was developed by the purpose-built variety theatres which sprang up in the 1850s and 60s. The first of these was the Canterbury, erected in Lambeth in 1852. Other 'palaces of variety' followed and the form survived well into the twentieth century.

★

from THE GOLDEN FLEECE
James Robinson Planché

A CLASSICAL EXTRAVAGANZA

The First Part
Entirely original, founded on the third and fourth books of 'the Argonautics', a poem by the late Apollonius Rhodius, Esq., principal Librarian to his Egyptian Majesty, Ptolemy Evergetes, professor of Greek Poetry in the Royal College of Alexandria, &c., &c., and entitled

JASON IN COLCHIS

Dramatis Personae

———

ÆETES, *King of Colchis (possessor of the original Golden Fleece)*
JASON, *Commander of the Argo and son of Æson, the deposed King of Iolchus*
ANONYMOUS, *Capt. of the Royal Guards*
MEDEA, *daughter of ÆETES, an enchanting creature*
ARGONAUTS, *i.e. crew of the Argo*
COLCHIAN NOBLES, SAGES, GUARDS &c.

THE PALACE OF ÆETES, KING OF COLCHIS

Three doors in centre; a large arch, R. & L.

As the curtain rises, the ship Argo, comes into port. ÆETES, *attended, enters
and takes his seat.* JASON *and the Argonauts enter. Enter* CHORUS *in front of
the raised stage, stopping* ÆETES, *who is about to speak.*

CHO: Friends, countrymen, lovers, first listen to me,
I'm the Chorus: Whatever you hear or you see,
That you don't understand, I shall rise to explain –
It's a famous old fashion that's come up again,
And will be of great service to many fine plays,
That nobody can understand now-a-days;
And think what a blessing, if found intervening,
When the author himself scarcely knows his own meaning.
You may reap from it, too, an advantage still further,
When an actor is bent upon marriage or murther,
To the Chorus his scheme he, in confidence, mentions,
'Stead of telling the pit all his secret intentions;
A wonderous improvement you all will admit,
And the secret is just as well heard by the pit.
Verbum sat: – To the wise, I'll not put one more word in,
Or instead of a Chorus they'll think me a burden,
But just say, this is Colchis, and that's King Æetes,
And this is young Jason, he coming to meet is.
And there are the forty odd friends of young Jason,
And that's their ship Argo, just entering the bason.
At the end of each scene I shall sing you some history
Or clear up whatever is in it of mystery,
But I can't tell you why – unless English I speak,
For this very plain reason – there's no Y in Greek. (*Retires.*)
ÆET: Ye who have dared to tread on Colchian ground,
Who and what are ye? whence and whither bound?
JAS: Hail, great Æetes, if you are no less –
My name is Jason, now perhaps you'll guess
My errand here?
ÆET: We are not good at guessing;
Speak, and remember whom you are addressing!
Son of the Sun, and grand-son of the Ocean,
Of anything like nonsense we've no notion!

AIR. – Jason.

'I am a brisk and lively lad.'

I am a brisk and lively lad
  As ever sail'd the seas on,
Cretheus was old Æson's dad,
  And I'm the son of Æson!
    With a yeo, yeo, yeo, yeo, &c.

A martyr to rheumatic gout,
  A feeble king was he, sir;
So uncle Pelias kicked him out,
  And packed me off to sea, sir.
    With a yeo, yeo, yeo, yeo, &c.

And now I've with a jolly crew,
  Sailed in the good ship Argo,
To rub off an old score with you,
  Then back again to Pa go.
    With a yeo, yeo, yeo, yeo, &c.

ÆET: Yeo! yeo! yeo! yeo! – I never heard such lingo,
Speak in plain words, you rascal, or by jingo –
JAS: In one word, – then you kill'd my cousin Phryxus,
And we are come for vengeance!
ÆET (*aside*):   There he nicks us.
My good young man, it is so long ago,
I scarce remember if I did or no;
Some little circumstance may have occurred
Of that description, but upon my word –
  JAS: Nay, no evasion, you owe reparation.
  ÆET: I plead the statute, then, of limitation.
  JAS: Of limitation, in a case of murther?
  ÆET: Why pursue such a subject any further?
  JAS: Pursue a subject! – I pursue a king,
And to the grindstone mean his nose to bring.
  ÆET (*aside*): Bring my nose to the grindstone! Father Phœbus!
There is no modus in this fellow's 'rebus';
He looks determined, bullying's no use,
To save my bacon I must cook his goose!
(*Aloud.*) What reparation then may purchase peace?
  JAS: The restoration of the golden fleece,

Of which you fleeced my cousin!

ÆET: Pray be cool,

All this great cry for such a little wool!
To take it if you can, sir, you are free,
No difficulty will be made by me;
But there are some obstructions in the way,
Which must all be surmounted in one day.

JAS: To them I beg immediate introduction.

ÆET: Two bulls are one.

JAS: One bull, or one obstruction?

ÆET: Two savage bulls, that breathe out fire and smoke,
You'll have to catch and break them to the yoke,
Then plough four acres, yonder crag beneath,
And sow them with a set of serpent's teeth,
From which will spring of soldiers a fine crop,
Whose heads, to save your own, you off must chop;
Then if the dragon set to guard the treasure
Will let you, you may take it at your pleasure.

JAS: In one day this must all be done!

ÆET: Just so.

JAS: Anything else in a small way?

ÆET: Why no.

There's nothing else occurs to me at present.

JAS: What will occur to me, is most unpleasant.

ÆET: It's optional, you know, you needn't do it
Unless you like.

JAS: Honour compels me to it.

OFFI: The princess.

    Enter MEDEA.

JAS: Gods! – a goddess, sure I gaze on.

ÆET: My daughter, sir, – Medea, Mr Jason! (*Introduces them.*)

QUARTETTO.

'Donna del Lago'
JASON, MEDEA, ÆETES, *and* ANONYMOUS.

JAS: To Kalon, – to sail on
In quest of, who would deign now?
Eureka! To seek a
Supremer bliss were vain now!
Pros Theon! my knee on!

I sink before such beauty!
Medea! to thee a
Poor Grecian pays his duty.
MED (*aside*): O Jason! thy face on
I wish I ne'er had look'd, sir!
So spicy and nice he,
Is – I'm completely hooked, sir!
His glances like lances,
Right through my heart he throws, O!
Enraptur'd! I'm captured
By that fine Grecian nose, O!
ÆET (*aside*): By Jupiter Ammon!
If me he thinks to gammon,
Despite of his mettle
His hash I soon will settle;
I'll hang at least forty
Of these bold Argonautæ,
I'll scuttle the Argo
And confiscate the cargo!
MED (*aside*): Sure there ne'er was such a duck, sir!
Down he seems upon his luck, sir!
I will cheer him – safely steer him;
I for him will run a muck, sir,
Teach him how to plough and sow.
JAS (*aside*): Overboard my cares I'd chuck, sir,
If to Greece with me she'd go.
ÆET (*to* JAS.): Pray walk in and take pot luck, sir.
(*Aside.*) For full soon to pot you go!
Staring like a pig that's stuck, sir,
To the ground he seems to grow!
ANON (*aside*): Down he seems upon his luck, sir,
To a goose he can't say 'boh!'
(*Exeunt* ÆT. JAS. & ARG.)
MED: Too lovely youth! wou'd I had ne'er set eyes on him!
Papa had better mind what tricks he tries on him.
Oh Eros! vulgarly called Cupid, Oh!
Thou god of love. In all the Greek I know,
And that's not much, I will apostrophize thee!
In vain the heart of mortal woman flies thee;
I, even I, feel sure that very soon I
Shall be on that young man, exceeding spoony!

AIR. – MEDEA.

'John Anderson'

You wanton son of Venus,
  My heart in twain you've rent;
Against no other maiden
  Could your wicked bow be bent?
It may seem very bold, but
  I love young Jason so;
If he were to pop the question, I
  Don't think I could say 'no.'

If he wool gathering go, love,
  My wits the wool shall gather –
In one boat we will row, love,
  In spite of wind and weather;
And if to Davy Jones, love,
  We hand and hand should go,
We'll sleep together in the old
  Boy's locker down below.

(*Exit* MED. – CHO. *advances.*)

CHO: Young ladies, I'm sure you need no explanation
Of the cause of Medea's extreme perturbation;
And yet he's so handsome – this young Grecian swain.
You'll none of you say that the cause is too plain.
However, my business at present is merely
To tell what may not have appeared quite so clearly:
The cause of the voyage, which the ship Argo
Young Jason has taken; and why this embargo
Is laid on the fleece, which lies here on the shelf;
And as I'm the Chorus I'll sing it myself.

SONG. – CHORUS.

'The Tight Little Island'

There reigned once on a time, o'er Bœotia's clime,
  A King, (Athamas he's known by name as;)
He pack'd off his first wife, and thought her the worst wife,
  Till the second the first proved the same as.
This second was Ino, who, you know,
  Was very displeasing to Juno,

And a shocking step-mother the children of t'other
  Found her to their cost, pretty soon, oh!

She threatened with slaughter her step-son and daughter
  But a ram with a fine golden fleece, sir,
Flew up thro' the sky, with them so very high,
  They could not see the least spot of Greece, sir!
They got in a deuce of a fright, sir,
  Poor Helle, she couldn't hold tight, sir!
She fell in the sea, but the young fellow, he
  Came over to Colchis, all right, sir!

What do you think this nice man did, as soon as he landed
  And found himself safe, the young sinner?
  He saw the King's daughter, made love to, and caught her,
  And had the poor ram killed for dinner.
'Twas very ungrateful you'll say, sir,
  But alas! of the world it's the way, sir,
When all a friend can, you have done for a man,
  He'll cut you quite dead the next day, sir!

But his father-in-law, who the golden fleece saw,
  Thought 'Oh! oh! two can play at that game, sir.'
And so one fine morning, without any warning,
  He served Master Phryxus the same, sir.
Before they knew what he was at, sir,
  He'd killed him as dead as a rat, sir,
He stuck him right thro', 'twas a wrong thing to do,
  But Kings don't stick at trifles like that, sir.

Well, to finish my song, which is getting too long,
  He hung up this famed golden fleece, sir,
On a tree in his park, and by way of a lark,
  Set a dragon to act as police, sir;
If Medea don't help him, you see, sir,
  Sharp work it for Jason will be, sir,
The Altar of Hecat'
  They're coming to speak at,
But of course that's betwixt you and me, sir. (CHO *retires*.)
      Enter MEDEA, *bearing a small golden box, and* JASON.
  JAS: Turn, fair enchantress, too bewitching maid!
A doating lover supplicates your aid;

A thousand charms all own that you possess,
Spare one to get me out of this sad mess.
Lo, I implore you! sinking on my sad knee –
Remember Theseus and Ariadne.
To thread the labyrinth a clue she gave him,
And from the beast (half bull, half man) to save him,
Went the whole hog.

MED: She did, I don't deny it,
And brought her pigs to a fine market by it.
Deceived, deserted, on destruction's brink,
She rushed to Bacchus – that is, took to drink.
To draw a parallel: – should Fate decree
As A to B, so C would be to D.

JAS: If I be C, and D my friend in need,
When C proves false to D may C be d—d!

MED: Great Hecate! hear my ditto to that oath,
And for the same dark journey book us both.
If true to Jason I do not remain,
Send me to Hades by the first down train.
Now mark this box of ointment, do not doubt –
Whate'er your foes this salve will sarve 'em out.
With it anointed, you may boldly take
Each bull by the horns, nor fear a bull to make.
Thro' the hard soil 'twill speed the plough, and bear,
In all thy labours, more than the plough's share.
When sown the serpent's teeth, prepare to fight;
It's no use showing teeth if you can't bite.
But as the soldiers rise, first take a sight at 'em,
Then pick up the first stone and shy it right at 'em;
On which, each thinking it was thrown by t'other,
They'll all draw swords and cut down one another.
An easy victory you thus may reap –
As to the dragon Pa has set to keep
Watch o'er the fleece, so vigilant and grim,
I'll mix a dose that soon shall doctor him.

JAS: My dear Medea! O, Medea my dear!
How shall I make my gratitude appear?
If I succeed. I swear, to Greece I'll carry you,
And there, as sure as you're alive, I'll marry you.

MED: Enough; I take your word and you my casket.
My heart was Jason's ere he came to ask it.

But oh, beware! I give you early warning;
If, your pledged faith and my fond passion scorning,
You with another venture to Philander,
To the infernal regions off I'll hand her
And lead you such a life as, on my word, will
Make e'en the cream of Tartarus to curdle.

DUO – JASON *and* MEDEA

'Ebben a té ferisce'

JAS: Ye Gods and little fishes,
Record my vows and wishes:
If from the walls of Æa
Thou'lt fly with me, Medea,
To fair Thessalia's shore,
Thee will I wed.
By Luna! thy mother,
And Phebus! her brother.

JAS: Thee will I   thee will I
                 marry;   marry, lawfully?
MED: Me will he   me will he

                              I adore!
The charmer – the charmer –
                              he adores!

'Giorno d'orrore.'

Bulls loudly roaring on mischief bent, O!
Broke to the yoke shall be in one moment, O!
Scores of old grinders drawn out for glory,
The unctuous spell shall quickly quell!
And grease for Greece fight con amore!

                        he over papa!
Oh how then, crow will
                        I o'er her papa!

MED: Then serenely to distant Thessalia,
Colchian Medea the sea will cross o'er;
JAS: There a queen, in all her regalia,
She a palace will reign in once more!
MED: Oh, an Alpha Cottage with thee, love,
I could share, nor deem it a bore!
JAS: And with thee, content I could be, love,
In the poorest attic floor!
But 'tis time that off I went, O!
Soon we meet to part no more!
MED: Be this charm a sweet memento

Of the maid whom you adore! (*Exit* JAS.)

MED: He's gone! and yet his God-like form before us (CHO *advances*.)
Appears to hover. Ah, my gentle Chorus,
You, the impartial confidant of all −
You, to whom every Colchian, great and small,
Imparts their hope or fear on this sad stage,
Have I done wrong with Jason to engage
In this great struggle 'gainst my royal sire?'

CHO: It's rather −

MED: Silence, sir, I don't require
To be told that, whatever it may be,
You were about to say; but answer me,
Have I done wrong?

CHO: You −

MED: Interrupt me not.
Have I done wrong, I ask? if so, in what?

CHO: I −

MED: Ah! your silence answers me too plainly.

CHO: But −

MED: And you offer consolation vainly.
'Gainst Fate's decree to strive, who has the brass?
For what must be comes usually to pass.
So let me haste, and pack up my portmanteau −
I've got that horrid dragon to enchant, too!

CHO: If I might ask −

MED: How that I mean to do?
In confidence, I don't mind telling you.
This dragon is a very artful dodger,
And sleeps with one eye open − the sly codger!
Now, as we daren't approach, a stick to pop in it,
The only chance is if he gets a drop in it;
For though notoriously a scaly fellow,
He has not the least objection to get mellow
At any one's expense except his own.
He's partial to an ardent spirit, known
By several names, and worshipped under all;
Some 'Cupid's eye water' the liquor call.
'White Satin' some, whilst others, wisely viewing
The baneful beverage, brand it as 'Blue Ruin.'
A plant called juniper the juice supplies,
And oft, beneath Hyperborean skies,

A bowl-full, mixed with raisins of the sun,
Gay youths and maidens set on fire for fun,
And call it snap-dragon. Now, my specific
Is this – I'll brew a potent soporific,
And in it steep a branch of this fell tree,
Which, when the dragon sniffs, with eager glee,
He'll fall, o'erpower'd by its strong aroma,
Into what doctors call a state of coma,
And if into his eye he gets a drop
'Twill change the coma into a full stop.
Then off with Jason and the Golden Fleece,
I fly to Thessaly, 'as slick as grease'.

DUO

French Air

MEDEA   *and*   CHORUS

Now farewell; for I must go, ... Oh.
To invoke my magic Ma, ... Ah.
Then to pack my portmanteau, ... Oh.
Ere I plunder poor Papa. .... Ah.
When from Colchis far away, ... Eh.
With the only Greek I know, ... Oh.
To my Jason I will say – .... Eh.
'Zoe mou sas agapo.' .... Oh.

(*Exit* MED.)

Æetes comes, looking as black as thunder,
And when you hear the cause you'll say, 'no wonder',
For Jason, aided by Medea's spell,
Has done the trick, and done the king as well.
You'll think, perhaps, you should have seen him do it,
But 'tisn't classical, you'll hear, not view it.
Whatever taxed their talent or their means,
These sly old Grecians did *behind* the scenes;
So, fired with their example, boldly we
Beg you'll suppose whate'er you wish to see.
        Enter ÆETES, *attended, and* JASON.

SONG and CHORUS – Jason, Æetes, Officer, and Chorus

Heiterersinn Polka

Æet: ⎧ Here's a precious row, sir!
Offi &:   ⎨   shall we
Cho: ⎩ What will you do now, sir!

He takes the bulls
And down he pulls,
And yokes them to the plough.
He tills the acres four, sir,
And, what's a greater bore, sir,
The teeth he sows,
And down he mows
My
   soldiers by the score!
Your

Jas: Glorious Apollo! the victory's mine!
Out of your son I have taken the shine –
Spite of his teeth and his troops of the line,
Cock of the walk am I!

Æet &c.: Here's a precious row, sir! &c.

Jas: Lo! King of Colchis, all my tasks are done,
And yet o'er Caucasus behold the sun.

Æet: Still from the dragon you the fleece must win,
Ere out of this you get in a whole skin.
Wound up, you'll find, his watch he'll always keep,
You sooner might a weazel catch asleep
And shave his eyebrow, so about it go;
If he don't eat you call and let me know. (*Exit.*)

Jas: So, then, I've work'd the whole day like a Nigger,
To cut at last this mighty silly figure!
Like a Lord Chancellor, compell'd to pack,
I've lost the wool and only got the sack;
For where's Medea, with her magic flagon –
The dose that was to doctor that deep dragon?
She's chang'd her mind, she neither comes nor sends,
And Fate cries, 'Kick him, he has got no friends.'
Embasian Phœbus! Thou ungrateful sun!
Was it for this, a salted Sally Lunn
We offered thee, the night before the day
The Minyans left the Pagasœan bay?

Wilt thou descend behind Promethean Caucasus,
Forgetful that on earth such creatures walk as us
Deaf on the shores of Aramanthine Phasis,
To him who made thy altars burn like blazes!
And vowed to roast whole oxen to thee, more
Than ever hail'd a son and heir before!
Magnus Apollo *thou?* – Pooh! go to bed,
In Tethis' lap hide thy diminished head.
No sun of mine! – to say it I am glad.
But were I Zeus, thy immortal dad,
I would myself the world, without a blush, light,
And cut you off without a farthing rushlight.

AIR – JASON.

'Then farewell, my trim-built Wherry'

Now farewell, my trim-built Argo!
Greece and Fleece, and all farewell;
Never more as super-cargo
Shall poor Jason cut a swell!

To the dragon, quite a stranger,
All alone, I'm left to go,
And to think upon my danger,
Makes me feel extremely low.

My catastrophe too plain is;
Hecate's daughter seals my doom!
Come then, friends to Jason's manes,
Sacrifice a Hetacomb!

What do I see? – oh, Sol, I ask your pardon,
I've been too hasty – yonder, through the garden,
Medea comes, to save her doating Jason.
> *Enter* MEDEA, *carrying a bowl of lighted spirits, and in the other a branch of*
> *Juniper.*
What's that she carries burning in a bason?
  MED: A dainty dish to set before the dragon.
His scaly shoulders how his head will wag on,
When first the odour of this branch he twigs!
But if a drop out of this bowl he swigs,
Deeming it gin! – All is not gold that glitters! –
To him 'twill prove a dose of gin and bitters.

Jas: Matchless Medea! I'm all admiration.
Med: Silence, whilst I commence my *gin*-cantation.

SONG – Medea

'The Mistletoe Bough'

The juniper bough to my aid I call!
Its spirit of millions has worked the fall,
And the dragon is longing snap-dragon to play,
Like a boy on a Christmas holiday.
Above him behold my father's pride,
The beautiful fleece – the golden ram's hide.
But stop till the monster asleep you see,
For he's mighty awkward company.
   Wave the juniper bough,
   Wave the juniper bough.
Behold, the monster, overcome by sleep,
Nods to his fall, like ruin on a steep
'Tis done! he sinks upon the ground, supine;
His end approaches, make it answer thine.
Hence! – with bold hand the fleecy treasure tear
Down from this beach, and hasten to that there.

                      (Exit Jas. *and returns with fleece.)*
    Jas: Arise, ye Minyans. *(Enter Argonauts.)* If again ye'd scan
Thessalia's shore, make all the sail you can.
For 'pris'ners base' you'll soon be, with your skipper,
If once her dad is roused to 'hunt the slipper'.

                              (Exeunt. Arg.)

    Med: With her bold Argonaut Medea flies,
Though 'Ah! go not,' the voice of duty cries.
With golden wool her ears sly Cupid stops,
And, like a detonator, off she pops,
In peace to pass with Jason all her days,
Till he or she the debt o' nature pays.

        (Exeunt. The Argo is seen leaving the Port. Shouts.)
    Enter Æetes.
    Æet: My mind misgives me, wherefore was that shout?
What ho! my slaves within, my guards without!
    Enter Guards and Sages.
We are betrayed! robbed! murdered! see, Oh treason!
Yonder he goes, that young son of – old Æson!

He's killed my dragon! stolen my Golden Fleece!
To arms, my Colchians! stop thief! police!

(Exeunt Guards.)

CHO (advancing): Be calm, great king! 'tis destiny's decree.
ÆET: How dare you talk of destiny to me!
What right have you with such advice to bore us?
CHO: Sir, I'm the Chorus.
ÆET: Sir, you're indecorous!
Where is my daughter?
CHO: Hopped off with the skipper!
ÆET: Impious Medea, may the furies whip her,
At the cart's tail of Thespis.
      Enter Officer and Guards.
                        Now, your news?
OFFI: Your son Absyrtus —
ÆET: Speak —
OFFI: My lips refuse
Almost, O King, to tell the horrid tale.
ÆET: My heir apparent?
OFFI: Dead as a door nail!
ÆET: Say in what manner hath his spirit fled?
OFFI: The fist of Jason punched his royal head;
Upon the shores of rapid rolling Ister,
The youthful prince o'ertook his faithless sister,
When Pelian Jason on his knowledge box,
Let fly a blow that would have felled an ox,
Black'd both his precious eyes, before so blue,
And from his nose the vital claret drew!
ÆET: Ah me! that blow has fallen on my pate.
CHO: In Jason's fist behold the hand of fate.
ÆET: I do, I do! that hit me right and left,
My daughter's stolen what I gained by theft.
Phryxus I slew, my son is now a shade,
Put me to bed ye Colchians, with a spade;
That fatal punch — I feel it in my noddle,
And down to Pluto I but ask to toddle!
CHO: Have patience man, and learn this truth sublime,
You can't go even there before your time!
      Thunder and Lightning. The Palace sinks, and the Argo is seen under sail,
      with JAS. MED. and the Argonauts.

[END OF PART FIRST.]

10 THE COLLEEN BAWN

Sensational scenes on stage were always a popular draw. When Planché looked back in old age on his long career he was anxious to dissociate himself from what he regarded as a degraded trend. In his 1872 *Recollections*, Planché condemned

> what is now distinguished as the sensational drama . . . on the grounds that the incidents are introduced for the purpose of affecting the nervous system only and not with the higher motive of pointing a moral, or the development of human passion. However cleverly constructed, they appeal to the lowest order of intellect; and the perils and atrocities represented being those most familiar to the public, from their daily occurrence in real life and graphic descriptions in the newspapers, the more naturally they are depicted, the more fearful and revolting is their effect.

Planché was speaking of a taste which pervaded all strata of the theatre. But there was one playwright in particular who capitalised on the love of sensation to the extent of creating a distinct genre of 'sensation drama'. 'Sensation is what the public wants and you cannot give them too much of it,' Dionysius Lardner Boucicault (1820–1890) informed the critic William Winter. Boucicault wrote plays which lived up to his striking name and racy reputation. Rumoured to be the natural son of a neighbour who was much younger than his legal father, the sudden death of Boucicault's first wife Anne Guiot aroused gossip that he had pushed her off a cliff. In 1885 he apparently committed bigamy by marrying an American actress while still hitched to Agnes, by whom he had four children. All his children went on the stage but his daughter Nina is perhaps the best remembered for being the first to play Peter Pan in the 1904 production of J.M. Barrie's play. Boucicault dominated the mid-century stage in England, and he was a major figure in New York where he lived from 1856–1860 and intermittently from 1872 until his death. *The Colleen Bawn; or, The Brides of Garryowen*, first performed in at Laura Keene's theatre in New York, was premiered in England at the Adelphi on Boucicault's return in 1860.

Boucicault came back to London in 1860 fresh from the controversy caused by his slavery play *The Octoroon*. Set in the American South, this was a spectacular work by any standards, featuring an exploding steamship and a camera which betrays the villain by photographing his evil deed. Exciting and successful as this was, it was too far removed from mainstream English concerns both intellectually and geographically and Boucicault chose to open in London with *The Colleen Bawn*. In New York he had titillated a populace on the cusp of a civil war over slavery with stereotypes of the 'barbaric' south; in London he turned to Ireland. Discard the local colour in each play – and here that word carries its full racial connotations – and it becomes apparent that Ireland and Louisiana are made use of in the same way, these plays are essentially fantasies of life and beliefs as they exist in 'civilised' regions made more exciting by being transplanted into picturesque and wild settings.

The Colleen Bawn thrilled audiences and set a fashion for plays with amazing scenes and cliffhanger perils. Its remarkable centrepiece was an attempted drowning, set in an Irish water cave, starring Boucicault and his wife Agnes. Twenty small boys stood in the wings shaking yards of blue gauze stretched across the stage to simulate water as the Colleen was pushed under by an evil hunchback. Boucicault played Myles-na-Coppaleen, a comic-pathetic former horse trader turned illicit whisky distiller – the very model of the stage 'oirishman' – while Agnes as the Colleen acted a beautiful peasant girl, married in secret to an Anglo-Irish gentleman ashamed of her broad brogue and working-class ways. The situation has plenty of potential for social and political comment, but as with *The Octoroon*, the story of a beautiful girl 'tainted' with the blood of a black African ancestor, Boucicault confines himself to the melodramatic, appealing to the emotions rather than the intelligence, and stops short of anything more cutting than mild comic joshing about accents. At their core, both plays are simple romantic dramas about unequal love. Hardress Cregan is unworthy of the Colleen Bawn because he rates his family pride too highly and not because she is the representative of a nation oppressed by his kind. His family pride and his desire to keep the foundering Cregan estate together reflect a commonplace, upper-middle-class Victorian concern, a situation, in essence, familiar to melodrama though usually represented at the other end of the social scale as affecting honest working people threatened by villainous landlords. Boucicault was right to choose *The Colleen Bawn* for London. The play ran for 230 performances, initiating the concept of the long run.

The Colleen Bawn resists allegorical interpretations; this is not an example of the Irish laughing at the English by pretending to laugh at themselves and nor is it, as is the case with Edmund Spenser's poem *The Faerie Queene* (1590–1596), alive with political and cultural nuances. Boucicault cut his cloth according to the prevailing fashion and *The Colleen Bawn* is very much a play for the English. All the more intriguing then is the fact is that Boucicault was Irish, born in Dublin of Huguenot extraction. Would *The Colleen Bawn* have been more political if it had been written in Ireland for an Irish audience? Later adaptations by Boucicault of *The Octoroon* suggest that Boucicault was more concerned with pandering to public taste than making provocative statements. When *The Octoroon* was finally staged in London in 1861, audiences objected to the sad ending which had the slave girl committing suicide. Boucicault hastily changed the closing scene to show the Octoroon alive and in the arms of her future husband, a white plantation owner. Londoners, it seems, were more tolerant than New Yorkers, at least when the action involved those far away in another country, and the comparison made them feel smugly enlightened. That same year Boucicault took a production of *The Colleen Bawn* to the Theatre Royal in Dublin where it played for 24 nights and was regarded as a great success. It would be interesting to know more about the composition of the audience and how the play's favourable reception by fashionable London society influenced the Irish reaction. Boucicault apparently had no sense that what he had written might offend. Forty years before the founding of the Abbey Theatre, Boucicault said he hoped that *The Colleen Bawn* would inspire others to write Irish plays drawing on Ireland's history and romance.

To the English of this period, Ireland was not quite another country but a nation defined by its relation to England. For many Londoners, 'the wild Irish' were near relations tainted with brutishness. The famine of the 1840s and the rise of Irish nationalism

The Colleen Bawn 133

created racist images in the English press of Ireland as a land of vicious, plebian monsters. A telling cartoon in *Punch* in 1843 represented Daniel O'Connell's Repeal Movement as Frankenstein's freak kicking England in the balls. *The Colleen Bawn* is silent about these political tensions but its gentler array of Irish stereotypes was made recognisable by the same popular discourse. Ireland proved a perfect fantasy land for Boucicault's London purposes and he went on to write two more sensational Irish dramas, *Arrah-na-Pogue* (1864) and *The Shaughraun* (1874). The success of these plays fed back into the popular imagination and strengthened an image which has, at its furthest reaches, resulted in Irish theme pubs and the Anglo-Irish novels of Molly Keane.

The Colleen Bawn and *The Octoroon* project strange lands with familiar outlines. Audiences on both sides of the Atlantic could enjoy the frisson of meeting a wilder version of themselves with the reassurance of an essential similarity. Differences were marked enough to be exotic but not so foreign as to disorientate. Boucicault's Irish peasants were fundamentally no different from the amusing freaks and tribal people who also shocked and titillated in the name of entertainment. Various Africans and native Americans caused sensations when they were displayed in England and historian Richard Altick has linked the exhibition of foreign people to the developing science of ethnology. In his seminal *The Shows of London* Altick wrote that 'living specimens of barbaric or savage races constituted prime material. Simultaneously, the imperialism that accompanied the early *pax Victoriana* was weaving ethnology, geography and the nation's economic and geopolitical aspirations into a single seamless pattern.'

In the year that *The Octoroon* premiered, Charles Darwin published *On The Origin of Species*. Although Darwin didn't specifically claim that people were descended from apes until he published *The Descent of Man* in 1871, the idea was inescapable – but venomously refuted in some quarters, partly, one suspects because it confirmed ancient, popular suspicions about the presence of the beast in humankind. Altick has asserted that most of the components of Darwin's theory of evolution were current knowledge in educated circles decades before the book was published and that sensation-mongers who exhibited foreign people were deliberately responding to this interest. 'In addition to the durable basic appeal of the remote and the strange, they now had working for them the strong feeling in favour of rational amusement, like the proprietors of certain freaks, but somewhat more plausibly, they could claim that their exhibitions contributed to scientific knowledge.'

The fear and fascination of the other, or the animal, lurking in the familiar was tirelessly manipulated by the Victorian theatre. We're back again with The Wild Man of the Prairies attempting to con his audience and being exposed as not real enough. Behind the Victorian search for sensation lay a desire for a dialogue with the exotic and it was the mechanisms of this hunger which produced freak shows, marvellous animals, spectacular stage effects and sensational plays.

★

THE COLLEEN BAWN;
OR, THE BRIDES OF GARRYOWEN

A DOMESTIC DRAMA IN THREE ACTS
Dion Boucicault

Dramatis Personæ

MRS CREGAN
ANNE CHUTE, *the Colleen Ruadh*
EILY O'CONNOR, *the Colleen Bawn*
SHEELAH
KATHLEEN CREAGH
DUCIE BLENNERHASSET
HARDRESS CREGAN, *son of Mrs Cregan*
KYRLE DALY, *a college friend to* HARDRESS
HYLAND CREAGH
BERTIE O'MOORE
SERVANT
FATHER TOM, *parish priest of Garryowen*
MR CORRIGAN, *a pettifogging attorney*
DANNY MANN, *the hunchbacked servant*
MYLES-NA-COPPALEEN
CORPORAL and SOLDIERS

ACT I

SCENE FIRST

(*Night*) — *Torc Cregan* — *the residence of Mrs Cregan on the Banks of Killarney. House, L. 2 E.; window facing audience (light behind — light to work in drop at back) — stage open at back. Music — seven bars before curtain.*

Enter HARDRESS CREGAN, *from house,* L.

HARD (*going up,* C.): Hist! Danny, are you there?

DANNY *appearing from below, at back.*

DANNY: Is it yourself, Masther Hardress?

HARD: Is the boat ready?

DANNY: Snug under the blue rock, sir.

HARD: Does Eily expect me to-night?

DANNY: Expict is it? Here is a lether she bade me give yuz; sure the young thing is never aisy when you are away. Look, masther, dear, do ye see that light, no bigger than a star beyant on Muckross Head?

HARD: Yes, it is the signal which my dear Eily leaves burning in our chamber.

DANNY: All night long she sits beside that light, wid her face fixed on that lamp in your windy above.

HARD: Dear dear Eily, after all here's asleep, I will leap from my window, and we'll cross the lake.

DANNY (*searching*): Where did I put that lether?

Enter KYRLE DALY *from house,* L.

KYRLE (L.): Hardress, who is that with you?

HARD (C.): Only Danny Mann, my boatman.

KYRLE: That fellow is like your shadow.

DANNY (R.): Is it a cripple like me, that would be the shadow of an illegant gintleman like Mr Hardress Cregan?

KYRLE (L.): Well, I mean that he never leaves your side.

HARD (C.): And he never *shall* leave me. Ten years ago he was a fine boy — we were foster-brothers and playmates — in a moment of passion, while we were struggling, I flung him from the gap rock into the reeks below, and thus he was maimed for life.

DANNY: Arrah! whist aroon! wouldn't I die for yez? didn't the same mother foster us? Why, wouldn't ye brake my back if it plazed ye, and welkim! Oh, Masther Kyrle, if ye'd seen him nursin' me for months, and cryin' over me, and keenin'! Sin' that time, sir, my body's been crimpin' up smaller and smaller every year, but my heart is gettin' bigger for him every day.

HARD: Go along, Danny.

DANNY: Long life t'ye, sir! I'm off. (*Runs up and descends rocks, C. to R.*)

KYRLE: Hardress, a word with you. Be honest with me – do you love Anne Chute?

HARD: Why do you ask?

KYRLE: Because we have been fellow-collegians and friends through life, and the five years that I have passed at sea have strengthened, but have not cooled, my feelings towards you. (*Offers hand.*)

 Enter MRS CREGAN, *from house,* L.

HARD (L.): Nor mine for you, Kyrle. You are the same noble fellow as ever. You ask me if I love my cousin Anne?

MRS C (C., *between them*): And I will answer you, Mr Daly.

HARD (R.): My mother!

MRS C (C.): My son and Miss Chute are engaged. Excuse me, Kyrle, for intruding on your secret, but I have observed your love for Anne with some regret. I hope your heart is not so far gone as to be beyond recovery.

KYRLE (L.): Forgive me, Mrs Cregan, but are you certain that Miss Chute really is in love with Hardress?

MRS C: Look at him! I'm sure no girl could do that and doubt it.

KYRLE: But I'm not a girl, ma'am; and sure, if you are mistaken –

HARD: My belief is that Anne does not care a token for me, and likes Kyrle better.

MRS C (C.): You are an old friend of my son, and I may confide to you a family secret. The extravagance of my husband left this estate deeply involved. By this marriage with Anne Chute we redeem every acre of our barony. My son and she have been brought up as children together, and don't know their true feelings yet.

HARD: Stop, mother, I know this: I would not wed my cousin if she did not love me, not if she carried the whole county Kerry in her pocket, and the barony of Kenmare in the crown of her hat.

MRS C: Do you hear the proud blood of the Cregans?

HARD: Woo her, Kyrle, if you like, and win her if you can. I'll back you.

 Enter ANNE CHUTE, *from house,* L.

ANNE (L. C.): So will I – what's the bet?

MRS C (C.): Hush!

ANNE: I'd like to have a bet on Kyrle.

HARD: Well, Anne, I'll tell you what it was.

MRS C (c.): Hardress!

ANNE (L. C.): Pull in one side, aunt, and let the boy go on.

HARD (R.): Kyrle wanted to know if the dark brown colt, Hardress Cregan, was going to walk over the course for the Anne Chute Stakes, or whether it was a scrub-race open to all.

ANNE: I'm free-trade — coppleens, mules and biddys.

MRS C: How can you trifle with a heart like Kyrle's?

ANNE: Trifle! his heart can be no trifle, if he's all in proportion.

Enter SERVANT *from house,* L.

SERVANT: Squire Corrigan, ma'am, begs to see you.

MRS C: At this hour, what can the fellow want? Show Mr Corrigan here.

Exit SERVANT *into house,* L.

I hate this man; he was my husband's agent, or what the people here call a middle-man — vulgarly polite, and impudently obsequious.

HARD (R.): Genus squireen — a half sir, and a whole scoundrel.

ANNE: I know — a potato on a silver plate: I'll leave you to peel him. Come, Mr Daly, take me for a moonlight walk, and be funny.

KYRLE: Funny, ma'am, I'm afraid I am —

ANNE: You are heavy, you mean; you roll through the world like a hogshead of whisky; but you only want tapping for pure spirits to flow out spontaneously. Give me your arm. (*Crossing,* R.) Hold that glove now. You are from Ballinasloe, I think?

KYRLE: I'm Connaught to the core of my heart.

ANNE: To the roots of your hair, you mean. I bought a horse at Ballinasloe fair that deceived me; I hope you won't turn out to belong to the same family.

KYRLE (R. C.): What did he do?

ANNE: Oh! like you, he looked well enough — deep in the chest as a pool a-dhiol, and broad in the back, as the Gap of Dunloe — but after two days' warm work he came all to pieces, and Larry, my groom, said he'd been stuck together with glue.

KYRLE (R.): Really, Miss Chute!

Music. — *Exeunt,* R. 1 E.

HARD (*advancing, laughing*): That girl is as wild as a coppleen — she won't leave him a hair on the head. (*Goes up.*)

Enter SERVANT, *shewing in* CORRIGAN *from house,* L. *Exit* SERVANT, L.

CORRIGAN (L.): Your humble servant, Mrs Cregan — my service t'ye, 'Squire — it's a fine night entirely.

MRS C (c.): May I ask to what business, sir, we have the honour of your call?

CORRIG (*aside,* L. C.): Proud as Lady Beelzebub, and as grand as a queen.

(*aloud*) True for you, ma'am; I would not have come but for a divil of a pinch I'm in entirely. I've got to pay £8,000 to-morrow, or lose the Knockmakilty farms.

Mrs C (c.): Well, sir?

Corrig: And I wouldn't throuble ye –

Mrs C: Trouble me, sir?

Corrig: Iss, ma'am – ye'd be forgettin' now that mortgage I have on this property. It ran out last May, and by rights –

Mrs C: It will be paid next month.

Corrig: Are you reckonin' on the marriage of Mister Hardress and Miss Anne Chute?

Hard (*advancing*, r.): Mr Corrigan, you forget yourself.

Mrs C: Leave us, Hardress, awhile. (Hardress *retires*, r.) Now, Mr Corrigan, state, in as few words as possible, what you demand.

Corrig: Mrs Cregan, ma'am, you depend on Miss Anne Chute's fortune to pay me the money, but your son does not love the lady, or, if he does, he has a mighty quare way of shewing it. He has another girl on hand, and betune the two he'll come to the ground, and so bedad will I.

Mrs C: That is false – it is a calumny, sir!

Corrig: I wish it was, ma'am. D'ye see that light over the lake? – your son's eyes are fixed on it. What would Anne Chute say if she knew that her husband, that is to be, had a mistress beyant – that he slips our every night after you're all in bed, and like Leandher, barrin' the wettin', he sails across to his sweetheart?

Mrs C: Is this the secret of his aversion to the marriage? Fool! fool! what madness, and at such a moment.

Corrig: That's what I say, and no lie in it.

Mrs C: He shall give up this girl – he must!

Corrig: I would like to have some security for that. I want by to-morrow Ann Chute's written promise to marry him or my £8,000.

Mrs C: It is impossible, sir; you hold ruin over our heads.

Corrig: Madam, it's got to hang over your head or mine.

Mrs C: Stay, you know that what you ask is out of our power – you know it – therefore this demand only covers the true object of your visit.

Corrig: 'Pon my honour! and you are as 'cute, ma'am, as you are beautiful!

Mrs C: Go on, sir.

Corrig: Mrs Cregan, I'm goin' to do a foolish thing – now, by gorra I am! I'm richer than ye think, maybe, and if you'll give me your *personal* security, I'll take it.

Mrs C: What do you mean?

CORRIG: I mean that I'll take a lien for life on *you*, instead of the mortgage I hold on the Cregan property. (*Aside.*) That's nate, I'm thinkin'.

MRS C: Are you mad?

CORRIG: I am – mad in love with yourself, and that's what I've been these fifteen years.

Music through dialogue till ANNE CHUTE *is off*

MRS C: Insolent wretch! my son shall answer and chastise you. (*Calls.*) Hardress!

HARD (*advancing*): Madam.

Enter ANNE CHUTE *and* KYRLE, R.

CORRIG: Miss Chute! ⎫
HARD: Well, mother? ⎬ (*together*)
ANNE: Well, sir? ⎭

MRS C (*aside*): Scoundrel! he will tell her all and ruin us! (*Aloud.*) Nothing. (*Turns aside.*)

CORRIG: Your obedient.

ANNE: Oh! (*Crosses with* KYRLE *and exit,* L.U.E)

Music ceases.

CORRIG: You are in my power, ma'am. See, now, not a sowl but myself knows of this secret love of Hardress Cregan, and I'll keep it as snug as a bug in a rug, if you'll only say the word.

MRS C: Contemptible hound, I loathe and despise you!

CORRIG: I've known that fifteen years, but it hasn't cured my heart ache.

MRS C: And you would buy my aversion and disgust!

CORRIG: Just as Anne Chute buys your son, if she knew but all. Can he love his girl beyant, widout haten this heiress he's obliged to swallow? – ain't you sthriven to sell him? But didn't feel the hardship of being sold till you tried it on yourself.

MRS C: I beg you, sir, to leave me.

CORRIG: That's right, ma'am – think over it, sleep on it. Tomorrow I'll call for your answer. Good evenin' kindly.

Music. – Exit CORRIGAN *in house,* L.

MRS C: Hardress.

HARD: What did he want?

MRS C: He came to tell me the meaning of yonder light upon Muckross Head.

HARD: Ah! has it been discovered. Well, mother, now you know the cause of my coldness, my indifference for Anne.

MRS C: Are you in your senses, Hardress? Who is this girl?

HARD: She is known at every fair and pattern in Munster as the Colleen Bawn – her name is Eily O'Connor.

MRS C: A peasant girl – a vulgar barefooted beggar.

HARD: Whatever she is, love has made her my equal, and when you set your foot upon her you tread upon my heart.

MRS C: 'Tis well, Hardress. I feel that perhaps I have no right to dispose of your life and your happiness – no, my dear son – I would not wound you – heaven knows how well I love my darling boy, and you shall feel it. Corrigan has made me an offer by which you may regain the estate, and without selling yourself to Anne Chute.

HARD: What is it? Of course you accepted it?

MRS C: No, but I will accept, yes, for your sake – I – I will. He offers to cancel this mortgage if – if – I will consent to – become his wife.

HARD: You – you, mother? Has he dared –

MRS C: Hush! he is right. A sacrifice must be made – either you or I must suffer. Life is before you – my days are well nigh past – and for your sake, Hardress – for yours; my pride, my only one. – Oh! I would give you more than my life.

HARD: Never – never! I will not cannot accept it. I'll tear that dog's tongue from his throat that dared insult you with the offer.

MRS C: Foolish boy, before to-morrow night we shall be beggars – outcasts from this estate. Humiliation and poverty stand like spectres at yonder door – to-morrow they will be realities. Can you tear out the tongues that will wag over our fallen fortunes? You are a child, you cannot see beyond your happiness.

HARD: Oh! mother, mother, what can be done? My marriage with Anne is impossible.

Enter DANNY MANN, up rock, at back.

DANNY (R. C.): Whisht, if ye plaze – ye're talkin' so loud she'll hear ye say that – she's comin'.

MRS C: Has this fellow overheard us?

HARD: If he has, he is mine, body and soul. I'd rather trust him with a secret than keep it myself.

MRS C (L. C.): I cannot remain to see Anne; excuse me to my friends. The night perhaps will bring counsel, or at least resolution to hear the worst! Good night, my son.

Music. – Exit into house, L.

DANNY (R. C.): Oh! masther, she doesn't know the worst! She doesn't know that you are married to the Colleen Bawn.

HARD: Hush! what fiend prompts you to thrust that act of folly in my face.

DANNY: Thrue for ye, masther! I'm a dirty mane scut to remind ye of it.

HARD: What will my haughty, noble mother say, when she learns the truth! how can I ask her to receive Eily as a daughter? – Eily, with her awkward manners, her Kerry brogue, her ignorance of the usages of society. Oh! what have I done?

DANNY: Oh! vo – vo, has the ould family come to this! Is it the daughter of Mihil-na-Thradrucha, the ould rope-maker of Garryowen, that 'ud take the flure as your wife?

HARD: Be silent, scoundrel! How dare you speak thus of my love? – wretch that I am to blame her! – poor, beautiful, angel-hearted Eily.

DANNY: Beautiful is it! Och – wurra – wurra, deelish! The looking-glass was never made that could do her justice; and if St Patrick wanted a wife, where would he find an angel that 'ud compare with the Colleen Bawn. As I row her on the lake, the little fishes come up to look at her; and the wind from heaven lifts up her hair to see what the devil brings her down here at all – at all.

HARD: The fault is mine – mine alone – I alone will suffer!

DANNY: Oh! why is'nt it mine? Why can't I suffer for yez, masther dear? Wouldn't I swally every tear in your body, and every bit of bad luck in your life, and then wid a stone round my neck, sink myself and your sorrows in the bottom of the lower lake.

HARD (*placing hand on* DANNY): Good Danny, away with you to the boat – be ready in a few moments, we will cross to Muckross Head. (*Looks at light at back.*)

Music. – *Exit* HARDRESS *into house,* L.

DANNY: Never fear, sir. Oh! it isn't that spalpeen, Corrigan, that shall bring ruin on that ould place. Lave Danny alone. Danny, the fox, will lade yez round and about, and cross the scint. (*takes off his hat – sees letter*) Bedad, here's the letter from the Colleen Bawn that I couldn't find awhile ago – it's little use now. (*goes to lower window, and reads by light from house*) 'Come to your own Eily, that has not seen you for two long days. Come, acushla agrah machree. I have forgotten how much you love me – Shule, shule, agrah. – Colleen Bawn.' Divil an address is on it.

Enter KYRLE *and* ANNE, L. U. E.

ANNE (C.): Have they gone?

KYRLE (L. C.): It is nearly midnight.

ANNE: Before we go in, I insist on knowing who is this girl that possesses your heart. You confess that you are in love – deeply in love.

KYRLE: I do confess it – but not even your power can extract that secret from me – do not ask me, for I could not be false, yet dare not be true. (*Exit* KYRLE *into house*, L.)

ANNE (L. C.): He loves me – oh! he loves me – the little bird is making a nest in my heart. Oh! I'm faint with joy.

DANNY (*as if calling after him*): Sir, sir!

ANNE: Who is that?

DANNY: I'm the boatman below, an' I'm waitin' for the gentleman.

ANNE: What gentleman?

DANNY: Him that's jist left ye, ma'am – I'm waitin' on him.

ANNE: Does Mr Kyrle Daly go out boating at this hour?

DANNY: It's not for me to say, ma'am, but every night at twelve o'clock I'm here wid my boat under the blue rock below, to put him across the lake to Muckross Head. I beg your pardon, ma'am, but here's a paper ye dropped on the walk beyant – if it's no vally I'd like to light my pipe wid it. (*Gives it.*)

ANNE: A paper I dropped! (*Goes to window – reads.*)

DANNY (*aside*): Oh, Misther Corrigan, you'll ruin masther will ye? asy now, and see how I'll put the cross on ye.

ANNE: A love-letter from some peasant girl to Kyrle Daly! Can this be the love of which he spoke? have I decieved myself?

DANNY: I must be off, ma'am; here comes the signal. (*Music.*)

ANNE: The signal?

DANNY: D'ye see yonder light upon Muckross Head? It is in a cottage windy; that light goes in and out three times winkin' that way, as much as to say, 'Are ye comin'?' Then if the light in that room there (*points at house above*) answers by a wink, it manes No! but if it goes out entirely, his honour jumps from the parlour windy into the garden behind and we're off. Look! (*Light in cottage disappears.*) That's one. (*Light appears.*) Now again. (*Light disappears.*) That's two. (*Light appears.*) What did I tell you? (*Light disappears.*) That's three, and here it comes again. (*Light appears.*) Wait now, and ye'll see the answer. (*Light disappears from window*, L.) That's my gentleman. (*Music change.*) You see he's goin' – good night, ma'am.

ANNE: Stay, here's money; do not tell Mr Daly that I know of this.

DANNY: Divil a word – long life t'ye. (*Goes up.*)

ANNE: I was not deceived; he meant me to understand that he loved me! Hark! I hear the sound of some one who leaped heavily on the garden walk. (*Goes to house*, L. – *looking at back.*)

Enter HARDRESS, *wrapped in a boat cloak*, L. U. E.

DANNY (*going down*, R. C.): All right, yer honour.

HARDRESS *crosses at back, and down rock*, R. C.

ANNE (*hiding*, L.): It is he, 'tis he. (*Mistaking Hardress for Daly – closed in.*)

SCENE SECOND

The Gap of Dunloe. (1st grooves.) Hour before sunrise.
Enter CORRIGAN, R. 1 E.

CORRIG: From the rock above I saw the boat leave Torc Cregan. It is now crossing the lake to the cottage. Who is this girl? What is this mysterious misthress of young Cregan? – that I'll find out.

MYLES *sings outside,* L.

'Oh! Charley Mount is a pretty place,
  In the month of July –'

CORRIG: Who's that? – 'Tis that poaching scoundrel – that horse stealer, Myles na Coppaleen. Here he comes with a keg of illicit whisky, as bould as Nebuckadezzar.

Enter MYLES *singing, with keg on his shoulder,* L.

Is that you, Myles?

MYLES: No! it's my brother.

CORRIG: I know ye, my man.

MYLES: Then why the divil did ye ax?

CORRIG: You may as well answer me kindly – civility costs nothing.

MYLES (L. C.): Ow now! don't it? Civility to a lawyer manes six-and-eight-pence about.

CORRIG (R. C.): What's that on your shoulder?

MYLES: What's that to you?

CORRIG: I am a magistrate, and can oblige you to answer.

MYLES: Well! it's a boulster belongin' to my mother's feather bed.

CORRIG: Stuff'd with whisky!

MYLES: Bedad! how would I know what it's stuff'd wid? I'm not an upholsterer.

CORRIG: Come, Myles, I'm not so bad a fellow as ye may think.

MYLES: To think of that now!

CORRIG: I am not the mane creature you imagine!

MYLES: Ain't ye now, sir? You keep up appearances mighty well, indeed.

CORRIG: No, Myles! I am not that blackguard I've been represented.

MYLES (*sits on keg*): See that now – how people take away a man's character. You are another sort of blackguard entirely.

CORRIG: You shall find me a gentleman – liberal, and ready to protect you.

MYLES: Long life t'ye, sir.

CORRIG: Myles, you have come down in the world lately; a year ago you were a thriving horse-dealer, now you are a lazy, ragged fellow.

MYLES: Ah, it's the bad luck, sir, that's in it.

CORRIG: No, it's the love of Eily O'Connor that's in it – it's the pride of Garryowen that took your heart away, and made ye what ye are – a smuggler and a poacher.

MYLES: Thim's hard words.

CORRIG: But they are true. You live like a wild beast in some cave or hole in the rocks above; by night your gun is heard shootin' the otter as they lie out on the stones, or you snare the salmon in your nets; on a cloudy night your whiskey still is going – you see, I know your life.

MYLES: Better than the priest, and devil a lie in it.

CORRIG: Now, if I put ye in a snug farm – stock ye with pigs and cattle, and rowl you up comfortable – o'ye think the Colleen Bawn wouldn't jump at ye?

MYLES: Bedad, she'd make a lape I b'leve – and what would I do for all this luck?

CORRIG: Find out for me who it is that lives at the cottage on Muckross Head.

MYLES: That's asy – it's Danny Mann – no less and his ould mother Sheelah.

CORRIG: Yes, Myles, but there's another – a girl who is hid there.

MYLES: Ah, now!

CORRIG: She only goes out at night.

MYLES: Like the owls.

CORRIG: She's the misthress of Hardress Cregan.

MYLES (seizing CORRIGAN): Thurra mon dhiol, what's that?

CORRIG: Oh, lor! Myles – Myles – what's the matter – are you mad?

MYLES: No – that is – why – why did ye raise your hand at me in that way?

CORRIG: I didn't.

MYLES: I thought ye did – I'm mighty quick at takin' thim hints, bein' on me keepin' agin' the gangers – go on – I didn't hurt ye.

CORRIG: Not much.

MYLES: You want to find out who this girl is?

CORRIG: I'll give £20 for the information – there's ten on account. (Gives money.)

MYLES: Long life t'ye; that's the first money I iver got from a lawyer, and bad luck to me but there's a cure for the evil eye in thim pieces.

CORRIG: You will watch to night?

MYLES: In five minutes I'll be inside the cottage itself.

CORRIG: That's the lad.

MYLES (*aside*): I was goin' there.

CORRIG: And to-morrow you will step down to my office with the particulars?

MYLES: To-morrow you shall breakfast on them.

CORRIG: Good night, entirely. (*Exit* CORRIGAN, L.)

MYLES: I'll give ye a cowstail to swally, and make ye think it's a chapter in St Patrick, ye spalpeen! When he called Eily the misthress of Hardress Cregan, I nearly shtretched him – begorra, I was full of sudden death that minute! Oh, Eily! acushla agrah asthore machree! as the stars watch over Innisfallen, and as the wathers go round it and keep it, so I watch and keep round you, avourneen!

SONG. – MYLES

Oh, Limerick is beautiful, as everybody knows.
The river Shannon's full of fish, beside the city flows;
But it is not the river, nor the fish that preys upon my mind,
Nor with the town of Limerick have I any fault to find.
The girl I love is beautiful, she's fairer than the dawn;
She lives in Garryowen, and she's called the Colleen Bawn.
As the river, proud and bold, goes by that famed city,
So proud and cold, widout a word, that Colleen goes by me!
Oh, hone! Oh, hone!

Oh, if I was the Emperor of Russia to command,
Or Julius Cæsar, or the Lord Lieutenant of the land,
I'd give up all my wealth, my manes, I'd give up my army.
Both the horse, the fut, and the Royal Artillery;
I'd give the crown from off my head, the people on their knees,
I'd give my fleet of sailing ships upon the briny seas,
And a beggar I'd go to sleep, a happy man at dawn,
If by my side, fast for my bride, I'd the darlin' Colleen Bawn.
Oh, hone! Oh, hone!

I must reach the cottage before the masther arrives; Father Tom is there waitin' for this keg o' starlight – it's my tithe; I call every tenth keg 'his riverince.' It's worth money to see the way it does the old man good, and brings the wather in his eyes; it's the only place I ever see any about him – heaven bless him! (*sings*)

Exit MYLES, R. – *Music.*

SCENE THIRD

Interior of Eily's Cottage on Muckross Head; fire burning, R. 3 E.*; table,* R. C.*; arm chair; two stools,* R. *of table; stool* L. *of table; basin, sugar spoon, two jugs, tobacco, plate, knife, and lemon on table.* FATHER TOM *discovered smoking in arm chair,* R. C. – EILY *in balcony, watching over lake.*

FATHER TOM (*sings*): 'Tobacco is an Injun weed.' And every weed wants wathering to make it come up; but tobacco bein' an Injun weed that is accustomed to a hot climate, water is entirely too cold for its warrum nature – it's whiskey and water it wants. I wonder if Myles has come; I'll ask Eily. (*Calls.*) Eily alanna! Eily a suilish machree!

EILY (*turning*): Is it me, Father Tom?

FATHER T: Has he come?

EILY: No, his boat is half a mile off yet.

FATHER T: Half a mile! I'll choke before he's here.

EILY: Do you mean Hardress?

FATHER T: No, dear! Myles na Coppaleen – cum spiritu Hiberncuse – which manes in Irish, wid a keg of puteen.

Enter MYLES, R. U. E.*, down* C.

MYLES: Here I am, your riverince, never fear. I tould Sheelah to hurry up with the materials, knowin' ye'd be dhry and hasty.

Enter SHEELAH, *with kettle of water,* R. U. E.

SHEELAH: Here's the hot water.

MYLES: Lave it there till I brew Father Tom a pint of mother's milk.

SHEELAH: We'ell thin, ye'll do your share of the work, and not a ha'porth more.

MYLES: Didn't I bring the sperrits from two miles and more? and I deserve to have the pref'rence to make the punch for his riverince.

SHEELAH: And didn't I watch the kettle all night, not to let it off the boil? – there now.

MYLES (*quarrelling with* SHEELAH): No, you did'nt, &c.

SHEELAH (*quarrelling*): Yes, I did, &c.

EILY: No, no; I'll make it, and nobody else.

FATHER T: Asy now, ye hocauns, and whist; Myles shall put in the whisky, Sheelah shall put in the hot water, and Eily, my Colleen, shall put the sugar in the cruiskeen. A blessin' on ye all three that loves the ould man. (MYLES *takes off hat* – WOMEN *curtsey* – *they make punch.*) See now, my children, there's a moral in everything, e'en in a jug of punch. There's the sperrit, which is the sowl and strength of the man. (MYLES *pours spirit from keg.*) That's the whiskey. There's the sugar, which is the smile of woman; (EILY *puts sugar.*) without that, life is without taste or sweetness. Then there's the lemon, (EILY *puts lemon.*) which is love; a squeeze now and again does a boy no harm; but not too much. And the hot water (SHEELAH *pours water.*) which is adversity — as little as possible if ye plaze — that makes the good things better still.

MYLES: And it's complate, ye see, for it's a woman that gets into hot wather all the while. (*Pours from jug to jug.*)

SHEELAH: Myles, if I hadn't the kettle, I'd bate ye.

MYLES: Then, why didn't ye let me make the punch? There's a guinea for your riverince that's come t'ye — one in ten I got awhile ago — it's your tithe — put a hole in it, and hang it on your watch chain, for it's a mighty grate charm entirely. (*They sit,* SHEELAH *near fire,* COLLEEN *on stool beside her,* FATHER TOM *in chair,* MYLES *on stool,* L. *of table.*)

FATHER T: Eily, look at that boy, and tell me, haven't ye a dale to answer for?

EILY: He isn't as bad about me as he used to be; he's getting over it.

MYLES: Yes, darlin', the storm has passed over, and I've got into settled bad weather.

FATHER T: Maybe, afther all, ye'd have done better to have married Myles there, than be the wife of a man that's ashamed to own ye.

EILY: He isn't — he's proud of me. It's only when I spake like the poor people, and say or do anything wrong, that he's hurt; but I'm gettin' clane of the brogue, and learnin' to do nothing — I'm to be changed entirely.

MYLES: Oh! if he'd lave me yer own self, and only take away wid him his improvements. Oh! murder — Eily, aroon, why wasn't ye twins, an' I could have one of ye, only nature couldn't make two like ye — it would be onreasonable to ax it.

EILY: Poor Myles, do you love me still so much?

MYLES: Didn't I lave the world to folly ye, and since then there's been neither night nor day in my life — I lay down on Glenna Point above, where I see this cottage, and I lived on the sight of it. Oh! Eily, if tears were pison to the grass there wouldn't be a green blade on Glenna Hill this day.

EILY: But you knew I was married, Myles.

MYLES: Not thin, aroon — Father Tom found me that way, and sat beside, and lifted up my soul. Then I confessed to him, and, sez he, 'Myles, go to Eily, she has something to say to you — say I sent you.' I came, and ye tould me ye were Hardress Cregan's wife, and that was a great comfort entirely. Since I knew that (*Drinks — voice in cup.*) I haven't been the blackguard I was.

FATHER T: See the beauty of the priest, my darlin' — *videte et admirate* — see and admire it. It was at confession that Eily tould me she loved Cregan, and what did I do? – sez I, 'Where did you meet your sweetheart?' 'At Garryowen,' sez she. 'Well,' says I; 'that's not the place.' 'Thrue, your riverince, it's too public entirely,' sez she. 'Ye'll mate him only in one place,' sez I; 'and that's the stile that's behind my chapel,' for, d'ye see, her mother's grave was forenint the spot, and there's a sperrit round the place,

MYLES *drinks*

that kept her pure and strong. Myles, ye thafe, drink faire.

SHEELAH: Come now, Eily, couldn't ye cheer up his riverince wid the tail of a song?

EILY: Hardress bid me not sing any ould Irish songs, he says the words are vulgar.

SHEELAH: Father Tom will give ye absolution.

FATHER T: Put your lips to that jug; there's only the sthrippens left. Drink! and while that thrue Irish liquor warms your heart, take this wid it. May the brogue of ould Ireland niver forsake your tongue – may her music niver lave yer voice – and may a true Irishwoman's virtue niver die in your heart!

MYLES: Come, Eily, it's my liquor – haven't ye a word to say for it?

SONG. – EILY

'Cruiskeen Lawn'

Let the farmer praise his grounds,
As the huntsman doth his hounds,
  And the shepherd his fresh and dewy morn;
But I, more blest than they,
Spend each night and happy day,
  With my smilin' little Cruiskeen Lawn, Lawn, Lawn.
Chorus (repeat) Gramachree, mavourneen, slanta gal avourneen,
Gramachree ma Cruiskeen Lawn, Lawn, Lawn,
With my smiling little Cruiskeen Lawn.
(*chorussed by* MYLES, FATHER T., *and* SHEELAH)

MYLES

And when grim Death appears
In long and happy years,
To tell me that my glass is run,
I'll say, begone, you slave,
For great Bacchus gave me lave
To have another Cruiskeen Lawn – Lawn – Lawn.
        Chorus. – Repeat

Gramachree, &c., &c.

HARD (*without*, L. U. E.): Ho! Sheelah — Sheelah!

SHEELAH (*rising*): Whisht! it's the master.

EILY (*frightened*): Hardress! oh, my! what will he say if he finds us here — run, Myles — quick, Sheelah — clear away the things.

FATHER T: Hurry now, or we'll get Eily in throuble. (*Takes keg* — MYLES *takes jugs* — SHEELAH *kettle.*)

HARD: Sheelah, I say!

> *Exeunt* FATHER TOM *and* MYLES, R. U. E., *quickly.*

SHEELAH: Comin', Sir, I'm puttin' on my petticoat. (*Exit* SHEELAH, R. U. E., *quickly.*)

> *Enter* HARDRESS *and* DANNY, L. U. E. *opening* — DANNY *immediately goes off,* R. U. E.

EILY (C.): Oh, Hardress, asthore!

HARD (L. C.): Don't call me by those confounded Irish words — what's the matter? you're trembling like a bird caught in a trap.

EILY: Am I, mavou — no I mean — is it tremblin' I am, dear?

HARD: What a dreadful smell of tobacco there is here, and the fumes of whiskey punch too, the place smells like a shebeen. Who has been here?

EILY: There was Father Tom an' Myles dhropped in.

HARD: Nice company for my wife — a vagabond.

EILY: Ah! who made him so but me, dear? Before I saw you, Hardress, Myles coorted me, and I was kindly to the boy.

HARD: Damn it, Eily, why will you remind me that my wife was ever in such a position?

EILY: I won't see him again — if yer angry, dear, I'll tell him to go away, and he will, because the poor boy loves me.

HARD: Yes, better than I do you mean?

EILY: No, I don't — oh! why do you spake so to your poor, Eily?

HARD: Spake so! Can't you say speak?

EILY: I'll thry, aroon — I'm sthrivin' — 'tis mighty hard, but what wouldn't I undert-tee-ta — undergo for your sa-se — for your seek.

HARD: Sake — sake!

EILY: Sake — seek — oh, it is to bother people entirely they mixed 'em up! Why didn't they make them all one way?

HARD (*aside*): It is impossible! How can I present her as my wife? Oh! what an act of madness to tie myself to one so much beneath me — beautiful — good as she is —

EILY: Hardress, you are pale — what has happened?

HARD: Nothing — that is nothing but what you will rejoice at.

EILY: What d'ye mane?

HARD: What do I mane! Mean – mean!

EILY: I beg your pardon, dear.

HARD: Well: I mean that after to-morrow there will be no necessity to hide our marriage, for I shall be a beggar, my mother will be an outcast, and amidst all the shame, who will care what wife a Cregan takes?

EILY: And d'ye think I'd like to see you dhragged down to my side – ye don't know me – see now – never call me wife again – don't let on to mortal that we're married – I'll go as a servant in your mother's house – I'll work for the smile ye'll give me in passing, and I'll be happy, if ye'll only let me stand outside and hear your voice.

HARD: You're a fool. I told you that I was betrothed to the richest heiress in Kerry; her fortune alone can save us from ruin. To-night my mother discovered my visits here, and I told her who you were.

EILY: Oh! what did she say?

HARD: It broke her heart.

EILY: Hardress! is there no hope?

HARD: None. That is none – that – that I can name.

EILY: There is one – I see it.

HARD: There is. We were children when we were married, and I could get no priest to join our hands but one, and he had been disgraced by his bishop. He is dead. There was no witness to the ceremony but Danny Mann – no proof but his word, and your certificate.

EILY (*takes paper from her breast*): This!

HARD: Eily! if you doubt my eternal love keep that security, it gives you the right to the shelter of my roof; but oh! if you would be content with the shelter of my heart.

EILY: And will it save ye, Hardress? and will your mother forgive me?

HARD: She will bless you – she will take you to her breast.

EILY: But you – another will take you to her breast.

HARD: Oh! Eily, darling – d'ye think I could forget you, machree – forget the sacrifice more than blood you give me.

EILY: Oh! when you talk that way to me, ye might take my life, and heart, and all. Oh! Hardress, I love you – take the paper and tare it.

HARDRESS *takes paper. Enter* MYLES, C., *opening.*

MYLES: No. I'll be damned if he shall.

HARD: Scoundrel! you have been listening?

MYLES: To every word. I saw Danny, wid his ear agin that dure, so as there was only one kay-hole I adopted the windy. Eily, aroon, Mr Cregan will giv' ye back that paper; you can't tare up an oath; will ye help him then to cheat this other girl, and to make her his mistress, for that's what she'll be if ye are his wife. An' after all, what is there agin' the crature? Only the money she's got. Will you stop lovin' him when his love belongs to another? No! I know it by myself; but if ye jine their hands together your love will be an adultery.

EILY: Oh, no!

HARD: Vagabond! outcast! jail bird! dare you prate of honor to me?

MYLES (C.): I am an outlaw, Mr Cregan – a felon may be – but if you do this thing to that poor girl that loves you so much – had I my neck in the rope – or my fut on the deck of a convict ship – I'd turn round and say to ye. 'Hardress Cregan, I make ye a present of the contempt of a rogue.' (*Snaps fingers.*)

> *Music till end of Act.* – *Enter* FATHER TOM, SHEELAH *and* DANNY, R. U. E. – HARDRESS *throws down paper* – *goes to table* – *takes hat.*

HARD: Be it so, Eily, farewell! until my house is clear of these vermin – (DANNY *appears at back*) – you will see me no more. (*Exit* HARDRESS, L. C., *followed by* DANNY.)

EILY: Hardress – Hardress! (*Going up.*) Don't leave me, Hardress!

FATHER T (*intercepts her*): Stop, Eily! (DANNY *returns and listens.*)

EILY: He's gone – he's gone!

FATHER T: Give me that paper, Myles. (MYLES *picks it up – gives it.*) Kneel down there, Eily, before me – put that paper in your breast.

EILY (*kneeling*): Oh! what will I do – what will I do!

FATHER T: Put your hand upon it now.

EILY: Oh, my heart – my heart!

FATHER T: Be the hush, and spake after me – by my mother that's in heaven.

EILY: By my mother that's in heaven.

FATHER T: By the light and the word.

EILY: By the light and the word.

FATHER T: Sleepin' or wakin'

EILY: Sleepin' or wakin'.

FATHER T: This proof of my truth.

EILY: This proof of my truth.

FATHER T: Shall never again quit my breast.

EILY: Shall never again quit my breast. (EILY *utters a cry and falls* – *Tableau.*)

ACT II

SCENE FIRST

(1st *grooves*) — *Gap of Dunloe; same as Second Scene, Act I.* — *Music.*
Enter HARDRESS *and* DANNY, L. 1 E.

HARD (R.): Oh! what a giddy fool I've been. What would I give to recall this fatal act which bars my fortune?

DANNY (L.): There's something throublin' yez, Masther Hardress. Can't Danny do something to aise ye? — spake the word and I'll die for ye.

HARD: Danny, I *am* troubled. I was a fool when I refused to listen to you at the chapel of Castle Island.

DANNY: When I warned ye to have no call to Eily O'Connor.

HARD: I was mad to marry her.

DANNY: I knew she was no wife for you. A poor thing widout manners, or money, or book larnin', or a ha'porth of fortin'. Oh! worra. I told ye dat, but ye bate me off, and here now is the way of it.

HARD: Well, it's done, and can't be undone.

DANNY: Bedad, I dun know that. Wouldn't she untie the knot herself — couldn't ye coax her?

HARD: No.

DANNY: Is that her love for you? You that giv' up the divil an all for her. What's *her* ruin to yours? Ruin — goredoutha — ruin is it? Don't I pluck a shamrock and wear it a day for the glory of St. Patrick, and then throw it away when it's gone by my likin'. What, is *she* to be ruined by a gentleman? Whoo! Mighty good, for the likes o' her.

HARD: She would have yielded, but —

DANNY: Asy now, an I'll tell ye. Pay her passage out to Quaybec, and put her aboord a three-master widout sayin' a word. Lave it to me. Danny will clare the road forenint ye.

HARD: Fool, if she still possesses that certificate — the proof of my first marriage — how can I dare to wed another? Commit bigamy — disgrace my wife — bastardize my children!

DANNY: Den' by the powers, I'd do by Eily as wid the glove there on yer hand; make it come off, as it come on — an' if it fits too tight, take the knife to it.

HARD (*turning to him*): What do you mean?

DANNY: Only gi' me the word, an' I'll engage that the Colleen Bawn will never throuble ye any more; don't ax me any questions at all. Only – if you're agreeable, take off that glove from yer hand and give it me for a token – that's enough.

HARD (*throws off cloak – seizes him – throws him down*): Villain! Dare you utter a word or meditate a thought of violence towards that girl –

DANNY: Oh! murder – may I never die in sin, if –

HARD: Begone! away, at once, and quit my sight. I have chosen my doom; I must learn to endure it – but, blood! and hers! Shall I make cold and still that heart that beats alone for me? – quench those eyes, that look so tenderly in mine? Monster! am I so vile that you dare to whisper such a thought?

DANNY: Oh! masther, divil burn me if I meant any harm.

HARD: Mark me well, now. Respect my wife as you would the queen of the land – whisper a word such as those you uttered to me, and it will be you last. I warn ye – remember and obey. (*Exit* HARDRESS, R.)

DANNY (*rises – picks up cloak*): Oh! the darlin' crature! would I harrum a hair of her blessed head? – no! Not unless you gave me that glove, and den I'd jump into the bottomless pit for ye. (*Exit* DANNY R.) –

Music – change.

SCENE SECOND

Room in Mrs Cregan's house; window, R. *in flat, backed by landscape; door,* L. *in flat; backed by interior.* (*lights up*)

Enter ANNE CHUTE, L. *in flat.*

ANNE: That fellow runs in my head. (*Looking at window.*) There he is in the garden, smoking like a chimney-pot. (*Calls.*) Mr Daly!

KYRLE (*outside window*): Good morning!

ANNE (*aside*): To think he'd smile that way, after going Leandering all night like a dissipated young owl. (*Aloud.*) Did you sleep well? (*Aside.*) Not a wink, you villain, and you know it.

KYRLE: I slept like a top.

ANNE (*aside*): I'd like to have the whipping of ye. (*Aloud.*) When did you get back?

KYRLE: Get back! I've not been out.

ANNE (*aside*): He's not been out! This is what men come to after a cruise at sea – they get sunburnt with love. Those foreign donnas teach them to make fire-places of their hearts, and chimney-pots of their mouths. (*Aloud.*) What are you doing down there? (*Aside.*) As if he was stretched out to dry.

Kyrle puts down pipe outside. Enter Kyrle *through window,* R., *in flat.*

Kyrle (R. C.): I have been watching Hardress coming over from Divil's Island in his boat – the wind was dead against him.

Anne (L. C.): It was fair for going to Divil's Island last night, I believe.

Kyrle: Was it?

Anne: You were up late, I think?

Kyrle: I was. I watched by my window for hours, thinking of her I loved – slumber overtook me and I dreamed of a happiness I never can hope for.

Anne: Look me straight in the face.

Kyrle: Oh! if some fairy could strike us into stone now – and leave us looking for ever into each other's faces, like the blue lake below and the sky above it.

Anne: Kyrle Daly! What would you say to a man who had two loves, one to whom he escaped at night and the other to whom he devoted himself during the day, what would you say?

Kyrle: I'd say he had no chance.

Anne: Oh! Captain Cautious! Well answered. Isn't he fit to take care of anybody? – his cradle was cut out of a witness box.

Enter Hardress *through window,* R., *in flat.*

Kyrle (R.): Anne! I don't know what you mean, but that I know that I love you, and you are sporting with a wretchedness you cannot console. I was wrong to remain here so long, but I thought my friendship for Hardress would protect me against your invasion – now I will go. (Hardress *advancing.*)

Hard (C.): No, Kyrle, you will stay. Anne he loves you, and I more than suspect you prefer him to me. From this moment you are free; I release you from all troth to me: in his presence I do this.

Anne (L.): Hardress!

Hard: There is a bar between us which you should have known before, but I could not bring myself to confess. Forgive me, Anne – you deserve a better man than I am. (*Exit,* L.)

Anne: A bar between us! What does he mean?

Kyrle: He means that he is on the verge of ruin: he did not know how bad things were till last night. His generous noble heart recoils from receiving anything from you but love.

Anne: And does he think I'd let him be ruined any way? Does he think I wouldn't sell the last rood o' land – the gown off my back, and the hair off my head before the boy that protected and loved me, the child, years ago, should come to a hap'orth of harrum. (*Crosses to* R.)

KYRLE: Miss Chute!

ANNE: Well, I can't help it. When I am angry the brogue comes out, and my Irish heart will burst through manners, and graces, and twenty stay-laces. (*Crosses to* L.) I'll give up my fortune, that I will.

KYRLE: You can't – you've got a guardian who cannot consent to such a sacrifice.

ANNE: Have I? then I'll find a husband that will.

KYRLE (*aside*): She means me – I see it in her eyes.

ANNE (*aside*): He's trying to look unconscious. (*Aloud.*) Kyrle Daly, on your honour and word as a gentleman, do you love me and nobody else?

KYRLE: Do you think me capable of contaminating your image by admitting a meaner passion into my breast?

ANNE: Yes, I do.

KYRLE: Then you wrong me.

ANNE: I'll prove that in one word. – Take care now – it's coming.

KYRLE: Go on.

ANNE (*aside*): Now I'll astonish him. (*Aloud.*) Eily!

KYRLE: What's that?

ANNE: 'Shule, shule, agrah!'

KYRLE: Where to?

ANNE: Three winks, as much as to say, 'Are you coming?' and an extinguisher above here means 'Yes.' Now you see I know all about it.

KYRLE: You have the advantage of me.

ANNE: Confess now, and I'll forgive you.

KYRLE: I will – tell me what to confess, and I'll confess it – I don't care what it is.

ANNE (*aside*): If I hadn't eye-proof he'd brazen it out of me. Isn't he cunning? He's one of those that would get fat where a fox would starve.

KYRLE: That was a little excursion into my past life – a sudden descent on my antecedents, to see if you could not surprise an infidelity – but I defy you.

ANNE: You do? I accept that defiance, and mind me, Kyrle, if I find you true, as I once thought, there's my hand; but if you are false in this, Anne Chute will never change her name for yours. (*He kisses her hand.*) Leave me now.

KYRLE: Oh! the lightness you have given to my heart. The number of pipes I'll smoke this afternoon will make them think we've got a haystack on fire. (*Exit* KYRLE, *through window,* R.)

ANNE (*rings bell on table,* R.): Here, Pat – Barney – some one.

Enter SERVANT, L. *door in flat.*

Tell Larry Dolan, my groom, to saddle the black mare, Fireball, but not bring her round the house – I'll mount in the stables.

Exit SERVANT, L. *door in flat.*

I'll ride over to Muckross Head, and draw that cottage; I'll know what's there. It mayn't be right, but I haven't a big brother to see after me – and self-protection is the first law of nature.

Exit ANNE, R. I E.

Music. – Enter MRS CREGAN *and* HARDRESS, L. *door in flat.*

MRS C (R. C.): What do you say, Hardress?

HARD (L. C.): I say, mother, that my heart and faith are both already pledged to another, and I cannot break my engagement.

MRS C: And this is the end of all our pride!

HARD: Repining is useless – thought and contrivance are of no avail – the die is cast.

MRS C: Hardress – I speak not for myself, but for you – and I would rather see you in your coffin than married to this poor, lowborn, silly, vulgar creature. I know you, my son, you will be miserable, when the infatuation of first love is past; when you turn from her and face the world, as one day you must do, you will blush to say, 'This is my wife.' Every word from her mouth will be a pang to your pride – you will follow her movements with terror – the contempt and derision she excites will rouse you first to remorse, and then to hatred – and from the bed to which you go with a blessing, you will rise with a curse.

HARD: Mother! mother! (*Throws himself in chair*, R.)

MRS C: To Anne you have acted a heartless and dishonourable part – her name is already coupled with yours at every fireside in Kerry.

Enter SERVANT, L. *door in flat.*

SERV: Mr Corrigan, ma'am.

MRS C: He comes for his answer. Shew him in.

Exit SERVANT, L. *door in flat.*

The hour has come, Hardress – what answer shall I give him?

HARD: Refuse him – let him do his worst.

MRS C: And face beggary! On what shall we live? I tell you the prison for debt is open before us. Can you work? No! Will you enlist as a soldier, and send your wife into service? We are ruined – d'ye hear – ruined. I must accept this man only to give you and yours a shelter, and under Corrigan's roof I may not be ashamed perhaps to receive your wife.

Enter SERVANT, *showing in* MR CORRIGAN, L. *door in flat.*

CORRIG (L.): Good morning, ma'am; I am punctual you perceive.

MRS C (C.): We have considered your offer, sir, and we see no alternative
– but – but –

CORRIG: Mrs Cregan, I'm proud, ma'am, to take your hand.

HARD (*starting up*): Begone – begone, I say – touch her and I'll brain you.

CORRIG: Squire! Sir! Mr Hardress.

HARD: Must I hurl you from the house?

Enter two SERVANTS, *door in flat.*

MRS C: Hardress, my darling boy, restrain yourself.

CORRIG: Good morning, ma'am. I have my answer. (*To* SERVANT.) Is
Miss Chute within?

SERV: No, sir, she's just galloped out of the stable yard.

CORRIG: Say I called to see her. I will wait upon her at this hour to-
morrow. (*Looking at the Cregans.*) To-morrow! to-morrow! (*Exit followed by*
SERVANTS, L. *door in flat.*)

MRS C: To-morrow will see us in Limerick Jail, and this house in the
hands of the sheriff.

HARD: Mother! heaven guide and defend me; let me rest for awhile –
you don't know all yet, and I have not the heart to tell you. (*Crosses* L.)

MRS C: With you, Hardress, I can bear anything – anything – but your
humiliation and your unhappiness —

HARD: I know it, mother, I know it. (*Exit,* L. 1 E. – *Music.*)

DANNY *appears at window,* R. *in flat.*

DANNY: Whisht – missiz – whisht.

MRS C (L. C.): Who's there?

DANNY: It's me sure, Danny – that is – I know the throuble that's in it.
I've been through it all wid him.

MRS C: You know, then – ?

DANNY: Everything, ma'am; and, shure, I sthruv hard and long to
impache him from doing id.

MRS C: Is he, indeed, so involved with this girl that he will not give her
up?

DANNY: No; he's got over the worst of it, but she holds him tight, and he
feels kindly and soft-hearted for her, and darn't do what another would.

MRS C: Dare not?

DANNY: Sure she might be packed off across the wather to Ameriky, or
them parts beyant? Who'd ever ax a word afther her? – barrin' the masther,
who'd murdher me if he knew I whispered such a thing.

MRS C: But would she go?

DANNY: Ow, ma'am, wid a taste of persuasion, we'd mulvather her
aboord. But there's another way again, and if ye'd only coax the masther to
send me his glove, he'd know the manin' of that token, and so would I.

Mrs C: His glove?

Danny: Sorra a haporth else. If he'll do that, I'll take my oath ye'll hear no more of the Colleen Bawn.

Mrs C: I'll see my son. (*Exit,* l. d. f.)

Danny: Tare an' 'ouns, that lively girl, Miss Chute, has gone the road to Muckross Head: I've watched her – I've got my eye on all of them. If she sees Eily – ow, ow, she'll get the ring itself in that helpin' of kale-canon. Be the piper, I'll run across the lake, and, maybe, get there first; she's got a long round to go, and the wind rising – a purty blast entirely. (*Goes to window – Music.*)

    Re-enter Mrs Cregan, l. d. f., *with glove.*

Mrs C (*aside*): I found his gloves in the hall, where he had thrown them in his hat.

Danny: Did ye ax him, ma'am?

Mrs C: I did – and here is the reply. (*Holds out glove.*)

Danny: He has changed his mind, then?

Mrs C: He has entirely.

Danny: And – and – I am – to – do it?

Mrs C: That is the token.

Danny: I know it – I'll keep my promise. I'm to make away with her?

Mrs C: Yes, yes – take her away – away with her! (*Exit* Mrs Cregan, l. door in flat.)

Danny: Never fear, ma'am. (*Going to window.*) He shall never see or hear again of the Colleen Bawn. (*Exit* Danny *through window – change.*)

SCENE THIRD

    Exterior of Eily's Cottage; Cottage, r. 3 e.; *set pieces, backed by Lake; table and two seats,* r. c.

    Sheelah *and* Eily *discovered knitting.*

Sheelah (r.): Don't cry, darlin' – don't, alaina!

Eily (l.): He'll never come back to me – I'll never see him again, Sheelah!

Sheelah: Is it lave his own wife?

Eily: I've sent him a letther by Myles, and Myles has never come back – I've got no answer – he won't spake to me – I am standin' betune him and fortune – I'm in the way of his happiness. I wish I was dead!

Sheelah: Whisht! be the husht! what talk is that? when I'm tuk sad that way, I go down to the chapel and pray a turn – it lifts the cloud off my heart.

EILY: I can't pray; I've tried, but unless I pray for him, I can't bring my mind to it.

SHEELAH: I never saw a colleen that loved as you love; sorra come to me, but I b'lieve you've got enough to supply all Munster, and more left over than would choke ye if you wern't azed of it.

EILY: He'll come back – I'm sure he will; I was wicked to doubt. Oh! Sheelah! what becomes of the girls he doesn't love. Is there anything goin' on in the world where he isn't?

SHEELAH: There now – you're smilin' again.

EILY: I'm like the first mornin' when he met me – there was dew on the young day's eye – a smile on the lips o' the lake. Hardress will come back – oh! yes; he'll never leave his poor Eily all alone by herself in this place. Whisht', now, an' I'll tell you.

Music.

SONG. – AIR

'Pretty Girl Milking her Cow.'

'Twas on a bright morning in summer,
    I first heard his voice speaking low,
As he said to a colleen beside me,
    'Who's that pretty girl milking her cow?'
And many times after he met me,
    And vow'd that I always should be
His own little darling alanna,
    Mavourneen a sweelish machree.

I haven't the manners or graces
    Of the girls in the world where ye move,
I haven't their beautiful faces,
    But I have a heart that can love.
If it plase ye, I'll dress in satins,
    And jewels I'll put on my brow,
But don't ye be after forgettin'
    Your pretty girl milking her cow.

SHEELAH: Ah, the birds sit still on the boughs to listen to her, and the trees stop whisperin'; she leaves a mighty big silence behind her voice, that nothin' in nature wants to break. My blessin' on the path before her – there's an angel at the other end of it. (*Exit* SHEELAH *in cottage,* R.)

EILY (*repeats last line of song*):

Enter ANNE CHUTE, L. U. E.

ANNE: There she is.

EILY (*sings till facing Anne – stops – they examine each other*)

ANNE: My name is Anne Chute.

EILY: I am Eily O'Connor.

ANNE: You are the Colleen Bawn – the pretty girl.

EILY: And you are the Colleen Ruaidh.

ANNE (*aside*): She is beautiful.

EILY (*aside*): How lovely she is.

ANNE: We are rivals.

EILY: I am sorry for it.

ANNE: So am I, for I feel that I could have loved you.

EILY: That's always the way of it; everybody wants to love me, but there's something spoils them off.

ANNE (*showing letter*): Do you know that writing?

EILY: I do, ma'am, well, though I don't know how you came by it.

ANNE: I saw your signals last night – I saw his departure, and I have come here to convince myself of his falsehood to me. But now that I have seen you, you have no longer a rival in his love, for I despise him with all my heart, who could bring one so beautiful and simple as you are to ruin and shame!

EILY: He didn't – no – I am his wife! Oh, what have I said!

ANNE: What?

EILY: Oh, I didn't mane to confess it – no, I didn't! but you wrung it from me in defence of him.

ANNE: You his wife?

Enter DANNY, L. U. E.

DANNY (*at back – aside*): The divil! they're at it – an' I'm too late!

ANNE: I cannot believe this – shew me your certificate.

EILY: Here it is.

DANNY (*advances between them*): Didn't you swear to the priest that it should niver lave your breast?

ANNE: Oh! you're the boatman.

DANNY: Iss, ma'am!

ANNE: Eily, forgive me for doubting your goodness, and your purity. I believe you. Let me take your hand. (*Crosses to her.*) While the heart of Anne Chute beats you have a friend that won't be spoiled off, but you have no longer a rival, mind that. All I ask of you is that you will never mention this visit to Mr Daly – and for you (*to* DANNY) this will purchase your silence. (*Gives money.*) Good-bye!

Exit ANNE, L. U. E.

DANNY: Long life t'ye. (*Aside.*) What does it mane? Hasn't she found me out?

EILY: Why did she ask me never to spake to Mr Daly of her visit here? Sure I don't know any Mr Daly.

DANNY: Didn't she spake of him before, dear?

EILY: Never!

DANNY: Nor didn't she name Master Hardress?

EILY: Well, I don't know; she spoke of him and of the letter I wrote to him, but I b'lieve she never named him intirely.

DANNY (*aside*): The divil's in it for sport; She's got 'em mixed yet.

Enter SHEELAH *from cottage,* R.

SHEELAH: What brings you back, Danny?

DANNY: Nothing! but a word I have from the masther for the Colleen here.

EILY: Is it the answer to the letter I sent by Myles?

DANNY: That's it, jewel, he sent me wid a message.

SHEELAH (C.): Somethin' bad has happened. Danny, you are as pale as milk, and your eye is full of blood – yez been drinkin'.

DANNY: May be I have.

SHEELAH: You thrimble, and can't spake straight to me. Oh! Danny, what is it, avick?

DANNY: Go on now, an' stop yer keenin'.

EILY: Faith, it isn't yourself that's in it, Danny; sure there's nothing happened to Hardress.

DANNY: Divil a word, good or bad, I'll say while the mother's there.

SHEELAH: I'm goin'. (*Aside.*) What's come to Danny this day, at all, at all; bedad, I don't know my own flesh and blood. (*Runs into cottage.*)

DANNY: Sorro' and ruin has come on the Cregans; they're broke intirely.

EILY: Oh, Danny.

DANNY: Whisht, now! You are to meet Masther Hardress this evenin', at a place on the Divil's Island, beyant. Ye'll niver breath a word to mortal to where yer goin', d'ye mind, now; but slip down, unbeknown, to the landin' below, where I'll have the boat waitin' for yez.

EILY: At what hour?

DANNY: Just after dark, there's no moon to-night, an' no one will see us crossin' the water.

Music till end of scene.

EILY: I will be there; I'll go down only to the little chapel by the shore, and pray there 'till ye come. (*Exit* EILY, *into cottage,* R.)

DANNY: I'm wake and cowld! What's this come over me? Mother, mother, acushla.

Enter SHEELAH, R.

SHEELAH: What is it, Danny?

DANNY (*staggering to table*): Give me a glass of spirits!

Falls in chair. – Change quickly.

SCENE FOURTH

The old Weir Bridge, or a Wood on the verge of the Lake – (1st grooves)
Enter ANNE CHUTE, R.

ANNE: Married! the wretch is married! and with that crime already on his conscience he was ready for another and similar piece of villany. It's the Navy that does it. It's my belief those sailors have a wife in every place they stop at.

MYLES (*sings outside*, R.)
'Oh! Eily astoir, my love is all crost,
Like a bud in the frost.'

ANNE: Here's a gentleman who has got my complaint – his love is all crost, like a bud in the frost.

Enter MYLES, R.

MYLES: 'And there's no use at all in my goin' to bed,
For it's drames, and not sleep, that comes into my head,
And it's all about you,' &c. &c.

ANNE: My good friend, since you can't catch your love, d'ye think you could catch my horse?

Distant thunder.

MYLES: Is it a black mare wid a white stockin' on the fore off leg?

ANNE: I dismounted to unhook a gate – a peal of thunder frightened her, and she broke away.

MYLES: She's at Torc Cregan stables by this time – it was an admiration to watch her stride across the Phil Dolan's bit of plough.

ANNE: And how am I to get home?

MYLES: If I had four legs, I wouldn't ax betther than to carry ye, an' a proud baste I'd be.

Thunder – rain.

ANNE: The storm is coming down to the mountain – is there no shelter near?

MYLES: There may be a corner in this ould chapel. (*Rain.*) Here comes the rain – murdher! ye'll be wet through. (*Music – pulls off coat.*) Put this round yez.

ANNE: What will you do? You'll catch your death of cold.

MYLES (*taking out bottle*): Cowld is it. Here's a wardrobe of top coats. (*Thunder.*) Whoo! this is a fine time for the water – this way, ma'am.

Exeunt MYLES *and* ANNE, L. *Enter* EILY, *cloak and hood*, R.

EILY: Here's the place where Danny was to meet me with the boat. Oh! here he is.

Enter DANNY, L.

How pale you are!

DANNY: The thunder makes me sick.

EILY: Shall we not wait till the storm is over?

DANNY: If it comes on bad we can put into the Divil's Island Cave.

EILY: I feel so happy that I am going to see him, yet there is a weight about my heart that I can't account for.

DANNY: I can. (*Aside.*) Are you ready now?

EILY: Yes; come – come.

DANNY (*staggering*): I'm wake yet. My throat is dry – if I'd a draught of whiskey now.

EILY: Sheelah gave you a bottle.

DANNY: I forgot – it's in the boat. (*Rain*)

EILY: Here comes the rain – we shall get wet.

DANNY: There's the masther's boat cloak below.

EILY: Come, Danny, lean on me. I'm afraid you are not sober enough to sail the skiff.

DANNY: Sober! The dhrunker I am the better I can do the work I've got to do.

EILY: Come, Danny, come – come!

Exeunt EILY *and* DANNY, R. – *Music ceases. Re-enter* ANNE CHUTE *and* MYLES, L.

MYLES: It was only a shower, I b'lieve – are ye wet, ma'am?

ANNE: Dry as a biscuit.

MYLES: Ah! then it's yerself is the brave and beautiful lady – as bould an' proud as a ship before the blast. (ANNE *looks off*, R.)

ANNE: Why, there is my mare, and who comes with – (*Crosses to* R.)

MYLES: It's Mr Hardress Cregan himself.

ANNE: Hardress here?

MYLES: Eily gave me a letter for him this morning.

Enter HARDRESS, R.

HARD: Anne, what has happened? Your horse galloped wildly into the stable – we thought you had been thrown.

MYLES: Here is the letther Eily tould me to give him. (*To* HARDRESS.) I beg your pardon, sir, but here's the taste of a letther I was axed to give your honor. (*Gives letter.*)

HARD (*aside*): From Eily!

ANNE: Thanks, my good fellow, for your assistance.

MYLES: Not at all, ma'am. Sure, there isn't a boy in the County Kerry that would not give two thumbs off his hands to do a service to the Colleen Ruaidh, as you are called among us – iss indeed, ma'am. (*Going – aside.*) Ah! then it's the purty girl she is in them long clothes. (*Exit* MYLES, R.)

HARD (*reads, aside*): 'I am the cause of your ruin; I can't live with that thought killin' me. If I do not see you before night you will never again be throubled with your poor Eily.' Little simpleton! she is capable of doing herself an injury.

ANNE: Hardress! I have been very blind and very foolish, but to-day I have learned to know my own heart. There's my hand, I wish to seal my fate at once. I know the delicacy which prompted you to release me from my engagement to you. I don't accept that release; I am yours.

HARD: Anne, you don't know all.

ANNE: I know more than I wanted, that's enough. I forbid you ever to speak on this subject.

HARD: You don't know my past life.

ANNE: And I don't want to know. I've had enough of looking into past lives; don't tell me anything you wish to forget.

HARD: Oh, Anne – my dear cousin; if I could forget – if silence could be oblivion.

Exeunt HARDRESS *and* ANNE, L.

SCENE FIFTH

Exterior of Myles's Hut. (1st grooves.)
Enter MYLES, R., *singing 'Brian O' Linn'.*

'Brian O' Linn had no breaches to wear.
So he bought him a sheepskin to make him a pair;
The skinny side out, the woolly side in,
"They are cool and convanient," said Brian O' Linn.'

(*Locks door of cabin.*) Now I'll go down to my whiskey-still. It is under my feet this minute, bein' in a hole in the rocks they call O'Donoghue's stables, a sort of water cave; the people around here think that the cave is haunted with bad spirits, and they say that of a dark stormy night strange onearthly noises is heard comin' out of it – it is me singing 'The Night before Larry was stretched.' Now I'll go down to that cave, and wid a sod of live turf under a kettle of worty, I'll invoke them sperrits – and what's more they'll come.

Exit MYLES *singing,* R. – *Music till* MYLES *begins to speak next scene.*

SCENE SIXTH

A Cave; through large opening at back is seen the Lake and Moon; rocks R. *and* L. – *flat rock,* R. C.; *gauze waters all over stage; rope hanging from* C., *hitched on wing,* R. U. E.

Enter MYLES *singing, top of rock,* R. U. E.

MYLES: And this is a purty night for my work! The smoke of my whiskey-still will not be seen; there's my distillery beyant in a snug hole up there, (*unfastens rope,* L.) and here's my bridge to cross over it. I think it would puzzle a gauger to folly me; this is a patent of my own – a tight-rope bridge. (*Swings across from* R. *to* L.) Now I tie up my drawbridge at this side till I want to go back – what's that – it was an otter I woke from a nap he was taken on that bit of rock there – ow! ye divil! if I had my gun I'd give ye a leaden supper, I'll go up and load it, may be I'll get a shot; them stones is the place where they lie out of a night, and many a one I've shot of them. (*Music. – disappears up rock,* L. U. E.)

A small boat with DANNY *and* EILY *appears, from* R., *and works on to rock,* C.

EILY: What place is this you have brought me to?

DANNY: Never fear – I know where I'm goin' – step out on that rock – mind yer footin'; 'tis wet there.

EILY: I don't like this place – it's like a tomb.

DANNY: Step out, I say; the boat is laking. (EILY *steps on to rock,* R. C.)

EILY: Why do you spake to me so rough and cruel?

DANNY: Eily, I have a word to say t'ye, listen now, and don't thrimble that way.

EILY: I won't, Danny – I won't.

DANNY: Wonst, Eily, I was a fine brave boy, the pride of my ould mother, her white haired darlin' – you wouldn't think it to look at me now. D'ye know how I got changed to this?

EILY: Yes, Hardress told me.

DANNY: He done it – but I loved him before it, an' I loved him afther it – not a dhrop of blood I have, but I'd pour out like wather for the masther.

EILY: I know what you mean – as he has deformed your body – ruined your life – made ye what ye are.

DANNY: Have you, a woman, less love for him than I, that you wouldn't give him what he wants of you, even if he broke your heart as he broke my back, both in a moment of passion? Did I ax him to ruin himself and his ould family, and all to mend my bones? No! I loved him and I forgave him that.

EILY: Danny, what d'ye want me to do?

DANNY *steps out on to rock.*

DANNY: Give me that paper in your breast? (*Boat floats off slowly,* R.)

EILY: I can't – I've sworn never to part with it! You know I have!

DANNY: Eily, that paper stands between Hardress Cregan and his fortune; that paper is the ruin of him. Give it, I tell yez.

EILY: Take me to the priest; let him lift the oath off me. Oh! Danny, I swore a blessed oath on my two knees, and ye would ax me to break that?

DANNY (*seizes her hands*): Give it up, and don't make me hurt ye.

EILY: I swore by my mother's grave, Danny. Oh! Danny dear, don't. Don't, acushla, and I'll do anything. See now, what good would it be: sure, while I live I'm his wife. (*Music changes.*)

DANNY: Then you've lived too long. Take your marriage lines wid ye to the bottom of the lake. (*He throws her from rock backwards into the water,* L. C., *with a cry; she reappears, clinging to rock.*)

EILY: No! save me. Don't kill me. Don't, Danny, I'll – do any thing, only let me live.

DANNY: He wants ye dead. (*Pushes her off.*)

EILY: Oh! Heaven help me. Danny – Dan – (*Sinks.*)

DANNY (*looking down*): I've done it. She's gone. (*Shot is fired,* L. U. E.; *he falls – rolls from the rock into the water,* R. C.)

MYLES *appears with gun on rock,* L. U. E.

MYLES: I hit one of them bastes that time. I could see well, though it was so dark. But there was somethin' moving on that stone. (*Swings across to* R. U. E.) Divil a sign of him. Stop! (*Looks down.*) What's this? it's a woman – there's something white there. (*Figure rises near rock,* R. U. E. – *kneels down; tries to take the hand of figure.*) Ah! that dress; it's Eily. My own darlin' Eily. (*Pulls off waistcoat – jumps off rock.* EILY *rises* R. – *then* MYLES *and* EILY *rise up,* C. – *he turns, and seizes rock,* R. C. – EILY *across left arm.*)

ACT III

SCENE FIRST

Interior of an Irish Hut; door and small opening R. C., *door* L. C. *flat.*
Truckle bed and bedding, R. C., *on which* DANNY MANN *is discovered; table*
with jug of water; lighted candle stuck in bottle, L.; *two stools –* SHEELAH *at*
table L. *– Music.*

DANNY (*in his sleep*): Gi' me the paper, thin – screeching won't save ye –
down, down! (*Wakes.*) Oh, mother, darlin' – mother!

SHEELAH (*waking*): Eh! did ye call me, Danny?

DANNY: Gi me a dhrop of wather – it's the thirst that's killin' me.

SHEELAH (*takes jug*): The fever's on ye mighty bad.

DANNY (*drinks, falls back, groans*): Oh, the fire in me won't go out! How
long have I been here?

SHEELAH: Ten days this night.

DANNY: Ten days dis night! have I been all that time out of my mind?

SHEELAH: Iss, Danny. Ten days ago, that stormy night, ye crawled in at
that dure, wake an' like a ghost.

DANNY: I remind me now.

SHEELAH: Ye tould me that ye'd been poachin' salmon, and had been
shot by the keepers.

DANNY: Who said I hadn't?

SHEELAH: Divil a one! Why did ye make me promise not to say a word
about it? didn't ye refuse even to see a doctor itself?

DANNY: Has anyone axed after me?

SHEELAH: No one but Mr Hardress.

DANNY: Heaven bless him.

SHEELAH: I told him I hadn't seen ye, and here ye are this day groanin'
when there's great doin's up at Castle Chute. To-morrow the masther will
be married to Miss Anne.

DANNY: Married! but – the – his —

SHEELAH: Poor Eily, ye mane?

DANNY: Hide the candle from my eyes, it's painin' me, shade it off. Go
on, mother.

SHEELAH: The poor Colleen! Oh, vo, Danny, I knew she'd die of the
love that was chokin' her. He didn't know how tindher she was, when he

give her the hard word. What was that message the masther sent to her, that ye wouldn't let me hear? It was cruel, Danny, for it broke her heart entirely she went away that night, and, two days after a cloak was found floatin' in the reeds, under Brikeen Bridge; nobody knew it but me. I turned away, and never said —. The crature is drowned, Danny, and wo to them as dhruv her to it. She has no father, no mother to put a curse on him, but there's the Father above that niver spakes till the last day, and then – (*She turns and sees* DANNY *gasping, his eyes fixed on her, supporting himself on his arms.*) Danny! Danny! he's dyin' – he's dyin'! (*Runs to him,* R. *of bed.*)

DANNY: Who said that? Ye lie! I never killed her – sure he sent me the glove – where is it?

SHEELAH: He's ravin' again.

DANNY: The glove, he sent it to me full of blood. Oh! master, dear, there's your token. I tould ye I would clear the path foreninst ye.

SHEELAH: Danny, what d'ye mane?

DANNY: I'll tell ye how I did it, masther; 'twas dis way, but don't smile like dat, don't, sir! she wouldn't give me de marriage lines, so I sunk her, and her proofs wid her! She's gone! she came up wonst, but I put her down agin! Never fear – she'll never throuble yer agin, never, never. (*Lies down, mutters –* SHEELAH *on her knees, in horror and prayer.*)

SHEELAH: 'Twas he! he! – my own son – he's murdered, her, and he's dyin' now – dyin', wid blood on his hands! Danny! Danny! Spake to me!

DANNY: A docther! will dey let me die like a baste, and never a docther?

SHEELAH: I'll run for one that'll cure ye. Oh! weerasthrue, Danny! Is it for this I've loved ye? No, forgive me, accushla, it isn't your own mother that 'ud add to her heart-breakin' and pain. I'll fetch the docther, avick. (*Music – puts on cloak, and pulls hood over her head.*) Oh! hone – oh! hone!

Exit SHEELAH, L. *door in flat – a pause – knock – pause – knock. Enter* CORRIGAN, *door in flat,* L. C.

CORRIG: Sheelah! Sheelah! Nobody here? – I'm bothered entirely. The cottage on Muckross Head is empy – not a sowl in it but a cat. Myles has disappeared, and Danny gone – vanished, bedad, like a fog. Sheelah is the only one remaining. I called to see Miss Chute; I was kicked out. I sent her a letther; it was returned to me unopened. Her lawyer has paid off the mortgage, and taxed my bill of costs – the spalpeen! (DANNY *groans*) What's that? Some one asleep there. 'Tis Danny!

DANNY: A docther – gi' me a doctor!

CORRIG: Danny here – concealed, too! Oh! there's something going on that's worth peepin' into. Whist! there's footsteps comin'. If I could hide a bit. I'm a magistrate, an' I ought to know what's goin' on – here's a turf hole wid a windy in it. (*Exit* CORRIGAN, *opening in flat,* R. C.)

Enter SHEELAH *and* FATHER TOM, L. C. *door.*

SHEELAH (*goes to* DANNY.): Danny!

DANNY: Is that you, mother?

SHEELAH: I've brought the docther, asthore. (DANNY *looks up.*)

DANNY: The priest!

SHEELAH (*on her knees* R. *of bed*): Oh! my darlin', don't be angry wid me, but dis is the docther you want; it is'nt in your body where the hurt is; the wound is in your poor sowl – there's all the harrum.

FATHER T: Danny, my son – (*sits* L. *of bed*) – it's sore-hearted I am to see you down this way.

SHEELAH: And so good a son he was to his ould mother.

DANNY: Don't say that – don't. (*Covering his face.*)

SHEELAH: I will say it – my blessin' on ye – see that now, he's cryin'.

FATHER T: Danny, the hand of death is on ye. Will ye lave your sins behind ye here below, or will ye take them with ye above, to show them on ye? Is there anything ye can do that'll mend a wrong? leave that legacy to your friend, and he'll do it. Do ye want pardon of any one down here – tell me, avick; I'll get it for ye, and send it after you – may be ye'll want it.

DANNY (*rising up on arm*): I killed Eily O'Connor.

SHEELAH (*covers her face with her hands*): Oh! oh!

FATHER T: What harrum had ye agin the poor Colleen Bawn? (CORRIGAN *takes notes.*)

DANNY: She stud in *his* way, and he had my heart and sowl in his keeping.

FATHER T: Hardress!

DANNY: Hisself! I said I'd do it for him, if he'd give me the token.

FATHER T: Did Hardress employ you to kill the girl?

DANNY: He sent me the glove; that was to be the token that I was to put her away, and I did – I – in the Pool a Dhiol. She wouldn't gi' me the marriage lines; I threw her in and then I was kilt.

FATHER T: Killed! by whose hand?

DANNY: I don't know, unless it was the hand of heaven.

FATHER T (*rising, goes down – aside*): Myles na Coppaleen is at the bottom of this; his whiskey still is in that cave, and he has not been seen for ten days past. (*Aloud – goes to* DANNY.) Danny, after ye fell, how did ye get home?

DANNY: I fell in the wather; the current carried me to a rock; how long I was there half drowned I don't know, but on wakin' I found my boat floatin' close by, an' it was still dark, I got in and crawled here.

FATHER T (*aside*): I'll go and see Myles – there's more in this than has come out.

SHEELAH: Won't yer riverince say a word of comfort to the poor boy? – he's in great pain entirely.

FATHER T: Keep him quiet, Sheelah. (*Music*) I'll be back again with the comfort for him. Danny, your time is short; make the most of it. (*Aside.*) I'm off to Myles na Coppaleen. Oh, Hardress (*Going up.*) Cregan, ye little think what a bridal day ye'll have! (*Exit door in flat,* L. C.)

CORRIG (*who has been writing in note-book, comes out – at back*): I've got down every word of the confession. Now, Hardress Cregan, there will be guests at your weddin' to-night ye little dhrame of. (*Exit door in flat,* L. C.)

DANNY (*rising up*): Mother, mother! the pain is on me. Wather – quick – wather!

> SHEELAH *runs to* L. *table – takes jug – gives it to* DANNY – *he drinks* –
> SHEELAH *takes jug –* DANNY *struggles – falls back on bed – close on picture*

SCENE SECOND

Chamber in Castle Chute. (1st grooves).
Enter KYRLE DALY *and* SERVANT, R.

KYRLE: Inform Mrs Cregan that I am waiting upon her.

Enter MRS CREGAN, L.

MRS C: I am glad to see you, Kyrle.

Exit SERVANT, L.

KYRLE (R. C.): You sent for me, Mrs Cregan. My ship sails from Liverpool to-morrow. I never thought I could be so anxious to quit my native land.

MRS C: I want you to see Hardress. For ten days past he shuns the society of his bride. By night he creeps out alone in his boat on the lake – by day he wanders round the neighbourhood pale as death. He is heartbroken.

KYRLE: Has he asked to see me?

MRS C: Yesterday he asked where you were.

KYRLE: Did he forget that I left your house when Miss Chute, without a word of explanation, behaved so unkindly to me?

MRS C: She is not the same girl since she accepted Hardress. She quarrels – weeps – complains, and has lost her spirits.

KYRLE: She feels the neglect of Hardress.

ANNE (*without,* R.): Don't answer me. Obey! and hold your tongue.

MRS C: Do you hear? she is rating one of the servants.

ANNE (*without*): No words – I'll have no sulky looks neither!

Enter ANNE, R., *dressed as a bride, with veil and wreath in her hand.*

ANNE: Is that the veil and wreath I ordered? How dare you tell me that. (*Throws it off*, R.)

MRS C: Anne! (ANNE *sees* KYRLE — *stands confused*.)

KYRLE: You are surprised to see me in your house, Miss Chute?

ANNE: You are welcome, sir.

KYRLE (*aside*): She looks pale! She's not happy — that's gratifying.

ANNE: He doesn't look well — that's some comfort.

MRS C: I'll try to find Hardress. — (*Exit* MRS CREGAN, L.)

KYRLE: I hope you don't think I intrude — that is — I came to see Mrs Cregan.

ANNE (*sharply*): I don't flatter myself you wished to see me, why should you?

KYRLE: Anne, I am sorry I offended you; I don't know what I did, but no matter.

ANNE: Not the slightest.

KYRLE: I released your neighbourhood of my presence.

ANNE: Yes, and you released the neighbourhood of the presence of somebody else — she and you disappeared together.

KYRLE: She!

ANNE: Never mind.

KYRLE: But I do mind. I love Hardress Cregan as a brother, and I hope the time may come, Anne, when I can love you as a sister.

ANNE: Do you? I don't.

KYRLE: I don't want the dislike of my friend's wife to part my friend and me.

ANNE: Why should it? I'm nobody.

KYRLE: If you were my wife, and asked me to hate any one, I'd do it — I couldn't help it.

ANNE: I believed words like that once when you spoke them, but I have been taught how basely you can deceive.

KYRLE: Who taught you?

ANNE: Who? — your wife.

KYRLE: My what?

ANNE: Your wife — the girl you concealed in the cottage on Muckross Head. Stop now, don't speak — save a falsehood, however many ye have to spare. I saw the girl — she confessed.

KYRLE: Confessed that she was my wife?

ANNE: Made a clean breast of it in a minute, which is more than you could do with a sixteen-foot waggon and a team of ten in a week.

KYRLE: Anne, hear me; this is a frightful error — the girl will not repeat it.

ANNE: Bring her before me and let her speak.

KYRLE: How do I know where she is?

ANNE: Well, bring your boatman then, who told me the same.

KYRLE: I tell you it is false; I never saw – never knew the girl!

ANNE: You did not? (*Shows* EILY's *letter.*) Do you know that? You dropped it, and I found it.

KYRLE (*takes letter*): This! (*Reads.*)
　　Enter HARDRESS, L.

ANNE: Hardress! (*Turns aside.*)

KYRLE: Oh! (*Suddenly struck with the truth – glances towards* ANNE *– finding her looking away, places letter to* HARDRESS.) Do you know that? – you dropped it.

HARD (*conceals letter*): Eh? – Oh!

KYRLE: 'Twas he. (*Looks from one to the other.*) She thinks me guilty; but if I stir to exculpate myself, he is in for it.

HARD: You look distressed, Kyrle. Anne, what is the matter?

KYRLE: Nothing, Hardress. I was about to ask Miss Chute to forget a subject which was painful to her, and to beg of her never to mention it again – not even to you, Hardress.

HARD: I am sure she will deny you nothing.

ANNE: I will forget, sir; (*Aside.*) but I will never forgive him – never.

KYRLE (*aside*): She loves me still, and he loves another, and I am the most miserable dog that ever was kicked. (*Crosses to* L.) Hardress, a word with you. (*Exit* KYRLE *and* Hardress, L.)

ANNE: And this is my wedding day. There goes the only man I ever loved. When he's here near by me, I could give him the worst treatment a man could desire, and when he goes away he takes the heart and all of me off with him, and I feel like an unfurnished house. This is pretty feelings for a girl to have, and she in her regimentals. Oh! if he wasn't married – but he is, and he'd have married me as well – the malignant! Oh! if he had, how I'd have made him swing for it – it would have afforded me the happiest moment of my life. (*Music. Exit* ANNE, L.)

SCENE THIRD

Exterior of Myles's Hut, door R. *in flat. (2nd grooves.)*
Enter FATHER TOM, L.

FATHER T: Here's Myles's shanty. I'm nearly killed with climbin' the hill.

I wonder is he at home? Yes, the door is locked inside. (*Knocks.*) Myles –
Myles, are ye at home?

MYLES (*outside*, R. 2 E.): No – I'm out.

Enter MYLES, R. 2. E.

Arrah! is it yourself, Father Tom, that's in it?

FATHER T: Let us go inside, Myles – I've a word to say t'ye.

MYLES: I – I've lost the key.

FATHER T: Sure it's sticken inside.

MYLES: Iss – I always lock the dure inside and lave it there when I go out,
for fear on losin' it.

FATHER T: Myles, come here to me. It's lyin' ye are. Look me in the face.
What's come to ye these tin days past – three times I've been to your door
and it was locked, but I heard ye stirrin' inside.

MYLES: It was the pig, yer riverince.

FATHER T: Myles, why did yer shoot Danny Mann?

MYLES: Oh, murther, who tould you that?

FATHER T: Himself.

MYLES: Oh, Father Tom, have ye seen him?

FATHER T: I've just left him.

MYLES: Is it down there ye've been?

FATHER T: Down where?

MYLES: Below, where he's gone to – where would he be, afther
murthering a poor creature?

FATHER T: How d'ye know that?

MYLES: How! how did I? – whisht, Father Tom, it was his ghost.

FATHER T: He is not dead, but dyin' fast, from the wound ye gave him.

MYLES: I never knew 'twas himself 'till I was tould.

FATHER T: Who tould you?

MYLES: Is it who?

FATHER T: Who? who? – not Danny, for he doesn't know who killed
him.

MYLES: Wait, an' I'll tell you. It was nigh twelve that night, I was comin'
home – I know the time, betoken Murty Dwyer made me step in his
shebeen, bein' the wake of the ould Callaghan, his wife's uncle – and a
dacent man he was. 'Murty,' ses I –

FATHER T: Myles, you're desavin' me.

MYLES: Is it afther desavin yer riverence I'd be?

FATHER T: I see the lie in yer mouth. Who tould ye it was Danny Mann
ye killed?

MYLES: You said so awhile ago.

FATHER T: Who tould ye it was Danny Mann?

MYLES: I'm comin to it. While I was at Murty's, yer riverince, as I was a-tellin' you – Dan Dayley was there – he had just kim'd in. 'Good morrow, – good day' – ses he. 'Good morrow, good Dan, ses I,' – jest that ways entirely – 'it's an opening to the heart to see you.' Well, yer riverence, as I ware sayin', – 'long life an' good wife to ye, Masther Dan,' ses I. 'Thank ye, ses he, and the likes to ye, anyway.' The moment I speck them words, Dan got heart, an' up an' tould Murty about his love for Murty's darter – the Colleen Rue. The moment he heard that, he puts elbows in himself, an' stood lookin' at him out on the flure. 'You flog Europe, for boldness,' ses he – 'get out of my sight,' ses he, – 'this moment,' ses he, – 'or I'll give yer a kick that will rise you from poverty to the highest pitch of affluence,' ses he – 'away out 'o that, you notorious delinquent; single yer freedom, and double yer distance,' ses he. Well, Dan was forced to cut an' run. Poor boy, I was sorry for his trouble; there isn't a better son nor brother this moment goin' the road than what he is – said – said – there wasn't a better, an', au' – oh! Father Tom, don't ax me; I've got an oath on my lips. (*Music.*) Don't be hard on a poor boy.

FATHER T: I lift the oath from ye. Tell me, avich, oh! tell me. Did ye search for the poor thing – the darlin' soft-eyed Colleen? Oh! Myles, could ye lave her to lie in the cowld lake all alone?

Enter EILY *from door* R. *flat.*

MYLES: No, I couldn't.

FATHER T (*turns – sees* EILY): Eily! Is it yerself, and alive – an' not – not – Oh! Eily, mavourneen. Come to my heart. (*Embraces* EILY.)

MYLES (*crosses to* L.): D'ye think ye'd see me alive if she wasn't? I thought ye knew me better – it's at the bottom of the Pool a Dhiol I'd be this minute if she wasn't to the fore.

FATHER T (C.): Speak to me – let me hear your voice.

EILY: Oh! father, father, won't ye take me, far far away from this place.

FATHER T: Why, did ye hide yourself, this way?

EILY: For fear *he'd* see me.

FATHER T: Hardress. You knew then that he instigated Danny to get rid of ye?

EILY: Why didn't I die – why am I alive now for him to hate me?

FATHER T: D'ye know that in a few hours he is going to marry another.

EILY: I know it, Myles tould me – that's why I'm hiding myself away.

FATHER T: What does she mean?

MYLES (L.): She loves him still – that's what she manes.

FATHER T: Love the wretch who sought your life!

EILY: Isn't it his own? It isn't his fault if his love couldn't last as long as mine. I was a poor, mane creature – not up to him any way; but if he'd only said, 'Eily, put the grave between us and make me happy,' sure I'd lain down, wid a big heart, in the loch.

FATHER T: And you are willing to pass a life of seclusion that he may live in his guilty joy?

EILY: If I was alive wouldn't I be a shame to him an' a ruin – ain't I in his way? Heaven help me – why would I trouble him? Oh! he was in great pain o' mind entirely when he let them put a hand on me – the poor darlin'.

FATHER T: And you mean to let him believe you dead?

EILY: Dead an' gone: then perhaps, his love for me will come back, and the thought of his poor, foolish little Eily that worshipped the ground he stood on, will fill his heart awhile.

FATHER T: And where will you go?

EILY: I don't know. Anywhere. What matters?

MYLES (*against wing,* L.): Love makes all places alike.

EILY: I'm alone in the world now.

FATHER T: The villain – the monster! He sent her to heaven because he wanted her there to blot out with her tears the record of his iniquity. Eily, ye have but one home, and that's my poor house. You are not alone in the world – there's one beside ye, your father, and that's myself.

MYLES: Two – bad luck to me, two. I am her mother; sure I brought her into the world a second time.

FATHER T (*looking,* R.): Whist! look down there, Myles – what's that on the road?

MYLES (*crosses,* R.): It's the sogers – a company of red-coats. What brings the army out? – who's that wid them? – it is ould Corrigan, and they are going towards Castle Chute. There's mischief in the wind.

FATHER T: In with you, an' keep close awhile; I'll go down to the castle and see what's the matter. (*Crosses* R.)

EILY: Promise me that you'll not betray me – that none but yourself and Myles shall ever know I'm livin'; promise me that, before you go.

FATHER T: I do. Eily; I'll never breathe a word of it – it is as sacred as an oath. (*Exit* L. – *music.*)

EILY (*going to cottage*): Shut me in, Myles, and take the key wid ye, this time. (*Exit in cottage,* R.C.)

MYLES (*locks door*): There ye are like a pearl in an oyster; now I'll go to my bed as usual on the mountain above – the bolster is stuffed wid rocks, and I'll have a cloud round me for a blanket. (*Exit* MYLES, R. 2. E.)

SCENE FOURTH

Outside of Castle Chute. (1st grooves)
Enter CORRIGAN *and six* SOLDIERS, R. 1 E.

CORRIG: Quietly, boys; sthrew yourselves round the wood – some of ye at the gate beyant – two more this way – watch the windies; if he's there to escape at all, he'll jump from a windy. The house is surrounded.

Quadrille music under stage. – Air, 'The Boulanger'.

Oh, oh! they're dancin' – dancin' and merry-making, while the net is closin' around 'em. Now Masther Hardress Cregan – I was kicked out, was I; but I'll come this time wid a call that ye'll answer wid your head instead of your foot. My letters were returned unopened; but here's a bit of writin' that ye'll not be able to hand back so easy.

Enter CORPORAL, R.

CORP: All right, sir.

CORRIG: Did you find the woman, as I told ye?

CORP: Here she is, sir.

Enter SHEELAH, *guarded by two* SOLDIERS, R.

SHEELAH (*crying*): What's this? Why am I thrated this way – what have I done?

CORRIG: You are wanted awhile – it's your testimony we require. Bring her this way. Follow me (*Exit*, L.)

SHEELAH (*struggling*): Let me go back to my boy. Ah! good luck t'ye, don't kape me from my poor boy! (*Struggling.*) Oh! you dirty blackguards, let me go – let me go!

Exit SHEELAH *and* SOLDIERS, L.

SCENE FIFTH

Ball Room in Castle Chute. Steps, C.; *platform – balustrades on top; backed by moonlight landscape – doors* R. *and* L.; *table* L. C.; *writing materials, books, papers on; chairs; chair* L. 2 E.; *chairs* R.; *chandeliers lighted.* LADIES *and* GENTLEMEN, WEDDING GUESTS *discovered,* HYLAND CREAGH, BERTIE O'MOORE, DUCIE, KATHLEEN CREAGH, ADA CREAGH, PATSIE O'MOORE, BRIDESMAIDS *and* SERVANTS *discovered. – Music going on under stage.*

HYLAND: Ducie, they are dancing the Boulanger, and they can't see the figure unless you lend them the light of your eyes.

KATHLEEN: We have danced enough; it is nearly seven o'clock.

DUCIE: Mr O'Moore; when is the ceremony to commence?

O'MOORE: The execution is fixed for seven – here's the scaffold, I presume. (*Points to table.*)

HYLAND: Hardress looks like a criminal. I've seen him fight three duels, and he never shewed such a pale face as he exhibits to-night.

DUCIE: He looks as if he was frightened at being so happy.

HYLAND: And Kyrle Daly wears as gay an appearance.

Enter KYRLE DALY, *down steps*, C.

DUCIE: Hush! here he is.

KYRLE: That need not stop your speech, Hyland. I don't hide my love for Anne Chute, and it is my pride, and no fault of mine if she has found a better man.

HYLAND: He is not a better man.

KYRLE: He is – she thinks so – what she says becomes the truth.

Enter MRS CREGAN, L. 2 E.

MRS C: Who says the days of chivalry are over? Come, gentlemen, the bridesmaids must attend the bride. The guests will assemble in the hall.

Enter SERVANT, R. 2 E., *with letter and card on salver.*

SERV: Mr Bertie O'Moore, if you please. A gentleman below asked me to hand you this card.

O'MOORE: A gentleman; what can he want? (*Reads card.*) Ah! indeed; this is a serious matter, and excuses the intrusion.

HYLAND: What's the matter?

O'MOORE: A murder has been committed.

ALL: A murder?

O'MOORE: The perpetrator of the deed has been discovered, and the warrant for his arrest requires my signature.

HYLAND: Hang the rascal. (*Goes up with* DUCIE.)

O'MOORE: A magistrate, like a doctor, is called on at all hours.

MRS C: We can excuse you for such a duty, Mr O'Moore.

O'MOORE (*crossing*, R.): This is the result of some brawl at a fair I suppose. Is Mr Corrigan below?

MRS C (*starting*): Corrigan?

O'MOORE: Shew me to him.

Exit O'MOORE *and* SERVANT, R. 2 E. – GUESTS *go up and off* L. U. E.

MRS C: Corrigan here! What brings that man to this house? (*Exit* MRS CREGAN, R. 3 E.)

Enter HARDRESS, *down steps*, C. *from* R., *pale.*

HARD (*sits*, L.): It is in vain – I cannot repress the terror with which I approach these nuptials – yet, what have I to fear? Oh! my heart is bursting with its load of misery.

Enter ANNE, *down steps*, C. *from* R.

ANNE: Hardress! what is the matter with you?

HARD (*rising* L. C.): I will tell you – yes, it may take this horrible oppression from my heart. At one time I thought you knew my secret: I was mistaken. – The girl you saw at Muckross Head —

ANNE (R. C.): Eily O'Connor.

HARD: Was my wife!

ANNE: Your wife?

HARD: Hush! Maddened with the miseries this act brought upon me, I treated her with cruelty – she committed suicide.

ANNE: Merciful powers!

HARD: She wrote to me bidding me farewell for ever, and the next day her cloak was found floating in the lake. (ANNE *sinks in chair.*) Since then I have neither slept nor waked – I have but one thought, one feeling; my love for her, wild and maddened, has come back upon my heart like a vengeance.

Music – tumult heard, R.

ANNE: Heaven defend our hearts, what is that?

Enter MRS CREGAN, *deadly pale,* R. 3 E. – *Locks door behind her.*

MRS C: Hardress! my child!

HARD: Mother!

ANNE: Mother, he is here. Look on him – speak to him – do not gasp and stare on your son in that horrid way. Oh! mother, speak, or you will break my heart.

MRS C: Fly – fly! (HARDRESS *going,* R.) Not that way. No – the doors are defended! there is a soldier placed at every entrance! You – you are trapped and caught – what shall we do? – the window in my chamber – come – come – quick – quick!

ANNE: Of what is he accused?

HARD: Of murder, I see it in her face. (*Noise,* R.)

MRS C: Hush! they come – begone! Your boat is below that window. Don't speak! when oceans are between you and danger – write! Till then not a word. (*Forcing him off,* L. 3 E. – *noise,* R.)

ANNE: Accused of murder! He is innocent!

MRS C: Go to your room! Go quickly to your room, you will betray him – you can't command your features.

ANNE: Dear mother, I will.

MRS C: Away, I say – you will drive me frantic, girl. My brain is stretched to cracking. Ha! (*Noise,* R.)

ANNE: There is a tumult in the drawing room.

MRS C: They come! You tremble! Go – take away your puny love – hide it where it will not injure him – leave me to face this danger!

ANNE: He is not guilty.

MRS C: What's that to me, woman? I am his mother – the hunters are after my blood! Sit there – look away from this door. They come!

Knocking loudly – crash – door R. 3 E. *opened – enter* CORPORAL *and* SOLDIERS *who cross stage, facing up to charge –* GENTLEMEN *with drawn swords on steps,* C.; LADIES *on at back –* O'MOORE, R. 3 E. *– enter* CORRIGAN, R. 3 E. *–* KYRLE *on steps,* C.

CORRIG: Gentlemen, put up your swords, the house is surrounded by a military force, and we are here in the king's name.

ANNE (R.): Gentlemen, come on, there was a time in Ireland when neither king nor faction could call on Castle Chute without a bloody welcome.

GUESTS: Clear them out!

KYRLE (*interposing*): Anne, are you mad. Put up your swords – stand back there – speak – O'Moore, what does this strange outrage mean?

SOLDIERS *fall back –* GENTLEMEN *on steps –* KYRLE *comes forward.*

O'MOORE: Mrs Cregan, a fearful charge is made against your son; I know – I believe he is innocent. I suggest, then, that the matter be investigated here at once, amongst his friends, so that this scandal may be crushed in its birth.

KYRLE: Where is Hardress?

CORRIG: Where? – why he's escaping while we are jabbering here. Search the house.

Exit two SOLDIERS, R. 3 E.

MRS C (L.): Must we submit to this, sir? Will you, a magistrate, permit –

O'MOORE: I regret, Mrs Cregan, but as a form –

MRS C: Go on sir!

CORRIG (*at the door,* L. 3 E): What room is this? 'tis locked –

MRS C: That is my sleeping chamber.

CORRIG: My duty compels me.

MRS C (*throws key down on ground*): Be it so, sir.

CORRIG (*picks up key – unlocks door*): She had the key – he's there.

Exit CORRIGAN, CORPORAL *and two* SOLDIERS.

MRS C: He has escaped by this time.

O'MOORE (*at* L. *table*): I hope Miss Chute will pardon me for my share in this transaction – believe me, I regret –

ANNE (R.): Don't talk to me of your regret, while you are doing your worst. It is hate, not justice, that brings this accusation against Hardress, and this disgrace upon me.

KYRLE: Anne!

ANNE: Hold *your* tongue – his life's in danger, and if I can't love him, I'll fight for him and that's more than any of you men can do. (*To* O'MOORE.) Go on with your dirty work. You have done the worst now – you have dismayed our guests, scattered terror amid our festival, and made the remembrance of this night, which should have been a happy one, a thought of gloom and shame.

MRS C: Hark! I hear – I hear his voice. It cannot be.

Re-enter CORRIGAN, L. 3 E.

CORRIG: The prisoner is here!

MRS C (C.): Ah, (*utters a cry*) is he? Dark bloodhound, have you found him? May the tongue that tells me so be withered from the roots, and the eye that first detected him be darkened in its sockets?

KYRLE: Oh, madam! for heaven's sake!

ANNE: Mother! mother!

MRS C: What! shall it be for nothing he has stung the mother's heart, and set her brain on fire?

Enter HARDRESS, *handcuffed, and two* SOLDIERS, L. 3 E.

I tell you that my tongue may hold its peace, but there is not a vein in all my frame but curses him. (*Turns – sees* HARDRESS; *falls on his breast.*) My boy! my boy!

HARD (L.): Mother, I entreat you to be calm. (*Crosses to* C.) Kyrle, there are my hands, do you think there is blood upon them?

KYRLE *seizes his hand –* GENTLEMEN *press round him, take his hand, and retire up.*

HARD: I thank you, gentlemen; your hands acquit me. Mother, be calm – sit there. (*Points to chair,* L.)

ANNE (R.): Come here, Hardress; your place is here by me.

HARD (R. C.): Now, sir, I am ready.

CORRIG (L. *of table*): I will lay before you, sir, the deposition upon which the warrant issues against the prisoner. Here is the confession of Daniel or Danny Mann, a person in the service of the accused, taken on his death-bed; in articulo mortis, you'll observe.

O'MOORE: But not witnessed.

CORRIG (*calling*): Bring in that woman.

Enter SHEELAH *and two* SOLDIERS, R. 3 E.

I have witnesses. Your worship will find the form of law in perfect shape.

O'MOORE: Read the confession, sir.

CORRIG (*reads*): 'The deponent being on his death-bed, in the presence of Sheelah Mann and Thomas O'Brien, parish priest of Kinmare, deposed and said' –

Enter FATHER TOM, R. 3 E.

Oh, you are come in time, sir.

FATHER T: I hope I am.

CORRIG: We may have to call your evidence.

FATHER T (C.): I have brought it with me.

CORRIG: 'Deposed and said, that he, deponent, killed Eily O'Connor; that said Eily was the wife of Hardress Cregan and stood in the way of his marriage with Miss Anne Chute; deponent offered to put away the girl, and his master employed him to do so.'

O'MOORE: Sheelah, did Danny confess this crime?

SHEELAH (L. C.): Divil a word – it's a lie from end to end, that ould thief was niver in my cabin – he invented the whole of it – sure you're the divil's own parverter of the truth!

CORRIG: Am I? Oh, oh! Father Tom will scarcely say as much? (*to him*) Did Danny Mann confess this in your presence?

FATHER T: I decline to answer that question!

CORRIG: Aha! you must – the law will compel you!

FATHER T: I'd like to see the law that can unseal the lip of the priest, and make him reveal the secrets of heaven.

ANNE: So much for your two witnesses. Ladies stand close. Gentlemen, give us room here.

BRIDESMAIDS *down*, R. *Exit* FATHER TOM, R. 3 E.

CORRIG: We have abundant proof, your worship – enough to hang a whole county. Danny isn't dead yet. Deponent agreed with Cregan that if the deed was to be done, that he, Cregan, should give his glove as a token.

MRS C: Ah!

HARD: Hold! I confess that what he has read is true. Danny did make the offer, and I repelled his horrible proposition.

CORRIG: Aha! but you gave him the glove?

HARD: Never, by my immortal soul – never!

MRS C (*advancing*): But I – I did! (*Movement of surprise.*) I, your wretched mother – I gave it to him – I am guilty! thank heaven for that! remove those bonds from his hands and put them here on mine.

HARD: 'Tis false, mother, you did not know his purpose – you could not know it. (CORPORAL *takes off handcuffs.*)

MRS C: I will not say anything that takes the welcome guilt from off me.

Enter MYLES *from steps.*

MYLES: Won't ye, ma'am? Well; if ye won't, I will.

ALL: Myles!

MYLES: Save all here. If you plaze, I'd like to say a word; there's been a murder done, and I done it.

ALL: You!

MYLES: Myself. Danny was killed by my hand. (*To* CORRIGAN.) Wor yez any way nigh that time?

CORRIG (*quickly*): No.

MYLES (*quickly*): That's lucky; then take down what I'm sayin'. I shot the poor boy – but widout manin' to hurt him. It's lucky I killed him that time, for it's lifted a mighty sin off the sowl of the crature.

O'MOORE: What does he mean?

MYLES: I mane, that if you found one witness to Eily O'Connor's death, I found another that knows a little more about it, and here she is.

Enter EILY *and* FATHER TOM *down steps.*

ALL: Eily!

MYLES: The Colleen Bawn herself!

EILY: Hardress!

HARD: My wife – my own Eily.

EILY: Here, darlin', take the paper, and tear it if you like. (*Offers him the certificate.*)

HARD: Eily, I could not live without you.

MRS C: If ever he blamed you, it was my foolish pride spoke in his hard words – he loves you with all his heart. Forgive me, Eily.

EILY: Forgive.

MRS C: Forgive your mother, Eily.

EILY (*embracing her*): Mother!

MRS C, HARDRESS, EILY, FATHER TOM *group together* – ANNE, KYRLE, *and* GENTLEMEN – LADIES *together* – *their backs to* CORRIGAN – CORRIGAN *takes bag, puts in papers, looks about, puts on hat, buttons coat, slinks up stage, runs up stairs and off* – MYLES *points off after him* – *several* GENTLEMEN *run after* CORRIGAN.

ANNE: But what's to become of me, in all my emotion to be summoned for nothing? Is my wedding dress to go to waste, and here's all my blushes ready? I must have a husband.

HYLAND *and* GENTLEMEN: Take me.

O'MOORE: Take me.

ANNE: Don't all speak at once! Where's Mr Daly!

KYRLE: Here I am, Anne!

ANNE: Kyrle, come here! You said you loved me, and I think you do.

KYRLE: Oh!

ANNE: Behave yourself now. If you'll ask me, I'll have you.

KYRLE (*embracing* ANNE): Anne! (*Shouts outside.*)

ALL: What's that?

MYLES (*looking off at back*): Don't be uneasy! it's only the boys outside that's caught ould Corrigan thryin' to get off, and they've got him in the horsepond.

KYRLE: They'll drown him.

MYLES: Nivir fear, he wasn't born to be drownded – he won't sink – he'll rise out of the world, and divil a fut nearer heaven he'll get than the top o' the gallows.

EILY (*to* HARDRESS): And ye won't be ashamed of me?

ANNE: I'll be ashamed of him if he does.

EILY: And when I spake – no – speak —

ANNE: Spake is the right sound. Kyrle Daly, pronounce that word.

KYRLE: That's right; if you ever spake it any other way I'll divorce ye – mind that.

FATHER T: Eily, darlin', in the middle of your joy, sure you would not forget one who never forsook you in your sorrow.

EILY: Oh, Father Tom!

FATHER T: Oh, it's not myself I mane.

ANNE: No, it's that marauder there, that lent me his top coat in the thunder storm. (*Pointing to* MYLES.)

MYLES: Bedad, ma'am, your beauty left a linin' in it that has kept me warm ever since.

EILY: Myles, you saved my life – it belongs to you. There's my hand, what will you do with it?

MYLES (*takes her hand and* HARDRESS'*s*): Take her, wid all my heart. I may say that, for ye can't take her widout. I am like the boy who had a penny to put in the poor-box – I'd rather keep it for myself. It's a shamrock itself ye have got, sir; and like that flower she'll come up every year fresh and green forent ye. When ye cease to love her may dyin' become ye, and when ye *do* die, lave yer money to the poor, your widdy to me, and we'll both forgive ye. (*Joins hands.*)

EILY: I'm only a poor simple girl, and it's frightened I am to be surrounded by so many.

ANNE: Friends, Eily, friends.

EILY: Oh, if I could think so – if I could hope that I had established myself in a little corner of their hearts, there wouldn't be a happier girl alive than THE COLLEEN BAWN.

SOLDIERS	SOLDIERS
GUESTS	GUESTS
	HYLAND
	O'MOORE SHEELAGH

KYRLE ANNE MYLES HARDRESS EILY FATHER TOM MRS CREEGAN

R.   L.

CURTAIN

Further Reading

Peter Ackroyd, *Dickens* (Sinclair-Stevenson, 1990). Readable biography.

Richard Altick, *The Shows of London* (Harvard University Press, 1978). Seminal account of freaks and shows. Everyone who writes about the exhibition of freaks in England is indebted to this book, as am I. Details of The Gnome Fly have been taken from this source.

Nina Auerbach, *Private Theatricals, The Lives of the Victorians* (Harvard University Press, 1990).

Peter Bailey, (ed.) *Music Hall: The Business of Pleasure* (Open University Press, 1986).

Henry Barton Baker, *The London Stage, its history and traditions from 1576–1888* (W. H. Allen, 1889).

Chris Baldick, *In Frankenstein's Shadow* (Oxford University Press, 1987).

William Gurney Benham, *John Vine of Colchester: A Remarkable Armless Artist* (Benham, 1931).

Michael Booth, *Victorian Spectacular Theatre 1850–1910* (Routledge and Kegan Paul, 1981).

J.S. Bratton (ed.) *Music Hall: Performance and Style* (Open University Press, 1986).

Charles Dickens, *Dickens' Journalism*, edited by Michael Slater (J.M. Dent, 1994). Includes *Sketches by Boz* and other early papers 1833–39.

Charles Dickens, *The Amusements of the People and Other Papers: Reports, Essays and Reviews, 1834–51* edited by Michael Slater (Ohio State University Press, 1996).

Richard Fawkes, *Dion Boucicault* (Quartet, 1979). Readable biography, full of dramatic information.

Leslie Fiedler, *Freaks: Myths and Images of the Secret Self* (Simon and Schuster 1978).

Edgar and Eleanor Johnson (eds), *The Dickens Theatrical Reader*

(Victor Gollancz, 1964). Useful compilation of Dickens' writings about theatrical matters.

David Krause, *The Dolmen Boucicault* (The Dolmen Press, 1964). Three Irish plays.

Sean McMahon, *The Wearing of the Green: The Irish Plays of Dion Boucicault* in Eire-Ireland, 2, 1957.

Henry Mayhew, *London Labour and the London Poor* (Griffin, Bohn and Co., 1851–1852). Still extraordinary. Worth reading in its entirety. Volume I has a section on penny gaffs from which my quotation is taken. Readers who are tempted to regard Mayhew's tone as quaint or laughable should read Nick Davies' *Dark Heart, The Shocking Truth about Hidden Britain* (Chatto and Windus, 1997) to put Mayhew's observations into perspective.

Elspeth Moncrieff with Stephen and Iona Joseph, *Farm Animal Portraits* (Antique Collectors' Club, 1996).

James Ollé, 'Where Crummles Played', *The Dickensian, vol 47* pages 143–7 (1951). Establishes likely source for Crummles and the Infant.

James Robinson Planché, *Recollections and Reflections* (Sampson Low, Marston and Co, 1901).

Jeffrey Richards, *Early American Drama* (Penguin Classics, 1997). Includes *The Octoroon* and sets Boucicault in his American context.

Harriet Ritvo, *The Animal Estate, The English and Other Creatures in the Victorian Age* (Harvard University Press, 1987).

A.H. Saxon, *Enter Foot and Horse. A History of Hippodrama in England and France* (Yale University Press, 1968). A marvellous book to which I am greatly indebted. Has a chapter on Shakespeare and circuses.

Lord George Sanger, *Seventy Years A Showman* (J. M. Dent, 1927). Reminiscences of one of the greatest Victorian showmen.

Paul Sheridan, *Penny Theatres of Victorian London*, (Denis Dobson, 1981). Full of amazing extracts.

R.S. Surtees, *Mr Sponge's Sporting Tour* (Bradbury and Evans, 1852).

Peter Thompson, *Plays by Dion Boucicault* (Cambridge University Press, 1984): Includes *The Octoroon* but not *The Colleen Bawn*.

Deborah Vlock, *Dickens' Novel Reading and Victorian Popular Theatre*

(Cambridge University Press, 1998). Argues that the voices in Dickens' narratives were conditioned by the culture of the stage.

Gaby Wood, *The Smallest Of All Persons Mentioned in The Records Of Littleness* (Profile Books, 1998). Expands Altick's original research into the Sicilian Fairy.

SOCIETY

11 THE BUSINESS OF MATRIMONY

Marriage was the glue that stuck Victorians together. Matrimony pasted everyone in place like so many photographs in an album and labelled them with a name and a station. Where there was dissention, trouble and unrest, marriage and the stable comforts of the domestic hearth were the cure proposed by much Victorian literature. Because writing for the stage was largely considered to be without literary merit, dramatists were free to reflect and comment upon social situations in a particularly straightforward way. The three plays and the libretto in this section show dramatists anatomising the society of their time, and their themes centre inevitably on matrimony.

The true social comment of the first play, John Walker's melodrama *The Factory Lad*, lies hidden behind its obvious attempt to be topical. It is ostensibly about a group of honest working men who lose their jobs when the wicked master converts his factory to steam. Written after the turmoil of the Luddite machine smashings and during a time of social unrest which later gave rise to the Chartist Movement, it is stuffed with muddled references to social injustices, including the game laws, the poor law, the workhouse and transportation. Closer study reveals that far from sympathising with the working men and inciting social change it actually recommends acquiescence with the status quo through virtuous domesticity.

We leap forward a generation for the next play. *Society* by T.W. Robertson, first performed in 1865, grandly proclaims its themes and then fails, as contemporary critics noted, to deliver quite what the title promises. Robertson is generally credited with ushering in a new type of stage play referred to by his contemporaries as 'talking drama' lacking the sensationalist scenes and effects popularised by Dion Boucicault. In a Robertson comedy the performance is focused upon the small-scale, middle-class domestic world familiar to well-off audiences. *Society* typically teases this audience's prejudices by pretending to question the class system but ends with a reassuring endorsement of things as they are. Comedy conventionally ends in marriage but here the proposed wedding stands for more than a throwaway, romantic flourish; it seals the characters into a correct social compact made perfect by Sidney Daryl's newly inherited title. Not everyone in *Society* is a nob. One scene is set in a seedy journalists' club and affectionately lampoons Robertson's circle of friends and fellow contributors to the magazine *Fun*. A gang from *Fun* attended *Society*'s first night and the group included William Schwenck Gilbert, then aged 28. It was Gilbert who later, in partnership with the composer Arthur Sullivan, evolved a comic form where serious, satirical bite was disguised as eccentric buffoonery. Gilbert's famously uneasy relationship with Sullivan produced twelve comic operas (not counting the very early *Thespis* or *Trial by Jury* – described by the press as 'an operatic trifle'). Five of the operas were definitive smash hits with *The Mikado* (1885) being the most popular of all.

The Savoy Operas are genuine hunks of Victoriana and their ponderous, often facetious nature is so out of temper with modern intellectual tastes that, despite their continued popularity, they have never achieved cultural respectability. Gilbert and Sullivan are usually regarded as beneath consideration and left out of discussions of Victorian theatre, although Gilbert's stage plays sometimes creep in for a mention as forerunners to the genius of Oscar Wilde. This is unfair since Gilbert's collaboration with Sullivan produced a hearty, 'healthy' form of theatre which was nevertheless more radical and socially challenging than the brittle, brilliant wit of the 1890s.

Victorian critics often disparaged the noisy world of the theatre and said that its entertainments were no good when read silently as printed texts. This, after all, was the age of the novel, when literature was measured by its ability to deliver a fully realised imaginative world to a reader sitting alone in a bedroom or study. Modern readers looking back across the perspective of a century or more may discover unintended benefits, as well as difficulties with dramatic material, flattened out on paper rather than given life on stage. Reading Gilbert's lyrics before hearing them sung provides useful insight into his methods and relationship with Sullivan and is revelatory enough to justify printing a libretto without the musical score. That said, it is impossible to understand *The Mikado* without hearing it – fortunately, productions are frequently staged and there are several versions available on video and CD. (Mike Leigh's film *Topsy-Turvy* adds an extra dimension.)

Dramatists themselves were sensitive to the carping of their peers and began to respond by making their work more readable. Arthur Wing Pinero's 1893 play *The Second Mrs Tanqueray* is a deliberately literary work which is notable for having some of the imaginative texture of a novel. It is also a play with a message and is significant for being one of the first pieces to examine the social problem posed by women who gain sexual experience before marriage.

The terms of the 1890s 'woman problem' debate were clearly set by Thomas Hardy in his 1891 novel *Tess of the D'Urbervilles*. Pinero took a great interest in Hardy's work and had borrowed his plots before, most acrimoniously for *The Squire* in 1881. For *Mrs Tanqueray* he was careful to shift the furniture around but the essential design remains the same as *Tess*; a pure woman has a hidden sexual past which re-emerges and destroys her. As the 1890s progressed, the argument broadened into more general feminist issues raised by the phenomenon of the New Woman. Yet it would be wrong to think this debate was essentially about sexual contact. At the heart of the 'woman problem' was an increasing social dissatisfaction and the ensuring discussion about women's roles magnified this. Both *Tess of the D'Urbervilles* and *The Second Mrs Tanqueray* develop a theme which had already been addressed; strongly by Gilbert and Pinero in the 1880s and weakly by Robertson in the 1860s. This theme was the inevitable rip and flaw caused by pinning together an unravelling social fabric with the instrument of marriage. Too much was expected of an institution with limited capacities. In a century of massive change which encouraged intellectual inquiry and exploration it was absurd to expect that static, conservative social values could remain intact.

12 THE FACTORY LAD

The Factory Lad is a melodrama that would like to be a revenge tragedy. Its simple plot is broken across a social dilemma concerning the disintegration of the old, feudal, agricultural-based relationship between master and servant and its replacement with a new, industrial order. Factory owner Squire Westwood converts his looms to steam power and modernises relations with his workforce, discharging most of his employees. In doing so he betrays the social obligations implied by his old-fashioned, landowning title of Squire. His men foolishly expect him to fulfil the duties his title traditionally entails and, when he reneges, they erupt into violence, arson and self-righteous, sub-Shakespearean language.

Both the factory hands and, ultimately, the play itself are crushed by the weight of history. This is not a subtle drama – John Walker is stunningly heavy-handed with the social and historial comment. Will Rushton, poacher and outcast, introduces himself in Act I scene ii with a rant about the Game Laws: 'As if a poor man hadn't as much right to the bird that flies, and the hare that runs, as the rich tyrants who want all, and gripe and grapple all too?' In the course of the play Rushton delivers himself of an astonishing range of complaints about injustice. He seems to have suffered all the criminal punishments possible, being whipped, imprisoned, transported and then seeing his wife and four children 'slaughtered by the natives, who hate white men and live on human flesh'.

How are we to take this type of thing today? The play's most ludicrous aspect is not its relentless appeal to the audience's emotions, after all we're used to TV drama following the traditions of melodrama. What sounds silliest to modern ears is the play's language, the actual words spoken by the characters as they protest against their fate. Blood boils several times, flesh is 'gored with the lash of power', brains grow giddy or frenzied and are crossed with wild dreams, chains and screams of death are heard, eyeballs crack and men call each other 'fiend'. Jane Allen falls on the 'cold ground' and fears her husband will be torn from her and taken 'to a loathsome dungeon' and Will Rushton rejoices to 'see the palace of the tyrant levelled to the ground – to hear his engines of gain cracking – to hear him call for help, and see the red flame laugh in triumph!'

Modern readers must resist the temptation to interpret this as camp. When *The Factory Lad* was first performed, melodrama was a popular, vibrant genre in no danger of decaying into parody. *The Factory Lad* is meant to be taken seriously and its sad ending and absence of comic relief are unusual for this genre. In his *Prefaces to Nineteenth Century Plays*, Professor Michael Booth says that the play's 'radical social consciousness is advanced even for socially aware domestic melodrama, and its unrelenting severity and power of serious dramatic expression also place it well ahead of its time'.

Walker worked within accepted conventions to produce a stirring play with a message. His intended message is simple; while engaging audience sympathy for the plight of the unemployed factory workers he quietly suggests that tragedy could have been averted. If it wasn't for the beer drunk in the pub and the incitement of Rushton the self-confessed incendiary, George Allen might have heeded his wife and stayed out of trouble. As Jane says to her foolish husband when the factory burns in Act II scene ii: 'Oh, George! bad advice has led you to this – I know you would not have done so of yourself.' Walker effectively recommends abstinence from alcohol, the removal of rebellious agitators, the influence of a good wife and domestic responsibility as excellent ways to maintain public order and social control. George Allen foolishly rejects a moderate measure of ale drunk mildly at home and chooses instead to down large amounts of beer in the intoxicating surroundings of The Harriers. The evil effects of excess liquor upon the working man was a well-worn Victorian obsession and the Temperance Movement campaigned to get men to sign the pledge and renounce the demon drink altogether. It's no coincidence that the plan to torch the factory is hatched in the inn and that the landlord is cast as a toady who is surprised at how much ale the men consume.

The Factory Lad is set in Lancashire and Walker makes a passable attempt at capturing the diction and speech patterns of working men from the north west. In Allen's first appeal to Westwood before it is obvious that all hope is lost he says: 'Things, mayhap, ha' run cross, so you be hasty.' This is credible, realistic speech from a plain, ill-educated worker. However, when Westwood refuses to capitulate Hatfield bursts forth with sudden, overworked eloquence and curses the squire in a new kind of language, using the insultingly familiar 'thou' and 'ye'.

> May thy endeavours be as sterile land, which the lightning has scath'd, bearing nor fruit, nor flower, nor blade, but never-dying thorns to pierce thee on thy pillow! Hard-hearted, vain pampered thing as thou art.
>
> (Act I scene i)

This sort of apparent overreaction is the essence of melodrama. The immediate impression is of borrowed words taken from a literary memory of Elizabethan and Jacobean dramatists and the Authorised Version of the Bible. Walker is not being flippant in choosing to call upon the past in this way, he does it because he really believes it will work. This mixed language is not so out of character as it might appear. Many dialects quite naturally retained the 'thou' forms of address and this has proved a difficult characteristic to get down convincingly in print; witness D.H. Lawrence's more risible passages in the early versions of *Lady Chatterley's Lover*. For Walker, the strength and justness of the factory men's cause resides in their connection with a mythic version of England's past. This inheritance is signalled in their faithful working habits and in their language. Squire Westwood's villainy is established in opposition to this tradition. He sacks his father's housekeeper and replaces her with a French cook, a man who delays taking up his post for an excursion to Brighton, notorious for its connection with the decadent Prince Regent. Hatfield and Sims wax indignant about Westwood's betrayal of the social contract. Hatfield says:

> Squire Westwood? Squire Hard-Heart! No man, no feeling! Call a man like that a squire! An English gentleman, a true English gentleman is he who feels for another, who relieves the distressed, and not turns out the honest hard-working man to beg or starve because he, forsooth, may keep his hunters and drink his foreign wines.

Sims replies:

> Aye, and go to foreign parts. Englishmen were happy when
> they knew nought but Englishmen – when they were plain,
> blunt, honest, upright and downright – the master an example
> to his servant, and both happy with the profits of their daily
> toil.

(Act I scene v)

For his part, Westwood rejects the past, saying: 'What, because
our fathers acted foolishly, shall we also plod on in the same dreary
route?' (Act I scene iv).

Westwood's treason carries the play's other message. Alongside
the remedy Walker trumpets for social injustice is another unbidden
but equally strident theme, one which imposed itself on nineteenth-
century theatre, painting and architecture, producing a type of art at
which the twentieth century tends to sneer. A technicolour vision of
England's medieval/Tudor centuries and its feudal brotherhood of
souls influenced Ruskin, Pugin, William Morris and the Pre-
Raphaelites who strove to reinvent its glorious traditions. In *The
Factory Lad*, Walker tries to reach back into this past and draw upon
memories of another type of play, just as his language tries to invoke
a remembered version of England. Rushton is a malcontent in role
as well as disposition; his sense of injustice prompts him to stir the
other characters to action and catalyses the plot. As a dramatic
character he is directly descended from Jacobean figures such as
Malevole in John Marston's *The Malcontent* (c1603).

Of course *The Factory Lad* is not a revenge tragedy. It lacks
darkness and glitter and is too open, too concerned with social
anguish. It makes too many recommendations about work and class
and it is too preoccupied with England's past and future. Little is
known about its author John Walker except that he wrote at least six
other melodramas, plus a comedy, between 1825 and 1843. The date
of *The Factory Lad* is uncertain. Two versions survive, the earliest in
Duncombe's *British Theatre vol 11*, is catalogued in the British Library
as 1825. The edition does not give a first performance date but states
this is the text as performed in the London theatres, suggesting it
already had a stage history. There is a later edition of 1888 in *Dicks
Standard Plays* number 930, which suggests that the play continued

to have some popularity. Written and performed before Victoria's accession, *The Factory Lad* contains within it the tensions and failures of domestic and industrial themes which are characteristically Victorian.

*

THE FACTORY LAD
John Walker

Dramatis Personæ

GEORGE ALLEN
FRANK WILSON
WALTER SIMS   } *Lately discharged from the Factory of* ★★★★★
JOE SMITH
JACK HATFIELD
WILL RUSHTON, *an Outcast*
SQUIRE WESTWOOD, *Master of the Factory*
TAPWELL, *Landlord of the 'Harriers'*
GRIMLEY
JUSTICE BIAS
CLERK
JANE ALLEN
MARY, *her eldest Girl, about* 11
MILLY, *her second, about* 6
A CHILD IN CRADLE
CONSTABLES
and SOLDIERS

ACT I

SCENE I

Exterior of a factory, lighted.

As the curtain rises the clock strikes eight, and the men, including ALLEN, WILSON, SMITH, SIMS, *and* HATFIELD, *enter from Factory.*

ALLEN: Now my lads, the glad sound – eight o'clock, Saturday night. Now for our pay, and for the first time from our new master, the son of our late worthy employer.

WILSON: The poor man's friend!

HATFIELD: And the poor man's father, too!

ALLEN: Aye, who, as he became rich by the industry of his men, would not desert them in a time of need, nor prefer steam machinery and other inventions to honest labour.

WILSON: May his son be like him!

ALLEN: Aye, he was a kind man truly; good as good could be, an enemy to no man; but the slothful. Ah! a tear almost starts when I think of him! May he be happy, – he must be as happy above as he made those on this earth. But come, come, we won't be melancholy. Saturday night! We won't put a dark side upon things, but let us hope his son, our present master, may be like his father, eh?

HATFIELD: Ah, half like, and I shall be content.

WILSON: And I, and all of us.

ALLEN: Hush! He comes.

Enter WESTWOOD, *from factory.*

WESTWOOD: Gentlemen!

HATFIELD (*aside to* ALLEN *and rest*): Gentlemen! There's a pleasing way.

ALLEN: Gentlemen, sir! We're no gentlemen, but only poor, hard-working men, at your honour's service.

HATFIELD: Hard-working, and honest, we hope.

WESTWOOD: Well, well; gentlemen or hard-working men, it's not what I've come about.

ALLEN: No complaint, I hope? Work all clean and right?

WESTWOOD: It may be.

HATFIELD: It may be! It is, or I'll forfeit my wages. Your father, sir, never spoke in doubt; but always looked, spoke his mind, and –

WESTWOOD: And that's what *I've* come to do – I've come to speak my mind. Times are now altered!

ALLEN: They are indeed, sir; a poor man has now less wages for more work.

WESTWOOD: The master having less money, resulting from there being less demand for the commodity manufactured.

ALLEN: Less demand!

WESTWOOD: Hear me: if not less demand, a greater quantity is thrown into the markets at a cheaper rate. Therefore to the business I've come about. As things go with the times, so must men. To compete with my neighbours – that is, if I wish to prosper as they do – in plain words, in future I have come to the resolution of having my looms propelled by steam.

ALLEN:
HATFIELD: } By steam!
WILSON:

WESTWOOD: Which will dispense with the necessity of manual labour, and save me some three thousand a year.

ALLEN: And not want us, who have been all our lives working here?

WESTWOOD: I can't help it – I am sorry for it; but I must do as others do.

ALLEN: What, and turn us out, to beg, starve, steal, or –

HATFIELD: Aye, or rot for what he cares.

WESTWOOD: Turn you out are words I don't understand. I don't want you, that's all. Surely I can say that? What is here is mine, left me by my father to do the best with, and that is now my intention. Steam supersedes manual labour; a ton of coals will do as much work as fifty men, and for less wages than ten will come to, is it not so?

ALLEN: It may be as you say, sir; but your poor father made the old plan do, and died, they say, rich. He was always well satisfied with the profits our industry brought him, he lived cheerful himself and made others so; and often I have heard him say his greatest pleasure was the knowledge that so many hard-working men could sit down to a Sunday's dinner in peace, and rear up their children decently through his means.

WILSON: Ah, heaven bless him!

HATFIELD: Heaven has blessed him, I trust, for he was a man – an Englishman! Who had feeling for his fellow creatures, and who would not, for the sake of extra gain, that he might keep his hounds and his hunters, turn the poor man from his door who had served him faithfully for years.

WESTWOOD: I hear you, and understand you, sir. Sentiments in theory sound well, but not in practice; and as you seem spokesman in this affair, I will – though I consider myself in no way compelled – reply to you in your own way. Don't you buy where you please, at the cheapest place? Would you have bought that jerkin of one man more than another, if he had charged you twice the sum for it, or even a sixpence more? Don't you, too, sow your garden as you please, and dig it as you please?

HATFIELD: Why, it's my own!

WESTWOOD: There it is. Then have *I* not the same right to do as I please with *my own*?

ALLEN: Then you discharge us?

HATFIELD: Oh, come along! What's the use of asking or talking either? You cannot expect iron to have feelings!

WESTWOOD: I stand not here to be insulted; so request you'll to the counting-house, receive your wages, and depart.

ALLEN: And for ever?

WESTWOOD: For ever! I want you not.

ALLEN: Will you not think of it again once more?

WESTWOOD: I'm resolved.

ALLEN (*aside*): My poor wife and children! (*To* WESTWOOD.) No, no; not quite – not quite resolved! Things, mayhap' ha' run cross, so you be hasty. Think, think again! (*Kneels.*) On my knees hear a poor man's prayer.

WESTWOOD: It is useless! I *have* thought and decided!

ALLEN (*rises*): My wife! My children! (*Rushes off. L.*)

WILSON: Poor fellow!

HATFIELD: Then, if ye will not hear a poor man's prayer, hear his curses! May thy endeavours be as sterile land, which the lightning has scath'd, bearing nor fruit, nor flower, nor blade, but never-dying thorns to pierce thee on thy pillow! Hard-hearted, vain, pampered thing as thou art. Remember, the day will come thou'lt be sorry for this night's work! Come, comrades – come!

HATFIELD, WILSON, SIMS, *and* SMITH *exit R*. WESTWOOD *into factory, sneeringly.*

SCENE II

A country lane. Dark.

Enter RUSHTON, *cautiously, with snare, bag, and gun. Sets a snare.*

RUSHTON: That be sure for a good 'un! Ha, ha! The Game Laws, eh? As if a poor man hadn't as much right to the bird that flies, and the hare that runs, as the rich tyrants who want all, and gripe and grapple all too? I care not for their laws. While I have my liberty, or power, or strength, I will live as well as the best of 'em. (*Noise without.*) But who comes here? Ah! what do I see? Some of the Factory lads, and this way too! What can this mean? I'll listen! (*Stands aside.*)

        Enter HATFIELD, WILSON, SIMS, *and* SMITH.

WILSON: Well, here's a pretty ending to all our labours, after nine years, as I've been –

SIMS: And I, ten.

SMITH: And I, since I was a lad.

HATFIELD: And I, all my life. But so it is. What are working men like us but the tools that make others rich, who, when we become old –

OMNES: Ah!

HATFIELD: We're kicked from our places, like dogs, to starve! Die, and rot, for what they care!

SIMS: Or beg!

HATFIELD: Ah! That I'll never do!

WILSON: Nor I!

SMITH: Nor I, either!

SIMS: Then rob, mayhap?

WILSON: That may be!

HATFIELD: Aye! Be like poor Will Rushton – an outcast, a poacher, or anything!

RUSHTON (*starting forward. The others stand amazed.*): Aye! Or a pauper; to go with your hat in your hand, and after begging and telling them what they know to be the truth; that you have a wife and five, six, or eight children, one, perhaps just born, another, mayhap' just dying – they'll give you eighteen pence to support them all for the week; and if you dare to complain, not a farthing! But place you in the stocks, or scourge you through the town as a vagabond! This is parish charity! I have known what it is. My back is still scored with the marks of their power. The slave abroad, the poor black whom they affect to pity, is not so trampled on! Hunted! and ill-used as the peasant, or hard-working fellows like yourselves; if once you have no home nor bread to give your children!

WILSON: But this I'll never submit to!

SIMS: Nor I!

SMITH: Nor I!

HATFIELD: Nor I! I'll hang first!

WILSON: Thank heaven, I have no children!

SMITH: Nor more have I, nor Sims; but some have both, wives and children.

WILSON: 'Tis true. I have a wife, but she's as yet young, healthy, and can work and does work; but think of poor Allen, with a wife and three small children and an aged mother to support.

RUSHTON: What! And is he discharged too? What, Allen – George Allen?

HATFIELD: Aye! Along with the rest. Not wanted now!

RUSHTON: My brother George, as I do call him still – for though my poor wife be dead and gone, she were his wife's sister. Ah! But let me not think of that. Where – where be poor George? He be not here!

WILSON: He rushed off home, I do believe, like to one broken-hearted.

RUSHTON: Ah! To his poor wife and children. There will I go to him, and say though all the world do forsake him, Will Rushton never will. No; while there be a hare or bird he shall have one; and woe to the man who dare prevent or hold my hand.

HATFIELD: You're a brave and staunch fellow.

RUSHTON: Aye! And desperate and daring, too.

WILSON: Give me your hand.

HATFIELD: And here's mine. What say you? Suppose we go to the 'Harriers', and, in the back room by ourselves, just ha' a drop of something and talk o' things a bit.

WILSON: We will go.

SMITH: Aye, we will.

HATFIELD (to RUSHTON): And you to George, and say where we are.

RUSHTON: I will – and bring him with me! But he'll not want asking. These times cannot last long. When man be so worried that he be denied that food that heaven sends for all, then heaven itself calls for vengeance! No; the time has come when the sky shall be like blood, proclaiming this shall be the reward of the avaricious, the greedy, the flinty-hearted, who, deaf to the poor man's wants, make him what he now is, a ruffian – an incendiary!

WILSON: Remember Allen. Yet stay! Now I think again, will it not alarm his wife to see you!

RUSHTON: Ah! (Approaches WILSON.)

HATFIELD: And bring things to mind that must not be – I don't mean together; but you know – not thought of just now.

RUSHTON: Ah, my wife –

HATFIELD: Was her sister. So, suppose Smith here goes instead. She do not know him, does she, Smith?

SMITH: But bare – perhaps not, I ha' passed her once or twice.

HATFIELD: 'Twill do then. You go then and whisper in his ear where we are.

SMITH: Aye, the 'Harriers'.

HATFIELD (to RUSHTON): What say you, isn't it better so?

RUSHTON: Aye, aye!

WILSON: 'Tis much better.

HATFIELD: Remember then, to the 'Harriers'!

RUSHTON: And shall I be there?

SMITH: To be sure.

WILSON: But won't our all meeting in a room by ourselves, and Will with us too, excite suspicion?

HATFIELD: That's well thought again. Then we'll drop in one by one, or two together so – and Will, you can look in too, as 'twere by accident, for a drink o' summat – that way.

RUSHTON: I care not how, lads. In Will Rushton you see one who has been so buffetted he thinks not of forms. But be it as you will. To the last drop I have, I'll be your friend – aye, the friend of poor George Allen!

HATFIELD: George! Away – away!

Music. They shake hands earnestly and exeunt.

SCENE III

Interior of ALLEN's house. Fireplace, saucepan on. A clock – time twenty minutes past eight. A cradle with child. JANE ALLEN, and MARY and MILLY assisting her in pearling lace, and drawing ditto.

MARY: I've done another length, mother, and that makes five, and sister hasn't done four yet.

JANE: Never mind! She does very well. You're both very good children! Only now you may lay the cloth, and get out the supper. It's past eight, and your father will be coming home, and he'll be very tired, I dare say, and hungry too, and at the end of the week a bit of supper and a draught of ale is a thing he looks for! And, his family around him, who so happy as George Allen?

MARY: And you too, mother, and me too, and sister too, and little brother in the cradle.

JANE: All – all, bless you, and thank heaven!

MARY: Then I'll not begin another, mother?

JANE: No; but make haste and lay the cloth.

MILLY: And shan't I finish mine neither, mother?

JANE: No, never mind, that's a good girl. Get out the bread, and be quick. (*Clock chimes half-past.*) Hear? It's half-past! A fork – the potatoes must be done.

MARY: Yes, mother.

Hands fork, JANE *goes to fire, and* MILLY *gets bread out.*

JANE: Oh, I think I hear him!

MARY: And so do I, mother – I can hear him! But oh dear, how he's banging to the gate!

Enter GEORGE ALLEN, *who throws himself in a chair fretfully.*

JANE: Why, George, what's the matter? Dear me, how pale you are! Are you not well, George? You seem feverish.

ALLEN: I am – I am!

JANE: You'll be better after supper. Children, quick!

MARY: Oh, father, we've been so busy, and done such a deal! See, father!

Shows him lace. ALLEN *takes it, throws it down, rises, and stamps on it.*

ALLEN: Curses on it!

MARY: Oh, mother – mother, father's thrown down all my work and has stamped on it, and I'm sure it's done very well! (*Cries.*)

MILLY: Oh, mother! See what father's done!

JANE: George, oh, tell me what means this!

ALLEN: It means that –

MARY: What, father? What makes you angry?

JANE: Say, George.

ALLEN (*looks at his children, and then clasping them, explains*): God – God bless you! (*Picks up the lace and gives it them.*) There, there! You're good children! (*Sits down.*)

MARY: I'm sure, father, I never do anything to make you angry.

MILLY: No more do I, father – do I?

MARY: Nor does mother, either?

ALLEN: No – no, I know she does not!

JANE: Then what is it, George? I never saw you thus before. You're so pale, and you tremble so. Why did you throw down the lace, that which is a living to us?

ALLEN: Because it will never be so again!

JANE: Not a living to us?

ALLEN: No! George Allen must beg now! Ah, beg or as bad – work and starve. And that I'll never do!

JANE: Oh, speak! Work and starve? Impossible!

ALLEN: Nought be impossible these days! What has ruined others will now ruin us. It's been others' turn first; now it be ours.

JANE: What, George?

ALLEN: That steam – that curse on mankind, that for the gain of a few, one or two, to ruin hundreds, is going to be at the factory! Instead of five-and-thirty good hands, there won't be ten wanted now, and them half boys and strangers. Yes, steam be now going to do all the work, and poor, hard-working, honest men, who ha' been for years toiling to do all for the good of a master, be now turned out o' doors to do what they can or what they like. And you know what that means, and what it must come to.

JANE: Oh, dreadful – dreadful! But don't fret, husband – don't fret! We will all strive to do something!

ALLEN (*again rising*): But what be that something? Think I can hear my children cry for food and run barefoot? Think I don't know what 'twill come to?

JANE: But some other place will perhaps give us employ?

ALLEN: Aye, some foreign outlandish place; to be shipped off like convicts to die and starve. Look at Will Rushton, who was enticed, or rather say ensnared there with his wife and four children. Were not the children slaughtered by the natives, who hate white men and live on human flesh? And was not his wife seized too, your own sister, and borne away and never returned; shared perhaps the same fate as her children, or perhaps worse? And has not poor Will, since he returned, been crazed, heart-broken; a pauper, a poacher, or anything?

JANE: Oh, no, no! We shall meet with friends here, George.

ALLEN: Aye, Jane, such friends that if thou wert dying! Starving! Our children stretched lifeless, and I but took a crust of bread to save thee, would thrust me in a prison, there to rot. I have read, Jane – I have seen, Jane, the fate of a poor man; and you know we have nothing now, no savings after the long sickness of father and burying, and the little one we lost, too.

JANE: They are in heaven now, I hope!

Door opens and SMITH *appears.*

ALLEN: Who's there?

SMITH: It's only me, George.

ALLEN: Ah! (SMITH *approaches and whispers in* ALLEN's *ear.*) I will!

JANE (*apart*): What can this mean?

SMITH: In secret.

ALLEN: As the grave!

SMITH (*whispers again*): There, too.

ALLEN: He will?

SMITH: As by chance, you know.

JANE (*apart*): Heaven! What can it mean?

ALLEN: I'll be there. (*Shakes* SMITH *by the hand, who leaves at door.*)

JANE: Oh, George – George, what is this, that your eyes roll so? Now think!

ALLEN: I do think, Jane.

JANE: Sit – come, come, sit – sit down and have some supper, then you'll be better! Remember it is Saturday night. I know it is enough to make you vexed; but think, George – think, and remember there is ONE who never forsakes the good man, if he will but pray to him.

ALLEN: I will – I will; but I must now to see the lads that be like myself, poor fellows – just to talk, you know – to think, as like – to plan – e'es to plan – merely to plan.

JANE: But not yet. Sit awhile. Take some ale.

ALLEN: Why, I can get ale there, and I can't eat, my tongue and throat be so dry. God bless you! (*Going.*)

MARY: Not going, father?

MILLY: Not going, father?

JANE: See, George! Don't go yet.

ALLEN (*kisses children*): I must – I must! Only for a short time, and it be growing late. (*Approaches door.*)

JANE: Don't! Stay, George – stay! (*Kneels and catches hold of him.*)

ALLEN: I must! I must! (*Rushes out. Music.* JANE *falls.*)

MARY (*cries*): Mother – mother! Oh, father!

They fall on their mother, and scene closes.

SCENE IV

An apartment in WESTWOOD'*s house.*
    Enter WESTWOOD.

WESTWOOD: I must be on the alert, and keep my doors well fastened, and have, too, an armed force to welcome these desperadoes if they should dare to violate the laws, well framed to subject them to obedience. I did not half like the menace of that fellow. However, I'll be secure, and if they dare, let them take the consequences. (*Muses, and repeats* HATFIELD'*s words.*) 'The day will come, I shall be sorry for what I have done!' Ha, ha! Sorry! Fool, and fools! What have I to fear or dread? Is England's proud aristocracy to tremble when brawling fools mouth and question? No; the hangman shall be their answer.

    Enter SERVANT.

SERVANT: The dinner's ready, sir.

WESTWOOD: Is it eight, then?

SERVANT: Yes, sir.

WESTWOOD: Is that old grumbler, my father's late housekeeper, gone, who dared to talk and advise, as she called it?

SERVANT: She went at six, sir. We trundled her out, sir.

WESTWOOD: And the French cook, is he arrived yet?

SERVANT: He has sent his valet to say he'll be here in three days after his excursion to Brighton. (*Exit.*)

WESTWOOD: What, because our fathers acted foolishly, shall we also plod on in the same dreary route? No; science has opened to us her stores, and we shall be fools indeed not to take advantage of the good it brings. The time must come, and shortly, when even the labourer himself will freely acknowledge that our improvements in machinery and the aid afforded us by the use of steam will place England on a still nobler eminence than the proud height she has already attained. (*Exit.*)

SCENE V

A room in the 'Harriers'.

> WILSON, SIMS, SMITH, *and* HATFIELD *discovered at a table, drinking.* TAPWELL, *the Landlord, just entering.*

TAPWELL: *Another* mug, did you say?

HATFIELD: Aye, and another to that! What stare you at?

TAPWELL: Eh? Oh, very well! (*Exit.*)

SIMS: Master Tapwell seems surprised at our having an extra pot.

HATFIELD: Let him be. We care not, no more will he, if we have twenty, so he gets the money.

WILSON (*to* SMITH): He said he'd come, did he – Allen?

SMITH: For certain.

HATFIELD: His wife, no doubt, was there? Did you manage all well? Whisper secretly.

SMITH: Not a word out.

HATFIELD: That's well, for women are bad to trust in these things. I've read in books where the best plots have failed through women being told what their husbands or their fathers were going to do, though it was to free a nation from the yoke of tyranny.

WILSON: Aye, right! And so have I.

> *Re-enter* TAPWELL, *with beer.*

TAPWELL: The beer. (*Holds out his hand without delivering it.*)

WILSON: What's that for?

TAPWELL: Another mug, and you didn't pay for the last, which makes one-and-fourpence.

HATFIELD: What, you know, do you, already, that we're discharged?

TAPWELL: Why, yes, if truth must be told, young Squire –

HATFIELD: Young who?

TAPWELL: Young Squire – Master Westwood.

HATFIELD: Young Damnation! Squire such a rascal as that again while we're here, and this pot with its contents shall make you call for a plaster quicker than you may like. Squire Westwood? Squire Hard-heart! No man, no feeling! Call a man like that a squire! An English gentleman, a true English gentleman is he who feels for another, who relieves the distressed, and not turns out the honest hard-working man to beg or starve because he, forsooth, may keep his hunters and drink his foreign wines.

SIMS: Aye; and go to foreign parts. Englishmen were happy when they knew nought but Englishmen – when they were plain, blunt, honest, upright and downright – the master an example to his servant, and both happy with the profits of their daily toil.

ALLEN *enters at door.*

SMITH: Allen!

HATFIELD (*to* TAPWELL): Off, thou lickshoe! There, take that. That will do, I suppose, for another pot, or a gallon?

Throws him down a crown piece on the floor.

TAPWELL: Oh, certainly, Master Hatfield – certainly gentlemen! Another pot now, did you say?

SMITH: Off! (*Thrusts him out and shuts the door.*)

HATFIELD (*to* ALLEN): Come, come, don't look so down – come, drink!

WILSON: Aye, drink!

ALLEN: Nay, I –

HATFIELD: Not drink? Not 'Destruction to steam machinery'?

ALLEN: Destruction to steam machinery? Aye, with all my heart! (*Drinks.*) Destruction to steam machinery!

HATFIELD: Aye, our curse – our ruin!

WILSON: Aye, aye; we've been talking about that, and one thing and t'other like, and about what we shall do, you know –

ALLEN: Ah!

SIMS: I say poaching.

ALLEN: And for a hare, to get sent away, perhaps, for seven long years.

SMITH: So I said.

SIMS: But we mayn't be caught, you know, not if we are true to each other. Four or five tightish lads like us, can't be easily taken, unless we like, you know!

ALLEN: And if we carry but a stick in our defence, and use it a bit, do you know the law? Hanging!

HATFIELD: Right! Hanging for a hare!

SIMS: Not so − not hanging! Don't Will Rushton carry on the sport pretty tidishly, and has only been −

ALLEN: In the stocks twice, whipped publicly thrice, and in gaol seven times. And what has he for his pains? Not a coat to his back worth a groat, no home but the hedge's shelter or an outhouse, and himself but to keep. What would he then do had he, as I have, a wife and three young children to support? Besides, isn't he at times wild with thinking of the past − of his lost wife and murdered children? He, poor unhappy wretch, cannot feel more or sink lower − the gaol to him is but a resting-place!

HATFIELD: 'Tis true, indeed. I remember him once a jovial fellow, the pride of all that knew him; but now −

ALLEN (*to* SMITH): But said you not he would be here?

WILSON: Aye, as by accident.

RUSHTON *partly opens door, when* TAPWELL *stops him.*

ALLEN: Ah! 'Tis he!

WILSON (*to* ALLEN): Be not over anxious.

TAPWELL: No, you can't. You remember the bag you left here the last time, and the scrape it got me into?

RUSHTON: But only a minute or so.

TAPWELL: Not for half a minute.

HATFIELD (*to* ALLEN): Shall I cleave the dastard down?

ALLEN: Leave it to me. (*Approaches* TAPWELL.) Come, sir landlord, mercy a bit, though you may not like his rags and for bread he snares a hare now and then, he may wear as honest a heart as many who wear a better garment; therefore, let him in. The outcast should sojourn with the outcast. Come, another gallon, and take that. (*Gives* TAPWELL *money.*)

TAPWELL: Oh well, certainly, if you have no objection, gentlemen, and he has no game or snares about him.

HATFIELD: Off!

Exit TAPWELL.

ALLEN: Rushton!

RUSHTON: Allen!

ALLEN: Thy hand.

RUSHTON: 'Tis here, with my heart.

ALLEN: Drink. (*Gives beer.*)

RUSHTON: Thanks! Many's the day since I was welcomed thus.

SIMS: Not since, I dare say, you lost your poor wife.

RUSHTON *stands transfixed.*

ALLEN: That was foolish to mention his wife.

SIMS: I forgot.

RUSHTON: Who spoke of my wife? Ah, did she call? Ah, she did – I hear her screams! They are – are tearing her from me! My children, too! I see their mangled forms, bleeding, torn piecemeal! My wife – my children! (*Subsides.*) My wife – my – (*Looks about.*) Where, where am I? (*Sees* ALLEN.) Allen! Allen!

ALLEN: To be sure – George Allen! Don't you know me? Your brother, your friend George, who –

RUSHTON: I know. Sent me food while I was in prison! (*Clasps* ALLEN'*s hand, and sobs.*) Heaven, heaven bless you!

ALLEN: Come, come, an end to this! I am now like thyself, an outcast – one driven, after years of hard toil, upon the world. These the same! (*Pointing to his comrades.*) Come now, say honestly, as a man who has seen much and whose hairs are gray, what would you advise us to do?

RUSHTON: I know all. You are discharged!

WILSON: Aye, from where we've worked since lads, nearly, if not all, and our fathers before us.

HATFIELD: And we are turned beggars on the world, for no reason but to make room for that which has ruined hundreds, to suit the whims and finery of a thing unworthy the name of man!

RUSHTON (*stands absorbed awhile*): I would, but I dare not advise, for my blood now boils, and my flesh is gored with the lash of power. Hush! Hither! (*Beckons them round him.*) A word! Are you all good here? (*Touching his heart.*) Sound? Prime?

HATFIELD: Who dare to doubt?

RUSHTON: Enough. Hush! (*Whispers in their ears, and ends with:*) Dare you?

HATFIELD: I dare!

SMITH: And I!

WILSON: And I!

SIMS: And I!

ALLEN: And I!

RUSHTON: 'Tis well! (*Shakes them by the hand.*) Now then, come lads, the time answers. Hush!

[*Music. Exeunt* OMNES *out of door.*]

SCENE VI

A country lane. Dark.
>   *Enter* RUSHTON, ALLEN, WILSON, SIMS, SMITH, *and* HATFIELD, *armed
>   variously.*

RUSHTON: Steady – steady, lads, and resolute!

WILSON: 'Tis well no one crosses our path.

HATFIELD: What if they did?

ALLEN: My heart almost begins to sicken; a fear, ever unknown to me, seems to shake me from head to foot.

RUSHTON: Pshaw! Fear! Fear is the coward's partner, and the companion of the guilty; not of men who are about to act in their own right, and crush oppression.

WILSON: 'Tis true we are oppressed!

SMITH: We are!

SIMS: Aye, we are!

HATFIELD: And we'll be revenged!

SIMS: Aye, revenged!

ALLEN: But if we meet with resistance – I mean if they attack us?

RUSHTON: Return their attack – blow for blow, if they will have it; aye, and blood for blood. Give in, and you're lost for ever! You'll have no mercy. Look at me, Will Rushton, honest Will Rushton that was once – hard-working Will Rushton. You know my fate – torture upon torture, the insult of the proud and the pity of the poor have been my lot for years. Trampled on! Crushed, and gored to frenzy! My blood boils now I think on't! The pale spectre of my wife, with my slaughtered children now beckons me on! Revenge! revenge! Come, revenge!

>   *Takes* ALLEN's *hand and exeunt.*

HATFIELD: Aye, revenge – revenge!

OMNES: Aye, revenge! (*They follow* RUSHTON *and* ALLEN.)

SCENE VII

Exterior of the factory. Dark.
>   *Enter* RUSHTON *with a torch, followed by* ALLEN, WILSON, SIMS, SMITH,
>   *and* HATFIELD.

RUSHTON: Now, to the work – to the work! Break, crack, and split into ten thousand pieces these engines of your disgrace! Your poverty, and your ruin! Now!

HATFIELD: Aye, now destruction!

WILSON: Aye, spare not a stick! Come, come, Allen!

RUSHTON, WILSON, SIMS, *and* SMITH *rush into the factory – the factory is seen blazing.*

WESTWOOD *rushes in, followed by* CONSTABLES.

WESTWOOD: Ah, villain, stay! It is as I was told; but little did I think they dared. Seize them!

HATFIELD: Ah, surprised!

RUSHTON *comes from the factory, with firebrand, followed by his comrades.*

WESTWOOD: Submit, I say!

RUSHTON: Ah!

Seizes him by the throat, hurls him to the earth, and waves the lighted ember above him in wild triumph.

ACT II

SCENE I

Moonlight. Open country, with view of factory burning in the distance. Enter RUSHTON, *with firebrand.*

RUSHTON: Ha! Ha! This has been a glorious night, to see the palace of the tyrant levelled to the ground – to hear his engines of gain cracking – to hear him call for help, and see the red flame laugh in triumph! Ah, many a day have I lain upon the cold damp ground, muttering curses – many a night have I called upon the moon, when she has frenzied my brain, to revenge my wrongs; for days and nights I have never slept – misery and want, and the smart of the lash, with visions of bygone days, have been like scorpions, rousing me to revenge, and the time has come. I have had partners, too, in the deed – men who, like myself, glory in the act. But where can Allen be, and the rest? They must away now. I'll to his cottage, and if the minions of power dare but touch a hair of his head, this brand shall lay them low. (*Exit.*)

SCENE II

Interior, as before, of ALLEN's *house. The casement open, and the blaze of the factory seen in the distance.*
JANE *watching at the window.* MARY *and* MILLY *near her.*

JANE: Oh, horror – horror!

MARY: It's not out yet, mother; it seems as if some other house was on fire.

MILLY: See, mother!

JANE: 'Tis too true, child! Oh, mercy – mercy! The flames have caught the farm next to it. I can no longer look. The worst of thoughts crowd upon my brain. My husband's absence – his wild and distracted look – the factory in flames!
Enter ALLEN, *hurriedly.*
Ah, my husband! Oh say, George, where – where is it you have been?

ALLEN: Jane – my children! (*Embraces them in silent anguish.*) Some ale, water, or something! My throat is parched!

MARY: Some ale, father?

JANE: You've seen the fire?

ALLEN: Yes, yes. Some ale, I said.

MARY: Here it is, father! (*Gives jug.* ALLEN *drinks.*)

ALLEN: Ah! That be sweet! (*To his wife in an undertone.*) Hush! Here – here, take this – (*Gives money.*) – it be all I have, and this, too. (*Gives watch.*) There be, too, a little up-stairs. Take care of thyself, Jane, and of children.

JANE: Oh, George, say not that! You would not leave your Jane, who has ever loved you, and ever will?

MARY: Oh, mother, don't cry!

ALLEN: Mother's not crying. (*Standing before her.*) See to the child; it wakes! (*Fire blazes vividly. To* JANE.) See you that? All be broken and burnt down. Say, if they come, you ha' not seen me, you know. They cannot harm thee.

JANE: Oh, George, say, for mercy's sake, you've had no hand in this!

ALLEN: What be done, Jane, cannot now be altered.

JANE: Oh, George! Bad advice has led you to this – I know you would not have done so of yourself.

ALLEN: It matters not now, Jane; it be done, and I must away; but you shall hear from me, Jane, where'er I be. I will send thee all I get.

A noise without.

JANE: Ah! That noise –

ALLEN: It be they come – come to take me.

JANE: Fly! Fly!

ALLEN *rushes towards the door, when* WESTWOOD *and* CONSTABLES *appear at the window.*

ALLEN: Ah! 'tis useless!

WESTWOOD: He's here.

Enter WESTWOOD *followed by* GRIMLEY *and* CONSTABLES.

Seize him. (*They seize* ALLEN.)

JANE (*kneels*): Oh, mercy! mercy! – spare him, – spare my husband.

MARY: Oh, spare my father!

MILLY: Don't hurt father.

JANE: He is not guilty – indeed he's not.

WESTWOOD: Not guilty, when I saw him with the rest?

JANE: But he did not set fire the place. I know he did not – he would not.

WESTWOOD: What matters what hand did the deed? – Is not all a heap of ashes – all burnt and destroyed!

JANE: Yet, mercy!

WESTWOOD: Mercy! What mercy had he to me? – Cast thy eye yonder, and petition to the flames.

JANE: Oh, George! George!

WESTWOOD: Away with him. Now for the outcast.

Enter RUSHTON, *frantically, with a piece of burnt machinery in his hand.*

RUSHTON: Who calls for the outcast? – Stay! – what are you about? Seizing an innocent man? Here stands the incendiary! I, Will Rushton, the outcast – the degraded – Ha! ha! Yes, and the revenged! 'Twas I led them on, and this hand lit the fire brand, and I am satisfied.

WESTWOOD: Seize him! 'tis the instigator – the ringleader!

They attempt to seize him.

RUSHTON (*in a menacing attitude*): Approach not, or your grave is at my feet. (*They retreat, intimidated.*)

WESTWOOD: Cowards! do you fear a madman? – Surrender, idiot, fiend, wretch, outcast – or this shall tame thee. (*Presents a pistol.*)

ALLEN: Rushton – you escape – I care not.

WESTWOOD: Ah! – then stir but one foot, and –

RUSHTON: And what – (*Seizes him by the collar and hurls him to the ground –* WESTWOOD *firing the pistol.*) Away! I say.

JANE: Oh, fly – fly George!

WESTWOOD *attempts to rise –* RUSHTON *stands over him, and waving the ember, secures the retreat of* ALLEN. *As he is rushing out, the scene closes.*

SCENE III

Exterior of an out-house or hovel, in lane. Moonlight.
Enter ALLEN, *frantic, as if pursued.*

ALLEN: Where shall I fly? My brain is giddy, my legs feeble. I can no further. – Oh, my wife – Jane – Jane – my children, too!

Falls exhausted. – WILSON *and* HATFIELD *look out from hovel.*

HATFIELD: It was Allen's voice, I'm sure – yet I see no one.

WILSON: See, who lies there? (*They come out.*)

HATFIELD: Ah! it is he.

WILSON: What is this? Not dead, – killed himself! (*Calls.*) Allen! Allen!

HATFIELD: Allen, lad!

ALLEN (*starting*): Ah! who calls on Allen? – Was't my wife – my children? I'm here – don't you see me? What – what's – (*Looks about wildly.*)

WILSON: Allen, it's but us, your old friends, Wilson and Hatfield – don't you know us?

ALLEN: Ah! – is it? – (*They assist him to rise – he clasps their hands earnestly.*) Have you seen my wife – my children?

HATFIELD: I thought you'd been to see them.

ALLEN: Ah, I remember! – like a wild dream, it comes across my brain; – but where – where's the rest? – Smith and – (*Voices without cry* 'This way! – this way!')

ALLEN: Ah! they come!

HATFIELD: In – in there; – would you be taken?

ALLEN: I care not. Ah! 'tis he! – 'tis Rushton. Never will I fly. He who would desert his comrade in the hour of peril, is worse than coward.

Enter RUSHTON *in haste, followed by* WESTWOOD *and* MILITARY.

WESTWOOD: Ah! here are the rest; seize them all and spare none!

RUSHTON: Hell-hounds! would you murder the poor wretches you have deprived of bread?

WESTWOOD: Villain! Have you not deprived me of bread, and set fire to my dwelling, reckless who might perish in the flames?

RUSHTON: That *you* had, then justice had been done and my revenge satisfied!

WESTWOOD: Officer! your duty. Let them not escape!

OFFICER: In the King's name I desire you to yield!

HATFIELD: Never!

RUSHTON: That's right, my lads, never yield! (*They stand on the defensive.*)

OFFICER: Then at your peril! (*Presents pistol.* SOLDIERS *advance, and a confused combat ensues, ending in the disarming of* HATFIELD *and* SMITH, *and capture of* ALLEN *with a wound across his forehead – at that moment,* JANE ALLEN *enters distracted.*)

JANE (*she screams on seeing her husband wounded and taken*): Oh, mercy! mercy! – my husband! Do not, do not murder him! Oh, George! (*Kneels and clasps him round the knee.*)

ALLEN: Who calls on George Allen?

JANE: It is thy wife! don't you know me! Thy wife, you know, George. Jane, Jane, thy wife!

ALLEN: Ah, Jane! my doom is fixed: leave me, and clasp those who are helpless, my little ones!

RUSHTON: There, monster? dost thou see that? – Thy doing.

WESTWOOD: 'Tis false! liar! fiend! reprobate!

RUSHTON: 'Tis true! liar! fiend! and reprobate again! Did'st thou not turn these poor men from their honest employ? to beg, steal, starve! or do as they have done – be revenged?

ALLEN: Peace, peace! it is over now. Jane, I feel my life fast ebbing! home – home!

WESTWOOD: Away with them!

JANE: Oh, pity! mercy! Tear him not away from me.

OFFICER: The law's imperative! (*The soldiers march them off,* JANE *falls fainting.*)

JANE *is lying senseless –* MARY, *her eldest child, enters.*

MARY: Mother, mother! where are you? Oh, what do I see on the cold ground? It can't be mother. Mother! (*Approaches nearer.*) Mother! Oh, it can't be my mother – she would hear me – yet it looks like my mother. Oh, dear! it is, I know it can be no other! Mother! Mother! (*Cries and falls on her mother.*) Mother, why don't you speak, mother! (*Kneels and kisses her –* JANE *recovering, looks about her in wild disorder.*)

JANE: Where am I?

MARY: Here, mother, on the cold ground!

JANE (*seeing her child*): Ah, my child! bless you! bless you! But what are we doing here in the open air?

MARY: You came out after father, mother.

JANE: Your father! (*Screams.*) Ah, I now remember all. They are tearing him from me, to take him to a loathsome dungeon! All now crosses me like a wild dream. The factory! the red sky! Flames whirling in the air! My eyeballs seem'd crack'd – my brain grows dizzy – I hear chains and screams of death! My husband – they shall not tear him from me!

MARY: Mother, mother! where are you going?

JANE: To thy father – to the gaol – they will not refuse his poor weak, and broken-hearted wife!

MARY: Nor me either – will they, mother?

JANE (*takes her up*): Bless you! Bless you! never, never shall they part us! (*Exit with child.*)

SCENE IV

Interior of a Justice Room.

> *The* JUSTICE *and* CLERK *discovered seated at Table.* GEORGE ALLEN, SIMS, WILSON, *and* HATFIELD, *discovered handcuffed –* WESTWOOD, CONSTABLES, OFFICER *and* SOLDIERS, *dragging in* RUSHTON, *struggling.*

RUSHTON: Why do you drag me thus? Do you think I'm afraid? Do you think I fear to own that I was the man who led them on? No. I glory in the act – 'tis the sweet triumph I've oft longed for.

BIAS: Silence, sirrah!

RUSHTON: I speak or am silent as I please! Talking is not hanging, is it? What are you more than I am? I remember when you were overseer – the man appointed to protect the poor.

BIAS: And what has that to do with the present business?

RUSHTON: It has this: to shew that an honest man at least, should sit in that seat, and not one who has crept into it by robbery and oppression.

BIAS: Maniac!

RUSHTON: Ay! but I was not so, when the cart, laden with provisions for the workhouse by your order, stopped at your own door, to pretend to deliver some articles ordered for yourself, but which belonged to the poor famished creatures, who had no redress, but the lash, if they dared to complain.

BIAS: It is false!

RUSHTON: Is it false, too, that through your means alone, when but seven years of age, I was condemned to six weeks hard labour in a prison, for stealing, as you called it – but a handful of apples from your orchard?

BIAS: 'Tis false! or why not have made your charge before? Is it to be supposed, one so vindictive, a common thief, an incendiary, would have concealed this so long? The law is open to you, is it not?

RUSHTON: No; I am poor.

BIAS: And what of that? The law is made alike for rich and poor.

RUSHTON: Is it? Why then does it so often lock the poor man in a jail, while the rich one goes free?

BIAS: No more of this – Clerk, draw out the commitment.

RUSHTON: Commitment! Who would you commit? Not these poor men. 'Twas I broke into and destroyed the engines of power. 'Twas I set fire to the mass, and reduced to ashes what has reduced others to beggary! Think you, I regret – think you I fear? No; I glory in the act. There! I have confessed; and as in me you see the avenger of the poor man's wrongs, on me, and me alone heap your vengeance.

BIAS: Clerk, record the prisoner's confession, and Charles George Westwood, proprietor of the factory and buildings joining thereunto, lately burnt, stand forth, and make your further allegations, and name the prisoners charged in this atrocious act.

WESTWOOD: I charge all the prisoners, now standing here, as being concerned in the destruction of the factory, dwelling house, and out-houses. First: their leader there, William, or Will Rushton as I believe he is called – second, John Hatfield – third, Walter Sims – fourth, Francis Wilson – fifth,

Joseph Sims, not here, through being wounded – sixth, and last, George Allen.

BIAS: And this you are willing to swear?

WESTWOOD: I am.

BIAS: Prisoners, you have heard the charge – have you aught to say?

HATFIELD: No; if it is to be, let it be; – we may as well die on a scaffold as be starved?

WILSON: Don't look down, George, let's bear it up like men.

ALLEN: Yet my wife and children.

BIAS: 'Tis well; this silence shows a proper sense of shame. 'Tis written, they who defy the law, must suffer by the law. Prisoners, though it is not my duty to pronounce judgment, still I deem it so, to apprize you of the fate likely to await you. Tomorrow will commence the assizes at the neighbouring town, where you will be removed, and arraigned before a tribunal, which will hear your defence, and give the verdict according to the evidence produced. Further I have nought to say. Officer, remove the prisoners.

JANE (*without*): Unhand me, I will enter! (*She enters –* ALLEN *conceals himself*.) He is here – must be here! Is it that agony has dimmed my sight, or that reason has left her seat and madness mocks me. (*Sees him*.) Ah, he's there! Oh, George! Is this the end of all our former bliss? Torn from me, and for ever? My husband! He whom I have pressed to my breast! My heart's blood – the father of my children! Oh, horror! horror! Exposed like a common felon to the gaze of thousands, on a gibbet! Hung! Oh, my heart sickens! No, no, it cannot be, must not be! Never shall it be said that my husband, George Allen, died like a felon; a common robber! A murderer!

BIAS: Seize this frantic woman, and let her be removed! (*They approach to take her*.)

JANE: Oh, touch me not! Off! off! I say! Yet have pity on me, I know not what I say – a whirlwind rushes through my brain! (*Falls at* WESTWOOD'*s feet, clasping his knees*.) Mercy! mercy! To you I kneel, pity my poor husband, and I will pray for thee, work for thee – my children, all, all, shall be your slaves – for ever – ever! But spare him!

WESTWOOD: Cling not to me; Justice shall have its due! (*Spurns her from him*.)

RUSHTON: Spurn a helpless and imploring woman! Whose heart is broken – whose mind is crazed! If her *voice* is weak, my *arm* is not. Justice shall have its due. Die! tyrant! Quick to where water quencheth not! (*Fires – * WESTWOOD *falls, and the Curtain drops on picture of,* RUSHTON *standing in centre, laughing hysterically, pointing at* WESTWOOD. JANE *in the arms of* ALLEN –

HATFIELD, SIMS, *and* WILSON, *in an attitude of surprise – the* SOLDIERS *with their musquets levelled at* RUSHTON.)

13 SOCIETY

The smart audiences who saw *Society* got what they liked – a bang up-to-date, fashionable, amusing play staged in a nice, clean theatre with carpet underfoot and white lace antimacassars in the stalls. The feminine touch came from theatre manager Marie Wilton, later Mrs Bancroft, who spent two years transforming a shabby playhouse nicknamed The Dusthole into The Prince of Wales. Wilton was an actress who had enough of playing breeches parts in burlesques and took over a theatre partly because she wanted to do legitimate comedy. An astute businesswoman, she hoped to succeed in management by providing a type of theatre-going experience not available elsewhere since the heyday of The Olympic under Madame Vestris in the 1830s. Wilton had little trouble creating the right atmosphere in her new theatre, her problem was finding a suitable play. It had to be a comedy, it must have a part for Wilton and it had to appeal to a sophisticated, largely middle-class audience satiated by the sensation drama of the past decade. Wilton was looking for something fresh and H.J. Byron, the playwright in residence at The Prince of Wales, hadn't supplied it.

In 1865 Byron recommended a play by an impoverished actor turned writer called Thomas William Robertson, though he warned that the work was dangerous and contained a scene certain to cause offence to the critics. Years later in her memoirs *On and Off the Stage* (1888), Mrs Bancroft said she took *Society* on because 'danger was better than dulness'. The scene in question was set in a seedy journalists' club called The Owl's Roost and included a satirical song with a verse poking fun at newspaper puffery. This particular verse was cut in performance (see commentary for Act II scene i) and although the scene did annoy some, it delighted others and the play as a whole proved a popular success, running for more than 140 initial performances and for four revivals under the Bancrofts.

Society wasn't Robertson's first play or even his first success. *David Garrick* adapted from a French source, had played in Birmingham and London the year before. Robertson (1829–1871) was the son of a large family of touring actors and by the time *Society* was staged in 1865 he was aged 36 and had connections throughout the theatrical world. Much has been made in retrospect of his stint as a prompter for Madame Vestris at the Lyceum in 1854. Here, it is claimed, he learned some of the tricks of realistic stage management which were to become the trademark of his productions. In fact, while he must have gained knowledge from Vestris and her partner Charles Mathews, much of his innovation was actually clever adoption of trends already well developed in other genres of Victorian theatre.

The Prince of Wales was a little place with seating for a maximum of about 800 people – this at a time when there were London theatres with room for 3,000. The theatre had an atmosphere of intimacy and the audience sat close to the stage, conditions which fostered Robertson's style of acting and production. While he drew heavily on the established Victorian predilection for realistic stage effects and scenery, Robertson rejected the mannered acting that often accompanied it. *Society* has precise stage directions which insist on naturalness and, in Victorian terms, an effacing anti-theatricality. His style of drama was to earn the nick-name of 'cup and saucer comedy' after a scene set in a kitchen in *Caste* (1867).

In practice, realism and naturalism are used to produce effects of artificial sophistication. For example, Sidney Daryl's tryst with Maud Hetherington in Act I scene ii happens in a garden square at evening and requires 'effect of setting sun in windows of houses; lights in some of the windows, etc; street lamps'. As the scene progresses, the light fades and the stage grows dark exactly as it would in a real square on an actual evening. The scene uses the natural process of sunset as a visual trick to condense time. Sidney keeps looking at his watch, the lighting hastens towards night and, in a typically topical reference, the newish Big Ben strikes nine, yet the whole scene which supposedly lasts half an hour could be played in ten minutes.

Robertson pays a great deal of attention to non-verbal stage business, controls it and works it into the action. Sidney's loose cuff link that won't fasten in Act II scene ii is a delightfully niggling example. Sidney enters with the stage direction 'he is pale and excited; one of the gold links of his wrist-band is unfastened'. Only an audience in a small theatre would notice such a detail. Throughout the scene he fiddles with the recalcitrant link, it becomes a piece of business for the actor. By the time he challenges Chodd Junior to bet on cards, the link has been worked up enough to carry a larger symbolic message about society, marriage and social ties. Robertson's strength as a playwright lies in the delicacy with which he does this; he never insists on the message and when the link has played its part he has Sidney give it to Chodd, turning it into a throw-away joke, literally. There is smartness in this lightness, a witty trifling that is characteristic of his best work.

Visual, playful jokery has its counterpart in the language Robertson uses. Puns, allusions and contemporary slang provide a kind of parlour game amusement beyond the character-driven action. The extended pun on printer's devil in Act II scene i is the most obvious, but there are others. During Sidney's battle of wits and luck against Chodd in Act II scene ii he offers Cloudwrays a regalia for keeping quiet about the gambling. Regalia was both the name for a large cigar and an old-fashioned term for a present of choice food or drink, or an entertainment. Sidney offers Cloudwrays both meanings; a cigar presumably since Cloudwrays loves to smoke and also the entertaining prospect of spectating at the contest. The Victorian mind relished finding fun in this sort of obscure conundrum. Unusually for Robertson, he draws on an obsolete meaning. More typically his language is marked by its up-to-dateness. Tom Stylus says he will 'vamoose', a piece of American slang which entered popular English usage in the later 1850s. For the *Earthquake*'s society gossip column Tom writes 'we hear a marriage is on the tapis', employing current newspaper slang which the *OED* records as being first used in the *York Herald* the same year that *Society* was premiered.

Robertson had an acute ear for colloquialisms which suggests he was good at remembering what others said. But it's not surprising that Sidney misquotes Tennyson's 'Locksley Hall' and drunken O'Sullivan blunders over *Hamlet*. The misquotes are actually part of the play's fashionable urbanity. Robertson didn't get it wrong by mistake. Gentlemen possessed of a literary education tend to misremember these things in a way that a desiccated scholar would not. In this context Tennyson and Shakespeare represent the cultural lumber of the educated man's mind and it's unlikely that those in the original audience would be pedantic enough to notice the inaccuracies in the midst of enjoying an entertaining night out.

What makes a gentleman? This is the real question *Society* poses and it delivers a stolidly conservative answer. There are three worlds in *Society*; there is the tarnished, somnolent aristocracy of Lord and Lady Ptarmigant which is burnished and revived by Sidney and Maud's marriage, there is the insufferable, pushy and vulgar lower-class milieu of the Chodds, and there is the lively, attractively disreputable circle of the Owl's Roost journalists which is linked through Sidney to the shady underworld of Sam Stunner, alias the Smiffel Lamb. All of these except the Chodds have their own code of honour. Sidney's gentlemanliness is so inherent that he is able to move amphibiously between all these worlds and, like a true gentleman, get on with anyone from any station, apart from the Chodds who are made to seem more offensive by his dislike. In joining battle with Chodd Junior, Sidney routs a repulsive tendency in society. In society money matters but it is not enough as is made clear when Tom takes Chodd Junior to the Owl's Roost and restrains him from standing a round of drinks. Chodd says: 'I suppose all these chaps are plaguy poor?' and Tom replies: 'Yes, they're poor; but they are *gent*lemen', with sarcastic emphasis as if he is educating an idiot. Chodd rejoins with an unattractive grin: 'I like that notion – a *poor* gentleman – it tickles me.' Tom in turn calls Chodd a 'Metallic snob!' a joke which has some of the modern day scorn nudists reserved for the clothed when they call them 'textiles'.

In 1897 Henry Arthur Jones criticised Robertson's intermingling of social types and called it 'false and theatrical – theatrical, that is, in the employment of a social contrast that was effective on the stage, but well nigh, if not quite, impossible in life'. This astonishing comment is really a backhanded compliment. All the 'cup and saucer' realism was a guise Robertson used to represent the social fantasies of his audience. The fact that it looked so dated by the turn of the century is a measure of how successfully it captured the temper of its time.

★

SOCIETY
Thomas William Robertson

A COMEDY IN THREE ACTS

Dramatis Personæ

LORD PTARMIGANT
LORD CLOUDWRAYS, M.P.
SIDNEY DARYL, *a barrister*
MR JOHN CHODD, SEN.
MR JOHN CHODD, JUN.
TOM STYLUS
O'SULLIVAN
MACUSQUEBAUGH
DOCTOR MAKVICZ
BRADLEY
SCARGIL
SAM STUNNER, P.R., *alias the Smiffel Lamb*
SHAMHEART
DODDLES
MOSES AARON, *a bailiff*
SHERIDAN TRODNON
LADY PTARMIGANT
MAUD HETHERINGTON
LITTLE MAUD
MRS CHURTON
A SERVANT
WAITERS, SERVANTS, ROUGHS
Optional characters: SIR FARINTOSH FADILEAF
                                    COLONEL BROWSER

ACT I

SCENE I

SIDNEY DARYL'S *Chambers, in Lincoln's Inn; set doorpiece* R. *and set doorpiece* L. *(to double up and draw off); the room to present the appearance of belonging to a sporting literary barrister; books, pictures, whips; the mirror stuck full of cards (painted on cloth); a table on* R., *chairs, &c. As the curtain rises a knock heard, and* DODDLES *discovered opening door,* L.

TOM (*without*): Mr Daryl in?

DODD: Not up yet.

Enter TOM STYLUS, CHODD, JUN., *and* CHODD, SEN.

CHODD, JUN. (L., *looking at watch*): Ten minutes to twelve, eh, guv?

TOM (R.C.): Late into bed; up after he oughter; out for brandy and sobering water.

SIDNEY (*within*): Doddles.

DODD (R., *an old clerk*): Yes, sir!

SIDNEY: Brandy and soda.

DODD: Yes, sir!

TOM: I said so! Tell Mr Daryl two gentlemen wish to see him on particular business.

CHODD, JUN. (*a supercilious, bad swell; glass in eye; hooked stick; vulgar and uneasy*): So this is an author's crib – is it? Don't think much of it, eh, guv? (*Crossing behind to* L.C.)

CHODD, SEN. (*a common old man, with a dialect*): Seems comfortable enough to me, Johnny.

CHODD, JUN.: Don't call me Johnny? I hope he won't be long. (*Looking at watch.*) Don't seem to me the right sort of thing, for two gentlemen to be kept waiting for a man they are going to employ.

CHODD, SEN.: Gently, Johnny. (CHODD, JUN., *looks annoyed.*) I mean gently without the Johnny – Mister –

TOM: Daryl – Sidney Daryl!

CHODD, SEN.: Daryl didn't know as we was coming!

CHODD, JUN. (*rudely to* TOM): Why didn't you let him know?

TOM (*fiercely*): How the devil could I? I didn't see you till last night. (CHODD, JUN., *retires into himself.*) You'll find Sidney Daryl just the man for you; young – full of talent – what I was thirty years ago; I'm old now, and not full of talent, if ever I was; I've emptied myself; I've missed my tip. You see I wasn't a swell – he is!

CHODD, JUN.: A swell – what a man who writes for his living?

DODDLES *enters door,* R.

DODD: Mr Daryl will be with you directly; will you please to sit down?

CHODD, SEN., *sits* L.C.; TOM *takes a chair* L. *of table;* CHODD, JUN., *waiting to have one given to him, is annoyed that no one does so, and sits on table.* DODDLES *goes round to* L.

CHODD, JUN.: Where is Mr Daryl?

DODD: In his bath!

CHODD, JUN. (*jumping off table*): What! You don't mean to say he keeps us here while he's washing himself?

Enter SIDNEY, *in morning jacket, door* R.

SIDNEY: Sorry to have detained you; how are you, Tom?

TOM *and* CHODD, SEN., *rise;* CHODD, JUN., *sits again on table and sucks cane.*

CHODD, SEN.: Not at all!

CHODD, JUN. (*with watch*): Fifteen minutes.

SIDNEY (*crossing,* C., *handing chair to* CHODD, JUN.): Take a chair!

CHODD, JUN.: This'll do.

SIDNEY: But you're sitting on the steel pens.

TOM: Dangerous things! pens.

CHODD, JUN., *takes a chair,* L.

SIDNEY: Yes! loaded with ink, percussion powder's nothing to 'em.

CHODD, JUN.: We came here to talk business. (*To* DODDLES.) Here, you get out!

SIDNEY (*surprised*): Doddles – I expect a lot of people this morning, be kind enough to take them into the library.

DODD (L.): Yes, sir! (*Aside, looking at* CHODD, JUN.) Young rhinocerous! (*Exit door,* L.)

SIDNEY: Now, gentlemen, I am – (*Crossing behind table to* R.)

TOM (L. *of table*): Then I'll begin. First let me introduce Mr Sidney Daryl to Mr John Chodd, of Snoggerston, also to Mr John Chodd, Jun., of the same place; Mr John Chodd, of Snoggerston, is very rich – he made a fortune by –

CHODD, SEN.: No! – my brother Joe made the fortune in Australey, by gold digging and then spec'lating; which he then died, and left all to me.

CHODD, JUN. (*aside*): Guv! cut it!

CHODD, SEN.: I shan't, – I ain't ashamed of what I was, nor what I am; it never was my way. Well, sir, I have lots of brass!

SIDNEY: Brass?

CHODD, SEN.: Money?

CHODD, JUN.: Heaps!

CHODD, SEN. (L.C.): Heaps; but having begun by being a poor man, without edication, and not being a gentleman –

CHODD, JUN. (*aside*): Guv! – cut it.

CHODD, SEN.: I shan't – I know I'm not, and I'm proud of it, that is, proud of knowing I'm not, and I won't pretend to be. Johnny don't put me out – I say I'm not a gentleman, but my son is.

SIDNEY (*looking at him*): Evidently.

CHODD, SEN.: And I wish him to cut a figure in the world – to get into Parliament.

SIDNEY: Very difficult.

CHODD, SEN.: To get a wife?

SIDNEY: Very easy.

CHODD, SEN.: And in short, to be a – a real gentleman.

SIDNEY: Very difficult.

CHODD, SEN.: } Eh?
CHODD, JUN.:

SIDNEY: I mean very easy.

CHODD, SEN.: Now, as I'm anxious he should be an M.P. as soon as –

SIDNEY: As he can.

CHODD, SEN.: Just so, and as I have lots of capital unemployed, I mean to invest it in –

TOM (*slapping* SIDNEY *on knees*): A new daily paper!

SIDNEY: By Jove!

CHODD, SEN.: A cheap daily paper, that could – that will – What will a cheap daily paper do?

SIDNEY: Bring the 'Court Circular' within the knowledge of the humblest.

TOM: Educate the masses – raise them morally, socially, politically, scientifically, geologically, and horizontally.

CHODD, SEN. (*delighted*): That's it – that's it, only it looks better in print.

TOM (*spouting*): Bring the glad and solemn tidings of the day to the labourer at his plough – the spinner at his wheel – the swart forger at his furnace – the sailor on the giddy mast – the lighthouse keeper as he trims his beacon lamp – the housewife at her pasteboard – the mother at her needle – the lowly lucifer seller, as he splashes his wet and weary way through the damp, steaming, stony streets, eh? – you know. (*Slapping* SIDNEY *on the knee – they both laugh.*)

CHODD, SEN. (*to* CHODD, JUN.): What are they a laughing at?

TOM: So my old friend, Johnny Prothero, who lives hard by Mr Chodd, knowing that I have started lots of papers, sent the two Mr Chodds, or the Messrs. Chodd – which is it? – you're a great grammarian – to me. I can find them an efficient staff, and you are the first man we've called upon.

SIDNEY: Thanks, old fellow. When do you propose to start it?

CHODD, SEN.: At once.

SIDNEY: What is it to be called?

CHODD, SEN.: We don't know.

CHODD, JUN.: We leave that to the fellows we pay for their time and trouble.

SIDNEY: You want something –

CHODD, SEN.: Strong.

TOM: And sensational.

SIDNEY: I have it. (*Rising.*)

TOM: ⎫
CHODD, SEN.: ⎬ What?
CHODD, JUN.: ⎭

SIDNEY: The 'Morning Earthquake'!

TOM: Capital!

CHODD, SEN. (*rising*): First-rate!

CHODD, JUN. (*still seated*): Not so bad. (*Goes up during next speech.*)

SIDNEY: Don't you see? In place of the clock, a mass of houses, factories, and palaces tumbling one over the other; and then the prospectus! 'At a time when thrones are tottering, dynasties dissolving – while the old world is displacing to make room for the new –'

TOM: Bravo!

CHODD, SEN. (*enthusiastically*): Hurray!

TOM: A second edition at 4 o'clock p.m. The 'Evening Earthquake,' eh? Placard the walls. 'The Earthquake,' one note of admiration; 'The Earthquake,' two notes of admiration; 'The Earthquake,' three notes of admiration. Posters: ' "The Earthquake" delivered every morning with your hot rolls.' 'With coffee, toast, and eggs, enjoy your "Earthquake" '!

CHODD, SEN. (*with pocket book*): I've got your name and address.

CHODD, JUN. (*who has been looking at cards stuck in glass,* C.): Guv.

Takes old CHODD *up and whispers to him.*

TOM (*to* SIDNEY): Don't like this young man!

SIDNEY: No.

TOM: Cub.

SIDNEY: Cad.

TOM: Never mind. The old un's not a bad 'un. We're off to a printer's.

SIDNEY: Good-bye, Tom, and thank ye.

TOM: How's the little girl?

SIDNEY: Quite well. I expect her here this morning.

CHODD, SEN.: Good morning.

Exeunt CHODD, SEN., *and* TOM, *door* L.

SIDNEY (*filling pipe, &c.*): Have a pipe?

CHODD, JUN. (*taking out a magnificent case*): I always smoke cigars.

SIDNEY: Gracious creature! Have some bitter beer? (*Getting it from locker.*)

CHODD, JUN.: I never drink anything in the morning.

SIDNEY: Oh!

CHODD, JUN.: But champagne.

SIDNEY: I haven't got any.

CHODD, JUN. (L.): Then I'll take beer. (*They sit.*) Business is business – so I'd best begin at once. The present age is, as you are aware – a practical age. I come to the point – it's my way. Capital commands the world. The capitalist commands capital, therefore the capitalist commands the world.

SIDNEY (R.): But you don't quite command the world, do you?

CHODD, JUN.: Practically, I do. I wish for the highest honours – I bring out my cheque-book. I want to go into the House of Commons – cheque-book. I want the best legal opinion in the House of Lords – cheque-book. The best house – cheque-book. The best turn out – cheque-book. The best friends, the best wife, the best trained children – cheque-book, cheque-book, and cheque-book.

SIDNEY: You mean to say with money you can purchase anything.

CHODD, JUN.: Exactly. This life is a matter of bargain.

SIDNEY: But 'honour, love, obedience, troops of friends'?

CHODD, JUN.: Can buy 'em all, sir, in lots, as at an auction.

SIDNEY: Love, too?

CHODD, JUN.: Marriage means a union mutually advantageous. It is a civil contract, like a partnership.

SIDNEY: And the old-fashioned virtues of honour and chivalry?

CHODD, JUN.: Honour means not being a bankrupt. I know nothing at all about chivalry, and I don't want to.

SIDNEY: Well yours is quite a new creed to me, and I confess I don't like it.

CHODD, JUN.: The currency, sir, converts the most hardened sceptic. I see by the cards on your glass that you go out a great deal.

SIDNEY: Go out?

CHODD, JUN.: Yes, to parties. (*Looking at cards on table.*) There's my Lady this, and the Countess t'other, and Mrs somebody else. Now that's what I want to do.

SIDNEY: Go into society?

CHODD, JUN.: Just so. You had money once, hadn't you.

SIDNEY: Yes.

CHODD, JUN.: What did you do with it?

SIDNEY: Spent it.

CHODD, JUN.: And you've been in the army?

SIDNEY: Yes.

CHODD, JUN.: Infantry?

SIDNEY: Cavalry.

CHODD, JUN.: Dragoons?

SIDNEY: Lancers.

CHODD, JUN.: How did you get out?

SIDNEY: Sold out.

CHODD, JUN.: Then you were a first-rate fellow, till you tumbled down?

SIDNEY: Tumbled down?

CHODD, JUN.: Yes, to what you are.

SIDNEY *about to speak is interrupted by* MOSES AARON, *without,* L.

MOSES: Tell you I musn't shee him.

Enter MOSES AARON *with* DODDLES, *door* L.

MOSES (*not seeing* CHODD, JUN., *going round behind table*): Sorry, Mister Daryl, but at the shoot of Brackersby and Co. (*Arrests him.*)

CHODD, JUN.: Je-hosophat! (*Rising.*)

SIDNEY: Confound Mr Brackersby! It hasn't been owing fifteen months! – How much?

MOSES: With exes, fifty four pun' two.

SIDNEY: I've got it in the next room. Have some beer?

MOSES: Thank ye, shir.

SIDNEY *pours it out.*

SIDNEY: Back directly. (*Exit door,* L.)

CHODD, JUN. (L.): This chap's in debt. Here you!

MOSES (R.): Shir.

CHODD, JUN.: Mr Daryl – does he owe much?

MOSES: Spheck he does, shir, or I shouldn't know him.

CHODD, JUN.: Here's half a sov. Give me your address?

MOSES (*gives card*): 'Orders executed with punctuality and despatch.'

CHODD, JUN.: If I don't get into society now, I'm a Dutchman.

Enter SIDNEY, R.

SIDNEY: Here you are – ten fives – two two's – and a half-a-crown for yourself.

MOSES: Thank ye, shir. Good mornin', shir

SIDNEY: Good morning.

Moses (*to* Chodd, Jun.): Good mornin', shir.

Chodd, Jun.: Such familiarity from the lower orders. (*Exit* Moses Aaron, *door* l.) You take it coolly. (*Sitting* l. *of table.*)

Sidney (*sitting*): I generally do.

Chodd, Jun. (*looking round*): You've got lots of guns?

Sidney: I'm fond of shooting.

Chodd, Jun.: And rods?

Sidney: I'm fond of fishing.

Chodd, Jun.: And books?

Sidney: I like reading.

Chodd, Jun.: And whips?

Sidney: And riding.

Chodd, Jun.: Why you seem fond of everything?

Sidney (*looking at him*): No; not everything.

  Doddles *enters, at door* l., *with card.*

Sidney (*reading*): 'Mr Sam. Stunner, P.R.'

Chodd, Jun.: 'P.R.' What's P.R. mean? Afternoon's P.M.?

Sidney: Ask him in.

  Exit Doddles.

Chodd, Jun.: Is he an author? or does P.R. mean Pre-Raphaelite?

Sidney: No; he's a prize-fighter – the Smiffel Lamb.

  Enter the Smiffel Lamb, l. *door.*

How are you, Lamb?

Lamb: Bleating, sir, bleating – thankee kindly.

Chodd, Jun. (*aside to* Sidney): Do prize-fighters usually carry cards?

Sidney: The march of intellect. Education of the masses – the Jemmy Masseys. Have a glass of sherry?

Lamb: Not a drain, thankee, sir.

Chodd, Jun. (*aside*): Offers that brute sherry, and makes me drink beer.

Lamb: I've jist bin drinkin' with Lankey Joe, and the Dulwich Duffer, at Sam Shoulderblows. I'm a going into trainin' next week to fight Australian Harry, the Boundin' Kangaroo. I shall lick him, sir. I know I shall.

Sidney: I shall back you, Lamb.

Lamb: Thankee, Mr Daryl. I knew you would. I always does my best for my backers, and to keep up the honour of the science; the Fancy, sir, should keep square. (*Looks at* Chodd, Jun., *hesitates, then walks to door, closes it, and walks sharply up to* Sidney Daryl – Chodd, Jun., *leaping up in alarm, and retiring to back – leaning on table and speaking close to* Sidney Daryl's *ear.*) I jist called in to give you the office, sir, as has always bin so kind to me, not to *put* any tin on the mill between the Choking Chummy and Slang's Novice. It's a cross sir, a reg'lar barney!

SIDNEY: Is it? Thank ye.

LAMB: That's wot I called for, sir; and now I'm hoff. (*Goes to door – turning.*) Don't *putt* a mag on it, sir; Choking Chummy's a cove as would sell his own mother; he once sold *me*, which is *wuss*. Good-day, sir.

    Exit LAMB, *door* L. CHODD, JUN., *reseats himself.*

CHODD, JUN.: As I was saying, you know lots of people at clubs, and in society.

SIDNEY: Yes.

CHODD, JUN.: Titles, and Honourables, and Captains, and that.

SIDNEY: Yes.

CHODD, JUN.: Tip-toppers. (*After a pause.*) You're not well off?

SIDNEY (*getting serious*): No.

CHODD, JUN.: I am. I've heaps of brass. Now I have what you haven't, and I haven't what you have. You've got what I want, and I've got what you want. That's logic, isn't it?

SIDNEY (*gravely*): What of it?

CHODD, JUN.: This; suppose we exchange or barter. You help me to get into the company of men with titles, and women with titles; swells, you know, real 'uns, and all that.

SIDNEY: Yes.

CHODD, JUN.: And I'll write you a cheque for any reasonable sum you like to name.

    SIDNEY *rises indignantly, at the same moment* LITTLE MAUD *and* MRS
    CHURTON *enter door,* L.

L. MAUD (*running to* SIDNEY): Here I am, uncle; Mrs Churton says I've been such a good girl.

SIDNEY (*kissing her*): My darling. How d'ye do, Mrs Churton. (*To* LITTLE MAUD.) I've got a waggon, and a baa-lamb that squeaks, for you. (*Then to* CHODD, JUN.) Mr Chodd, I cannot entertain your very commercial proposition. My friends are my friends; they are not marketable commodities. I regret that I can be of no assistance to you. With your appearance, manners, and cheque-book, you are sure to make a circle of your own.

CHODD, JUN.: You refuse, then –

SIDNEY: Absolutely. Good morning.

CHODD, JUN.: Good morning. (*Aside.*) And if I don't have my knife into you, my name's not John Chodd, Jun.

    Exeunt SIDNEY, LITTLE MAUD *and* MRS CHURTON, *door* R. CHODD,
    JUN., *door* L.

SCENE II

The Interior of a Square at the West End. Weeping ash over a rustic chair, C., *trees, shrubs, walks, rails, gates, &c.; houses at back. Time evening – effect of setting sun in windows of houses; lights in some of the windows, &c.; street lamps.* MAUD *discovered in rustic chair reading; street band heard playing in the distance.*

MAUD: I can't see to read any more. Heigho! how lonely it is! and that band makes me so melancholy – sometimes music makes me feel – (*Rising.*) Heigho! I suppose I shall see nobody to-night; I must go home. (*Starts.*) Oh! (SIDNEY *appears at* L. *gate.*) I think I can see to read a few more lines. (*Sits again, and takes book.*)

SIDNEY (*feeling pockets*): Confound it! I've left the key at home. (*Tries gate.*) How shall I get in! (*Looking over rails.*) I'll try the other. (*Goes round at back to opposite gate.*)

MAUD: Why, he's going! He doesn't know I'm here. (*Rises, calling.*) Sid – No I won't, the idea of his – (*Sees* SIDNEY *at gate,* R.) Ah! (*Gives a sigh of relief, reseats herself and reads.*)

SIDNEY (*at gate,* R.): Shut too! (*Trying gate.*) Provoking! What shall I – (*Sees* NURSEMAID *approaching with* CHILD *from* L. *1* E. – *drops his hat into square.*) Will you kindly open this? I've forgotten my key. (GIRL *opens gate.*) Thanks! (SIDNEY *enters square;* GIRL *and* CHILD *go out at gate;* LIFE GUARDSMAN *enters,* R.U.E., *speaks to* GIRL; *they exeunt,* L.U.E. SIDNEY *sighs on seeing* MAUD.) There she is! (*Seats himself by* MAUD.) Maud!

MAUD (L., *starting*): Oh! is that you? Who would have thought of seeing you here?

SIDNEY (R.): Oh, come – don't I know that you walk here after dinner? and all day long I've been wishing it was half-past eight.

MAUD (*coquetting*): I wonder, now, how often you've said that, this last week.

SIDNEY: Don't pretend to doubt me, that's unworthy of you. (*A pause.*) Maud!

MAUD: Yes.

SIDNEY: Are you not going to speak?

MAUD (*dreamily*): I don't know what to say.

SIDNEY: That's just my case. When I'm away from you, I feel I could talk to you for hours; but when I'm with you, somehow or other, it seems all to go away. (*Getting closer to her, and taking her hand.*) It is such happiness to be with you, that it makes me forget everything else. (*Takes off his gloves and puts them on seat.*) Ever since I was that high, in the jolly old days down at Springmead, my greatest pleasure has been to be near you. (*Looks at watch.*) Twenty to nine. When must you return?

MAUD: At nine.

SIDNEY: Twenty minutes. How's your aunt?

MAUD: As cross as ever.

SIDNEY: And Lord Ptarmigant?

MAUD: As usual – asleep.

SIDNEY: Dear old man! how he does doze his time away. (*Another pause.*) Anything else to tell me?

MAUD: We had such a stupid dinner; such odd people.

SIDNEY: Who?

MAUD: Two men by the name of Chodd.

SIDNEY (*uneasily*): Chodd!

MAUD: Isn't it a funny name? – Chodd.

SIDNEY: Yes, it's a Chodd name – I mean an odd name. Where were they picked up?

MAUD: I don't know. Aunty says they are both very rich.

SIDNEY (*uneasily*): She thinks of nothing but money. (*Looks at watch.*) Fifteen to nine (*Stage has grown gradually dark.*) Maud?

MAUD (*in a whisper*): Yes

SIDNEY: If I were rich – if you were rich – if we were rich.

MAUD: Sidney! (*Drawing closer to him.*)

SIDNEY: As it is, I almost feel it's a crime to love you.

MAUD: Oh, Sidney!

SIDNEY: You who might make such a splendid marriage.

MAUD: If you had – money – I couldn't care for you any more than I do now.

SIDNEY: My darling! (*Looks at watch.*) Ten minutes. I know you wouldn't. Sometimes I feel mad about you – mad when I know you are out a smiling upon others – and – and waltzing.

MAUD: I can't help waltzing when I'm asked.

SIDNEY: No, dear, no; but when I fancy you are spinning round with another's arm about your waist. (*His arm round her waist.*) Oh! – I feel –

MAUD: Why, Sidney. (*Smiling.*) You are jealous!

SIDNEY: Yes, I am.

MAUD: Can't you trust me?

SIDNEY: Implicitly. But I like to be with you all the same.

MAUD (*whispering*): So do I with you.

SIDNEY: My love! (*Kisses her, and looks at watch.*) Five minutes.

MAUD: Time to go?

SIDNEY: No! (MAUD, *in taking out her handkerchief, takes out a knot of ribbon.*) What's that?

MAUD: Some trimmings I'm making for our fancy fair.

SIDNEY: What colour is it. Scarlet?

MAUD: Magenta.

SIDNEY: Give it to me?

MAUD: What nonsense.

SIDNEY: Won't you?

MAUD: I've brought something else.

SIDNEY: For me?

MAUD: Yes.

SIDNEY: What?

MAUD: These. (*Producing small case, which* SIDNEY *opens.*)

SIDNEY: Sleeve links!

MAUD: Now, which will you have, the links or the ribbon?

SIDNEY (*after reflection*): Both.

MAUD: You avaricious creature!

SIDNEY (*putting the ribbons near his heart*): It's not in the power of words to tell you how I love you. Do you care for me enough to trust your future with me? Will you be mine?

MAUD: Sidney?

SIDNEY: Mine, and none other's; no matter how brilliant the offer – how dazzling the position?

MAUD (*in a whisper – leaning towards him*): Yours and yours only!

   Clock strikes nine.

SIDNEY (*with watch*): Nine! Why doesn't time stop, and big Ben refuse to toll the hour?

   LADY *and* LORD PTARMIGANT *appear and open gate,* R.

MAUD (*frightened*): My aunt!

   SIDNEY *gets to back, round* L. *of square.* LORD *and* LADY PTARMIGANT *advance.*

LADY P. (*a very grand acid old lady*): Maud!

MAUD: Aunty, I was just coming away.

LADY P.: No one in the square? Quite improper to be here alone. Ferdinand!

LORD P. (*a little old gentleman*): My love!

LADY P.: What is the time?

LORD P.: Don't know – watch stopped – tired of going, I suppose, like me.

LADY P. (*sitting on chair – throws down the gloves left by* SIDNEY *with her dress*): What's that? (*Picking them up.*) Gloves?

MAUD (*frightened*): Mine, aunty!

LADY P.: Yours? You've got yours on! (*Looking at them.*) These are Sidney Daryl's. I know his size – seven-and-a-half. I see why you are so fond of walking in the square; for shame! (*Turning to* SIDNEY, *who has just got the* R. *gate open, and is going out.*) Sidney! (*Fiercely.*) I see you! There is no occasion to try and sneak away. Come here. (SIDNEY *advances. With ironical politeness.*) You have left your gloves.

All are standing except LORD PTARMIGANT, *who lies at full length on chair and goes to sleep.*

SIDNEY (*confused*): Thank you, Lady Ptarm –

LADY P.: You two fools have been making love. I've long suspected it. I'm shocked with both of you; a penniless scribbler, and a dependent orphan, without a shilling or an expectation. Do you (*To* SIDNEY.) wish to drag my niece, born and bred a lady, to a back parlour, and bread and cheese? Or do you (*To* MAUD.) wish to marry a shabby writer, who can neither feed himself nor you? I can leave you nothing, for I am as well bred a pauper as yourselves. (*To* MAUD.) To keep appointments in a public square! your conduct is disgraceful – worse – it is unladylike; and yours (*To* SIDNEY.), is dishonourable, and unworthy, to fill the head of a foolish girl with sentiment and rubbish. (*Loudly.*) Ferdinand!

LORD P. (*waking up*): Yes, dear.

LADY P.: Do keep awake; the Chodds will be here directly; they are to walk home with us, and I request you to make yourself agreeable to them.

LORD P.: Such canaille.

LADY P.: Such cash!

LORD P.: Such cads.

LADY P.: Such cash! Pray, Ferdinand, don't argue (*Authoritatively.*)

LORD P.: I never do. (*Goes to sleep again.*)

LADY P.: I wish for no esclandre. Let us have no discussion in the square. Mr Daryl, I shall be sorry if you compel me to forbid you my house. I have other views for Miss Hetherington. (SIDNEY *bows.*)

The two CHODDS, *in evening dress, appear at gate,* R.; *they enter.*

LADY P.: My dear Mr Chodd, Maud has been so impatient. (*The* CHODDS *do not see* SIDNEY – *to* CHODD, SEN.) I shall take your arm, Mr Chodd. (*Very sweetly.*) Maud, dear, Mr John will escort you.

Street band heard playing 'Fra Poco' in distance; MAUD *takes* CHODD, JUN.'*s arm; the two couples go off* R. *gate; as* MAUD *turns, she looks an adieu at* SIDNEY, *who waves the bunch of ribbon, and sits down on chair in a reverie, not perceiving* LORD PTARMIGANT'*s legs;* LORD PTARMIGANT *jumps up with pain;* SIDNEY *apologises. Curtain quick.*

ACT II

SCENE I

Parlour at the 'Owl's Roost' Public-house. Cushioned seats all round the apartment; gas lighted R. *and* L. *over tables; splint boxes, pipes, newspapers, &c., on table; writing materials on* R. *table (near door); gong bell on* L. *table; door of entrance* C.; *clock above door (hands set to half-past nine); hat pegs and hats on walls. In the chair at* L. *table head is discovered* O'SULLIVAN; *also, in the following order,* MACUSQUE-BAUGH, AUTHOR, *and* DR MAKVICZ; *also at* R. *table,* TRODNON *(at head),* SHAMHEART, BRADLEY, SCARGIL; *the* REPORTER *of 'Belgravian Banner' is sitting outside the* R. *table, near the head, and with his back turned to it, smoking a cigar. The* CHARACTERS *are all discovered drinking and smoking, some reading, some with their hats on.*

OMNES: Bravo! Hear, hear! Bravo!

O'SULL. (*on his legs, a glass in one hand, and terminating a speech, in Irish accent*): It is, therefore, gintlemen, with the most superlative felicitee, the most fraternal convivialitee, the warmest congenialitee, the most burning friendship, and ardent admiration, that I propose his health!

OMNES: Hear, hear! &c.

O'SULL.: He is a man, in the words of the divine bard –

TROD (*in sepulchral voice*): Hear! hear!

O'SULL.: Who, in 'suffering everything, has suffered nothing'.

TROD: Hear, hear!

O'SULL.: I have known him when, in the days of his prosperitee, he rowled down to the House of Commons in his carriage.

MACU.: 'Twasn't his own – 'twas a job!

OMNES: Silence! Chair! Order!

O'SULL.: I have known him when his last copper, and his last glass of punch, has been shared with the frind of his heart!

OMNES: Hear, hear!

O'SULL.: And it is with feelings of no small pride that I inform ye that that frind of his heart was the humble individual who has now the honour to address ye!

OMNES: Hear, hear! &c.

O'SULL.: But, prizeman at Trinity, mimber of the bar, sinator, classical scholar, or frind, Desmond MacUsquebaugh has always been the same – a gintleman and a scholar; and that highest type of that glorious union – an Irish gintleman and scholar. Gintlemen, I drink his health – Desmond, my long loved frind, bless ye! (*All rise solemnly and drink* – 'Mr MacUsquebaugh.') Gintlemen, my frind, Mr MacUsquebaugh will respond.

OMNES: Hear, hear!

Enter WAITER *with glasses, tobacco, &c., and receives orders – changes* O'SULLIVAN*'s glass and exits,* C. *Enter* TOM STYLUS *and* CHODD, JUN., C. TOM *has a greatcoat on, over an evening dress.*

CHODD, JUN: Thank you; no, not anything.

TOM: Just a wet – an outrider – or advanced guard, to prepare the way for the champagne.

CHODD, JUN: No.

As soon as the sitters see TOM STYLUS *they give him a friendly nod, looking inquiringly at* CHODD, *and whisper each other.*

TOM (R.): You'd better. They are men worth knowing. (*Pointing them out.*) That is the celebrated Olinthus O'Sullivan, Doctor of Civil Laws.

O'SULLIVAN *is at this moment reaching to the gaslight to light his pipe.*

CHODD, JUN. (L.): The gent with the long pipe?

TOM: Yes; one of the finest classical scholars in the world; might have sat upon the woolsack if he'd chosen, but he didn't. (O'SULLIVAN *is now tossing with* MACUSQUEBAUGH.) That is the famous Desmond MacUsquebaugh, late M.P. for Killcrackskullcoddy, county Galway, a great patriot and orator; might have been Chancellor of the Exchequer if he'd chosen, but he didn't. (SCARGIL *reaches to the gaslight to light his pipe.*) That's Bill Bradley (*Pointing to* BRADLEY, *who is reading paper with double eye-glass.*), author of the famous romance of 'Time and Opportunity'; ran through ten editions. He got two thousand pounds for it, which was his ruin.

CHODD, JUN.: How was he ruined by getting two thousand pounds?

TOM: He's never done anything since. We call him 'One book Bradley.' That gentleman fast asleep – (*Looking towards* AUTHOR *at table,* L.) has made the fortune of three publishers, and the buttoned-up one with the shirt front of beard is Herr Makvicz, the great United German. Dr Scargil, there, discovered the mensuration of the motive power of the cerebral organs.

SCARGIL *takes a pinch of snuff from a box on the table.*

CHODD, JUN.: What's that?

TOM: How many million miles per minute thought can travel. He might have made his fortune if he'd chosen.

CHODD, JUN.: But he didn't. Who is that mild-looking party, with the pink complexion, and the white hair! (*Looking towards* SHAMHEART.)

TOM: Sam Shamheart, the professional philanthropist. He makes it his business and profit to love the whole human race. (SHAMHEART *puffs a huge cloud of smoke from his pipe.*) Smoke, sir; all smoke. A superficial observer would consider him only a pleasant oily humbug, but I, having known him two and twenty years, feel qualified to pronounce him one of the biggest villains untransported.

CHODD, JUN.: And that man asleep at the end of the table.

TOM: Trodnon, the eminent tragedian.

TRODNON *raises himself from the table, yawns, stretches himself, and again drops head on table.*

CHODD, JUN.: I never heard of him.

TOM: Nor anybody else. But he's a confirmed tippler, and here we consider drunkenness an infallible sign of genius – we make that a rule.

CHODD, JUN.: But if they are all such great men, why didn't they make money by their talents?

TOM (R.): Make money! They'd scorn it! they wouldn't do it – that's another rule. That gentleman there (*Looking towards a very seedy man with eyeglass in his eye.*) does the evening parties on the 'Belgravian Banner.'

CHODD, JUN. (*with interest*): Does he? Will he put my name among the fashionables to-night?

TOM: Yes.

CHODD, JUN.: And that we may know who's there and everything about it – you're going with me?

TOM: Yes, I'm going into *society*; thanks to your getting me the invitation. I can dress up an account, not a mere list of names, but a picturesque report of the soirée, and show under what brilliant auspices you entered the beau-monde.

CHODD, JUN.: Beau-monde. What's that?

TOM (*chaffing him*): Every man is called a cockney who is born within the sound of the beau-monde.

CHODD, JUN. (*not seeing it*): Oh! Order me two hundred copies of the 'Belgravian' – What's its name?

TOM: 'Banner.'

CHODD, JUN.: The day my name's in it – and put me down as a regular subscriber. I like to encourage high-class literature. By the way, shall I ask the man what he'll take to drink?

TOM: No, no.

CHODD, JUN.: I'll pay for it. I'll stand, you know. (*Going to him,* TOM *stops him.*)

Tom: No, no – he don't know you, and he'd be offended.

Chodd, Jun.: But, I suppose all these chaps are plaguy poor?

Tom: Yes, they're poor; but they are *gentlemen*.

Chodd, Jun. (*grinning*): I like that notion – a *poor* gentleman – it tickles me. (*Going up* R.)

Tom (*crossing into* L. *corner*): Metallic snob!

Chodd, Jun.: I'm off now (*Going up*, R.) You'll come to my rooms and we'll go together in the brougham. I want to introduce you to my friends, Lady Ptarmigant and Lord Ptarmigant?

Tom: I must wait here for a proof I expect from the office.

Chodd, Jun.: How long shall you be?

Tom (*looking at clock*): An hour.

Chodd, Jun.: Don't be later.

> *Exit* Chodd, Jun., C. – *the* Reporter *rises, gets paper from* L. *table, and shows it to* Shamheart, *sitting next him on his* L. *hand.*

O'Sull.: Sit down, Tommy, my dear boy. Gintlemen, Mr Desmond MacUsquebaugh will respond.

> *Tapping with hammer. Enter* Waiter, C., *and gives* Bradley *a glass of grog.*

MacU. (*rising*): Gintlemen.

> Tom *taking his coat off, shows evening dress.*

Tom: A go of whiskey.

Waiter: Scotch or Irish?

Tom: Irish.

> *Exit* Waiter, C. *All are astonished at* Tom's *costume – they cry* 'By Jove! there's a swell,' &c.

O'Sull.: Why, Tom, my dear friend – are ye going to be married to-night, that ye're got up so gorgeously?

MacU.: Tom, you're handsome as an angel.

O'Sull.: Or a duke's footman. Gintlemen, rise and salute our illustrious brother.

> *All rise and make* Tom *mock bows.*

Brad: The gods preserve you, noble sir.

Sham: May the bill of your sublime highness's washerwoman be never the less.

MacU.: And may it be paid.

> *A general laugh.*

O'Sull.: Have you come into a fortune?

Dr M.: Or married a widow?

Sham: Or buried a relation?

A general laugh.

By my soul, Tom, you look an honour to humanity!

O'SULL.: And your laundress.

A general laugh.

BRAD: Gentlemen, Mr Stylus's health and shirt front.

A general laugh – all drink and sit.

TOM (C.): Bless ye, my people, bless ye! (*Sits, and takes out short pipe and smokes.*)

O'SULL.: Gintlemen. (*Rising.*) My friend, Mr MacUsquebaugh, will respond.

OMNES: Hear, hear!

MacU. (*rising*): Gintlemen –

Enter SIDNEY, *in evening dress and wrapper. Enter* WAITER *and* TOM'*s grog.*

OMNES: Hallo, Daryl!

SIDNEY: How are ye, boys? Doctor, how goes it? (*Shaking hands.*) Mac. How d'ye do, O'Sullivan? Tom, I want to speak to you.

O'SULL.: Ah, Tom, this is the rale metal – the genuine thing; compared to him you are a sort of Whitechapel would-if-I-could-be. (*To* SIDNEY.) Sit down, my gorgeous one, and drink with me.

SIDNEY: No, thanks.

SIDNEY and TOM *sit at* R. *table head.*

O'SULL.: Waiter, take Mr Daryl's orders.

SIDNEY: Brandy cold.

Exit WAITER, C.

MacU.: Take off your wrap, rascal, and show your fine feathers.

SIDNEY: No; I'm going out, and I shall smoke my coat.

TOM *extinguishing his pipe, and puts it in his dresscoat pocket, then puts on his greatcoat with great solemnity.*

O'SULL.: Going?

TOM: No.

O'SULL.: Got the rheumatism?

TOM: No; but I shall smoke my coat.

General laugh.

Enter WAITER, C. *He gives glass of brandy and water to* SIDNEY, *and glass of grog to* SHAMHEART.

O'SULL.: What news, Daryl?

SIDNEY: None, except that the Ministry is to be defeated.

O'SULLIVAN pays WAITER.

ALL: No!

SIDNEY: I say, yes. They're whipping up everything to vote against Thunder's motion. Thunder is sure of a majority, and out they go. Capital brandy. (*Coming forward.*) Tom! (TOM *rises; they come down stage.*) I am off to a soirée.

TOM (R., *aside*): So am I; but I won't tell him.

SIDNEY (L.): I find I've nothing in my portmonnaie but notes. I want a trifle for a cab. Lend me five shillings.

TOM: I haven't got it, but I can get it for you.

SIDNEY: There's a good fellow, do. (*Returns to seat.*)

TOM (*to* MACUSQUEBAUGH, *after looking round*): Mac. (*Whispering.*) Lend me five bob.

MACU.: My dear boy, I haven't got so much.

TOM: Then don't lend it.

MACU.: But I'll get it for you. (*Crosses to* BRADLEY – *whispers.*) Bradley lend me five shillings.

BRAD.: I haven't it about me, but I'll get it for you. (*Crosses to* O'SULLIVAN – *whispers.*) O'Sullivan, lend me five shillings.

O'SULL.: I haven't got it, but I'll get it for you. (*Crossing to* SCARGIL – *whispers.*) Scargil, lend me five shillings.

SCARG.: I haven't got it, but I'll get it for you. (*Crossing to* MAKVICZ – *whispers.*) Doctor, lend me five shillings.

DR M.: I am waiting for chaange vor a zoveren; I'll give it you when de waiter brings to me.

SCARG.: All right! (*To* O'SULLIVAN.) All right!

O'SULL.: All right! (*To* BRADLEY.) All right!

BRAD.: All right! (*To* MACUSQUEBAUGH.) All right!

MACU.: All right! (*To* TOM.) All right!

TOM (*to* SIDNEY): All right!

O'SULL. (*tapping*): Gintlemen, my friend, Mr MacUsquebaugh will respond to the toast that –

MACU. (*rising*): Gintlemen –

SIDNEY: Oh, cut the speechifying, I hate it! you ancients are so fond of spouting; let's be jolly, I've only a few minutes more.

BRAD.: Daryl, sing us 'Cock-a-doodle-doo.'

SIDNEY: I only know the first two verses.

TOM: I know the rest.

　　Enter WAITER, *gives glass of grog to* MAKVICZ.

SIDNEY: Then here goes. Waiter, shut the door, and don't open it till I've done. Now then, ready.

Exit WAITER. O'SULLIVAN *taps.*

SIDNEY (*giving out*): Political: –
(*sings*)   When Ministers in fear and doubt,
            That they should be from place kicked out,
            Get up 'gainst time and sense to spout
                A long dull evening through,
            What mean they then by party clique,
            Mob orators and factions weak?
            'Tis only would they truth then speak
                But cock-a-doodle-doo!
            Cock-a-doodle, cock-a-doodle, cock-a-doodle-doo.

CHORUS (*gravely and solemnly shaking their heads*): Cock-a-doodle, &c.

SIDNEY (*speaking*): Commercial: –
(*sings*)   When companies, whose stock of cash
            Directors spend to cut a dash,
            Are formed to advertise and smash,
                And bankruptcy go through.
            When tradesfolks live in regal state,
            The goods they sell adulterate,
            And puff in print, why what's their prate
                But cock-a-doodle-doo?
            Cock-a-doodle, cock-a-doodle, &c.

CHORUS (*as before*): Cock-a-doodle, &c.

Enter WAITER, C.

O'SULL.: How dare you come in and interrupt the harmony!

WAITER: Beg pardon, sir, but there's somebody says as he must see Mr Stylus.

TOM: Is he a devil?

WAITER: No, sir, he's a juvenile. (*A general laugh.*)

TOM: Send in some whiskey – Irish – and the devil.

WAITER: Hot, sir? (*A general laugh.*)

TOM *nods to* WAITER, *who exits,* C. *door.*

SIDNEY: Why can't you see your proofs at the office?

TOM: I'm in full fig, and can't stew in that atmosphere of steam and copperas.

Enter PRINTER'S BOY, C.; *he goes up to* TOM *at head of* R. *table. Enter* WAITER *with tray, hot-water jug, &c.; he gives change in silver to* MAKVICZ, *who crosses to* SCARGIL. WAITER *puts hot-water jug and whisky before* TOM, *and exits,* C. *door.*

DR M.: Here! (*Giving two half-crowns to* SCARGIL.) Scargil!

SCARG. (*crossing in same manner to* O'SULLIVAN): Here, O'Sullivan.

O'SULL. (*crossing to* BRADLEY): Here, Bradley.

BRAD. (*crossing to* MACUSQUEBAUGH): Here, Mac.

MACU. (*crossing to* TOM): Here, Tom.

PRINTER'S BOY (*to* TOM): Please, sir, Mr Duval said would you add this to it? (*Giving* TOM *a proof slip.*)

TOM: All right – wait outside – I'll bring it to you.

> *Exit* BOY, C.

TOM (*draws writing pad towards him, takes his grog, and is about to pour hot water from pewter jug into it, when he burns his fingers, starts up and dances*): Confound it!

ALL: What's the matter?

TOM: I've scalded my fingers with the hot water.

SIDNEY (*taking up pen*): Here, I'll correct it for you.

TOM: Thank you.

O'SULL.: Gintlemen, proceed with the harmony. Mr Stylus –

TOM: One minute. (*To* SIDNEY.) Just add this to it. (SIDNEY *sits down to write,* TOM *standing over him, reading slip.*) 'Fashionable Intelligence. – We hear a marriage is on the tapis between Mr John Chodd, Junior, son of the celebrated millionaire, and Miss Maud Hetherington, daughter of the late Colonel Hetherington.'

> SIDNEY *starts.*

TOM: What's the matter?

SIDNEY: Nothing!

> *He goes on writing –* O'SULLIVAN *taps hammer.*

TOM (*speaking*): Amatory: –

(*sings*)   When woman, lovely woman sighs,
           You praise her form, her hair, her eyes;
           Would link your heart by tend'rest ties,
                And vow your vows are true.
           She answers tenderly and low,
           Though from her lips the words that flow,
           So softly sweet, are nought we know
                But cock-a-doodle-doo!
                     &c., &c., &c.

TOM *throws five shillings to* SIDNEY, *which rattle on the table.* SIDNEY *gives him back the proof; his face is deadly pale; as his head falls on the table the Chorus is singing,* 'Cock-a-doodle-doo,' &c. – *closed in.*

SCENE II

A Retiring Room at SIR FARINTOSH FADILEAF'S *(2nd grooves); large archway or alcove,* L*., with curtain drawn or doors leading to ballroom; small arch or alcove,* R*., leading to supper-room, with drawn curtain; centre opening curtains drawn; the room is decorated for a ball; candelabra, flowers. &c.*[1]

'LADY P. *(without)*: Very pretty – very pretty indeed, Sir Farintosh; all very nice.'

LADY PTARMIGANT *enters from* R*., with* 'SIR FARINTOSH,' LORD PTARMIGANT, *and* MAUD, *all in evening dress.*

'SIR F. *(an old beau)*: So kind of you, Cousin Ptarmigant, to take pity on a poor old widower, who has no womankind to receive for him, and all that.

'LADY P.: Not at all – not at all; I am only too glad to be useful.'

LORD P. *(speaking off,* R. 1 E.): Bring chairs.

LADY P.: Ferdinand, you can't want to go to sleep again!

LORD P.: I know I can't, but I do.

SERVANT *brings two chairs and a small table,* R.

LADY P.: Besides I don't want chairs here, young men get lolling about, and then they don't dance. (LORD PTARMIGANT *sits,* R*., and closes his eyes.*) 'Farintosh, '(*Knocks heard.*) the arrivals are beginning.

'SIR F.: But, Lady Ptarmigant, if –

'LADY P.: Remember that the old Dowager Countess of McSwillumore has plenty of whisky toddy in a green glass, to make believe hock.

'SIR F.: But if –'

LADY P.: 'Now go. Oh dear me! (*Almost forces* SIR FARINTOSH *off,* L.*')* Now, Maud, one word with you; you have been in disgrace all this last week about that writing fellow.

MAUD (L*., indignant*): What writing fellow?

LADY P.: Don't echo me if you please. You know who I mean – Daryl!

MAUD: Mr Daryl is a relation of your ladyship's – the son of the late Sir Percy Daryl, and brother of the present Baronet.

LADY P. (R.): And when the present Baronet, that precious Percy, squandered everything at the gaming table, dipped the estates, and ruined himself, Sidney gave up the money left him by his mother, to reinstate a dissolute beggared brother! I don't forget that.

MAUD (*with exultation*): I do not forget it, I never shall. To give up all his

---

[1] The lines between inverted commas can be omitted.

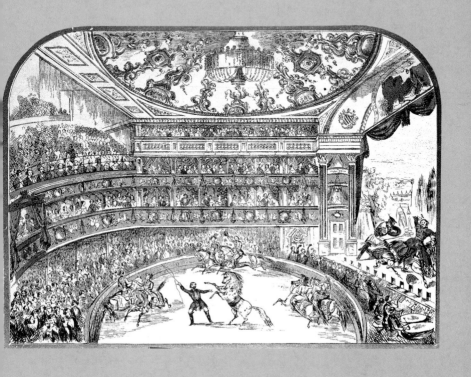

Interior of the fourth Astley's *c.*1856 showing *Richard III* in progress on the stage. Note the exciting circus-style presentation occurring simultaneously in the ring below the stage.
(© The Board of the Trustees of the Victoria & Albert Museum)

MASTER VINE.

Left: John Vine, the remarkable armless artist, who began his career as a curiosity exhibited at travelling fairs. These two pictures show him as a child and an adult. The print of Vine as a child in the 1810s suggests he produced sketches on request for his audience. (Artist unknown, © British Museum)

Above: This extraordinary photograph was taken by Ernest Mason of Colchester, probably in the 1860s. Vine married a Colchester girl and opened a studio in the town in about 1830. By the 1840s his practice was well-established and he continued painting until his death in 1867. (© Colchester Museum)

ROYAL AMPHITHEATRE, under the Management of Messrs. Ducrow and West, Jun.

Last 3 Weeks OF PERFORMING.

MONDAY, Sept. 17th, 1838, and 5 following Evenings,

SECOND WEEK OF

VAN AMBURGH's New Feats

AND EXTRAORDINARY PERFORMANCE WITH THE

Bengal Tiger!!

LIVING LIONS

TIGERS, LEOPARDS,

&c. &c. (which generally commences AT HALF PAST SEVEN O'CLOCK.) in the

BRUTE TAMER OF POMPEII!

To the above Attraction, will be added, (for the Last Week,) the Splendid Military Equestrian Spectacle of the BURNING of

MOSCOW!

After which, the admired SCENES of the CIRCLE will introduce the Splendid Rustic Pageant of The

FLITCH OF BACON!

By all the HORSES and EQUESTRIANS.

MR. DUCROW WILL APPEAR

And introduce the extraordinary Exercises of his

HORSE, BEAUTY!!

Messrs. Hillars and Clarke will be introduced as the CHINESE BROTHERS:—The INFANT EQUESTRIAN WONDERS will give their Extravagance of LITTLE

RED RIDING HOOD!

The Performance will conclude with the interesting Legend and favorite Equestrian Delineation of

TURPIN's Ride to York!

Mr. DUCROW will shortly appear as the IDIOT of HEIDELBURG.

Seaton, Printer, Bridge Road, Lambeth.

Left: Astley's playbill from 1838. The folk legend of *Turpin's Ride to York* was already an established feature of the popular theatre. (© The Board of the Trustees of the Victoria & Albert Musuem)

Above: The Bower Saloon in London was renowned for its dog melodramas. This playbill from the 1850s shows the period's fascination with animals and theatrical novelties. (© The Board of the Trustees of the Victoria & Albert Musuem)

POSITIVELY THE LAST WEEK !!

J. MARSH,

HAS PURCHASED A

GREAT NOVELTY !!

Which may be SEEN ALIVE !!

AT THE

STAR YARD, OXFORD,

A WONDERFULLY

LARGE PIG,

Weighing 68 Score 12 lbs.,

From the Birmingham Cattle Show, Bred and Exhibited by W. B. Wainman, Esq., Yorkshire.

This is the Largest Pig ever seen and has gained 14 Prizes.

Admission, 2d., Children & Schools, 1d.

The PIG will be on her legs at 12, 2, 4, and 6 o'clock.

Hall and Son. Printers. New Road, Oxford.

There were two sides to animal theatricality – the animals that performed wonders such as the Bower Saloon dogs, and the animals that were themselves wondrous, like this Large Pig. Notable for its physical characteristics, this mammoth sow did no more than stand up for the delight, and perhaps terror, of her rustic audience. Other pigs were more talented, Toby the celebrated Sapient Pig, could read, spell, play cards and tell the time.

(© Rural History Centre, University of Reading)

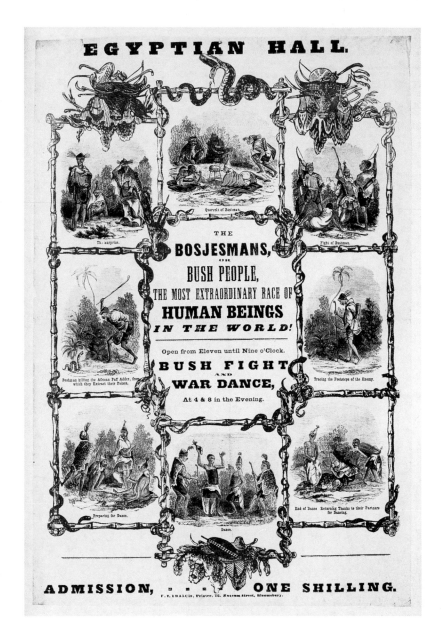

The Bush People were typical of successive groups of foreign tribal people exhibited in London throughout the century. The Egyptian Hall specialised in human exhibits; it was here that the Gnome Fly, Harvey Leech, impersonated the Wild Man of the Prairies. Promoters often made up ridiculous names for their acts if they thought they could create a greater stir. Other shows in London during the period included the Famous Amazons of Dahomey, supposedly a regiment of female warriors. Not all the exhibits were alive – the Aztec Lilliputians, who were billed as an entirely new race of people when they visited London, were reproduced as wax models for Reimer's Anatomical and Ethnological Museum in Leicester Square. (© Bodleian Library, John Johnson Collection)

Playbill for the English Opera House. Harvey Leech played the title role in the original version of this play, *Tale of Enchantment; or, The Gnome Fly* at the Bowery Theatre in New York in 1840. His performance there earned him his striking sobriquet.
(© Bodleian Library, John Johnson Collection)

fortune, to ruin his bright prospects to preserve his brother, and his brother's wife and children, to keep unsullied the honour of his name, was an act –

LADY P.: Of a noodle, and now he hasn't a penny save what he gets by scribbling – a pretty pass for a man of family to come to. You are my niece, and it is my solemn duty to get you married if I can. Don't thwart me, and I will. Leave sentiment to servant wenches who sweetheart the policemen; it's unworthy of a lady. I've a man in my eye – a rich one – young Chodd.

MAUD (*with repugnance*): Such a commonplace person.

LADY P.: With a very uncommonplace purse. He will have eighteen thousand a year. I have desired him to pay you court, and I desire you to receive it.

MAUD: He is so vulgar.

LADY P.: He is so rich. When he is your husband put him in a back study, and don't show him.

MAUD: But I detest him.

LADY P.: What on earth has that to do with it? You wouldn't love a man before you were married to him, would you? Where are your principles? Ask my lord how I treated him before our marriage. (*Hitting* LORD PTARMIGANT *with her fan.*) Ferdinand!

LORD P. (*awakening*): My love!

LADY P.: Do keep awake.

LORD P.: 'Pon my word you were making such a noise I thought I was in the House of Commons. (*With fond regret.*) I used to be allowed to sleep so comfortably there.

LADY P.: Are you not of opinion that a match between Mr Chodd and Maud would be most desirable.

LORD P. (*looking at* LADY PTARMIGANT): Am I not of opinion – my opinion – what is my opinion?

LADY P. (*hitting him with fan*): Yes, of course.

LORD P.: Yes – of course – my opinion is yes, of course. (*Aside, crossing* C. *with chair.*) Just as it used to be in the House. I always roused in time to vote as I was told to.

MAUD: But, uncle, one can't purchase happiness at shops in packets, like bon-bons. A thousand yards of lace cost so much, they can be got at the milliner's; but an hour of home or repose can only be had for love. Mere wealth –

LORD P.: My dear, wealth, if it does not bring happiness, brings the best imitation of it procurable for money. There are two things – wealth and poverty. The former makes the world a place to live in; the latter a place to – go to sleep in – as I do. (*Leans back in chair and dozes.*)

'*Enter* SIR FARINTOSH, COLONEL BROWSER, *and* LORD CLOUDWRAYS, L.C.

'SIR F.: Have you heard the news? The division is to come off to-night. Many men won't be able to come. I must be off to vote. If the Ministry go out –

'COL. B.: They won't go out – there'll be a dissolution!

'SIR F.: And I shall have to go down to be re-elected. Cloudwrays, will you come and vote?

'LORD C. (*languidly*): No.

'SIR F.: Why not?

'LORD C.: I'm dying for a weed.

'SIR F.: You can smoke in the smoking-room!

'LORD C.: So I can – that didn't occur to me!

'SIR F.: Ptarmigant, cousin, you do the honours for me. My country calls, you know, and all that. Come on, Cloudwrays; how slow are you. Hi, tobacco!

'CLOUDWRAYS *rouses himself. Exeunt* SIR FARINTOSH *and* LORD CLOUDWRAYS. LORD PTARMIGANT *dozes.*

'COL. B. (*who has been talking to* LADY PTARMIGANT, *turns to* LORD PTARMIGANT): As I was saying to her ladyship –

'LADY P.: Ferdinand, do wake up!

'LORD P.: Hear, hear! (*Waking.*) My dear!'

Enter SERVANT, R. 1 E.

PAGE: Mr Chodd, Mr John Chodd, and Mr Stylus.

Enter CHODD, JUN., CHODD, SEN. *and* TOM, R. 1 E. *Exit* SERVANT, R. 1 E.

LADY P. (L.C.): My dear Mr Chodd, how late you are! Maud dear, here is Mr Chodd. Do you know we were going to scold you, you naughty men!

CHODD, SEN. (R.C., *astonished, aside*): Naughty men! Johnny, her ladyship says we're naughty men; we've done something wrong!

CHODD, JUN. (R.): No, no – it's only her ladyship's patrician fun. Don't call me Johnny. I'm sure I hurried here on the wings of – (*Crossing* L.C., *falls over* LORD PTARMIGANT'*s feet, who rises and turns his chair the reverse way;* CHODD, *seeing* MAUD, *repellant.*) – a brougham and pair. Lady Ptarmigant, let me introduce a friend of mine. Lady Ptarmigant – Mr Stylus, whom I took the liberty of –

LADY P. (R.C.): Charmed to see any friend of yours!

TOM *advances from back,* R., *abashed; as he is backing and bowing he falls over* LORD Ptarmigant'*s legs;* LORD PTARMIGANT *rises with a look of annoyance; they bow;* LORD PTARMIGANT *again turns chair and sits.*

'LADY P.: Mr Chodd, take me to the ballroom. (CHODD, SEN., *offers his arm.*) You will look after Maud, I'm sure. (*To* CHODD, JUN.*, who smilingly offers his arm to* MAUD*, who, with a suppressed look of disgust, takes it.*) Mr Silen-us.

'TOM: Stylus – ma'am – my lady.

'LADY P.: Stylus – pardon me – will you be kind enough to keep my lord awake? (*Significantly.*) Maud! Now, dear Mr Chodd.

'CHODD, JUN.: Guv!

'*Exeunt* LADY PTARMIGANT, MAUD*, and the* CHODDS, L.

'TOM (*aside*): These are two funny old swells!

'COL. B.: Odd looking fellow. (*To* TOM.) Nice place this!

'TOM: Very.

'COL. B.: And charming man, Fadileaf.

'TOM: Very. I don't know him, but I should say he must be very jolly.

'COL. B. (*laughing*): Bravo! Why you're a wit!

'TOM: Yes! (*Aside.*) What does he mean?

'COL. B. (*offering box*): Snuff? Who's to win the Leger? Diadeste?

'TOM: I don't know – not in my department.

'COL. B. (*laughing*): Very good.

'TOM: What is? (*Innocently.*)

'COL. B.: You are. Do you play whist?

'TOM: Yes; cribbage, and all fours, likewise.

'COL. B.: We'll find another man, and make up a rubber.

'TOM (*pointing to* LORD PTARMIGANT *asleep*): He'll do for dummy.

'COL. B. (*laughing*): Capital!

'TOM: What a queer fellow this is – he laughs at everything I say.

Dance music.

'COL. B.: They've begun.

'TOM (*waking up* LORD PTARMIGANT): My lady said I was to keep you awake.

'LORD P.: Thank you.

'COL. B.: Come and have a rubber! Let's go and look up Chedbury.

'LORD P.: Yes.

'COL. B. (*to* TOM): You'll find us in the card-room.

'*Exeunt* LORD PTARMIGANT *and* COLONEL BROWSER, L.'

[NOTE. – *If preceeding lines be omitted, the following sentence and business.*]

LADY P.: Ferdinand! (*Going up* C. *to* LORD PTARMIGANT*, who awakes.*) Do rouse yourself, and follow me to the ballroom.

Exeunt all but TOM, L. 2 E. LORD PTARMIGANT *returns, and drags chair off after him.*

TOM: Here I am in society, and I think society is rather slow; it's much jollier at the 'Owl,' and there's more to drink. If it were not wicked to say it, how I should enjoy a glass of gin and water!

Enter LADY PTARMIGANT, L.

LADY P. (L.): Mr Si–len–us!

TOM (L., *abashed*): Stylus, ma'am – my lady!

LADY P.: Stylus! I beg pardon. You're all alone.

TOM: With the exception of your ladyship!

LADY P.: All the members have gone down to the House to vote, and we are dreadfully in want of men – I mean dancers! You dance, of course?

TOM: Oh! of course – I – (*Abashed.*)

LADY P.: As it is Leap-year, I may claim the privilege of asking you to see me through a quadrille!

TOM (R., *frightened*): My lady! I –

LADY P. (L., *aside*): He's a friend of the Chodds, and it will please them. Come then. (*She takes his arm; sniffing.*) Dear me! What a dreadful smell of tobacco! (*Sniffing.*)

TOM (*awfully self-conscious – sniffing*): Is there?

LADY P. (*sniffing*): Some fellow must have been smoking.

TOM (*sniffing*): I think some fellow must, or some fellow must have been where some other fellows have been smoking. (*Aside.*) It's that beastly parlour at the 'Owl'. (*In taking out his pocket-handkerchief his pipe falls on floor.*)

LADY P.: What's that?[1]

TOM (*in torture*): What's what? (*Turning about and looking through eye-glass at the air.*)

LADY P. (*pointing*): That!

TOM (*as if in doubt*): I rather think – it – is – a pipe!

LADY P.: I'm sure of it. You'll join me in the ball-room. (*Going up* C. *to* L.)

TOM: Instantly your ladyship (*Exit* LADY PTARMIGANT, L. *Looking at pipe, he picks it up.*) If ever I bring you into society again – (*Drops it.*) Waiter! (*Enter* PAGE, R. 1. E.) Somebody's dropped something. Remove the Whatsoname. (*Quadrille music in ballroom;* PAGE *goes off,* R. 1. E., *and returns with tray and sugar tongs, with which he picks up pipe with an air of ineffable disgust and goes off,* R. 1. E.) Now to spin round the old woman in the mazy waltz. (*Splits kid gloves in drawing them on.*) There goes one-and-nine.

Exit TOM, L. *Enter* SIDNEY, L. *He is pale and excited; one of the gold links of his wrist-band is unfastened.*

SIDNEY: I have seen her – she is smiling – dancing, but not with him. She

---

[1] This incident is taken from M. Emile Augier's admirable comedy of 'Les Effrontés.' – T.W.R.

looked so bright and happy. I won't think of her. How quiet it is here: so different to that hot room, with the crowd of fools and coquettes whirling round each other. I like to be alone – alone! I am now thoroughly – and to think it was but a week ago – one little week – I'll forget her – forget, and hate her. Hate her – Oh, Maud, Maud, till now, I never knew how much I loved you; loved you – loved you – gone; shattered; shivered; and for whom? For one of my own birth? For one of my own rank? No! for a common clown, who – confound this link – but he is rich – and – it won't hold. (*Trying to fasten it – his fingers trembling.*) I've heard it all – always with her, at the Opera and the Park, attentive and obedient – and she accepts him. My head aches. (*Louder.*) I'll try a glass of champagne.

TOM (*without, R.*): Champagne – here you are! (*Draws curtain. Enter* TOM, R. 2 E., *with champagne glass from supper-room; portion of supper table seen in alcove; seeing* SIDNEY.) Sidney!

SIDNEY: Tom! you here!

TOM: Very much here. (*Drinking.*) I was brought by Mr Chodd.

SIDNEY (L.): Chodd?

TOM (R.): Don't startle a fella. You look pale – aren't you well?

SIDNEY (*rallying*): Jolly, never better.

TOM: Have some salmon.

SIDNEY: I'm not hungry.

TOM: Then try some jelly, it's no trouble to masticate and is emollient and agreeable to the throat and palate.

SIDNEY: No, Tom, champagne.

TOM: There you are. (*Fetching bottle from table.*)

SIDNEY: I'll meet her eye to eye. (*Drinks.*) Another, Tom – and be as smiling and indifferent. As for that heavy-metalled dog – thanks, Tom. (*Drinks.*) Another.

TOM: I've been dancing with old lady Ptarmigant.

SIDNEY: Confound her.

TOM: I did. As I was twirling her round I sent my foot through her dress and tore her skirt out of the gathers.

SIDNEY (*laughing hysterically*): Good! Good! Bravo! Tom! Did she row you?

TOM: Not a bit. She said it was of no consequence; but her looks were awful.

SIDNEY: Ha! ha! ha! Tom, you're a splendid fellow, not like these damned swells, all waistcoat and shirt front.

TOM: But I like the swells. I played a rubber with them and won three pounds, then I showed them some conjuring tricks – you know I'm a famous conjuror (*Taking a pack of cards out of his pocket.*) By Jupiter! Look here, I've brought the pack away with me; I didn't know I had. I'll go and take it back.

SIDNEY (*taking cards from him absently*): No, never mind, stay with me, I don't want you to go.

TOM: I find high life most agreeable, everybody is so amiable, so thoughtful, so full of feeling.

SIDNEY: Feeling! Why man, this is a flesh market where the match-making mammas and chattering old chaperons have no more sense of feeling than drovers – the girls no more sentiment than sheep, and the best man is the highest bidder; that is, the biggest fool with the longest purse.

TOM: Sidney, you're ill.

SIDNEY: You lie, Tom – never better – excellent high spirits – confound this link!

Enter LORD CLOUDWRAYS *and* 'SIR FARINTOSH,' L.

LORD C: ⎱
'SIR F:' ⎰ By Jove! Ha, Sidney, heard the news?

SIDNEY (C.): News – there is no news! The times are bankrupt, and the assignees have sold off the events.

LORD C: ⎱
'SIR F:' ⎰ The Ministry is defeated.

TOM (R.): No.

LORD C: ⎱
'SIR F:' ⎰ Yes; by a majority of forty-six.

SIDNEY: Serve them right.

LORD C: ⎱
'SIR F:' ⎰ Why?

SIDNEY: I don't know! Why, what a fellow you are to want reasons.

LORD C.: Sidney!

SIDNEY: Hullo, Cloudwrays! my bright young British senator – my undeveloped Chatham, and mature Raleigh.

TOM: Will they resign?

SIDNEY: Of course they will: resignation is the duty of every man, or Minister, who can't do anything else.

TOM: Who will be sent for to form a Government?

SIDNEY: Cloudwrays.

LORD C.: How you do chaff a man!

SIDNEY: Why not? Inaugurate a new policy – the policy of smoke – free-trade in tobacco! Go in, not for principles, but for Principes – our hearths – our homes, and 'bacca boxes!

TOM: If there's a general election?

SIDNEY: Hurrah, for a general election! eh, Cloudwrays? – 'eh, Farintosh?' What speeches you'll make – what lies you'll tell, and how your constituents *won't* believe you!

LORD C:
'SIR F:' } How odd you are.

LORD C: Aren't you well?

SIDNEY: Glorious! only one thing annoys me.

LORD C:
'SIR F:' } What's that?

SIDNEY: They won't give me any more champagne.

'Enter COLONEL BROWSER, L.'

LORD C: } Lady Ptarmigant sent me here to say –
'COL. B: } Farintosh,' the ladies want partners.

*'*COLONEL *and* SIR FARINTOSH *go off,* L.'

SIDNEY: Partners! Here are partners for them – long, tall, stout, fat, thin, poor, rich. (*Crossing,* C.) Cloudwrays, you're the man! (*Enter* CHODD, JUN., L. SIDNEY *sees and points to him.*) No; this is the man!

CHODD, JUN. (L.): Confound this fellow! (*Aside.*)

SIDNEY (L.C.): This, sir, is the 'Young Lady's Best Companion,' well bound, Bramah-locked, and gilt at the edges – mind, gilt only at the edges. This link will *not* hold. (*Sees the pack of cards in his hand.*) Here, Chodd, take these – no, cut for a ten-pound note. (*Puts cards on small table,* R.)

CHODD, JUN. (L.C., *quickly*): With pleasure. (*Aside.*) I'll punish this audacious pauper in the pocket. (*Crossing to table.*)

LORD C.: You mustn't gamble here.

SIDNEY: Only for a frolic!

CHODD, JUN.: I'm always lucky at cards!

SIDNEY: Yes, I know an old proverb about that.

CHODD, JUN.: Eh?

SIDNEY (R.): Lucky at play, unlucky in – This link will not hold.

CHODD, JUN. (L.C., *maliciously*): Shall we put the stakes down first?

SIDNEY (*producing portmonnaie*): With pleasure!

LORD C.: But I don't think it right –

Advancing – CHODD, JUN. *stays him with his arm.*

TOM: Sidney!

SIDNEY: Nonsense! hold your tongue, Cloudwrays, and I'll give you a regalia. Let's make it for five-and-twenty?

CHODD, JUN.: Done!

SIDNEY: Lowest wins – that's in your favour.

CHODD, JUN.: Eh?

SIDNEY: Ace is lowest. (*They cut.*) Mine! Double the stakes?

CHODD, JUN.: Done! (*They cut.*)

SIDNEY: Mine again! Double again?

CHODD, JUN.: Done! (*They cut.*)

SIDNEY: You're done again! I'm in splendid play to-night. One hundred, I think?

CHODD, JUN.: I'd play again (*Handing notes.*) but I've no more with me.

SIDNEY: Your word's sufficient – you can send to my chambers – besides, you've got your cheque-book. A hundred again?

CHODD, JUN.: Yes. (*They cut.*)

SIDNEY: Huzzah! Fortune's a lady! Again? (CHODD, JUN., *nods – they cut.*) Bravo! Again? (CHODD, JUN. *nods – they cut.*) Mine again! Again? (CHODD, JUN., *nods – they cut.*) Mine again! Again? (CHODD, JUN., *nods – they cut.*) Same result! That makes five! Let's go in for a thousand?

CHODD, JUN.: Done!

LORD C. (*advancing*): No!

CHODD, JUN. (*savagely*): Get out of the way! (LORD CLOUDWRAYS *looks at him through eye-glass in astonishment.*)

SIDNEY: Pooh! (*They cut.*) Mine! Double again?

CHODD, JUN.: Yes.

LORD C. (*going round to back of table and seizing the pack*): No; I can't suffer this to go on – Lady Ptarmigant would be awful angry. (*Going off,* L.)

SIDNEY: Here, Cloudwrays! What a fellow you are. (*Exit* LORD CLOUDWRAYS, L.C. *Turning to* CHODD, JUN.) You owe me a thousand!

CHODD, JUN.: I shall not forget it.

SIDNEY: I don't suppose you will. Confound – (*Trying to button sleeve link, crossing* C.) Oh, to jog your memory, take this.

    Gives him sleeve link, which he has been trying to button, and goes off after LORD CLOUDWRAYS, L.C.

CHODD, JUN.: And after I have paid you, I'll remember and clear off the old score.

TOM (R., *taking his arm as he is going*): Going into the ballroom?

CHODD, JUN. (L., *aghast at his intrusion*): Yes!

TOM (R.): I'll go with you.

CHODD, JUN. (L., *disengaging his arm*): I'm engaged!

    Exit CHODD, JUN., R. *Music till end.*

TOM: You've an engaging manner! I'm like a donkey between two bundles of hay. On one side woman – lovely woman! on the other, wine and wittles. (*Taking out a sovereign.*) Heads, supper – tails, the ladies. (*Tosses at table.*) Supper! Sweet goddess Fortune, accept my thanks!

    Exit into supper-room, R. *Enter* MAUD *and* CHODD, JUN., L.

MAUD (L.): This dreadful man follows me about everywhere.

CHODD, JUN. (R.): My dear Miss Hetherington!

MAUD: I danced the last with you.

CHODD, JUN.: That was a quadrille. (*Enter* SIDNEY, L.) This is for a polka.

SIDNEY (*advancing between them*): The lady is engaged to me.

CHODD, JUN. (*aside*): This fellow's turned up again. (*To him.*) I beg your pardon.

SIDNEY: I beg yours! I have a prior claim. (*Bitterly.*) Ask the lady – or perhaps I had better give her up to you.

MAUD: The next dance with you, Mr Chodd; this one –

CHODD, JUN.: Miss, your commands are Acts of Parliament. (*Looking spitefully at* SIDNEY *as he crosses,* L.) I'll go and see what Lady Ptarmigant has to say to this.

Exit CHODD, JUN. *Music changes to a slow waltz.*

SIDNEY: Listen to me for the last time. My life and being were centred in you. You have abandoned me for money! You accepted me; you now throw me off, for money! You gave your hand, you now retract, for money! You are about to wed – a knave, a brute, a fool, whom in your own heart you despise, for money!

MAUD: How dare you?

SIDNEY: Where falsehood is, shame cannot be. The last time we met (*Producing ribbon.*) you gave me this. See, 'tis the colour of a man's heart's blood. (*Curtains or doors at back draw apart.*) I give it back to you. (*Casting the bunch of ribbon at her feet.* LORD CLOUDWRAYS, 'SIR FARINTOSH, COLONEL BROWSER,' TOM, LORD PTARMIGANT, *and* LADY PTARMIGANT, CHODD, JUN., *and* CHODD, SEN., *appear at back.* GUESTS *seen in ballroom.*) And tell you, shameless girl, much as I once loved, and adored, I now despise and hate you.

LADY P. (*advancing,* C., *in a whisper to* SIDNEY): Leave the house, sir! How dare you – go!

SIDNEY: Yes; anywhere.

Crash of music. MAUD, *is nearly falling when* CHODD, JUN., *appears near her; she is about to lean on his arm, but recognising him, retreats and staggers.* SIDNEY *is seen to reel through ballroom full of dancers. Drop.*

GUESTS.

SIDNEY.

CLOUDWRAYS.   'SIR F.'

TOM   COL. B

LORD PTARMIGANT.   CHODD, SEN.

LADY PTARMIGANT.   CHODD, JUN.   MAUD.

ACT III

SCENE I

The 'Owl's Roost.' (same as Scene I, Act II.) Daylight; the room in order.
Tom discovered writing at table, R. Boy sitting on table, L., and
holding the placard on which is printed – 'Read the "Morning
Earthquake" – a first-class daily paper,' &c. On the other, 'The
"Evening Earthquake" – a first-class daily paper – Latest Intelligen-
ce,' &c.

Tom: Um! It'll look well on the walls, and at the railway stations. Take these back to the office (Boy *jumps down.*) – to Mr Piker, and tell him he must wait for the last leader – till it's written. (*Exit* Boy, C. Tom *walks to and fro, smoking long clay pipe.*) The M.E. – that is, the 'Morning Earthquake,' shakes the world for the first time to-morrow morning, and everything seems to have gone wrong with it. It is a crude, unmanageable, ill-disciplined, ill-regulated earthquake. Heave the first – Old Chodd behaves badly to me. After organising him a first-rate earthquake, engaging him a brilliant staff, and stunning reporters, he doesn't even offer me the post of sub-editor – ungrateful old humbug! Heave the second – no sooner is he engaged than our editor is laid up with the gout; and then Old Chodd asks me to be a literary warming-pan, and keep his place hot, till colchicum and cold water have done their work. I'll be even with Old Chodd, though! I'll teach him what it is to insult a man who has started eighteen daily and weekly papers – all of them failures. Heave the third – Sidney Daryl won't write the social leaders. (*Sits* L., *at end of table.*) Poor Sidney! (*Takes out the magenta ribbon which he picked up at the ball.*) I shan't dare to give him this – I picked it up at the ball, at which I was one of the distinguished and illustrious guests. Love is an awful swindler – always drawing upon Hope, who never honours his drafts – a sort of whining beggar, continually moved on by the maternal police. But 'tis a weakness to which the wisest of us are subject – a kind of manly measles which this flesh is heir to, particularly when the flesh is heir to nothing else – even I have felt the divine damnation – I mean emanation. But the lady united herself to another, which was a very good thing for me, and anything but misfortune for her. Ah! happy days of youth! – Oh! flowing fields of Runnington-cum-Wapshot – where the yellow corn waved, our young loves ripened, and the new gaol now stands. Oh! Sally, when I think of you and the past, I feel that (*Looking into his pot.*) the pot's empty, and I could drink another pint. (*Putting the ribbon in his pocket.*) Poor Sidney – I'm afraid he's going to the bad. (*Enter* SIDNEY, C.; *he strikes bell on* L. *table and sits at the head, his appearance altered.*) Ha! Sid, is that you? Talk of the – how d'e do?

SIDNEY: Quite well – how are you?

TOM: I'm suffering from an earthquake in my head, and a general printing office in my stomach. Have some beer?

    Enter WAITER, C.

SIDNEY: No thanks – brandy –

TOM: So early?

SIDNEY: And soda. I didn't sleep last night.

TOM: Brandy and soda, and beer again.

    Exit WAITER, *with pint pot off* R. *table.*

SIDNEY: I never do sleep now – I can't sleep.

TOM: Work hard.

    Enter WAITER, C.

SIDNEY: I do – it is my only comfort – my old pen goes driving along, at the rate of – (WAITER *after placing pint of porter before* TOM, *places tray with brandy and soda before* SIDNEY.) That's right! (WAITER *uncorks and exits*, C.) What a splendid discovery was brandy. (*Drinks.*)

TOM: Yes, the man who invented it deserves a statue.

SIDNEY: That's the reason that he doesn't get one.

TOM (*reading paper*): 'Election intelligence.' There's the general election – why not go in for that.

SIDNEY: Election – pooh! what do I care for that!

TOM: Nothing, of course, but it's occupation.

SIDNEY (*musing*): I wonder who'll put up for Springmead!

TOM: Your brother's seat, wasn't it?

SIDNEY: Yes, our family's for years. By-the-way, I'd a letter from Percy last mail; he's in trouble, poor fellow – his little boy is dead, and he himself is in such ill-health that they have given him sick leave. We are an unlucky race, we Daryls. Sometimes, Tom, I wish that I were dead.

TOM: Sidney!

SIDNEY: It's a bad wish, I know; but what to me is there worth living for?

TOM: What! oh, lots of things. Why, there's the police reports – mining intelligence – hop districts – the tallow market – ambition – Society!

SIDNEY (*heartily*): Damn Society!

TOM: And you know, Sid, there are more women in the world than one.

SIDNEY: But only one a man can love.

TOM: I don't know about that: temperaments differ.

SIDNEY (*pacing about and reciting*): 'As the husband, so the wife is.'
> 'Thou art mated to a clown:
> And the grossness of his nature
> Shall have power to drag thee down;
> He will hold thee when his passion
> Shall have spent its novel force,
> Something better than his dog, and
> Little dearer than his horse.'

I'm ashamed of such a want of spirit – ashamed to be such a baby! And you, Tom, are the only man in the world I'd show it to; but I – I can think of nothing else but her – and – and of the fate in store for her. (*Sobs and leans on table with his face in his hands.*)

TOM: Don't give way, Sid; there are plenty of things in this life to care for.

SIDNEY: Not for me – not for me.

TOM: Oh yes! there's friendship; and – and – the little girl, you know!

SIDNEY: That reminds me, I wrote a week ago to Mrs Churton, asking her to meet me with Mau – with the little darling in the square. I always asked them to come from Hampstead to the square, that I might look up at her window as I passed. What a fool I've been – I can't meet them this morning! Will you go for me?

TOM: With pleasure.

SIDNEY: Give Mrs Churton this. (*Wrapping up money in paper from* TOM's *case.*) It's the last month's money. Tell her I'm engaged, and can't come – and – (*Putting down money.*) buy the baby a toy, bless her! What a pity to think she'll grow to be a woman!

Enter MACUSQUEBAUGH, O'SULLIVAN, *and* MAKVICZ.

MACU. (*entering*): A three of whisky, hot!

O'SULL.: The same for me – neat.

DR M.: A pint of stoot. (*All sit,* R.)

O'SULL.: Tom, mee boy, what news of the 'Earthquake'?

Enter WAITER *with orders, and gives* TOM *a note.*

TOM: Heaving, sir – heaving. (TOM *opens note;* SIDNEY *sits abstracted.*) Who's going electioneering?

DR M.: I am.

O'SULL.: And I.

MACU.: And so am I.

TOM: Where?

MACU.: I don't know.

O'SULL.: Somewhere – anywhere.

TOM (*reading note*): From Chodd, Senior – the old villain! (*Reads.*) 'Dear Sir, – Please meet me at Lady Ptarmigant's at eleven p.m.' (*Suddenly.*) Sidney!

SIDNEY (*moodily*): What?

TOM (*reading note*): 'I am off to Springmead-le-Beau by the train at two-fifty. My son, Mr John Chodd, Junior, is the candidate for the seat for the borough.'

SIDNEY (*rising*): What! – that hound! – that cur! – that digesting cheque-book – represent the town that my family have held their own for centuries. I'd sooner put up for it myself. (*Rising.*)

TOM (*rising*): Why not? Daryl for Springmead – here's occupation – here's revenge!

SIDNEY: By heaven, I will! (*Crosses to* R., *and returns.*)

TOM (C.): Gentlemen, the health of Mr Daryl, M.P. for Springmead.

SIDNEY *crosses to* L.

OMNES (*rising and drinking*): Hurrah!

TOM: We'll canvass for you. (*Aside.*) And now, Mr Chodd, Senior, I see the subject for the last leader. I'll fetter you with your own type. (*Down,* L.)

SIDNEY (*crosses,* C.): I'll do it! I'll do it! When does the next train start?

MACU. (*taking 'Bradshaw' from table,* R.): At two-fifty – the next at five.

SIDNEY (*crossing to* L.): Huzza! (*With excitement.*) I'll rouse up the tenants – call on the tradesmen! (*Crossing to* C.)

O'SULL.: But the money?

SIDNEY (C.): I'll fight him with the very thousand that I won of him. Besides, what need has a Daryl of money at Springmead?

TOM: We can write for you.

O'SULL. (R.C.): And fight for you.

SIDNEY: I feel so happy – Call cabs.

MACU.: How many?

SIDNEY: The whole rank! (*Goes up,* C.)

TOM: But Sidney, what colours shall we fight under?

SIDNEY: What colours? (*Feels in his breast and appears dejected;* TOM *hands him the ribbons; he clutches them eagerly.*) What colours? Magenta!

OMNES: Huzzah! (*Closed in as they go up.*)

	O'SULLIVAN.	SIDNEY.	
	MACUSQUEBAUGH.		TOM.
MAKVICZ.			
R.			L.

SCENE II

An Apartment at LORD PTARMIGANT'*s (1st grooves)*

LADY P. (*without,* L. 1 E.): Good-bye, dear Mr Chodd. A pleasant ride, and all sorts of success. (*Enter* LADY PTARMIGANT, L. 1 E.) Phew! there's the old man gone. Now to speak to that stupid Maud. (*Looking off,* R.) There she sits in the sulks – a fool! Ah, what wise folks the French were before the Revolution, when there was a Bastille or a convent in which to pop dangerous young men and obstinate young women. (*Sweetly.*) Maud dear! I'll marry her to young Chodd, I'm determined.

    Enter MAUD, R. 1 E., *very pensive.*

LADY P.: Maud, I wish to speak to you.

MAUD: Upon what subject, aunt?

LADY P. (L.): One that should be very agreeable to a girl of your age – marriage.

MAUD (R.): Mr Chodd again?

LADY P.: Yes, Mr Chodd again.

MAUD: I hate him!

LADY P.: You wicked thing! How dare you use such expressions in speaking of a young gentleman so rich?

MAUD: Gentleman?

LADY P.: Yes, gentleman! – at least he will be.

MAUD: Nothing can make Mr Chodd – what a name! – anything but what he is.

LADY P.: Money can do everything.

MAUD: Can it make me love a man I hate?

LADY P.: Yes; at least, if it don't, it ought. I suppose you mean to marry somebody?

MAUD: No.

LADY P.: You audacious girl! How can you talk so wickedly? Where do you expect to go to?

MAUD: To needlework! Anything from this house; and from this persecution.

LADY P.: Miss Hetherington!

MAUD: Thank you, Lady Ptarmigant, for calling me by my name; it reminds me who I am, and of my dead father, 'Indian Hetherington,' as he was called. It reminds me that the protection you have offered to his orphan daughter has been hourly embittered by the dreadful temper, which is an equal affliction to you as to those within your reach. It reminds me that the daughter of such a father should not stoop to a mésalliance. (*Crossing to* L.)

LADY P.: Mésalliance! How dare you call Mr Chodd a mésalliance? And you hankering after that paltry, poverty-stricken, penny-a-liner?

MAUD: Lady Ptarmigant, you forget yourself; and you are untruthful. Mr Daryl is a gentleman by birth and breeding! I loved him – I acknowledge it – I love him still!

LADY P.: You shameless girl! and he without a penny! After the scene he made!

MAUD: He has dared to doubt me, and I have done with him for ever. From the moment he presumed to think that I could break my plighted word – that I could be false to the love I had acknowledged – the love that was my happiness and pride – all between us is over.

LADY P. (*aside*): That's some comfort. (*Aloud.*) Then what do you intend to do?

MAUD: I intend to leave the house.

LADY P.: To go where?

MAUD: Anywhere from you!

LADY P.: Upon my word! (*Aside.*) She has more spirit than I gave her credit for. (*Aloud.*) And do you mean to tell me that that letter is not intended for that fellow Daryl?

MAUD (*giving letter*): Read it.

LADY P. (*opens it and reads*): 'To the Editor of the "Times." Please insert the enclosed advertisement for which I send stamps. Wanted a situation as governess by' – (*Embracing* MAUD.) Oh, my dear – dear girl! you couldn't think of such a thing – and you a lady, and my niece.

MAUD (*disengaging herself*): Lady Ptarmigant, please don't!

LADY P. (*thoroughly subdued*): But, my love, how could I think –

MAUD: What Lady Ptarmigant thinks is a matter of the most profound indifference to me.

LADY P. (*aside*): Bless her! Exactly what I was at her age. (*Aloud.*) But my dear Maud, what is to become of you?

MAUD: No matter what! welcome poverty – humiliation – insult – the contempt of fools – welcome all but dependence! I will neither dress myself at the expense of a man I despise, control his household, owe him duty, or lead a life that is a daily lie; neither will I marry one I love, who has dared to doubt me, to drag him into deeper poverty. (*Crossing to* R.)

Enter SERVANT, L. 1 E.

SERVANT: My Lady, there is a gentleman inquiring for Mr Chodd.

LADY P.: Perhaps some electioneering friend. Show him here. (*Exit* SERVANT.) Don't leave the room, Maud, dear.

MAUD: I was not going – why should I?

SERVANT *shows in* TOM *with* LITTLE MAUD, L. 1 E.

LADY P.: It's the tobacco man!

TOM (*to* CHILD): Do I smell of smoke? I beg your ladyship's pardon, but Mr Chodd, the old gentleman, wished me to meet him here.

LADY P.: He has just driven off to the station.

TOM: I know I'm a few minutes behind time – there's the young lady. Good morning, Miss – Miss – I don't know the rest of her – I – I – have been detained by the – this little girl –

LADY P. (C.): A sweet little creature, Mr Silenus.

TOM (L.): Stylus.

LADY P.: Stylus, pardon me.

TOM (*aside*): This old lady will insist on calling me Silenus! She'd think me very rude if I called her Ariadne.

LADY P.: Sweet little thing! Come here, my dear! (LITTLE MAUD *crosses to her.*) Your child, Mr – Stylus?

TOM: No, my lady, this is Mr Sidney Daryl's protégé.

LADY P. (*moving from* LITTLE MAUD): Whose?

TOM: Sidney Daryl's (MAUD *advances.*)

LADY P.: Nasty little wretch! How do you mean? Speak, quickly!

TOM: I mean that Sidney pays for her education, board, and all that. Oh, he's a splendid fellow – a heart of gold! (*Aside.*) I'll put in a good word for him, as his young woman's here. I'll make her repent!

MAUD (R.): Come to me, child. (LITTLE MAUD *crosses to her.*) Who are you?

L. MAUD: I'm Mrs Churton's little darling, and Mr Daryl's little girl.

Crosses to TOM, *as* MAUD *moves away.*

LADY P. (C.): His very image. (*Goes to* MAUD.)

TOM (L.): Bless her little tongue! I took her from the woman who takes care of her. She's going down with me to Springmead. I've bought her a new frock, all one colour, magenta. (*Aside.*) That was strong.

LADY P.: Did I tell you Mr Chodd had gone?

TOM: I'm one too many here. I'll vamoose! Good morning, my lady.

LADY P.: Good morning, Mr – Bacchus.

TOM: Stylus – Stylus! I shall have to call her Ariadne. Um! They might have asked the child to have a bit of currant cake, or a glass of currant wine. Shabby devils!

Exeunt TOM *and* LITTLE MAUD, L. 1 E. *A pause.*

LADY P. (*aside*): Could anything have happened more delightfully?

MAUD (*throwing herself into* LADY PTARMIGANT'*s arms*): Oh, aunty! Forgive me – I was wrong – I was ungrateful – forgive me! Kiss me, and forgive me! I'll marry Mr Chodd – anybody – do with me as you please.

LADY P.: My dear niece! (*Affected.*) I – I – feel for you. I'm – I'm not so heartless as I seem. I know I'm a harsh, severe old woman, but I am a woman, and I can feel for you. (*Embracing her.*)

MAUD: And to think that with the same breath he could swear that he loved me, while another – this child, too! (*Bursts into a flood of tears.*) There, aunt, I won't cry. I'll dry my eyes – I'll do your bidding. You mean me well, while he – oh! (*Shudders.*) Tell Mr Chodd I'll bear his name, and bear it worthily! (*Sternly.*)

LADY P. (*embracing – kissing her at each stop*): Men are a set of brutes, I was jilted myself when I was twenty-three – and, oh, how I loved the fellow! But I asserted my dignity, and married Lord Ptarmigant, and *he*, and *he* only, can tell you how I have avenged my sex! Cheer up, my darling! Love, sentiment, and romance are humbug! – But wealth, position, jewels, balls, presentations, a country house, town mansion, society, power – that's true, solid happiness, and if it isn't, I don't know what is?

Exeunt, R. 1 E.

SCENE III

The Wells at Springmead-le-Beau. An avenue of elms, sloping off to R.U.E., *on* L. *House with windows, &c., on to lawn; railings at back of stage. Garden seats, chairs, lounges, small tables, &c., discovered near house,* L. LORD PTARMIGANT *discovered asleep in garden chair against house,* L., *his feet resting on another. Enter* CHODD, SEN., *down avenue,* R.

CHODD, SEN.: Oh, dear! Oh, dear! What a day this is! There's Johnny to be elected, and I'm expecting the first copy of the 'Morning Earthquake' – my paper! my own paper! – by the next train. Then here's Lady Ptarmigant says that positively her niece will have Johnny for her wedded husband, and in one day my Johnny is to be a husband, an M.P., and part proprietor of a daily paper! Whew! how hot it is! It's lucky that the wells are so near the hustings – one can run under the shade and get a cooler. Here's my lord! (*Waking him.*) My lord!

LORD P. (*waking*): Oh! eh! Mr Chodd – good morning! – how d'e do?

CHODD, SEN. (*sitting on stool,* L.): Oh, flurried, and flustered, and worritted. You know to-day's the election.

Lord P.: Yes, I believe there is an election going on somewhere. (*Calling.*) A tumbler of the waters No. 2.

Enter Waitress *from house,* l*., places tumbler of water on table, and exits.*

Chodd, Sen.: Oh, what a blessing there is no opposition! If my boy is returned – (*Rising.*)

Enter Chodd, Jun*., agitated, a placard in his hand,* r. 2 e.

Chodd, Jun.: Look here, guv! Look here!

Chodd, Sen.: What is it, my Johnny!

Chodd, Jun.: Don't call me Johnny! Look here! (*Shows electioneering placard,* 'Vote for Daryl!'*.*)

Chodd, Sen.: What?

Chodd, Jun.: That vagabond has put up as candidate? His brother used to represent the borough.

Chodd, Sen.: Then the election will be contested?

Chodd, Jun.: Yes.

Chodd, Sen*., sinks on garden chair.*

Lord P. (*rising and taking tumbler from table*): Don't annoy yourself, my dear Mr Chodd; these accidents will happen in the best regulated constituencies.

Chodd, Jun.: Guv, don't be a fool!

Lord P.: Try a glass of the waters.

Chodd, Sen*., takes tumbler and drinks, and the next moment ejects the water with a grimace, stamping about.*

Chodd, Sen.: Oh, what filth! O-o-o-o-o-oh!

Lord P.: It is an acquired taste. (*To* Waiter.) Another tumbler of No. 2.

Chodd, Sen.: So, Johnny, there's to be a contest, and you won't be M.P. for Springmead after all.

Chodd, Jun.: I don't know that.

Chodd, Sen.: What d'ye mean?

Chodd, Jun.: Mr Sidney Daryl may lose, and, perhaps, Mr Sidney Daryl mayn't show. After that ball –

Chodd, Sen.: Where you lost that thousand pounds?

Chodd, Jun.: Don't keep bringing that up, guv'nor. After that I bought up all Mr Daryl's bills – entered up judgment, and left them with Aaron. I've telegraphed to London, and if Aaron don't nab him in town he'll catch him here.

Chodd, Sen.: But, Johnny, isn't that rather mean?

Chodd, Jun.: All's fair in love and Parliament.

Enter Country Boy *with newspaper,* r. 1 e.

Boy: Mr Chodd?

CHODD, SEN. ⎫
CHODD, JUN. ⎭ Here!

BOY: Just arrived.

CHODD, JUN.: The 'Morning Earthquake.'

They both clutch at it eagerly; each secures a paper, and sit under tree, R.

CHODD, SEN. (R., *reading*): Look at the leader. 'In the present aspect of European politics –'

CHODD, JUN. (L.): 'Some minds seem singularly obtuse to the perception of an idea.'

CHODD, SEN.: Johnny!

CHODD, JUN.: Guv!

CHODD, SEN.: Do you see the last leader?

CHODD, JUN.: Yes.

CHODD, SEN. (*reading*): 'The borough of Springmead-le-Beau has for centuries been represented by the house of Daryl.'

CHODD, JUN. (*reading*): 'A worthy scion of that ancient race intends to offer himself as candidate at the forthcoming election, and, indeed, who will dare to oppose him?'

CHODD, SEN.: 'Surely not a Mister –'

CHODD, JUN.: 'Chodd.' (*They rise and come down.*)

CHODD, SEN.: 'Whoever he may be.'

CHODD, JUN.: 'What are the Choddian antecedents?'

CHODD, SEN.: 'Whoever heard of Chodd?'

CHODD, JUN.: 'To be sure, a young man of that name has recently been the cause of considerable laughter at the clubs on account of his absurd attempts to become a man of fashion.' (*Both crossing* L. *and* R.)

CHODD, SEN. (R.): 'And to wriggle himself into Society.' (*Crossing again.*)

CHODD, JUN. (R.): Why, it's all in his favour. (*In a rage.*)

CHODD, SEN.: In our own paper, too! Oh, that villain Stylus! (*Crossing* R.)

CHODD, JUN. (*crossing* R.): There are no more of these in the town, are there?

BOY: Yes, sir. A man came down with two thousand; he's giving them away everywhere.

CHODD, JUN.: Confound you! (*Pushes him off,* R. 1 E. *– follows.*)

CHODD, SEN.: Oh, dear! oh, dear! oh, dear! Now, my lord, isn't that too bad. (*Sees him asleep.*) He's off again! (*Waking him.*) My lord, here's the 'Earthquake'! (*Half throwing him off his seat.*)

LORD P.: Earthquake! Good gracious! I didn't feel anything. (*Rising.*)

CHODD, SEN.: No, no, the paper.

LORD P.: Ah, most interesting. (*Drops paper, and leisurely reseats himself.*) My dear Mr Chodd, I congratulate you.

CHODD, SEN.: Congratulate me? (*Looks at watch.*) I must be off to the committee.

Exit CHODD, SEN., L. 2 E.

LORD P.: Waiter! am I to have that tumbler of No. 2?

Band heard playing 'Conquering Hero', and loud cheers as LORD PTARMIGANT *goes into house,* L., *and enter* SIDNEY, O'SULLIVAN, MACUSQUEBAUGH, *and* DR MAKVICZ, R.U.E. SIDNEY *bowing off as he enters. Cheers.*

SIDNEY: So far so good. I've seen lots of faces that I knew. I'll run this Dutch-metalled brute hard, and be in an honourable minority anyhow.

Enter TOM, *hastily,* R. 1 E.

TOM: Daryl.

SIDNEY: Yes.

TOM: Look out.

SIDNEY: What's the matter?

TOM: I met our friend Moses Aaron on the platform. He didn't see you, but what does he want here?

SIDNEY: Me, if anybody. (*Musing.*) This is a shaft from the bow of Mr John Chodd, Junior. I see his aim.

TOM: What's to be done? The voters are warm, but, despite the prestige of the family name, if you were not present –

SIDNEY: Besides, I couldn't be returned from Cursitor Street, M.P. for the Queen's Bench. (*Thinking.*) Did the Lamb come down with us?

TOM: Yes – second class.

SIDNEY: Let him stop the bailiffs – Aaron is as timid as a girl. I'll go through here, and out by the grand entrance. Let in the Lamb, and –

TOM: I see.

SIDNEY: Quick!

Exit TOM, R. 1 E.

O'SULL.: Daryl, is there any fighting to be done?

MACU.: Or any drinking?

DR M.: If so, we shall be most happy.

SIDNEY: No, no, thanks. Come with me – I've a treat for you.

OMNES: What?

SIDNEY (*laughing*): The chalybeate waters.

Exeunt OMNES *into house,* L. *Enter* CHODD, JUN., *and* AARON, R. 1 E.

CHODD, JUN.: You saw him go in – arrest him. The chaise is ready – take him to the next station, and all's right. I'll stay and see him captured. (CHODD *in great triumph.*)

AARON: Very good, shur – do it at vunsh.

Is going into the house, when the LAMB *springs out;* AARON *staggers back;*

the LAMB *stands in boxing attitude before the door;* TOM *and* SIX *or* EIGHT
ROUGHS *enter by avenue,* R.

LAMB (*with back half turned to audience*): Now, then, where are *you* a
shovin' to?

AARON: I want to passh by.

LAMB: Then you can't.

AARON: Why not?

LAMB (*doggedly*): 'Cos I'm doorkeeper, and you haven't got a check.

AARON: Now, Lamb, dooty'sh dooty, and –

LAMB (*turning with face to audience, and bringing up the muscle of his right
arm*): Feel that!

AARON (*alarmed*): Yesh, shur. (*Feels it slightly.*)

LAMB: You can't come in.

CHODD, JUN. (*crossing to* LAMB *fussily*): Why not?

LAMB (*looks at him, half contemptuously, half comically*): 'Cos that sez I
mustn't let you. Feel it! (*Taps muscle.*)

CHODD, JUN.: Thank you, some other time.

Crossing, R. *The* ROUGHS *surround him, jeer, and prepare to hustle him.*
TOM *mounts seat,* R.

TOM: Vote for Daryl!

LAMB (*making up to* AARON *in sparring attitude, who retreats in terror*): Are yer
movin'?

CHODD, JUN.: Do your duty.

ROUGHS *laugh.*

AARON: I can't – they are many, I am a few.

Cheers without, R.

CHODD, JUN. (*losing his presence of mind*): Particular business requires me
at the hustings. (*Goes off,* R., *midst jeers and laughter of* ROUGHS.)

LAMB (*at same time advancing upon* AARON): Are yer movin'?

AARON: Yesh, Mr Lamb.

By this time he has backed close to TOM, *perched upon the seat, who bonnets
him.*

TOM: Vote for Daryl!

AARON *is hustled off,* R. 1 E., *by* MOB, *followed leisurely by* LAMB.

TOM (*on chair*): Remember, gentlemen, the officers of the law – the
officers of the sheriff – are only in the execution of their duty. (*Shouts and
uproar without.*) Don't offer any violence. (*Shouts.*) Don't tear them limb
from limb!

Shouts, followed by a loud shriek. TOM *leaps from chair, dances down stage,
and exits,* R.U.E. *Enter* LADY PTARMIGANT *and* CHODD, SEN., R. 2 E.

LADY PTARMIGANT *is dressed in mauve.* CHODD, SEN. *escorts her to house,* L.

CHODD, SEN.: But if he is absent from his post?

LADY P.: His post must get on without him. Really, my dear Mr Chodd, you must allow me to direct absolutely. If you wish your son to marry Miss Hetherington, now is the time – now or never.

Exit into house, L. CHODD, SEN., *exits,* R. 1 E. *Enter* CHODD, JUN., *and* MAUD, *dressed in mauve,* R.U.E.

CHODD, JUN.: Miss Hetherington, allow me to offer you a seat. (*She sits under tree,* R.; *aside.*) Devilish awkward! Lady Ptarmigant says, 'Strike while the iron's hot'; but I want to be at the hustings. I've made my speech to the electors, and now I must do my courting. She looks awfully proud. I wish I could pay some fellow to do this for me. Miss Hetherington a – a – a – I got the speech I spoke just now off by heart. I wish I'd got this written for me, too. Miss Hetherington, I – I am emboldened by the – by what I have just been told by our esteemed correspondent, Lady Ptar – I mean by your amiable aunt. I – I – (*Boldly.*) I have a large fortune, and my prospects are bright and brilliant – bright and brilliant. I – I am of a respectable family, which has always paid its way. I have entered on a political career, which always pays its way; and I mean some day to make my name famous. My lady has doubtless prepared you for the hon – I offer you my – my humble hand, and large – I may say colossal fortune.

MAUD (L.): Mr Chodd I will be plain with you.

CHODD, JUN. (R.): Impossible for Miss Hetherington to be plain.

MAUD: You offer me your hand; I will accept it.

CHODD, JUN.: Oh, joy! Oh – (*Endeavouring to take her hand.*)

MAUD: Please hear me out. On these conditions.

CHODD, JUN.: Pin money no object. Settle as much on you as you like.

MAUD: I will be your true and faithful wife – I will bear your name worthily; but you must understand our union is a union of convenience.

CHODD, JUN.: Convenience!

MAUD: Yes; that love has no part in it.

CHODD, JUN.: Miss Hetherington – may I say Maud? – I love you – I adore you with my whole heart and fortune. (*Aside.*) I wonder how they are getting on at the hustings.

MAUD: I was saying, Mr Chodd –

CHODD, JUN.: Call me John – your own John! (*Seizing her hand; she shudders and withdraws it.*)

MAUD (*struggling with herself*): I was saying that the affection which a wife should bring the man she has elected as – (*Cheers without.*)

SIDNEY (*speaking without*): Electors of Springmead.

MAUD: We hardly know sufficient of each other to warrant –
SIDNEY (*without*): I need not tell you who I am.
Cheers. MAUD *trembles.*
MAUD: We are almost strangers.
SIDNEY: Nor what principles I have been reared in.
CHODD, JUN.: The name of Chodd, if humble, is at least wealthy.
SIDNEY: I am a Daryl; and my politics those of the Daryls. (*Cheers.*)
CHODD, JUN. (*aside*): This is awkward. (*To* MAUD.) As to our being strangers –
SIDNEY: I am no stranger. (*Cheers.*) I have grown up to be a man among you. There are faces I see in the crowd I am addressing, men of my own age, whom I remember children. (*Cheers.*) There are faces among you who remember me when I was a boy. (*Cheers.*) In the political union between my family and Springmead, there is more than respect and sympathy, there is sentiment. (*Cheers.*)
CHODD, JUN.: Confound the fellow! Dearest Miss Hetherington – Dearest Maud – you have deigned to say you will be mine.
SIDNEY: Why, if we continue to deserve your trust, plight your political faith to another?
MAUD (*overcome*): Mr Chodd, I –
CHODD, JUN.: My own bright, particular Maud!
SIDNEY: Who is my opponent?
TOM (*without*, R.): Nobody. (*A loud laugh.*)
SIDNEY: What is he?
TOM: Not much. (*A roar of laughter.*)
SIDNEY: I have no doubt he is honest and trustworthy, but why turn away an old servant to hire one you don't know? (*Cheers.*) Why turn off an old love that you have tried and proved for a new one? (*Cheers.*) I don't know what the gentleman's politics may be. (*Laugh.*) Or those of his family. (*Roar of laughter.*) I've tried to find out, but I can't. To paraphrase the ballad: –

> I've searched through Hansard, journals,
> Books, De Brett, and Burke, and Dodd,
> And my head – my head is aching,
> To find out the name of Chodd.

Loud laughter and three cheers. MAUD *near fainting.*
CHODD, JUN.: I can't stand this; I must be off to the hustings, Miss Heth –! Oh! she's fainting. What shall I do? Lady Ptarmigant! Oh, here she comes! Waiter, a tumbler of No. 2. (*Runs off,* 2. R.E.)
SIDNEY (*without*): And I confidently await the result which will place me at the head of the poll. (*Cheers.*)

Enter LORD *and* LADY PTARMIGANT, *from house,* L. LADY PTARMIGANT *attends to* MAUD.

MAUD: 'Twas nothing — a slight faintness — an attack of —

LORD P.: An attack of Chodd, I think! What a dreadful person my lady is, to be sure. (*Aside, sits,* L.)

LADY P. (*to* MAUD): Have you done it?

MAUD: Yes.

LADY P.: And you are to be his wife?

MAUD: Yes. (*Cheers.*)

Enter SIDNEY, O'SULLIVAN, MACUSQUEBAUGH, *and* DOCTOR MAK-VICZ, R. 2 E.

SIDNEY (*coming down,* L.): Tom, I feel so excited — so delighted — so happy — so — (*Sees* MAUD *stops; takes his hat off;* MAUD *bows coldly.*) In my adversary's colours!

LADY P. (R.): That fellow, Sidney!

MAUD (C., *aside*): It seems hard to see him there, and not to speak to him for the last time.

Is about to advance when TOM *brings on* LITTLE MAUD, R.U.E., *dressed in magenta.* MAUD *recedes.* LORD PTARMIGANT *goes to sleep in garden seat,* L.

LADY P.: The tobacco man!

TOM (*down,* L.): Ariadne!

SIDNEY *kisses* LITTLE MAUD. *Enter* CHODD, JUN., R.U.E., *and down,* R.

LADY P. (*with a withering glance at* SIDNEY): Maud, my child, here's Mr Chodd.

CHODD, JUN., *crossing* R.C., *gives his arm to* MAUD. SIDNEY *stands with* LITTLE MAUD, L.C. *All go off,* R.U.E., *except* LADY PTARMIGANT, SIDNEY, LITTLE MAUD, TOM, *and* LORD PTARMIGANT

SIDNEY (L.): On his arm! Well, I deserve it! I am poor!

LADY P. (R.): Mr Daryl.

SIDNEY *bows.*

TOM (L.): Ariadne is about to express her feelings; I shall go! (*Exit,* R.U.E.)

LADY P.: I cannot but express my opinion of your conduct. For a long time I have known you to be the associate of prize-fighters, betting men, racehorses, authors, and other such low persons; but despite that I thought you had some claims to be a gentleman.

SIDNEY: In what may have I forfeited Lady Ptarmigant's good opinion?

LADY P.: In what, sir? In daring to bring me, your kinswoman, and a lady — in daring to bring into the presence of the foolish girl you professed to love — that child — your illegitimate offspring!

LORD PTARMIGANT *awakes.*

SIDNEY (*stung*): Lady Ptarmigant, do you know who that child is?

LADY P.: Perfectly! (*With a sneer.*)

SIDNEY: I think not. She is the lawful daughter of your dead and only son, Charles!

LADY P.: What?

SIDNEY: Two days before he sailed for the Crimea, he called at my chambers, and told me that he felt convinced he should never return. He told me, too, of his connection with a poor and humble girl, who would shortly become the mother of his child. I saw from his face that the bullet was cast that would destroy him, and I begged him to legitimatise one who, though of his blood, might not bear his name. Like a brave fellow, a true gentleman, on the next day he married.

LADY P.: How disgraceful!

SIDNEY: Joined his regiment, and, as you know, fell at Balaclava.

LADY P.: My poor – poor boy.

SIDNEY: His death broke his wife's heart – she, too, died.

LADY P.: What a comfort!

SIDNEY: I placed the child with a good motherly woman, and I had intended, for the sake of my old friend, Charley, to educate her, and to bring her to you, and say. Take her, she is your lawful grandchild, and a lady *pur sang*; love her, and be proud of her, for the sake of the gallant son, who galloped to death in the service of his country.

LADY P. (*affected*): Sidney!

SIDNEY: I did not intend that you should know this for some time. I had some romantic notion of making it a reason for your consent to my marriage with – (LADY PTARMIGANT *takes* LITTLE MAUD.) with Miss Hetherington – that is all over now. The ill opinion with which you have lately pursued me has forced this avowal from me.

LADY P. (*to child*): My darling! Ah! my poor Charley's very image! My poor boy! My poor boy!

LORD P. (*who has been listening, advancing*, L.): Sidney, let my son Charley's father thank you. You have acted like a kinsman and a Daryl! (*Affected.*)

LADY P.: Sidney, forgive me!

SIDNEY (C.): Pray forget it, Lady Ptarm –

LADY P.: I will take care that Miss Hetherington shall know –

SIDNEY (*hotly*): What! did she, too, suspect! Lady Ptarmigant, it is my request – nay, if I have done anything to deserve your good opinion, my injunction – that Miss Hetherington is not informed of what has just passed. If she has thought that I could love another – she is free to her opinion! (*Goes up, and comes down,* R.*, with the child.*)

LORD P.: But *I* shall tell her.

LADY P. (*astonished*): You! (*Aside.*) Don't you think, under the circum-stances, it would be better –

LORD P.: I shall act as I think best.

LADY P.: Ferdinand! (*Authoritatively.*)

LORD P.: Lady Ptarmigant, it is not often I speak, goodness knows! But on a question that concerns my honour and yours, I shall *not* be silent.

LADY P. (c.): Ferdinand! (*Imploringly.*)

LORD P.: Lady Ptarmigant, I am *awake*, and you will please to follow my instructions. (*Crossing,* c.) What is my granddaughter's name?

L. MAUD: Maud.

LORD P.: Maud, Maud – is it Maud? (*Playfully.*)

LORD PTARMIGANT *lifts her in his arms, and is carrying her off.*

LADY P.: My lord! Consider – people are looking!

LORD P.: Let 'em look – they'll know I'm a *grandfather!*

Exit LORD PTARMIGANT, *with* LITTLE MAUD, *and* LADY PTARMIGANT, R.U.E. *avenue.* TOM *runs on,* R.U.E.

TOM (L.): It's all right, Sid! Three of Chodd's committee have come over to us. They said that so long as a Daryl was not put up, they felt at liberty to support him, but now – (*Seeing that* SIDNEY *is affected.*) What's the matter?

SIDNEY (R.): Nothing.

TOM: Ah, that means love! I hope to be able to persuade the majority of Chodd's committee to resign; and, if they resign, he must too, and we shall walk over the course. (SIDNEY *goes up and sits,* L. TOM, *aside.*) Cupid's carriage stops the way again. Confound that nasty, naughty, naked little boy! I wonder if he'd do less mischief if they put him into knickerbockers. (*Exit,* R. 1 E.)

SIDNEY: Mr Chodd shall not have Springmead.

Enter MAUD, *leading* LITTLE MAUD *by the hand,* R.U.E. SIDNEY's *face is buried in his hands on the table.*

MAUD (*kissing the child, then advancing slowly to* SIDNEY): Sidney!

SIDNEY (*rising*): Maud – Miss Hetherington!

L. MAUD: Uncle, this is my new aunt. She's my aunt and you're my uncle. You don't seemed pleased to see each other, though – ain't you? Aunt, why don't you kiss uncle?

MAUD (R., *after a pause*): Sidney, I have to beg your forgiveness for the – the mistake which –

SIDNEY (L.): Pray don't mention it, Maud – Miss Hetherington. It is not of the –

MAUD (R.): It is so hard to think ill of those we have known.

CHILD *goes up,* R.

SIDNEY: I think that it must be very easy! Let me take this opportunity of apologising personally, as I have already done by letter, for my misconduct at the ball. I had heard that you were about to – to –

MAUD: Marry! Then you were in error. Since then I have accepted Mr Chodd. (*Pause.*)

SIDNEY: I congratulate you. (*Turns his face aside.*)

MAUD: You believed me to be false – believed it without inquiry!

SIDNEY: As you believed of me!

MAUD: Our mutual poverty prevented.

SIDNEY (*bursting out*): Oh, yes, we are poor! We are poor! We loved each other – but we were poor! We loved each other – but we couldn't take a house in a square! We loved each other – but we couldn't keep a carriage! We loved each other – but we had neither gold, purple, plate, nor mansion in the country! You were right to leave me, and to marry a *gentleman* – rich in all these assurances of happiness!

MAUD: Sidney, you are cruel.

SIDNEY: I loved you, Maud; loved you with my whole heart and soul since we played together as children, and you grew till I saw you a lovely blushing girl, and now – pshaw! This is folly, sentiment, raving madness! Let me wish you joy – let me hope you will be happy.

L. MAUD (*coming down*, C.): Uncle, you mustn't make my new aunt cry. Go and make it up with her, and kiss her.

LADY PTARMIGANT, LORD PTARMIGANT, *and* LORD CLOUDWRAYS *have entered during the last speech*, R.U.E.

MAUD: Farewell, Sidney! (*Holding out her hand.*)

SIDNEY: Farewell!

LADY P. (*advancing*, C.): Farewell! What nonsense; two young people so fond of each other. Sidney – Maud, dear, you have my consent.

SIDNEY (L.C., *astonished*): Lady Ptarmigant!

LADY P. (R.C.): I always liked you, Sidney, though, I confess, I didn't always show it.

LORD P. (L.): I can explain my lady's sudden conversion – at least, Cloudwrays can.

LORD C. (R.): Well, Sid, I'm sorry to be the bearer of good news – I mean of ill news; but your brother – poor Percy – he – a –

SIDNEY: Dead!

LORD C.: The news came by the mail to the club, so as I'd nothing to do, I thought I'd come down to congratulate – I mean condole with you.

LORD P.: Bear up, Sidney, your brother's health was bad before he left us.

SIDNEY: First the son, and then the father.

MAUD (L.C.): Sidney!

SIDNEY (*catching her hand*): Maud!

MAUD: No, no – not now – you are rich, and I am promised.

LADY P.: Why, you wicked girl; you wouldn't marry a man you didn't love, would you? Where are your principles?

Lord Ptarmigant sits on garden seat, L., with Little Maud.

MAUD: But – but – Mr Chodd?

LADY P.: What on earth consequence is Mr Chodd?

Enter Chodd, Sen., and Chodd, Jun., avenue R.

CHODD, SEN.: My lady, it's all right, Johnny has been accepted!

Maud goes up and sits, L.C. Sidney and Lord Cloudwrays also go up with her.

LADY P. (L.): By whom?

CHODD, SEN. (R.): By Miss Hetherington – by Maud!

LADY P.: Why, you must be dreaming, the election has turned your brain – my niece marry a Chodd!

CHODD, SEN.: ⎱
                   ⎰ My lady!
CHODD, JUN.: ⎰

LADY P.: Nothing of the sort; I was only joking, and thought you were, too. (*Aside.*) The impertinence of the lower classes in trying to ally themselves with us! (*Going up, L.*)

CHODD, JUN.: Guv.

CHODD, SEN.: Johnny!

CHODD, JUN.: We're done. (*Crosses, L.*)

Loud cheering. Enter Tom, R.U.E., who whispers and congratulates Sidney. Enter a Gentleman, R. 1 E., who whispers to Chodd, Sen., condolingly, and exits, R. 1 E.

CHODD, SEN. (R., *shouting*): Johnny!

CHODD, JUN. (L.): Guv.

CHODD, SEN.: They say there's no hope, and advise us to withdraw from the contest.

All congratulate Sidney, up stage.

LADY P.: Sir Sidney Daryl, M.P., looks like old times. (*To Lord Ptarmigant.*) My lord, congratulate him.

LORD P. (*waking and shaking Chodd, Jun., by the hand*): Receive my congratulations.

LADY P.: Oh! It's the wrong man!

CHODD, SEN. (R.): Mr Stylus, I may thank you for this.

TOM (R.C.): And yourself, you may. I brought out your journal, engaged your staff, and you tried to throw me over. You've got your reward. Morning paper! (*Throws paper in the air.*)

Enter Aaron, with hat broken and head bound up, R.U.E.

AARON (C., *to Sidney*): Arresht you at the shoot of –

The Chodds rub their hands in triumph.

TOM (R.C.): Too late! too late! He's a member of Parliament.

CHODD, JUN., and CHODD, SEN., *turn into* R. *and* L. *corners.*

SIDNEY (L.C. *to* TOM): I haven't taken the seat or the oaths yet.

TOM (R.C.): They don't know that.

SIDNEY: We can settle it another way. (*Taking out pocket-book and looking at* CHODD, JUN.) Some time ago I was fortunate enough to win a large sum of money; this way if you please. (*Goes up with* AARON, *and gives money, notes, &c.*)

CHODD, JUN.: Pays his own bills, which I'd bought up, with my money.

CHODD, SEN. (*crossing,* L.): Then, Johnny, you won't get into Society.

LADY P. (*coming down,* R.): Never mind, Mr Chodd, your son shall marry a lady.

CHODD, JUN: } Eh!
CHODD, SEN: }

LADY P.: I promise to introduce you to one of blue blood.

CHODD, JUN.: Blue bl – I'd rather have it the natural colour.

> *Cheers. Enter* O'SULLIVAN *and* COMMITTEE, R.U.E. *Stage full. Church bells heard.*

O'SULL. (R.): Sir Sidney Daryl, we have heard the news. In our turn we have to inform you that your adversaries have retired from the contest, and you are member for Springmead. (*Cheers.*) We, your committee, come to weep with you for the loss of a brother, to joy with you on your accession to a title and your hereditary honours. Your committee most respectfully beg to be introduced to Lady Daryl. (*With intention and Irish gallantry.*)

> SIDNEY *shows* MAUD *the magenta ribbon; she places her hand in his.*

SIDNEY (C.): Gentlemen, I thank you; I cannot introduce you to Lady Daryl, for Lady Daryl does not yet exist. In the meantime I have permission to present you to Miss Hetherington.

TOM (*leaping on chair,* R., *and waving handkerchief*): Three cheers for my lady!

> *All cheer. Church bells; band plays 'Conquering Hero'.* GIRL *at window of house waves handkerchief, and* CHILD *a stick with magenta streamer attached.* COUNTRYMEN, *&c., wave hats; band plays, &c.*

> ROUGHS.   COUNTRYFOLKS.   GIRL *and* CHILD.
> SIDNEY *and* MAUD.
> MAKVICZ, TOM.   LORD P., L. MAUD.
> MACUSQUEBAUGH.   LADY P., LORD C.
> O'SULLIVAN   CHODD, SEN.
> CHODD, JUN.

CURTAIN.

14 THE MIKADO

> Flirting is the only crime punishable with decapitation, and married men never flirt.
>
> (Act II, Ko-Ko to Nanki-Poo)

The Mikado is a satire which attacks Gilbert's favourite target: the regulation of society by ludicrous laws and cumbersome bureaucracy. Rank and office are ridiculed and the function of marriage as a social mechanism called into question. Underneath the catchy tunes and silly plot there is a sour savagery which mocks the good humour. The opera was a smash hit in 1885, lasting for an initial run of 672 performances at the Savoy Theatre and inspiring *Mikado* mania across North America. It is still performed frequently and is particularly popular with amateur operatic societies, which is in itself enough to make the intellectually fastidious turn away in disgust.

The works of Gilbert and Sullivan attract incredible devotion. When a heart attack struck the Mikado in the middle of the Romsey Amateur Operatic and Dramatic Society's 1997 performance, singer Ivan Cotter carried on to the end of 'A more humane Mikado' before staggering off-stage and collapsing. His condition was serious – his heart stopped several times in the ambulance on the way to hospital and he had to undergo a triple bypass operation. The blackly absurd situation, with its mix of light comedy and near death, is perfectly Gilbertian. Mr Cotter adhered to his duty and risked his life for the sake of a comic opera. The fact that he suffered a heart disorder makes the situation all the more fitting. Perhaps there is something in the nature of comedy which invites heart attacks – maybe it's the breathless stress induced night after night, the public pressure to be amusing and the cruelty inherent in laughter. Whatever it is, many famous comics have succumbed: Sid James, Tommy Cooper, Les Dawson. Gilbert himself died a true comic's death, not on stage, but in the absurder setting of his own lake, into which he dived to save a teenage girl who cried out that she was drowning. Gilbert had developed heart problems and the shock of the cold water as he 'threw himself into the billowy wave' brought on cardiac arrest. The girl was fine.

More apocryphal stories collect around William Schwenck Gilbert (1836–1911) than any other dramatist of his day. He allegedly had a room in his house called the Flirtorium, he took pretty girls on holiday with his wife, he argued constantly with Arthur Sullivan, he was vain, quarrelsome, litigious and a boaster. Some of these allegations were made by a disgruntled actress in an 1877 pamphlet entitled *A Letter from Miss Henrietta Hodson, An Actress, to the Members of the Dramatic Profession. Being a Relation of the Persecutions which She has Suffered from Mr William Schwenck Gilbert, a Dramatic Author.* Other stories were fostered by Gilbert, who collaborated in his own myth-making and cracked jokes about himself which his enemies took seriously. There is no evidence, for instance, to support the famous confabulation he told his first biographer of how he was kidnapped by Italian bandits when he was less than two years old. Preposterous tales such as this reveal Gilbert's lively, contradictory character and his talent for invention. They are, in their way, verbal versions of the *Bab Ballads*, the grotesque, mocking verses he wrote and illustrated for *Fun* magazine in the 1860s and 70s.

The *Bab Ballads* invent a topsy-turvy world peopled by oddly-named characters such as the Bishop of Rum-ti-Foo. They took their title from Gilbert's childhood nickname Bab, short for Baby. In the *Ballads*, Gilbert uses tightly correct metrical structures to play about with rhyme, making light verse, says the critic Eric Griffiths, 'by pretending to slight the rules of light verse', a technique Gilbert uses to excess in his librettos.

The *Mikado* exercises Gilbert's notion of a topsy-turvy society. He originally planned to set the action in the court of Henry VIII, but a Japanese sword falling from the wall of his study (another unreliable story) supposedly gave him the brilliant idea of transferring it to Japan. A more likely explanation is that Gilbert was influenced by the Japanese Village exhibition which opened in Knightsbridge in January 1885, and by talks with Algernon Mitford, a former Secretary of the British Legation at Tokyo. It may have been Mitford who gave Gilbert the genuine Japanese song of the Mikado's troops. Either way, the Japanese setting is merely a fashionably topical diversion taking advantage of the interest in a country which had recently begun to establish contact with Europe. *The Mikado* was Gilbert's ninth collaboration with Sullivan and by then the partnership was wracked with rows about money involving Richard D'Oyly Carte, owner of the Savoy Theatre, and 'artistic differences' between the collaborators. Sullivan was composing right up to the night before the dress rehearsal and on the opening night Gilbert suddenly decided to cut the Mikado's solo 'A more humane Mikado' because he thought it covered the same material as Ko-Ko's 'little list'. Fortunately, singer Richard Temple persuaded him differently and the showstopper was preserved. There were other changes made during the first performances: Ko-Ko's list moved forward, Yum-Yum's 'The sun whose rays' went into Act II and the character Go-To had to be invented because Frederick Bovill, who played Pish-Tush, couldn't reach the lowest notes of the madrigal.

The plot is childishly logical. The Mikado has ruled that the penalty for flirting is decapitation, and so to circumvent this the citizens of Titipu appoint a condemned flirter to the post of executioner on the understanding that he can't cut off his own head. The flirter, Ko-Ko, is betrothed to his ward Yum-Yum. Meanwhile, the Mikado's son Nanki-Poo has fled the court rather than marry middle-aged, bossy Katisha. In disguise as a musician he falls in love with Yum-Yum and, thinking that her betrothed has been executed, he comes to claim her. From here onwards the plot twists and doubles. Eventually there is a happy ending with Nanki-Poo married to Yum-Yum and Ko-Ko to Katisha.

Katisha is a stock Gilbertian figure. The plain, late-middle-aged woman without a husband is derived partly from the pantomime dame tradition and features in previous operas. She begins, feebly, as Lady Sangazure in *The Sorcerer*, is rather fun as Buttercup the Bumboat Woman in *HMS Pinafore*, takes control as Ruth in *The Pirates of Penzance*, gains gravitas as Lady Jane in *Patience* and is spiteful as Lady Blanche in *Princess Ida*. But it is as Katisha that she becomes terrifying. Katisha and, to a lesser extent, her predecessors expose the true nature of the man-trap set by marriage. Nanki-Poo thinks he's escaped Katisha for a sweet young girl but Katisha represents the truth of what his bride will mature into; an ugly harridan full of her own importance who orders men about. This is the real meaning behind Katisha's scornful 'Pink cheek, that rulest / Where wisdom serves!' at the end of Act I. It's easy to see Katisha as an expression of Gilbert's misogynistic tendencies, a caricature of the frustrated middle-aged woman who, without youth, beauty and 'girlish glee', has lost all reason to exist. To believe in this interpretation is to fall victim to Gilbert's deadpan satire.

To understand Katisha better it's helpful to consider *The Mikado* alongside a stage play which came out in the same year – *The Magistrate* by Arthur Wing Pinero. Both works show an inverted image of Victorian society. While Gilbert transposes his action to a foreign country, Pinero uses London but sets it within the conventions of farce, a form which trades on the ludicrous. Liberty granted, both Gilbert and Pinero address a common theme. This is the question of what happens when women age in a society which compels them to seek partners in the marriage market. Both authors take it for granted that the destiny of their male and female characters is marriage. This assumption goes beyond the demands of a convenient comedic plot device.

In *The Magistrate* a bufferish magistrate in late middle-age marries a widow, Agatha, with a son called Cis. To make herself more attractive and marriageable, Agatha lops five years off her real age, thus making her 19-year-old son a bare 14. The poor lad is ignorant of his real age, despite the fact that he has the inclinations and tastes of a young man about town. A series of farcical incidents driven by Agatha's wish to keep her secret combined with Cis' forward preferences leads to everyone getting caught in a shady hotel drinking after hours. The Poskets do not recognise each other and while Mr Posket evades arrest, his wife spends the night in the cells. All is finally unmasked in the dock of the magistrates court when Agatha appears before Mr Posket.

In each work the law is presented as an ass for attempting to regulate domestic issues. In the absence of any real crime in *The Mikado*, laws are passed which restrict private behaviour and criminals guilty of social offence are made to pay with fitting punishments. In *The Magistrate* the law is mocked for punishing people who are not really guilty. The worlds of both dramas are safe from any true criminal malevolence. Even Mr Posket's servants, all judged guilty in court, make reliable domestic staff in his home.

Both Agatha and Katisha are set in relief against younger, prettier women courting young men. While Agatha accepts that age is unattractive and tries to hide her maturity, Katisha revels in her ugliness, deluding herself that it is beauty and telling Pooh-Bah: 'You hold that I am not beautiful because my face is plain. But you know nothing . . . Learn, then, that it is not in the face alone that beauty is to be sought' (Act II). This being Gilbert, the joke doubles back on her as she exhibits her ugliness: 'My right elbow has a fascination that few can resist.' He makes her monstrous, but curiously sympathetic. Gilbert and Pinero waste no time trying to persuade the audience why these characters want to be married in the first place. After all, they are writing within a culture founded on the institution. But the question is there in embryo, an inescapable doubt which in a few years was to surface and shape itself into what became known as the 'woman problem'.

★

THE MIKADO;
OR, THE TOWN OF TITIPU
William Schwenck Gilbert

Dramatis Personæ

The MIKADO *of Japan*

NANKI-POO, *his son, disguised as a wandering minstrel, and in love with* YUM-YUM

KO-KO, *Lord High Executioner of Titipu*

POOH-BAH, *Lord High Everything Else*

PISH-TUSH, *a Noble Lord*

YUM-YUM ⎫
PITTI-SING ⎬ *Three sisters − Wards of* KO-KO
PEEP-BO ⎭

KATISHA, *an elderly Lady, in love with* NANKI-POO

Chorus of school-girls, nobles, guards and coolies

ACT I

SCENE

Court-yard of Ko-Ko's *Palace in Titipu. Japanese nobles discovered standing and sitting in attitudes suggested by native drawings.*

CHORUS

If you want to know who we are,
  We are gentlemen of Japan:
On many a vase and jar –
  On many a screen and fan,
    We figure in lively paint:
    Our attitudes queer and quaint –
    You're wrong if you think it ain't.

If you think we are worked by strings,
  Like a Japanese marionette,
You don't understand these things:
  It is simply Court etiquette.
    Perhaps you suppose this throng
    Can't keep it up all day long?
    If that's your idea, you're wrong.

Enter Nanki-Poo *in great excitement. He carries a native guitar on his back, and a bundle of ballads in his hand.*

RECIT – Nanki-Poo

Gentlemen, I pray you tell me,
Where a lovely maiden dwelleth.
Named Yum-Yum, the ward of Ko-Ko?
In pity speak – oh speak, I pray you!

A Noble: Why, who are you who ask this question?

Nank: Come gather round me, and I'll tell you.

SONG – Nanki-Poo

A wandering minstrel I –
  A thing of shreds and patches,

Of ballads, songs and snatches,
And dreamy lullaby!

My catalogue is long,
      Through every passion ranging,
      And to your humours changing
I tune my supple song!

         Are you in sentimental mood?
            I'll sigh with you,
               Oh, willow, willow!
         On maiden's coldness do you brood?
            I'll do so, too –
               Oh, willow, willow!
         I'll charm your willing ears
         With songs of lover's fears,
         While sympathetic tears
            My cheeks bedew –
               Oh, willow, willow!

But if patriotic sentiment is wanted,
   I've patriotic ballads cut and dried;
For where'er our country's banner may be planted,
   All other local banners are defied!
Our warriors, in serried ranks assembled,
   Never quail – or they conceal it if they do –
And I shouldn't be surprised if nations trembled
   Before the mighty troops of Titipu!

And if you call for a song of the sea,
   We'll heave the capstan round,
With a yeo heave ho, for the wind is free,
Her anchor's a-trip and her helm's a-lee,
   Hurrah for the homeward bound!
      Yeo-ho – heave ho –
   Hurrah for the homeward bound!

To lay aloft in a howling breeze
   May tickle a landsman's taste,
But the happiest hours a sailor sees
      Is when he's down
      At an inland town,
With his Nancy on his knees, yeo ho!

And his arm around her waist!

Then man the capstan – off we go,
As the fiddler swings us round,
With a yeo heave ho,
And a rumbelow,
Hurrah for the homeward bound!

A wandering minstrel I, &c.

Enter PISH-TUSH.

PISH: And what may be your business with Yum-Yum?

NANK: I'll tell you. A year ago I was a member of the Titipu town band. It was my duty to take the cap round for contributions. While discharging this delicate office, I saw Yum-Yum. We loved each other at once, but she was betrothed to her guardian Ko-Ko, a cheap tailor, and I saw that my suit was hopeless. Overwhelmed with despair, I quitted the town. Judge of my delight when I heard, a month ago, that Ko-Ko had been condemned to death for flirting! I hurried back at once, in the hope of finding Yum-Yum at liberty to listen to my protestations.

PISH: It is true that Ko-Ko was condemned to death for flirting, but he was reprieved at the last moment, and raised to the exalted rank of Lord High Executioner under the following remarkable circumstances: –

SONG – PISH-TUSH
Our great Mikado, virtuous man,
When he to rule our land began,
Resolved to try
A plan whereby
Young men might best be steadied.
So he decreed, in words succinct,
That all who flirted, leered, or winked,
(Unless connubially linked),
Should forthwith be beheaded.

And I expect you'll all agree
That he was right to so decree.
And I am right,
And you are right,
And all is right as right can be!

CHORUS: And I expect, &c.

This stern decree, you'll understand,
Caused great dismay throughout the land;

> For young and old
> And shy and bold
> Were equally affected.
> The youth who winked a roving eye,
> Or breathed a non-connubial sigh,
> Was thereupon condemned to die –
> He usually objected.

> And you'll allow, as I expect,
> That he was right to so object.
> And I am right,
> And you are right,
> And everything is quite correct!

CHORUS: And you'll allow, as I expect, &c.

> And so we straight let out on bail
> A convict from the county jail,
> Whose head was next
> On some pretext
> Condemned to be mown off,
> And made *him* Headsman, for we said
> 'Who's next to be decapitated
> Cannot cut off another's head
> Until he's cut his own off.'

> And we are right, I think you'll say,
> To argue in this kind of way.
> And I am right,
> And you are right,
> And all is right – too-lorral-lay!

CHORUS: And they were right, &c.

Exeunt CHORUS. *Enter* POOH-BAH

NANK: Ko-Ko, the cheap tailor, Lord High Executioner of Titipu! Why, that's the highest rank a citizen can attain!

POOH: It is. Our logical Mikado, seeing no moral difference between the dignified judge, who condemns a criminal to die, and the industrious mechanic who carries out the sentence, has rolled the two offices into one, and every judge is now his own executioner.

NANK: But how good of you (for I see that you are a nobleman of the highest rank) to condescend to tell all this to me, a mere strolling minstrel!

POOH: Don't mention it. I am, in point of fact, a particularly haughty and exclusive person, of pre-Adamite ancestral descent. You will understand this when I tell you that I can trace my ancestry back to a protoplasmal primordial atomic globule. Consequently my family pride is something inconceivable. I can't help it. I was born sneering. But I struggle hard to overcome this defect. I mortify my pride continually. When all the great officers of State resigned in a body, because they were too proud to serve under an ex-tailor, did I not unhesitatingly accept all their posts at once?

PISH: And the salaries attached to them? You did.

POOH: It is consequently my degrading duty to serve this upstart as First Lord of the Treasury, Lord Chief Justice, Commander-in-Chief, Lord High Admiral, Master of the Buckhounds, Groom of the Back Stairs, Archbishop of Titipu, and Lord Mayor, both acting and elect, all rolled into one. And at a salary! A Pooh-Bah paid for his services! I a salaried minion! But I do it! It revolts me, but I do it.

NANK: And it does you credit.

POOH: But I don't stop at that. I go and dine with middle-class people on reasonable terms. I dance at cheap suburban parties for a moderate fee. I accept refreshments at any hands, however lowly. I also retail State secrets at a very low figure. For instance, any further information about Yum-Yum would come under the head of a State secret. (NANKI-POO *takes the hint, and gives him money.*) (*Aside.*) Another insult, and I think a light one!

SONG – POOH-BAH
Young man, despair,
    Likewise go to,
Yum-Yum the fair
    You must not woo.
    It will not do:
    I'm sorry for you,
You very imperfect ablutioner!
    This very day
        From school Yum-Yum
Will wend her way,
        And homeward come
        With beat of drum,
        And a rum-tum-tum,
To wed the Lord High Executioner!
        And the brass will crash,
        And the trumpets bray,
    And they'll cut a dash
        On their wedding day.

From what I say, you may infer
It's as good as a play for him and her,
She'll toddle away, as all aver,
With the Lord High Executioner!

It's a hopeless case
As you may see,
And in your place
Away I'd flee;
But don't blame me —
I'm sorry to be
Of your pleasure a diminutioner.
They'll vow their pact
Extremely soon,
In point of fact
This afternoon
Her honeymoon
With that buffoon
At seven, commences, so *you* shun her!

ALL: The brass will crash, &c.

RECIT

NANK: And have I journeyed for a month, or nearly,
To learn that Yum-Yum, whom I love so dearly,
This day to Ko-Ko is to be united!

POOH: The fact appears to be as you've recited:
But here he comes, equipped as suits his station:
He'll give you any further information.

Enter KO-KO, *attended.*

CHORUS

Behold the Lord High Executioner!
A personage of noble rank and title —
A dignified and potent officer,
Whose functions are particularly vital.
Defer, defer,
To the noble Lord High Executioner!

Solo KO-KO.

Taken from the county jail
By a set of curious chances;

Liberated then on bail,
  On my own recognizances;
Wafted by a favouring gale
  As one sometimes is in trances,
To a height that few can scale,
  Save by long and weary dances;
Surely, never had a male
  Under such like circumstances
So adventurous a tale,
  Which may rank with most romances.

CHORUS
Behold the Lord High Executioner, &c.

KO: Gentlemen, – I'm much touched by this reception. I can only trust that by strict attention to duty I shall ensure a continuance of those favours which it will ever be my study to deserve. If I should ever be called upon to act professionally, I am happy to think that there will be no difficulty in finding plenty of people whose deaths will be a distinct gain to society at large.

SONG – KO-KO
As some day it may happen that a victim must be found,
  I've got a little list – I've got a little list
Of social offenders who might well be underground,
  And who never would be missed – who never would be missed!
There's the pestilential nuisances who write for autographs –
All people who have flabby hands and irritating laughs –
All children who are up in dates, and floor you with 'em flat –
All persons who in shaking hands, shake hands with you like *that* –
And all third persons who on spoiling *tête–à-têtes* insist –
  They'd none of 'em be missed – they'd none of 'em be missed!

CHORUS: He's got 'em on the list – he's got 'em on the list;
And they'll none of 'em be missed, – They'll none of 'em be missed.

There's the nigger serenader, and the others of his race,
  And the piano organist – I've got him on the list!
And the people who eat peppermint and puff it in your face,
  They never would be missed – they never would be missed!
Then the idiot who praises, with enthusiastic tone,

All centuries but this, and every country but his own;
And the lady from the provinces, who dresses like a guy,
And who doesn't think she waltzes, but would rather like to try;
And that singular anomaly, the lady novelist –
    I don't think she'd be missed – I'm *sure* she'd not be missed!

    CHORUS: He's got her on the list – he's got her on the list;
And I don't think she'll be missed – I'm sure she'll not be missed!

And that *Nisi Prius* nuisance, who just now is rather rife,
    The Judicial humorist – I've got *him* on the list!
All funny fellows, comic men, and clowns of private life –
    They'd none of 'em be missed – they'd none of 'em be missed.
And apologetic statesmen of a compromising kind,
Such as – what d'ye call him – Thing'em bob, and likewise Never Mind,
And 'St – 'st – 'st – and What's-his-name, and also You-know-who –
The task of filling up the blanks I'd rather leave to *you*.
But it really doesn't matter whom you put upon the list,
    For they'd none of 'em be missed – they'd none of 'em be missed!

    CHORUS: You may put 'em on the list – you may put 'em on the list;
And they'll none of 'em be missed – they'll none of 'em be missed!

    KO: Pooh-Bah, it seems that the festivities in connection with my approaching marriage must last a week. I should like to do it handsomely, and I want to consult you as to the amount I ought to spend upon them.
    POOH: Certainly. In which of my capacities? As First Lord of the Treasury, Lord Chamberlain, Attorney-General, Chancellor of the Exchequer, Privy Purse, or Private Secretary?
    KO: Suppose we say as Private Secretary.
    POOH: Speaking as your Private Secretary, I should say that as the city will have to pay for it, don't stint yourself, do it well.
    KO: Exactly – as the city will have to pay for it. That is your advice.
    POOH: As Private Secretary. Of course you will understand that, as Chancellor of the Exchequer, I am bound to see that due economy is observed.
    KO: Oh. But you said just now 'don't stint yourself, do it well'.
    POOH: As Private Secretary.
    KO: And now you say that due economy must be observed.
    POOH: As Chancellor of the Exchequer.
    KO: I see. Come over here, where the Chancellor can't hear us. (*They*

cross stage.) Now, as my Solicitor, how do you advise me to deal with this difficulty?

POOH: Oh, as your Solicitor, I should have no hesitation in saying 'chance it –'

KO: Thank you. (*Shaking his hand*.) I will.

POOH: If it were not that, as Lord Chief Justice, I am bound to see that the law isn't violated.

KO: I see. Come over here where the Chief Justice can't hear us. (*They cross the stage*.) Now, then, as First Lord of the Treasury?

POOH: Of course, as First Lord of the Treasury, I could propose a special vote that would cover all expenses, if it were not that, as leader of the Opposition, it would be my duty to resist it, tooth and nail. Or, as Paymaster-General, I could so cook the accounts, that as Lord High Auditor I should never discover the fraud. But then, as Archbishop of Titipu, it would be my duty to denounce my dishonesty and give myself into my own custody as First Commissioner of Police.

KO: That's extremely awkward.

POOH: I don't say that all these people couldn't be squared; but it is right to tell you that I shouldn't be sufficiently degraded in my own estimation unless I was insulted with a very considerable bribe.

KO: The matter shall have my careful consideration. But my bride and her sisters approach, and any little compliment on your part, such as an abject grovel in a characteristic Japanese attitude, would be esteemed a favour.

Enter procession of YUM-YUM's *schoolfellows, heralding* YUM-YUM, PEEP-BO, *and* PITTI-SING.

CHORUS
Comes a train of little ladies
From scholastic trammels free,
Each a little bit afraid is,
Wondering what the world can be!

Is it but a world of trouble –
Sadness set to song?
Is its beauty but a bubble
Bound to break ere long?

Are its palaces and pleasures
Fantasies that fade?
And the glory of its treasures
Shadow of a shade?

Schoolgirls we, eighteen and under,
From scholastic trammels free,
And we wonder – how we wonder! –
What on earth the world can be!

TRIO.

YUM-YUM, PEEP-BO, *and* PITTI-SING

THE THREE: Three little maids from school are we,
Pert as a school girl well can be,
Filled to the brim with girlish glee,
Three little maids from school!
YUM-YUM: Everything is a source of fun. (*Chuckle.*)
PEEP-BO: Nobody's safe, for we care for none! (*Chuckle.*)
PITTI-SING: Life is a joke that's just begun! (*Chuckle.*)
THE THREE: Three little maids from school!
ALL (*dancing*): Three little maids who, all unwary,
Come from a ladies' seminary,
Freed from its genius tutelary –
THE THREE (*suddenly demure*): Three little maids from school!
YUM-YUM: One little maid is a bride, Yum-Yum –
PEEP-BO: Two little maids in attendance come –
PITTI-SING: Three little maids is the total sum.
THE THREE: Three little maids from school!
YUM-YUM: From three little maids take one away –
PEEP-BO: Two little maids remain, and they –
PITTI-SING: Won't have to wait very long, they say –
THE THREE: Three little maids from school!
ALL (*dancing*): Three little maids who, all unwary,
Come from a ladies' seminary,
Freed from its genius tutelary –
THE THREE (*suddenly demure*): Three little maids from school!

KO: At last, my bride that is to be! (*About to embrace her.*)
YUM: You're not going to kiss me before all these people?
KO: Well, that was the idea.
YUM (*aside to* PEEP-BO): It seems odd, don't it.
PEEP: It's rather peculiar.
PITTI: Oh, I expect it's all right. Must have a beginning, you know.
YUM: Well, of course I know nothing about these things; but I've no objection if it's usual.

KO: Oh, it's quite usual, I think. Eh, Lord Chamberlain? (*Appealing to* POOH-BAH.)

POOH: I have known it done. (KO-KO *embraces her.*)

YUM: That's over! (*Sees* NANKI-POO, *and rushes to him.*) Why, that's never you? (*The Three Girls rush to him and shake his hands, all speaking at once.*)

> YUM: Oh, I'm so glad! I haven't seen you for ever so long, and I'm right at the top of the school, and I've got three prizes, and I've come home for good, and I'm not going back any more!
>
> PEEP: And have you got an engagement? – Yum-Yum's got one, but she don't like it, and she'd ever so much rather it was you. I've come home for good, and I'm not going back any more!
>
> PITTI: Now tell us all the news, because you go about everywhere, and we've been at school, but thank goodness that's all over now, and we've come home for good, and we're not going back any more!

These three speeches are spoken together in one breath.

KO: I beg your pardon. Will you present me?

YUM: ⎧ Oh, this is the musician who used –
PEEP: ⎨ Oh, this is the gentleman who used –
PITTI: ⎩ Oh, it is only Nanki-Poo who used –

KO: One at a time, if you please.

YUM: He's the gentleman who use to play so beautifully on the – on the –

PITTI: On the Marine Parade.

YUM: Yes, I think that was the name of the instrument.

NANKI: Sir, I have the misfortune to love your ward, Yum-Yum – oh, I know I deserve your anger!

KO: Anger! not a bit, my boy. Why, I love her myself. Charming little girl, isn't she? Pretty eyes, nice hair. Taking little thing, altogether. Very glad to hear my opinion backed by a competent authority. Thank you very much. Good bye. (*To* PISH-TUSH.) Take him away. (PISH-TUSH *removes him.*)

PITTI (*who has been examining* POOH-BAH): I beg your pardon, but what is this? Customer come to try on?

KO: That is a Tremendous Swell. (*She starts back in alarm.*)

POOH: Go away, little girls. Can't talk to little girls like you. Go away, there's dears.

KO: Allow me to present you, Pooh-Bah. These are my three wards. The one in the middle is my bride elect.

POOH: What do you want me to do to them? Mind, I *will not* kiss them.

KO: No, no, you sha'n't kiss them: a little bow — a mere nothing — you needn't mean it, you know.

POOH: It goes against the grain. They are not young ladies, they are young persons.

KO: Come, come, make an effort, there's a good nobleman.

POOH (*aside to* KO-KO): Well, I sha'n't mean it. (*With a great effort.*) How de do, how de do, little girls! (*Aside.*) Oh my protoplasmal ancestor!

KO: That's very good. (*Girls indulge in suppressed laughter.*)

POOH: I see nothing to laugh at. It is very painful to me to have to say 'How de do, how de do, little girls,' to young persons. I'm not in the habit of saying 'How de do, how de do, little girls' to anybody under the rank of a Stockbroker.

KO (*aside to girls*): Don't laugh at him — he's under treatment for it. (*Aside to* POOH-BAH.) Never mind them, they don't understand the delicacy of your position.

POOH: We know how delicate it is, don't we?

KO: I should think we did! How a nobleman of your importance can do it at all is a thing I never can, never shall understand. (*Retires up and goes off.*)

QUARTET AND CHORUS
YUM-YUM, PEEP-BO, *and* PITTI-SING

So please you, sir, we much regret
If we have failed in etiquette
Towards a man of rank so high —
We shall know better by and bye.

But youth, of course, must have its fling,
  So pardon us,
  So pardon us,
And don't, in girlhood's happy spring,
  Be hard on us,
  Be hard on us
If we're disposed to dance and sing,
  Tra la la, &c. (*Dancing.*)

CHORUS OF GIRLS: But youth, of course, &c.

POOH: I think you ought to recollect
      You cannot show too much respect
      Towards the highly-titled few;
      But nobody does, and why should you?

> That youth at us should have its fling,
>> Is hard on us,
>> Is hard on us;
> To our prerogative we cling –
>> So pardon us,
>> So pardon us,
> If we decline to dance and sing –
>> Tra la la, &c. (*Dancing.*)

CHORUS OF GIRLS: But youth, of course, must have its fling, &c.

Exeunt all but YUM-YUM. *Enter* NANKI-POO.

NANK: Yum-Yum, at last we are alone! I have sought you night and day for three weeks, in the belief that your guardian was beheaded, and I find that you are about to be married to him this afternoon!

YUM: Alas, yes!

NANK: But you do not love him?

KO: Alas, no!

NANK: Modified rapture! But why do you not refuse him?

YUM: What good would that do? He's my guardian, and he wouldn't let me marry you!

NANK: But I would wait until you were of age!

YUM: You forget that in Japan girls do not arrive at years of discretion until they are fifty.

NANK: True; from seventeen to forty-nine are considered years of indiscretion.

YUM: Besides – a wandering minstrel, who plays a wind instrument outside tea-houses, is hardly a fitting husband for the ward of a Lord High Executioner.

NANK: But – (*Aside.*) Shall I tell her? Yes! She will not betray me! (*Aloud.*) What if it should prove that, after all, I am no musician!

YUM: There! I was certain of it, directly I heard you play!

NANK: What if it should prove that I am no other than the son of his Majesty the Mikado?

YUM: The son of the Mikado! But why is your Highness disguised? And what has your Highness done? And will your Highness promise never to do it again?

NANK: Some years ago I had the misfortune to captivate Katisha, an elderly lady of my father's court. She misconstrued my customary affability into expressions of affection, and claimed me in marriage, under my father's law. My father, the Lucius Junius Brutus of his race, ordered me to marry her within a week, or perish ignominiously on the scaffold. That night I fled his court, and, assuming the disguise of a Second Trombone, I joined the band in which you found me when I had the happiness of seeing you! (*Approaching her.*)

YUM (*retreating*): If you please, I think your Highness had better not come too near. The laws against flirting are excessively severe.

NANK: But we are quite alone, and nobody can see us.

YUM: Still that don't make it right. To flirt is illegal, and we must obey the law.

NANK: Deuce take the law!

YUM: I wish it would, but it won't!

NANK: If it were not for that, how happy we might be!

YUM: Happy indeed!

NANK: If it were not for the law, we should now be sitting side by side, like that. (*Sits by her.*)

YUM: Instead of being obliged to sit half a mile off, like that. (*Crosses and sits on other side of stage.*)

NANK: We should be gazing into each other's eyes, like that. (*Approaching and gazing at her sentimentally.*)

YUM: Breathing vows of unutterable love – like that. (*Sighing and gazing lovingly at him.*)

NANK: With our arms round each other's waists, like that. (*Embracing her.*)

YUM: Yes, if it wasn't for the law.

NANK: If it wasn't for the law.

YUM: As it is, of course, we couldn't do anything of the kind.

NANK: Not for worlds!

YUM: Being engaged to Ko-Ko, you know!

NANK: Being engaged to Ko-Ko!

DUET – YUM-YUM *and* NANKI-POO

NANK: Were you not to Ko-Ko plighted,
    I would say in tender tone,
    'Loved one, let us be united –
    Let us be each other's own!'
I would merge all rank and station,
    Worldly sneers are nought to us,
And, to mark my admiration,
    I would kiss you fondly thus – (*Kisses her.*)

$$\text{BOTH:} \quad \begin{cases} \begin{matrix} \text{I} \\ \text{He} \end{matrix} & \text{would kiss} & \begin{Bmatrix} \text{you} \\ \text{me} \end{Bmatrix} & \text{fondly thus} - (\textit{Kiss.}) \\ \begin{matrix} \text{I} \\ \text{He} \end{matrix} & \text{would kiss} & \begin{Bmatrix} \text{you} \\ \text{me} \end{Bmatrix} & \text{fondly thus} - (\textit{Kiss.}) \end{cases}$$

YUM: But as I'm engaged to Ko-Ko,
    To embrace you thus, *con fuoco*,
    Would distinctly be no *gioco*,
    And for yam I should get toco –

BOTH: Toco, toco, toco, toco!

NANK: So, in spite of all temptation,
      Such a theme I'll not discuss,
    And on no consideration
      Will I kiss you fondly thus – (*Kissing her.*)
    Let me make it clear to you,
      This, oh this, oh this, oh this (*Kissing her.*)
    This is what I'll never do!

    Exeunt in opposite directions.
    Enter KO-KO.

KO (*looking after* YUM-YUM): There she goes! To think how entirely my future happiness is wrapped up in that little parcel! Really, it hardly seems worth while! Oh, matrimony! – (*Enter* POOH-BAH *and* PISH-TUSH.) Now then, what is it? Can't you see I'm soliloquizing? You have interrupted an apostrophe, sir!

PISH: I am the bearer of a letter from His Majesty the Mikado.

KO (*taking it from him reverentially*): A letter from the Mikado! What in the world can he have to say to me? (*Reads letter.*) Ah, here it is at last! I thought it would come! The Mikado is struck by the fact that no executions have taken place in Titipu for a year, and decrees that unless somebody is beheaded within one month, the post of Lord High Executioner shall be abolished, and the city reduced to the rank of a village!

PISH: But that will involve us all in irretrievable ruin!

KO: Yes. There's no help for it, I shall have to execute somebody. The only question is, who shall it be?

POOH: Well, it seems unkind to say so, but as you're already under sentence of death for flirting, everything seems to point to *you*.

KO: To me? What are you talking about? I can't execute myself, Recorder!

POOH: Why not?

KO: Why not? Because in the first place, self-decapitation is an extremely difficult, not to say dangerous, thing to attempt; and, in the second, it's suicide, and suicide is a capital offence.

POOH: That is so, no doubt.

PISH: We might reserve that point.

POOH: True, it could be argued six months hence, before the full Court.

KO: Besides, I don't see how a man *can* cut off his own head.

POOH: A man might try.

PISH: Even if you only succeeded in cutting it half off, that would be something.

POOH: It would be taken as an earnest token of your desire to comply with the Imperial will.

KO: No. Pardon me, but there I am adamant. As official Headsman, my reputation is at stake, and I can't consent to embark on a professional operation unless I see my way to a successful result.

POOH: This professional conscientiousness is highly creditable to *you*, but it places us in a very awkward position.

KO: My good sir, the awkwardness of your position is grace itself compared with that of a man engaged in the act of cutting off his own head.

PISH: I am afraid that, unless you can obtain a substitute –

KO: A substitute? Oh, certainly – nothing easier (*To* POOH-BAH.) Pooh-Bah, I appoint you my substitute.

POOH: I should like it above all things. Such an appointment would realize my fondest dreams. But no, at any sacrifice, I must set bounds to my insatiable ambition!

TRIO

KO-KO	POOH-BAH	PISH-TUSH
My brain it teams	I am so proud,	I heard one day,
With endless schemes,	If I allowed	A gentleman say
Both good and new	My family pride	That criminals who
For Titipu;	To be my guide,	Are cut in two
But if I flit,	I'd volunteer	Can hardly feel
The benefit	To quit these sphere	The fatal steel,
That I'd diffuse	Instead of you,	And are so slain
The town would lose!	In a minute or two,	Without much pain.
Now every man	But family pride	If this is true
To aid his clan	Must be denied,	It's jolly for you;
Should plot and plan	And set aside,	Your courage screw
As well as he can,	And mortified,	To bid us adieu,
And so,	And so,	And go
Although	Although	And show

I'm ready to go,	I wish to go,	Both friend and foe
Yet recollect	And greatly pine	How much you dare.
'Twere disrespect	To brightly shine,	I'm quite aware
Did I neglect	And take the line	It's your affair,
To thus effect	Of a hero fine,	Yet I declare
This aim direct,	With grief condign	I'd take your share,
So I object –	I must decline –	But I don't much care –
So I object –	I must decline –	I don't much care –
So I object –	I must decline –	I don't much care –

ALL: To sit in solemn silence in a dull, dark dock,
     In a pestilential prison, with a life-long lock,
     Awaiting the sensation of a short, sharp shock,
     From a cheap and chippy chopper on a big black block!

Exeunt all but KO-KO

KO: This is simply appalling! I, who allowed myself to be respited at the last moment, simply in order to benefit my native town, am now required to die within a month, and that by a man whom I have loaded with honours! Is this public gratitude? Is this – (*Enter* NANKI-POO *with a rope in his hands.*) Go away, sir! how dare you? Am I never to be permitted to soliloquize?

NANK: Oh, go on – don't mind me.

KO: What are you going to do with that rope?

NANK: I am about to terminate an unendurable existence.

KO: Terminate your existence? Oh nonsense! What for?

NANK: Because you are going to marry the girl I adore.

KO: Nonsense, sir. I won't permit it. I am a humane man, and if you attempt anything of the kind I shall order your instant arrest. Come, sir, desist at once, or I summon my guard.

NANK: That's absurd. If you attempt to raise an alarm, I instantly perform the Happy Despatch with this dagger.

KO: No, no, don't do that. This is horrible! (*Suddenly.*) Why, you cold-blooded scoundrel, are you aware that, in taking your life, you are committing a crime which – which – which is – Oh! (*Struck by an idea.*)

NANK: What's the matter?

KO: It is *absolutely certain* that you are resolved to die?

NANK: Absolutely!

KO: Will *nothing* shake your resolution?

NANK: Nothing.

KO: Threats, entreaties, prayers – all useless?

NANK: All! My mind is made up.

KO: Then, if you really mean what you say, and if you are absolutely resolved to die, and if nothing whatever will shake your determination – don't spoil yourself by committing suicide, but be beheaded handsomely at the hands of the Public Executioner!

NANK: I don't see how that would benefit me.

KO: You don't? Observe: you'll have a month to live, and you'll live like a fighting cock at my expense. When the day comes there'll be a grand public ceremonial – you'll be the central figure – no one will attempt to deprive you of that distinction. There'll be a procession – bands – dead march – bells tolling – all the girls in tears – Yum-Yum distracted – then, when it's all over, general rejoicings, and a display of fireworks in the evening. *You* won't see them, but they'll be there all the same.

NANK: Do you think Yum-Yum would really be distracted at my death?

KO: I am convinced of it. Bless you, she's the most tender-hearted little creature alive.

NANK: I should be sorry to cause her pain. Perhaps, after all, if I were to withdraw from Japan, and travel in Europe for a couple of years, I might contrive to forget her.

KO: Oh, I don't think you could forget Yum-Yum so easily, and, after all, what is more miserable than a love-blighted life?

NANK: True.

KO: Life without Yum-Yum – why it seems absurd!

NANK: And yet there are a good many people in the world who have to endure it.

KO: Poor devils, yes! You are quite right not to be of their number.

NANK (*suddenly*): I *won't* be of their number!

KO: Noble fellow!

NANK: I'll tell you how we'll manage it. Let me marry Yum-Yum tomorrow, and in a month you may behead me.

KO: No, no. I draw the line at Yum-Yum.

NANK: Very good. If you can draw the line, so can I. (*Preparing rope.*)

KO: Stop, stop – listen one moment – be reasonable. How can I consent to your marrying Yum-Yum if I'm going to marry her myself?

NANK: My good friend, she'll be a widow in a month, and you can marry her then.

KO: That's true, of course. I quite see that, but, dear me, my position during the next month will be most unpleasant – most unpleasant!

NANK: Not half so unpleasant as my position at the end of it.

KO: But – dear me – well – I agree – after all, it's only putting off my wedding for a month. But you won't prejudice her against me, will you?

You see I've educated her to be my wife; she's been taught to regard me as a wise and good man. Now I shouldn't like her views on that point disturbed.

NANK: Trust me, she shall never learn the truth from me.

FINALE

Enter CHORUS, POOH-BAH, *and* PISH-TUSH.

CHORUS

With aspect stern
And gloomy stride,
We come to learn
How you decide.

Don't hesitate
Your choice to name,
A dreadful fate
You'll suffer all the same.

POOH: To ask you what you mean to do we punctually appear.

KO: Congratulate me, gentlemen, I've found a Volunteer!

ALL: The Japanese equivalent for Hear, Hear, Hear!

KO (*presenting him*): 'Tis Nanki-Poo!

ALL: Hail, Nanki-Poo!

KO: I think he'll do?

ALL: Yes, yes, he'll do!

KO: He yields his life if I'll Yum-Yum surrender;
Now I adore that girl with passion tender,
And could not yield her with a ready will,
     Or her allot,
     If I did not
Adore myself with passion tenderer still!

ALL: Ah, yes!
He loves himself with passion tenderer still!

KO (*to* NANKI-POO): Take her — she's yours!

Enter YUM-YUM, PEEP-BO, *and* PITTI-SING.

NANK *and* YUM-YUM: Oh, rapture!

ENSEMBLE

YUM-YUM *and* NANKI-POO: The threatened cloud has passed away,
And brightly shines the dawning day;
What though the night may come too soon,
There's yet a month of afternoon!
     Then let the throng
     Our joy advance,

> With laughing song,
> And merry dance,
> With joyous shout and ringing cheer,
> Inaugurate our brief career!

CHORUS: Then let the throng, &c.

PITTI-SING: A day, a week, a month, a year –
> Or be it far, or be it near,
> Life's eventime comes much too soon,
> You'll live at least a honeymoon!

ALL: Then let the throng, &c.

SOLO – POOH-BAH

> As in three weeks you've got to die,
> If Ko-Ko tells us true,
> 'Twere empty compliment to cry
> Long life to Nanki-Poo!
> But as you've got three weeks to live
> As fellow citizen,
> This toast with three times three we'll give –
> 'Long life to you – till then!'

CHORUS: May all good fortune prosper you,
> May you have health and riches too,
> May you succeed in all you do.
> Long life to you – till then!

DANCE

Enter KATISHA *melodramatically.*

KAT: Your revels cease – assist me all of you!

CHORUS: Why, who is this whose evil eyes
> Rain blight on our festivities?

KAT: I claim my perjured lover, Nanki-Poo!
> Oh, fool! to shun delights that never cloy!
> Come back, oh, shallow fool! come back to joy!

CHORUS: Go, leave thy deadly work undone;
> Away, away! ill-favoured one!

NANK (*aside to* YUM-YUM):   Ah!
> 'Tis Katisha!
> The maid of whom I told you (*About to go.*)

KAT (*detaining him*):   No!
> You shall not go,
> These arms shall thus enfold you!

SONG – KATISHA
(*addressing* NANKI-POO):
Oh fool, that fleest
   My hallowed joys!
Oh blind, that seest
   No equipoise!
Oh rash, that judgest
   From half, the whole?
Oh base, that grudgest
   Love's lightest dole!
   Thy heart unbind,
   Oh fool, oh blind!
   Give me my place,
   Oh rash, oh base!

CHORUS: If she's thy bride, restore her place,
   Oh fool, oh blind, oh rash, oh base!

KAT (*addressing* YUM-YUM): Pink cheek, that rulest
   Where wisdom serves!
Bright eye, that foolest
   Steel-tempered nerves;
Rose-lip, that scornest
   Lore-laden years –
Sweet tongue, that warnest
   Who rightly hears –
   Thy doom is nigh,
   Pink cheek, bright eye!
   Thy knell is rung,
   Rose-lip, sweet tongue!

CHORUS: If true her tale, thy knell is rung,
   Pink cheek, bright eye, rose-lip, sweet tongue!

PITTI-SING: Away, nor prosecute your quest –
   From our intention well expressed,
   You cannot turn us!
The state of your connubial views
Towards the person you accuse
   Does not concern us!
For he's going to marry Yum-Yum –

ALL: Yum-Yum!

PITTI: Your anger pray bury,
   For all will be merry,
I think you had better succumb –

ALL: Cumb – cumb!
PITTI: And join our expressions of glee,
                  On this subject I pray you be dumb –
ALL: Dumb – dumb!
PITTI: You'll find there are many
                        Who'll wed for a penny –
                  The word for your guidance is, 'Mum' –
ALL: Mum – mum!
PITTI: There's lots of good fish in the sea!
ALL: There's lots of good fish in the sea!
                     And you'll find there are many, &c

                         SOLO – KATISHA
                        The hour of gladness
                           Is dead and gone;
                        In silent sadness
                           I live alone!
                        The hope I cherished
                           All lifeless lies,
                        And all has perished
                           Save love, which never dies!
                  Oh, faithless one, this insult you shall rue!
                  In vain for mercy on your knees you'll sue.
                     I'll tear the mask from you disguising!
NANK (*aside*):   Now comes the blow!
KAT: Prepare yourself for news surprising!
NANK (*aside*):   How foil my foe?
KAT: No minstrel he, despite bravado!
YUM (*aside, struck by an idea*): Ha! ha! I know!
KAT: He is the son of your –
      NANKI-POO *and* YUM-YUM, *interrupting, sing Japanese words, to drown
      her voice.*
                     O ni! bikkuri shakkuri to!
                     O sa! bikkuri shakkuri to!
KAT: In vain you interrupt with this tornado:
         He is the only son of your –
ALL: O ni! bikkuri shakkuri to!
KAT: I'll spoil –
ALL: O ni! bikkuri shakkuri to!
KAT: Your gay gambado!
      He is the son –

ALL: O ni! bikkuri shakkuri to!
KAT: Of your —
ALL: O ni! bikkuri shakkuri to!

ENSEMBLE

KATISHA	THE OTHERS
Ye torrents roar!	We'll hear no more
Ye tempests howl!	Ill-omened owl,
Your wrath outpour	To joy we soar,
With angry growl!	Despite your scowl
Do ye your worst, my vengeance call	The echoes of our festival
Shall rise triumphant over all!	Shall rise triumphant over all!
Prepare for woe,	Away you go,
Ye haughty lords,	Collect your hordes;
At once I go	Proclaim your woe
Mikado-wards,	In dismal chords;
And when he learns his son is found,	We do not heed their dismal sound,
My wrongs with vengeance will be	For joy reigns everywhere around!
crowned!	

KATISHA *rushes furiously up stage, clearing the crowd away right and left, finishing on steps at the back of stage.*

ACT II

SCENE – Ko-Ko's *Garden*

Yum-Yum *discovered seated at her bridal toilet, surrounded by maidens, who are dressing her hair and painting her face and lips, as she judges of the effect in a mirror.*

Chorus
Braid the raven hair –
    Weave the supple tress –
Deck the maiden fair
In her loveliness –
Paint the pretty face –
    Dye the coral lip –
Emphasize the grace
    Of her ladyship!
Art and nature, thus allied,
Go to make a pretty bride!

SOLO – Pitti-Sing
Sit with downcast eye –
    Let it brim with dew –
Try if you can cry –
    We will do so, too.
When you're summoned, start,
    Like a frightened roe –
Flutter, little heart,
    Colour, come and go!
Modesty at marriage tide
    Well become a pretty bride!

Chorus
Braid the raven hair, &c.
Exeunt Chorus.

Yum (*looking at herself in glass*): Yes, I am indeed beautiful! Sometimes I sit and wonder, in my artless Japanese way, why it is that I am so much more attractive than anybody else in the whole world? Can this be vanity? No!

Nature is lovely and rejoices in her loveliness. I am a child of Nature, and take after my mother.

SONG – YUM-YUM

The sun, whose rays
Are all ablaze
    With ever living glory,
Does not deny
His majesty –
    He scorns to tell a story!
He don't exclaim
'I blush for shame,
    So kindly be indulgent.'
But, fierce and bold,
In fiery gold,
    He glories all effulgent!

I mean to rule the earth,
    As he the sky –
We really know our worth,
    The sun and I!

Observe his flame,
That placid dame,
    The moon's Celestial Highness;
There's not a trace
Upon her face
    Of diffidence or shyness:
She borrows light
That, through the night,
    Mankind may all acclaim her!
And, truth to tell,
She lights up well,
    So I, for one, don't blame her!

Ah, pray make no mistake,
    We are not shy;
We're very wide awake,
    The moon and I!

YUM: Yes, everything seems to smile upon me. I am to be married today to the man I love best, and I believe I am the very happiest girl in Japan!

PEEP: The happiest girl indeed, for she is indeed to be envied who has attained happiness in all but perfection.

YUM: In 'all but' perfection?

PEEP: Well, dear, it can't be denied that the fact that your husband is to be beheaded in a month is, in its way, a drawback.

PITTI: I don't know about that. It all depends!

PEEP: At all events, *he* will find it a drawback.

PITTI: Not necessarily. Bless you, it all depends!

YUM (*in tears*): I think it very indelicate of you to refer to such a subject on such a day. If my married happiness *is* to be – to be –

PEEP: Cut short.

YUM: Well, cut short – in a month, can't you let me forget it? (*Weeping.*)
 Enter NANKI-POO *followed by* PISH-TUSH.

NANK: Yum-Yum in tears – and on her wedding morn!

YUM (*sobbing*): They've been reminding me that in a month you're to be beheaded! (*Bursts into tears.*)

PITTI: Yes, we've been reminding her that you're to be beheaded. (*Bursts into tears.*)

PEEP: It's quite true, you know, you *are* to be beheaded! (*Bursts into tears.*)

NANK (*aside*): Humph! How some bridegrooms would be depressed by this sort of thing! (*Aloud.*) A month? Well, what's a month? Bah! These divisions of time are purely arbitrary. Who says twenty-four hours make a day?

PITTI: There's a popular impression to that effect.

NANK: Then we'll efface it. We'll call each second a minute – each minute an hour – each hour a day – and each day a year. At that rate we've about thirty years of married happiness before us!

PEEP: And at that rate, this interview has already lasted four hours and three quarters! (*Exit* PEEP-BO.)

YUM (*still sobbing*): Yes. How time flies when one is thoroughly enjoying one's self!

NANK: That's the way to look at it! Don't let's be downhearted! There's a silver lining to every cloud.

YUM: Certainly. Let's – let's be perfectly happy! (*Almost in tears.*)

PISH: By all means. Let's – let's thoroughly enjoy ourselves.

PITTI: It's – it's absurd to cry! (*Trying to force a laugh.*)

YUM: Quite ridiculous! (*Trying to laugh.*)
 All break into a forced and melancholy laugh.

QUARTETTE
YUM-YUM, PITTI-SING, NANKI-POO, *and* PISH-TUSH

Brightly dawns our wedding day;
　　Joyous hour, we give thee greeting!
　　Whither, whither art thou fleeting?
Fickle moment, prithee stay!
　　What though mortal joys be hollow?
　　Pleasures come, if sorrows follow:
Though the tocsin sound, ere long,
　　Ding dong! Ding dong!
Yet until the shadows fall
Over one and over all,
Sing a merry madrigal –
　　　　　A madrigal!

Fal-la – fal-la! &c. (*Ending in tears.*)

Let us dry the ready tear,
　　Though the hours are surely creeping,
　　Little need for woeful weeping,
Till the sad sundown is near.
　　All must sip the cup of sorrow –
　　I to-day and thou to-morrow:
This the close of every song –
　　Ding dong! Ding dong!
What, though solemn shadows fall,
Sooner, later, over all?
Sing a merry madrigal –
　　　　　A madrigal!
Fal-la – fal-la! &c. (*Ending in tears.*)

Exeunt PITTI-SING *and* PISH-TUSH. NANKI-POO *embraces* YUM-YUM.
– *Enter* KO-KO – NANKI-POO *releases* YUM-YUM.

KO: Go on – don't mind me.

NANK: I'm afraid we're distressing you.

KO: Never mind, I must get used to it. Only please do it by degrees. Begin by putting your arm round her waist. (NANKI-POO *does so.*) There; let me get used to that first.

YUM: Oh, wouldn't you like to retire? It must pain you to see us so affectionate together!

KO: No, I must learn to bear it! Now oblige me by allowing her head to rest on your shoulder. (*He does so – KO-KO much affected.*) I am much obliged to you. Now – kiss her! (*He does so – KO-KO writhes with anguish.*) Thank you – it's simple torture!

YUM: Come, come, bear up. After all, it's only for a month.

KO: No. It's no use deluding oneself with false hopes.

NANK: ⎫
YUM: ⎭ What do you mean?

KO (*to* YUM-YUM): My child – my poor child. (*Aside.*) How shall I break it to her? (*Aloud.*) My little bride that was to have been –

YUM (*delighted*): *Was* to have been!

KO: Yes, you never can be mine!

YUM (*in ecstasy*): What!!!

KO: I've just ascertained that, by the Mikado's law, when a married man is beheaded his wife is buried alive.

NANK: ⎫
YUM: ⎭ Buried alive!

KO: Buried alive. It's a most unpleasant death.

NANK: But whom did you get that from?

KO: Oh, from Pooh-Bah. He's my solicitor.

YUM: But he may be mistaken!

KO: So I thought, so I consulted the Attorney-General, the Lord Chief Justice, the Master of the Rolls, the Judge Ordinary, and the Lord Chancellor. They're all of the same opinion. Never knew such unanimity on a point of law in my life!

NANK: But stop a bit! This law has never been put in force?

KO: Not yet. You see, flirting is the only crime punishable with decapitation, and married men never flirt.

NANK: Of course they don't. I quite forgot that! Well, I suppose I may take it that my dream of happiness is at an end!

YUM: Darling – I don't want to appear selfish, and I love you with all my heart – I don't suppose I shall ever love anybody else half as much – but when I agreed to marry you – my own – I had no idea – pet – that I should have to be buried alive in a month!

NANK: Nor I! It's the very first I've heard of it!

YUM: It – it makes a difference, don't it?

NANK: It *does* make a difference, of course!

YUM: You see – burial alive – it's such a stuffy death! You see my difficulty, don't you?

NANK: Yes, and I see my own. If I insist on your carrying out your promise, I doom you to a hideous death; if I release you, you marry Ko-Ko at once!

TRIO — YUM-YUM, NANKI-POO, *and* KO-KO

YUM:
Here's a how-de-do!
If I marry you,
When your time has come to perish,
Then the maiden whom you cherish
Must be slaughtered too!
Here's a how-de-do!

NANK:
Here's a pretty mess!
In a month, or less,
I mut die without a wedding!
Let the bitter tears I'm shedding
Witness my distress,
Here's a pretty mess!

KO:
Here's a state of things!
To her life she clings!
Matrimonial devotion
Doesn't seem to suit her notion —
Burial it brings!
Here's a state of things!

ENSEMBLE

YUM-YUM *and* NANKI-POO	KO-KO
With a passion that's intense	With a passion that's intense
I worship and adore,	You worship and adore,
But the laws of common sense	But the laws of common sense
We oughtn't to ignore.	You oughtn't to ignore.
If what he says is true,	If what I say is true,
It is death to marry you!	It is death to marry you!
Here's a pretty state of things!	Here's a pretty state of things!
Here's a pretty how-de-do!	Here's a pretty how-de-do!

Exit YUM-YUM

KO (*going up to* NANKI-POO): My poor boy, I'm really very sorry for you.

NANK: Thanks, old fellow. I'm sure you are.

KO: You see I'm quite helpless.

NANK: I quite see that.

KO: I can't conceive anything more distressing than to have one's marriage broken off at the last moment. But you shan't be disappointed of a wedding — you shall come to mine.

NANK: It's awfully kind of you, but that's impossible.

KO: Why so?

NANK: To-day I die.

KO: What do you mean?

NANK: I can't live without Yum-Yum. This afternoon I perform the Happy Despatch.

KO: No, no – pardon me – I can't allow that.

NANK: Why not?

KO: Why, hang it all, you're under contract to die by the hand of the Public Executioner in a month's time! If you kill yourself, what's to become of me? Why, I shall have to be executed in your place!

NANK: It would certainly seem so!

Enter POOH-BAH.

KO: Now then, Lord Mayor, what is it?

POOH: The Mikado and his suite are approaching the city, and will be here in ten minutes.

KO: The Mikado! He's coming to see whether his orders have been carried out! (*To* NANKI-POO.) Now look here, you know – this is getting serious – a bargain's a bargain, and you really mustn't frustrate the ends of justice by committing suicide. As a man of honour and a gentleman, you are bound to die ignominiously by the hands of the Public Executioner.

NANK: Very well, then – behead me.

KO: What now?

NANK: Certainly; at once.

KO: My good sir, I don't go about prepared to execute gentlemen at a moment's notice. Why, I never even killed a blue-bottle!

POOH: Still, as Lord High Executioner, –

KO: My good sir, as Lord High Executioner I've got to behead him in a month. I'm not ready yet. I don't know how it's done. I'm going to take lessons. I mean to begin with a guinea pig, and work my way through the animal kingdom till I come to a second trombone. Why, you don't suppose that, as a humane man, I'd have accepted the post of Lord High Executioner if I hadn't thought the duties were purely nominal? I *can't* kill you – I can't kill anything! (*Weeps.*)

NANK: Come, my poor fellow, we all have unpleasant duties to discharge at times; after all, what is it? If I don't mind, why should you? Remember, sooner or later it must be done.

KO (*springing up suddenly*): *Must it?* I'm not so sure about that!

NANK: What do you mean?

KO: Why should I kill you when making an affidavit that you've been executed will do just as well? Here are plenty of witnesses – the Lord Chief Justice and Lord High Admiral, Commander-in-Chief, Secretary of State for the Home Department, First Lord of the Treasury, and Chief Commissioner of Police. They'll all swear to it – won't you? (*To* POOH-BAH.)

POOH: Am I to understand that all of us high Officers of State are required to perjure ourselves to ensure your safety?

KO: Why not? You'll be grossly insulted, as usual.

POOH: Will the insult be cash down, or at a date?

KO: It will be a ready-money transaction.

POOH (*aside*): Well, it will be a useful discipline. (*Aloud.*) Very good. Choose your fiction, and I'll endorse it! (*Aside.*) Ha! ha! Family Pride, how do you like *that*, my buck?

NANK: But I tell you that life without Yum-Yum –

KO: Oh, Yum-Yum, Yum-Yum! Bother Yum-Yum! Here, Commissionaire (*To* POOH-BAH.), go and fetch Yum-Yum. (*Exit* POOH-BAH.) Take Yum-Yum and marry Yum-Yum, only go away and never come back again. (*Enter* POOH-BAH *with* YUM-YUM *and* PITTI-SING.) Here she is. Yum-Yum, are you particularly busy?

YUM: Not particularly.

KO: You've five minutes to spare?

YUM: Yes.

KO: Then go along with his Grace the Archbishop of Titipu; he'll marry you at once.

YUM: But if I'm to be buried alive?

KO: Now don't ask any questions, but do as I tell you, and Nanki-Poo will explain all.

NANK: But one moment –

KO: Not for worlds. Here comes the Mikado, no doubt to ascertain whether I've obeyed his decree, and if he finds you alive, I shall have the greatest difficulty in persuading him that I've beheaded you. (*Exeunt* NANKI-POO *and* YUM-YUM, *followed by* POOH-BAH.) Close thing that, for here he comes!

March. – *Enter procession, heralding* MIKADO, *with* KATISHA

CHORUS
'*March of the Mikado's troops*'

Miya sama, miya sama,
On ma no mayé ni
Pira-Pira suru no wa
Nan gia na
Toko tonyaré tonyaré na!

DUET – MIKADO *and* KATISHA

MIKADO: From every kind of man
                    Obedience I expect;
                 I'm the Emperor of Japan –

KAT: And I'm his daughter-in-law elect!
                    He'll marry his son
                    (He has only got one)
                 To his daughter-in-law elect.

MIK: My morals have been declared
                 Particularly correct;

KAT: But they're nothing at all, compared
                    With those of his daughter-in-law elect!
                    Bow – Bow –
                 To his daughter-in-law elect!

ALL: Bow – Bow –
                 To his daughter-in-law elect.

MIK: In a fatherly kind of way
                 I govern each tribe and sect,
              All cheerfully own my sway –

KAT: Except his daughter-in-law elect!
                    As tough as a bone,
                    With a will of her own,
                 Is his daughter-in-law elect!

MIK: My nature is love and light –
                 My freedom from all defect –

KAT: Is insignificant quite,
                    Compared with his daughter-in-law elect
                    Bow! Bow!
                 To his daughter-in-law elect!

                    Bow! Bow!
                 To his daughter-in-law elect.

SONG – MIKADO
A more humane Mikado never
Did in Japan exist,
To nobody second,
I'm certainly reckoned

A true philanthropist.
It is my very humane endeavour
To make, to some extent,
    Each evil liver
    A running river
Of harmless merriment.

My object all sublime
I shall achieve in time –
To let the punishment fit the crime
    The punishment fit the crime;
And make each prisoner pent
Unwillingly represent
A source of innocent merriment,
    Of innocent merriment!

All prosy dull society sinners,
    Who chatter and bleat and bore,
        Are sent to hear sermons
        From mystical Germans
    Who preach from ten to four.
The amateur tenor, whose vocal villanies
    All desire to shirk,
        Shall, during off-hours,
        Exhibit his powers
    To Madame Tussaud's waxwork.

The lady who dies a chemical yellow,
    Or stains her grey hair puce,
        Or pinches her figger,
        Is blacked like a nigger
    With permanent walnut juice.
The idiot who, in railway carriages,
    Scribbles on window panes,
        We only suffer
        To ride on a buffer
    In Parliament trains.

        My object my sublime, &c

The advertising quack who wearies
    With tales of countless cures,
        His teeth, I've enacted,

Shall all be extracted
By terrified amateurs.
The music hall singer attends a series
Of masses and fugues and 'ops'
By Bach, interwoven
With Spohr and Beethoven,
At classical Monday Pops.

The billiard sharp whom any one catches,
His doom's extremely hard –
He's made to dwell –
In a dungeon cell
On a spot that's always barred.
And there he plays extravagant matches
In fitless finger-stalls
On a cloth untrue
With a twisted cue,
And elliptical billiard balls!

My object all sublime, &c.

Enter POOH-BAH, *who hands a paper to* KO-KO.

Ko: I am honoured in being permitted to welcome your Majesty. I guess the object of your Majesty's visit – your wishes have been attended to. The execution has taken place.

MIK: Oh, you've had an execution, have you?

Ko: Yes. The Coroner has just handed me his certificate.

POOH: I am the Coroner. (KO-KO *hands certificate to* MIKADO.)

MIK (*reads*): 'At Titipu in the presence of the Lord Chancellor, Lord Chief Justice, Attorney-General, Secretary of State for the Home Department, Lord Mayor and Groom of the Second Floor Front.'

POOH: They were all present, your Majesty. I counted them myself.

MIK: Very good house. I wish I'd been in time for the performance.

Ko: A tough fellow he was, too – a man of gigantic strength. His struggles were terrific. It was really a remarkable scene.

TRIO – KO-KO, PITTI-SING, *and* POOH-BAH

Ko: The criminal cried, as he dropped him down,
In a state of wild alarm –
With a frightful, frantic, fearful frown
I bared my big right arm.
I seized him by his little pig-tail,
And on his knees fell he,

As he squirmed and struggled
And gurgled and guggled,
I drew my snickersnee!
Oh never shall I
Forget the cry,
Or the shriek that shriekèd he,
As I gnashed my teeth,
When from its sheath
I drew my snickersnee:

CHORUS
We know him well,
He cannot tell
Untrue or groundless tales –
He always tries
To utter lies,
And every time he fails.

PITTI-SING: He shivered and shook as he gave the signs
For the stroke he didn't deserve;
When all of a sudden his eye met mine,
And it seemed to brace his nerve,
For he nodded his head and kissed his hand,
And he whistled an air, did he,
As the sabre true
Cut cleanly through
His cervical vertebrae!
When a man's afraid,
A beautiful maid
Is a cheering sight to see
And it's oh, I'm glad,
That moment sad
Was soothed by sight of me!

CHORUS
Her terrible tale
You can't assail,
With truth it quite agrees;
Her taste exact
For faultless fact
Amounts to a disease.

POOH:
    Now though you'd have said that head was dead
      (For its owner dead was he),
    It stood on its neck with a smile well bred,
    And bowed three times to me!
    It was none of your impudent off-hand nods,
      But as humble as could be.
        For it clearly knew
        The deference due
    To a man of pedigree!
        And it's oh, I vow,
        This deathly bow
    Was a touching sight to see;
        Though trunkless, yet
        It couldn't forget
    The deference due to me!

CHORUS
    This haughty youth
    He speaks the truth
  Whenever he finds it pays,
    And in this case
    It all took place
  Exactly as he says!
Exeunt CHORUS.

MIK: All this is very interesting, and I should like to have seen it. But we came about a totally different matter. A year ago my son, the heir to the throne of Japan, bolted from our imperial court.

KO: Indeed? Had he any reason to be dissatisfied with his position?

KAT: None whatever. On the contrary, I was going to marry him – yet he fled!

POOH: I am surprised that he should have fled from one so lovely!

KAT: That's not true. You hold that I am not beautiful because my face is plain. But you know nothing; you are still unenlightened. Learn then, that it is in the face alone that beauty is to be sought. But I have a left shoulder-blade that is a miracle of loveliness. People come miles to see it. My right elbow has a fascination that few can resist. It is on view Tuesdays and Fridays, on presentation of visiting card. As for my circulation, it is the largest in the world. Observe this ear.

KO: Large.

KAT: Large? Enormous! But think of its delicate internal mechanism. It is fraught with beauty! As for this tooth, it almost stands alone. Many have tried to draw it, but in vain.

KO: And yet he fled!

MIK: And is now masquerading in this town, disguised as a second trombone.

KO:
POOH: } A second trombone!
PITTI:

MIK: Yes; would it be troubling you too much if I asked you to produce him? He goes by the name of Nanki-Poo.

KO: Oh, no; not at all − only −

MIK: Yes?

KO: It's rather awkward, but in point of fact, he's gone abroad!

MIK: Gone abroad? His address!

KO: Knightsbridge!

KAT (*who is reading certificate of death*): Ha!

MIK: What's the matter?

KAT: See here − his name − Nanki-Poo − beheaded this morning. Oh, where shall I find another! Where shall I find another!

Ko-Ko, Pooh-Bah, *and* Pitti-Sing, *fall on their knees.*

MIK (*looking at paper*): Dear, dear, dear; this is very tiresome. (*To* Ko-Ko.) My poor fellow, in your anxiety to carry out my wishes, you have beheaded the heir to the throne of Japan!

Together { KO: But I assure you we had no idea −
POOH: But, indeed, we didn't know −
PITTI: We really hadn't the least notion −

MIK: Of course you hadn't. How could you? Come, come, my good fellow, don't distress yourself − it was no fault of yours. If a man of exalted rank chooses to disguise himself as a second trombone, he must take the consequences. It really distresses me to see you take on so. I've no doubt he thoroughly deserved all he got. (*They rise.*)

KO: We are infinitely obliged to your Majesty −

MIK: Obliged? not a bit. Don't mention it. How *could* you tell?

POOH: No, of course we couldn't know that he was the Heir Apparent.

PITTI: It wasn't written on his forehead, you know.

KO: It might have been on his pocket-handkerchief, but Japanese don't use pocket-handkerchiefs! Ha! ha! ha!

MIK: Ha! ha! ha! (*To* KAT.) I forget the punishment for compassing the death of the Heir Apparent.

Ko:
Pooh: } Punishment! (*They drop down on their knees again.*)
Pitti:

MIK: Yes. Something lingering with boiling oil in it, I fancy. Something of that sort. I think boiling oil occurs in it, but I'm not sure. I know it's something humorous, but lingering, with either boiling oil or melted lead. Come, come, don't fret – I'm not a bit angry.

KO (*in abject terror*): If your Majesty will accept our assurance, we had no idea –

MIK: Of course you hadn't. That's the pathetic part of it. Unfortunately the fool of an act says 'compassing the death of the Heir Apparent'. There's not a word about a mistake, or not knowing, or having no notion. There should be, of course, but there isn't. That's the slovenly way in which these acts are drawn. However, cheer up, it'll be all right. I'll have it altered next session.

KO: What's the good of that?

MIK: Now let's see – will after luncheon suit you? Can you wait till then?

KO, PITTI, *and* POOH: Oh yes – we can wait till then!

MIK: Then we'll make it after luncheon. I'm really very sorry for you all, but it's an unjust world, and virtue is triumphant only in theatrical performances.

GLEE
MIKADO KATISHA, KO-KO, POOH-BAH, *and* PITTI-SING

MIK *and* KAT: See how the Fate of their gifts allot,
                  For A is happy – B is not.
                  Yet B is worthy, I dare say,
                  Of more prosperity than A!

KO, POOH, *and* PITTI: *Is* B more worthy?

MIK *and* KAT: I should say
                  He's worth a great deal more than A.

ENSEMBLE: {
                  Yet A is happy!
                  Oh so happy
                  Laughing, Ha! ha!
                  Chaffing, Ha! ha!
                  Nectar quaffing, Ha! ha! ha! ha
                  Ever joyous, ever gay,
                  Happy, undeserving A!

KO, POOH, *and* PITTI: If I were Fortune – which I'm not –
B should enjoy A's happy lot,
And A should die in miserie,
That is, assuming I am B.

MIK, *and* KAT: But *should* A perish?

KO, POOH, *and* PITTI: That should he,
(Of course assuming I am B).
B should be happy!
Oh so happy!
Laughing, Ha! ha!
Chaffing, Ha! ha!
Nectar quaffing, Ha! ha! ha! ha!
But condemned to die is he,
Wretched, meritorious B!

Exeunt MIKADO *and* KATISHA.

KO: Well! a nice mess you've got us into, with your nodding head and the deference due to a man of pedigree!

POOH: Merely corroborative detail, intended to give artistic verisimilitude to a bald and unconvincing narrative.

PITTI: Corroborative detail indeed! Corroborative fiddlestick!

KO: And you're just as bad as he is with your cock-and-a-bull stories, about catching his eye, and his whistling an air. But that's so like you! You must put in your oar!

POOH: But how about your big right arm?

PITTI: Yes, and your snickersnee!

KO: Well, well, never mind that now. There's only one thing to be done. Nanki-Poo hasn't started yet – he must come to life again at once – (*Enter* NANKI-POO *and* YUM-YUM *prepared for journey.*), here he comes. Here, Nanki-Poo, I've good news for you – you're reprieved.

NANK: Oh, but it's too late. I'm a dead man, and I'm off for my honeymoon.

KO: Nonsense. A terrible thing has just happened. It seems you're the son of the Mikado.

NANK: Yes, but that happened some time ago.

KO: Is this a time for airy persiflage? You're father is here, and with Katisha!

NANK: My father! And with Katisha!

KO: Yes, he wants you particularly.

POOH: So does she.

YUM: Oh, but he's married now.

KO: But, bless my heart, what has that to do with it.

NANK: Katisha claims me in marriage, but I can't marry her because I'm married already − consequently she will insist on my execution, and if I'm executed, my wife will have to be buried alive.

YUM: You see our difficulty.

KO: Yes, I don't know what's to be done.

NANK: There's one chance for you. If you could persuade Katisha to marry you, she would have no further claim on me, and in that case I could come to life without any fear of being put to death.

KO: I marry Katisha!

YUM: I really think it's the only course.

KO: But, my good girl, have you seen her? She's something appalling!

PITTI: Ah, that's only her face. She has a left elbow which people come miles to see!

POOH: I am told that her right heel is much admired by connoisseurs.

KO: My good sir, I decline to pin my heart upon any lady's right heel.

NANK: It comes to this: while Katisha is single, I prefer to be a disembodied spirit. When Katisha is married, existence will be as welcome as the flowers in spring.

DUET
NANKI-POO and KO-KO

NANK: The flowers that bloom in the spring,
        Tra la,
    Breathe promise of merry sunshine −
    As we merrily dance and we sing,
        Tra la,
    We welcome the hope that they bring,
        Tra la,
        Of a summer of roses and wine;
            And that's what we mean when we say that a thing
            Is welcome as flowers that bloom in the spring.
                Tra la la la la la, &c

ALL: And that's what we mean,&c.

KO: The flowers that bloom in the spring,
        Tra la,
    Have nothing to do with the case.
I've got to take under my wing,
        Tra la,
A most unattractive old thing,
        Tra la,

With a caricature of a face;
   And that's what I mean when I say, or I sing,
   'Oh, bother the flowers that bloom in the spring!'
       Tra la la la la la, &c.
ALL: And that's what he means when he ventures to sing, &c.
   Dance and exeunt NANKI-POO, YUM-YUM, POOH-BAH, *and* PITTI-
SING.

   Enter KATISHA

RECITATIVE
Alone, and yet alive! Oh, sepulchre!
My soul is still my body's prisoner!
Remote the peace that Death alone can give –
My doom, to wait! my punishment, to live!

SONG
Hearts do not break!
They sting and ache
For old sake's sake,
      But do not die!
Though with each breath
They long for death,
As witnesseth
      The living I!
      Oh, living I!
      Come, tell me why,
      When hope is gone
      Dost thou stay on?
      Why linger here,
      Where all is drear?
   May not a cheated maiden die?

KO (*approaching her timidly*): Katisha!
KAT: The miscreant who robbed me of my love! But vengeance pursues
– they are heating the cauldron!
KO: Katisha – behold a suppliant at your feet! Katisha – mercy!
KAT: Mercy? Had you mercy on him? See here, you! You have slain my
love. He did not love *me*, but he would have loved me in time. I am an
acquired taste – only the educated palate can appreciate *me*. I was educating
his palate when he left me. Well, he is dead, and where shall I find another?
It takes years to train a man to love me – am I to go through the weary
round again, and, at the same time, implore mercy for you who robbed me

of my prey – I mean my pupil – just as his education was on the point of completion? Oh, where shall I find another!

KO (*suddenly, and with great vehemence*): Here! – Here!

KAT: What!!!

KO (*with intense passion*): Katisha, for years I have loved you with a white-hot passion that is slowly but surely consuming my very vitals! Ah, shrink not from me! If there is aught of woman's mercy in your heart, turn not away from a love-sick suppliant whose every fibre thrills at your tiniest touch! True it is that, under a poor mask of disgust, I have endeavoured to conceal a passion whose inner fires are broiling the soul within me. But the fire will not be smothered – it defies all attempts at extinction, and, breaking forth, all the more eagerly for its long restraint, it declares itself in words that will not be weighed – that cannot be schooled – that should not be too severely criticised. Katisha, I dare not hope for your love – but I will not live without it!

KAT: You, whose hands still reek with the blood of my betrothed, dare to address words of passion to the woman you have so foully wronged!

KO: I do – accept my love, or I perish on the spot!

KAT: Go to! Who knows so well as I that no one ever yet died of a broken heart!

KO: You know not what you say. Listen!

SONG – KO-KO

On a tree by a river a little tom-tit
    Sang 'Willow, titwillow, titwillow!'
And I said to him, 'Dicky-bird, why do you sit
    Singing 'Willow, titwillow, titwillow'?
'Is it weakness of intellect, birdie?' I cried,
'Or a rather tough worm in your little inside?'
With a shake of his poor little head he replied,
    'Oh willow, titwillow, titwillow!'

He slapped at his chest, as he sat on that bough,
    Singing 'Willow, titwillow, titwillow!'
And a cold perspiration bespangled his brow,
    'Oh willow, titwillow, titwillow!'
He sobbed and he sighed, and a gurgle he gave,
Then he threw himself into the billowy wave,
And an echo arose from the suicide's grave –
    'Oh willow, titwillow, titwillow!'

Now I feel just as sure as I'm sure that my name

Isn't Willow, titwillow, titwillow,
That 'twas blighted affection that made him exclaim,
'Oh willow, titwillow, titwillow!'

And if you remain callous and obdurate, I
Shall perish as he did, and you will know why,
Though I probably shall not exclaim as I die,
'Oh willow, titwillow, titwillow!'

During this song KATISHA *has been greatly affected, and at the end is almost in tears.*

KAT (*whimpering*): Did he really die of love?

KO: He really did.

KAT: All on account of a cruel little hen?

KO: Yes.

KAT: Poor little chap!

KO: It's an affecting tale, and quite true. I knew the bird intimately.

KAT: Did you? He must have been very fond of her!

KO: His devotion was something extraordinary.

KAT (*still whimpering*): Poor little chap! And — and if I refuse you, will you go and do the same?

KO: At once.

KAT: No, no — you mustn't! Anything but that! (*Falls on his breast.*) Oh, I'm a silly little goose!

KO (*making a wry face*): You are!

KAT: And you won't hate me because I'm just a little teeny weeny wee bit blood-thirsty, will you?

KO: Hate you? Oh Katisha! is there not beauty even in blood-thirstiness?

KAT: My idea exactly.

DUET — KO-KO *and* KATISHA

KAT: There is beauty in the bellow of the blast,
            There is grandeur in the growling of the gale,
                  There is eloquent out-pouring
                  When the lion is a-roaring,
            And the tiger is a-lashing of his tail!

KO: Yes, I like to see a tiger
                  From the Congo or the Niger,
            And especially when lashing of his tail!

KAT: Volcanoes have a splendour that is grim,
            And earthquakes only terrify the dolts,
                  But to him who's scientific

There's nothing that's terrific
In the falling of a flight of thunderbolts!

KO: Yes, in spite of all my meekness,
If I have a little weakness,
It's a passion for a flight of thunderbolts.

BOTH: If that is so,
Sing derry down derry!
It's evident, very,
Our tastes are one.

Away we'll go,
And merrily marry,
Nor tardily tarry,
'Till day is done!

KO: There is beauty in extreme old age –
Do you fancy you are elderly enough?
Information I'm requesting
On a subject interesting:
Is a maiden all the better when she's tough?

KAT: Throughout this wide dominion
It's the general opinion
That she'll last a good deal longer when she's tough.

KO: Are you old enough to marry, do you think?
Won't you wait 'till you are eighty in the shade?
There's a fascination frantic
In a ruin that's romantic;
Do you think you are sufficiently decayed?

KAT: To the matter that you mention
I have given some attention,
And I think I am sufficiently decayed.

BOTH: If that is so,
Sing derry down derry!
It's evident, very,
Our tastes are one!

Away we'll go,
And merrily marry,
Nor tardily tarry,
Till day is done!

Exeunt together.
Flourish. Enter the MIKADO, *attended by* PISH-TUSH *and Court.*

MIK: Now then, we've had a capital lunch, and we're quite ready. Have all the painful preparations been made?

PISH: Your Majesty, all is prepared.

MIK: Then produce the unfortunate gentleman and his two well-meaning but misguided accomplices.

 Enter KO-KO, KATISHA, POOH-BAH, *and* PITTI-SING. *They throw themselves at the* MIKADO'*s feet.*

KAT: Mercy! Mercy for Ko-Ko! Mercy for Pitti-Sing! Mercy even for Pooh-Bah!

MIK: I beg your pardon, I don't think I quite caught that remark.

KAT: Mercy! My husband that was to have been is dead, and I have just married this miserable object.

MIK: Oh! You've not been long about it!

KO: We were married before the Registrar.

POOH: *I* am the Registrar.

MIK: I see. But my difficulty is that, as you have slain the Heir-Apparent –

 Enter NANKI-POO *and* YUM-YUM. *They kneel.*

NANK: The Heir-Apparent is *not* slain.

MIK: Bless my heart, my son!

YUM: And your daughter-in-law elected!

KAT (*seizing* KO-KO): Traitor, you have deceived me!

MIK: Yes, you are entitled to a little explanation, but I think he will give it better whole than in pieces.

KO: Your Majesty, it's like this. It is true that I stated that I had killed Nanki-Poo –

MIK: Yes, with most affecting particulars.

POOH: Merely corroborative detail intended to give verisimilitude to a bald and –

KO: *Will* you refrain from putting in your oar? (*To* MIK.) It's like this: when your Majesty says, 'Let a thing be done,' it's as good as done – practically, it *is* done – because your Majesty's will is law. Your Majesty says, 'Kill a gentleman,' and a gentleman is told off to be killed. Consequently, that gentleman is as good as dead – practically, he *is* dead – and if he is dead, why not say so?

MIK: I see. Nothing could possibly be more satisfactory!

FINALE

PITTI: For he's gone and he's married Yum-Yum –

ALL: Yum-Yum!

PITTI: Your anger pray bury,

         For all will be merry,

I think you had better succumb –

ALL: Cumb-cumb!

PITTI: And join our expressions of glee!

KO: On this subject I pray you be dumb –

ALL: Dumb-Dumb!

KO: Your notions, though many,
                                      Are not worth a penny,
                          The word for your guidance is 'Mum' –

ALL: Mum-mum

KO: You've a very good bargain in me.

YUM *and* NANK: The threatened cloud has passed away,
                                  And brightly shines the dawning day;
                                  What though the night may come too soon,
                                  We've years and years of afternoon!

ALL: Then let the throng
                                          Our joy advance,
                                      With laughing song
                                          And merry dance,
                              With joyous shout and ringing cheer,
                              Inaugurate our new career!
                                  Then let the throng, &c.

THE END.

15 THE SECOND MRS TANQUERAY

The Second Mrs Tanqueray (1893) straddles the world of the old Victorian theatre and the new drama of the 1890s. It is a play with the imaginative texture of a novel that bears up to being read alone. It is more interested in inner states of mind than external action. Yet it is unashamedly melodramatic and uses tricks and effects common in the theatre of the 1850s and 60s. Set beside later plays by Wilde and Shaw it looks clunky and old-fashioned, but it is different in tone and intention from preceding plays of the 1880s. The best comparison is not with other plays but with a novel, *Tess of the D'Urbervilles* by Thomas Hardy, published two years earlier in 1891.

Arthur Wing Pinero (1855–1934) was a prolific, professional playwright whose career lasted nearly 60 years. *The Second Mrs Tanqueray* was his most performed work and the lead role will forever be associated with the actress Mrs Patrick Campbell who made her name playing the contradictory, wilful, wronged Paula. It is usually regarded as a 'problem play' because it examines the difficult social question of the unmarried woman burdened with a sexual history. Paula is, we assume, the lover of widower Aubrey Tanqueray, who honourably decides to marry her even though he knows she has 'kept house' for other men. This euphemism for her disgrace is suitably domestic and dutiful because Paula is a good woman, not a blowsy, fun-loving tart like her friend Lady Orreyed, formerly an actress.

Pinero makes it extremely clear from the beginning of Act I that he does not excuse Paula's misdemeanour. She may be more sinned against than sinning, but there is no escaping the fact that she has done wrong. This belief that she has been warped and tainted, 'a good woman, as it were, maimed', compels Pinero to write the unhappy ending. Once the situation has been established, there is no alternative but to let fate take its inexorable course. The most Pinero can do in his role as heavyweight, social philosopher is to explore Paula's breakdown. Her suicide, when it comes, is off-stage, vague and unrealistic, the cause of death unclear. It doesn't matter; with the inevitable conclusion fulfilled, Pinero tries to wrench another message from the ending and makes Ellean, Aubrey's cold and conventional daughter, blame herself for Paula's death. But he refuses to pursue this and brings the curtain down quick to stop it going any further.

It is possible to sit quietly at home in undramatic surroundings reading *The Second Mrs Tanqueray* and still enter its imaginative world in a form of reading experience usually reserved for prose fiction. Earlier Victorian drama with its terse code of stage directions and reliance on actorly effect insists on its need to be performed. *The Second Mrs Tanqueray* does not. Although Robertson employed equally detailed stage directions, he didn't blend them into the speech so that they function as a narrator's voice would in a novel, albeit in an abbreviated form. A progress can be traced through nineteenth-century plays; earlier writers leave most of the 'business' to the actors, Robertson exercises dramatic control by putting instructions in, Pinero explains what's happening. Of course *The Second Mrs Tanqueray* was written to be performed and there are moments and scenes of high dramatic effect, but the play still hangs together as an interior mental experience. This is a new development for the drama of its time and must at least in part be a conscious response to years of dominance by the novel.

Dramatically, the play is a wobbly combination of accomplished effects and clumsy plotting. In Act IV, during the crisis between Ellean and Paula, the younger woman cries out 'You hurt me!' as Paula shakes her. It's a nice moment when action and deeper meaning converge. Similarly, in Act II Ellean wails, 'It's so difficult to seem what one is not!' which is both in character for the priggish Ellean, extends her character by telling more about her, and again has a wider resonance in a play exploring the strain of trying to appear what one is not. Touches like these have to survive cumbersome plotting such as the sudden return of Ellean and Mrs Cortelyon which jolts the action back into play-world artificiality.

Mrs Tanqueray is not a wholly serious play. Farce lurks behind the high drama and there is a broad streak of conventional comedy. The 'orrible Orreyeds provide comic relief through a rather sneaky social double standard. Sir George Orreyed is an upper-class fool and a drunk, a degenerate who cannot be taken seriously. He is a character from the earlier Victorian stage, as the directions in Act III make clear where he is described as, 'a man of about thirty-five, with a low forehead, a receding chin, a vacuous expression, and an ominous redness about the nose'. This is not the portrait of a character from new, sophisticated, psychological drama. His red nose, presumably achieved with stage make-up, draws on the traditions of melodrama, where costume and make-up acted as signals of character type. In melodrama virtuous young women had pale faces while hearty youths sported ruddy complexions. Greasepaint arrived from the Continent in 1877 and thereafter these visual indications settled into a hieratic code. Just as Robertson was careful to present undeserving and unlikeable lower-class characters alongside more deserving types, so Pinero plays the affected and corrupt Lady Orreyed off against Paula.

Paula's tragedy is the same at heart as that of Thomas Hardy's 'pure woman' Tess Durbeyfield. There are plot similarities, specifically the confessional letter which, by remaining unread, converts the truth into a poison which will eventually kill the heroine. Both Hardy and Pinero make a case for their heroine but are forced by moral logic to do her in and start again with a better version. Tess is replaced in her husband's affections by her almost identical but virginal younger sister, while Ellean as Paula's substitute literally fills the dramatic space left behind on stage. Both Hardy and Pinero struggle to shift the blame on to a man, the woman's original corrupter, and both go to some lengths to flesh out the figure of the seducer. Both develop curiously sympathetic villains and discover that if they blame them and make the women into victims they dissolve their heroines' capacity to be responsible for their actions. A rigid moral code of precisely the type they argue against then becomes a logical necessity to protect other such women. Of course there are differences, Tess is an innocent child of nature, a dairymaid who has one previous lover, while Paula is an older, more experienced woman about town, but all this really illustrates is the gap between rural and urban fictions.

There can be little doubt that Pinero knew of Hardy's novel when he wrote *Mrs Tanqueray*. The publication of *Tess of the D'Urbervilles* caused a public stir and Pinero had a history of borrowing from Hardy. Twelve years previously he had angered the novelist with an unauthorised adaptation of *Far from the Madding Crowd*. Pinero denied that *The Squire* (1881) was in any way connected to the novel and there was a sharp exchange of letters. Hardy's own frustrated ambitions as a dramatist probably exacerbated his irritation with Pinero. Ultimately, however, the idea that it might be excusable for certain women to have sexual experience before marriage was neither Hardy's nor Pinero's. It was one of the current issues of the time and part of an on-going debate about women's position and role in society. This circular flow of ideas between stage and novel was completed in 1895 when Grant Allen's novel *The Woman Who Did* took the same theme and seemingly updated it with an 'advanced' heroine conscientiously opposed to marriage. As in *Mrs Tanqueray*, the plot ends with the heroine forced into suicide by her virginal daughter's wedding expectations.

All these works explore matrimonial conventions, the structures which regulate men and women's behaviour to each other. The true subject of *Mrs Tanqueray* is not sexual contact but social contract. Although Aubrey accepts Paula's past, his mistake lies in expecting society to do the same. Paula despairs when she realises that she is nothing without the social status respectability confers. In Act IV she faces the same nasty truth which preoccupied Gilbert in *The Mikado* and Pinero in *The Magistrate*, which is that, like all women, she will have nothing to sustain her when her beauty is gone. 'That horrid, irresistible truth that physical repulsion forces on men and women will come . . . You'll see me just as your daughter does now, as all wholesome folks see women like me. And I shall have no weapon to fight with – not one serviceable little bit of prettiness left to defend myself with!' Paula is neurotic but this is more than a crazy rant by an insecure wife. Her vehemence expresses a fundamental inequality between the sexes and draws the battle lines for future conflict.

★

THE SECOND MRS TANQUERAY
Arthur Wing Pinero

Dramatis Personæ

AUBREY TANQUERAY
PAULA
ELLEAN
CAYLEY DRUMMLE
MRS ALICE CORTELYON
CAPTAIN HUGH ARDALE
GORDON JAYNE, M.D.
FRANK MISQUITH, Q.C., M.P.
SIR GEORGE ORREYED
LADY ORREYED
MORSE

The present day.

The scene of the first act is laid at MR TANQUERAY'S *rooms at The Albany in the month of November; the occurrences of the succeeding acts take place at his house 'Highercoombe', near Willowmere, Surrey, during the early part of the following year.*

THE FIRST ACT

AUBREY TANQUERAY's *Chambers in the Albany – a richly and tastefully decorated room, elegantly and luxuriously furnished: on the right a large pair of doors opening into another room, on the left at the further end of the room a small door leading to a bedchamber. A circular table is laid for a dinner for four persons which has now reached the stage of dessert and coffee. Everything in the apartment suggests wealth and refinement. The fire is burning brightly.*

AUBREY TANQUERAY, MISQUITH, and JAYNE ae seated at the dinner-table. AUBREY is forty-two, handsome, winning in manner, his speech and bearing retaining some of the qualities of young-manhood. MISQUITH is about forty-seven, genial and portly. JAYNE is a year or two MISQUITH's senior; soft-speaking and precise – in appearance a type of the prosperous town physician. MORSE, AUBREY's servant, places a little cabinet of cigars and the spirit-lamp on the table beside AUBREY, and goes out.

MISQUITH: Aubrey, it is a pleasant yet dreadful fact to contemplate, but it's nearly fifteen years since I first dined with you. You lodged in Piccadilly in those days, over a hat-shop. Jayne, I met you at the dinner, and Cayley Drummle.

JAYNE: Yes, yes. What a pity it is that Cayley isn't here tonight.

AUBREY: Confound the old gossip! His empty chair has been staring us in the face all through dinner. I ought to have told Morse to take it away.

MISQUITH: Odd, his sending no excuse.

AUBREY: I'll walk round to his lodgings later on and ask after him.

MISQUITH: I'll go with you.

JAYNE: So will I.

AUBREY (*opening the cigar-cabinet*): Doctor, it's useless to tempt you, I know. Frank – (MISQUITH *and* AUBREY *smoke.*) I particularly wished Cayley Drummle to be one of us tonight. You two fellows and Cayley are my closest, my best friends –

MISQUITH: My dear Aubrey!

JAYNE: I rejoice to hear you say so.

AUBREY: And I wanted to see the three of you round this table. You can't guess the reason.

MISQUITH: You desired to give us a most excellent dinner.

JAYNE: Obviously.

AUBREY (*hesitatingly*): Well – I – (*Glancing at the clock.*) – Cayley won't turn up now.

JAYNE: H'm, hardly.

AUBREY: Then you two shall hear it. Doctor, Frank, this is the last time we are to meet in these rooms.

JAYNE: The last time?

MISQUITH: You're going to leave the Albany?

AUBREY: Yes. You've heard me speak of a house I built in the country years ago, haven't you?

MISQUITH: In Surrey.

AUBREY: Well, when my wife died I cleared out of that house and let it. I think of trying the place again.

MISQUITH: But you'll go raving mad if ever you find yourself down there alone.

AUBREY: Ah, but I sha'n't be alone, and that's what I wanted to tell you. I'm going to be married.

JAYNE: Going to be married?

MISQUITH: Married?

AUBREY: Yes – tomorrow.

JAYNE: Tomorrow?

MISQUITH: You take my breath away! My dear fellow, I – I – of course, I congratulate you.

JAYNE: And – and so do I – heartily.

AUBREY: Thanks – thanks.

There is a moment or two of embarrassment.

MISQUITH: Er – ah – this is an excellent cigar.

JAYNE: Ah – um – your coffee is remarkable.

AUBREY: Look here; I daresay you two old friends think this treatment very strange, very unkind. So I want you to understand me. You know a marriage often cools friendships. What's the usual course of things? A man's engagement is given out, he is congratulated, complimented upon his choice; the church is filled with troops of friends, and he goes away happily to a chorus of good wishes. He comes back, sets up house in town or country, and thinks to resume the old associations, the old companionships. My dear Frank, my dear good doctor, it's very seldom that it can be done. Generally, a worm has begun to eat its way into those hearty, unreserved, prenuptial friendships; a damnable constraint sets in and acts like a wasting disease; and so, believe me, in nine cases out of ten a man's marriage severs for him more close ties than it forms.

MISQUITH: Well, my dear Aubrey, I earnestly hope –

AUBREY: I know what you're going to say, Frank. I hope so, too. In the meantime let's face dangers. I've reminded you of the *usual* course of things, but my marriage isn't even the conventional sort of marriage likely to satisfy society. Now, Cayley's a bachelor, but you two men have wives. By-the-bye, my love to Mrs Misquith and to Mrs Jayne when you get home – don't forget that. Well, your wives may not – like – the lady I'm going to marry.

JAYNE: Aubrey, forgive me for suggesting that the lady you are going to marry may not like our wives – mine at least; I beg your pardon, Frank.

AUBREY: Quite so; then I must go the way my wife goes.

MISQUITH: Come, come, pray don't let us anticipate that either side will be called upon to make such a sacrifice.

AUBREY: Yes, yes, let us anticipate it. And let us make up our minds to have no slow bleeding-to-death of our friendship. We'll end a pleasant chapter here tonight, and after tonight start afresh. When my wife and I settle down at Willowmere it's possible that we shall all come together. But if this isn't to be, for Heaven's sake let us recognise that it is simply because it *can't* be, and not wear hypocritical faces and suffer and be wretched. Doctor, Frank – (*Holding out his hands, one to* MISQUITH, *the other to* JAYNE.) Good luck to all of us!

MISQUITH: But – but – do I understand we are to ask nothing? Not even the lady's name, Aubrey?

AUBREY: The lady, my dear Frank, belongs to the next chapter, and in that her name is Mrs Aubrey Tanqueray.

JAYNE (*raising his coffee-cup*): Then, in an old-fashioned way, I propose a toast. Aubrey, Frank, I give you 'The Next Chapter!'

They drink the toast, saying, 'The Next Chapter!'

AUBREY: Doctor, find a comfortable chair; Frank, you too. As we're going to turn out by-and-by, let me scribble a couple of notes now while I think of them.

MISQUITH *and* JAYNE: Certainly – yes, yes.

AUBREY: It might slip my memory when I get back. (*Sits at a writing-table at the other end of the room, and writes.*)

JAYNE (*to* MISQUITH, *in a whisper*): Frank – (MISQUITH *quietly leaves his chair and sits nearer to* JAYNE.) What is all this? Simply a morbid crank of Aubrey's with regard to ante-nuptial acquaintances?

MISQUITH: H'm! Did you notice *one* expression he used?

JAYNE: Let me think –

MISQUITH: 'My marriage is not even the conventional sort of marriage likely to satisfy society.'

JAYNE: Bless me, yes! What does that suggest?

MISQUITH: That he has a particular rather than a general reason for anticipating estrangement from his friends, I'm afraid.

JAYNE: A horrible *mésalliance!* A dairymaid who has given him a glass of milk during a day's hunting, or a little anaemic shopgirl! Frank, I'm utterly wretched!

MISQUITH: My dear Jayne, speaking in absolute confidence, I have never been more profoundly depressed in my life.

MORSE *enters.*

MORSE (*announcing*): Mr Drummle.

CAYLEY DRUMMLE *enters briskly. He is a neat little man of about five-and-forty, in manner bright, airy, debonair, but with an undercurrent of seriousness.* MORSE *retires.*

DRUMMLE: I'm in disgrace; nobody realises that more thoroughly than I do. Where's my host?

AUBREY (*who has risen*): Cayley.

DRUMMLE (*shaking hands with him*): Don't speak to me till I have tendered my explanation. A harsh word from anybody would unman me.

MISQUITH *and* JAYNE *shake hands with* DRUMMLE.

AUBREY: Have you dined?

DRUMMLE: No – unless you call a bit of fish, a cutlet, and a pancake dining.

AUBREY: Cayley, this is disgraceful.

JAYNE: Fish, a cutlet, and a pancake will require a great deal of explanation.

MISQUITH: Especially the pancake. My dear friend, your case looks miserably weak.

DRUMMLE: Hear me! hear me!

JAYNE: Now then!

MISQUITH: Come!

AUBREY: Well!

DRUMMLE: It so happens that tonight I was exceptionally early in dressing for dinner.

MISQUITH: For which dinner – the fish and cutlet?

DRUMMLE: For *this* dinner, of course – really, Frank! At a quarter to eight, in fact, I found myself trimming my nails, with ten minutes to spare. Just then enter my man with a note – would I hasten, as fast as cab could carry me, to old Lady Orreyed in Bruton Street? – 'sad trouble'. Now, recollect, please, I had ten minutes on my hands, old Lady Orreyed was a very dear friend of my mother's, and was in some distress.

AUBREY: Cayley, come to the fish and cutlet?

MISQUITH *and* JAYNE: Yes, yes, and the pancake!

DRUMMLE: Upon my word! Well, the scene in Bruton Street beggars description; the women servants looked scared, the men drunk; and there was poor old Lady Orreyed on the floor of her boudoir like Queen Bess among her pillows.

AUBREY: What's the matter?

DRUMMLE (*to everybody*): You know George Orreyed?

MISQUITH: Yes.

JAYNE: I've met him.

DRUMMLE: Well, he's a thing of the past.

AUBREY: Not dead!

DRUMMLE: Certainly, in the worse sense. He's married Mabel Hervey.

MISQUITH: What!

DRUMMLE: It's true – this morning. The poor mother showed me his letter – a dozen curt words, and some of those ill-spelt.

MISQUITH (*walking up to the fireplace*): I'm very sorry.

JAYNE: Pardon my ignorance – who *was* Mabel Hervey?

DRUMMLE: You don't – ? Oh, of course not. Miss Hervey – Lady Orreyed, as she now is – was a lady who would have been, perhaps has been, described in the reports of the Police or the Divorce Court as an actress. Had she belonged to a lower stratum of our advanced civilisation she would, in the event of judicial inquiry, have defined her calling with equal justification as that of a dressmaker. To do her justice, she is a type of a class which is immortal. Physically, by the strange caprice of creation, curiously beautiful; mentally, she lacks even the strength of deliberate viciousness. Paint her portrait, it would symbolise a creature perfectly patrician; lance a vein of her superbly-modelled arm, you would get the poorest *vin ordinaire!* Her affections, emotions, impulses, her very existence – a burlesque! Flaxen, five-and-twenty, and feebly frolicsome; anybody's, in less gentle society I should say everybody's, property! That, doctor, was Miss Hervey who is the new Lady Orreyed. Dost thou like the picture?

MISQUITH: Very good, Cayley! Bravo!

AUBREY (*laying his hand on* DRUMMLE's *shoulder*): You'd scarcely believe it, Jayne, but none of us really know anything about this lady, our gay young friend here, I suspect, least of all.

DRUMMLE: Aubrey, I applaud your chivalry.

AUBREY: And perhaps you'll let me finish a couple of letters which Frank and Jayne have given me leave to write. (*Returning, to the writing table.*) Ring for what you want, like a good fellow! (*Resumes his writing.*)

MISQUITH (*to* DRUMMLE): Still, the fish and cutlet remain unexplained.

DRUMMLE: Oh, the poor old woman was so weak that I insisted upon her taking some food, and felt there was nothing for it but to sit down opposite her. The fool! the blackguard!

MISQUITH: Poor Orreyed! Well, he's gone under for a time.

DRUMMLE: For a time! My dear Frank, I tell you he has absolutely ceased to be. (AUBREY, *who has been writing busily, turns his head towards the speakers and listens. His lips are set, and there is a frown upon his face.*) For all practical purposes you may regard him as the late George Orreyed. To-morrow the very characteristics of his speech, as we remember them, will have become obsolete.

JAYNE: But surely, in the course of years, he and his wife will outlive –

DRUMMLE: No, no, doctor, don't try to upset one of my settled beliefs. You may dive into many waters, but there is *one* social Dead Sea – !

JAYNE: Perhaps you're right.

DRUMMLE: Right! Good God! I wish you could prove me otherwise! Why, for years I've been sitting, and watching and waiting.

MISQUITH: You're in form to-night, Cayley. May we ask where you've been in the habit of squandering your useful leisure?

DRUMMLE: Where? On the shore of that same sea.

MISQUITH: And, pray, what have you been waiting for?

DRUMMLE: For some of my best friends *to come up.* (AUBREY *utters a half-stifled exclamation of impatience; then he hurriedly gathers up his papers from the writing-table. The three men turn to him.*) Eh?

AUBREY: Oh, I – I'll finish my letters in the other room if you'll excuse me for five minutes. Tell Cayley the news. (*He goes out.*)

DRUMMLE (*hurrying to the door*): My dear fellow, my jabbering has disturbed you! I'll never talk again as long as I live!

MISQUITH: Close the door, Cayley.

DRUMMLE *shuts the door.*

JAYNE: Cayley –

DRUMMLE (*advancing to the dinner table*): A smoke, a smoke, or I perish! (*Selects a cigar from the little cabinet.*)

JAYNE: Cayley, marriages are in the air.

DRUMMLE: Are they? Discover the bacillus, doctor, and destroy it.

JAYNE: I mean, among our friends.

DRUMMLE: Oh, Nugent Warrinder's engagement to Lady Alice Tring. I've heard of that. They're not to be married till the spring.

JAYNE: Another marriage that concerns us a little takes place tomorrow.

DRUMMLE: Whose marriage?

JAYNE: Aubrey's.

DRUMMLE: Aub – ! (*Looking towards* MISQUITH.) Is it a joke?

MISQUITH: No.

DRUMMLE (*looking from* MISQUITH *to* JAYNE): To whom?

MISQUITH: He doesn't tell us.

JAYNE: We three were asked here tonight to receive the announcement.

Aubrey has some theory that marriage is likely to alienate a man from his friends, and it seems to me he has taken the precaution to wish us good-bye.

MISQUITH: No, no.

JAYNE: Practically, surely.

DRUMMLE (*thoughtfully*): Marriage in general, does he mean, or *this* marriage?

JAYNE: That's the point. Frank says –

MISQUITH: No, no, no; I feared it suggested –

JAYNE: Well, well. (*To* DRUMMLE.) What do you think of it?

DRUMMLE (*after a slight pause*): Is there a light there? (*Lighting his cigar.*) He – wraps the lady – in mystery – you say?

MISQUITH: Most modestly.

DRUMMLE: Aubrey's – not – a very – young man.

JAYNE: Forty-three.

DRUMMLE: Ah! *L'age critique!*

MISQUITH: A dangerous age – yes, yes.

DRUMMLE: When you two fellows go home, do you mind leaving me behind here?

MISQUITH: Not at all.

JAYNE: By all means.

DRUMMLE: All right. (*Anxiously.*) Deuce take it, the man's second marriage mustn't be another mistake! (*With his head bent he walks up to the fireplace.*)

JAYNE: You knew him in his short married life, Cayley. Terribly unsatisfactory, wasn't it?

DRUMMLE: Well – (*Looking at the door.*) I quite closed that door?

MISQUITH: Yes.

Settles himself on the sofa; JAYNE *is seated in an armchair.*

DRUMMLE (*smoking, with his back to the fire*): He married a Miss Herriott; that was in the year eighteen – confound dates – twenty years ago. She was a lovely creature – by Jove, she was; by religion a Roman Catholic. She was one of your cold sort, you know – all marble arms and black velvet. I remember her with painful distinctness as the only woman who ever made me nervous.

MISQUITH: Ha, ha!

DRUMMLE: He loved her – to distraction, as they say. Jupiter, how fervently that poor devil courted her! But I don't believe she allowed him even to squeeze her fingers. She *was* an iceberg! As for kissing, the mere contact would have given him chapped lips. However, he married her and took her away, the latter greatly to my relief.

JAYNE: Abroad, you mean?

DRUMMLE: Eh? Yes. I imagine he gratified her by renting a villa in Lapland, but I don't know. After a while they returned, and then I saw how woefully Aubrey had miscalculated results.

JAYNE: Miscalculated –?

DRUMMLE: He had reckoned, poor wretch, that in the early days of marriage she would thaw. But she didn't. I used to picture him closing his doors and making up the fire in the hope of seeing her features relax. Bless her, the thaw never set in! I believe she kept a thermometer in her stays and always registered ten degrees below zero. However, in time a child came – a daughter.

JAYNE: Didn't that –?

DRUMMLE: Not a bit of it; it made matters worse. Frightened at her failure to stir up in him some sympathetic religious belief, she determined upon strong measures with regard to the child. He opposed her for a miserable year or so, but she wore him down, and the insensible little brat was placed in a convent, first in France, then in Ireland. Not long afterwards the mother died, strangely enough, of fever, the only warmth, I believe, that ever came to that woman's body.

MISQUITH: Don't, Cayley!

JAYNE: The child is living, we know.

DRUMMLE: Yes, if you choose to call it living. Miss Tanqueray – a young woman of nineteen now – is in the Loretto convent at Armagh. She professes to have found her true vocation in a religious life, and within a month or two will take final vows.

MISQUITH: He ought to have removed his daughter from the convent when the mother died.

DRUMMLE: Yes, yes, but absolutely at the end there was reconciliation between husband and wife, and she won his promise that the child should complete her conventual education. He reaped his reward. When he attempted to gain his girl's confidence and affection he was too late; he found he was dealing with the spirit of the mother. You remember his visit to Ireland last month?

JAYNE: Yes.

DRUMMLE: That was to wish his girl good-bye.

MISQUITH: Poor fellow?

DRUMMLE: He sent for me when he came back. I think he must have had a lingering hope that the girl would relent – would come to life, as it were – at the last moment, for, for an hour or so, in this room, he was terribly shaken. I'm sure he'd clung to that hope from the persistent way in which he kept breaking off in his talk to repeat one dismal word, as if he couldn't realise his position without dinning this damned word into his head.

JAYNE: What word was that?

DRUMMLE: Alone – alone.

AUBREY enters.

AUBREY: A thousand apologies!

DRUMMLE (*gaily*): We are talking about you, my dear Aubrey.

During the telling of the story, MISQUITH has risen and gone to the fire, and DRUMMLE has thrown himself full-length on the sofa. AUBREY now joins MISQUITH and JAYNE.

AUBREY: Well, Cayley, are you surprised?

DRUMMLE: Surp –! I haven't been surprised for twenty years.

AUBREY: And you're not angry with me?

DRUMMLE: Angry! (*Rising.*) Because you considerately withhold the name of a lady with whom it is now the object of my life to become acquainted? My dear fellow, you pique my curiosity, you give zest to my existence! And as for a wedding, who on earth wants to attend that familiar and probably draughty function? Ugh! My cigar's out.

AUBREY: Let's talk about something else.

MISQUITH (*looking at his watch*): Not tonight, Aubrey.

AUBREY: My dear Frank!

MISQUITH: I go up to Scotland tomorrow, and there are some little matters –

JAYNE: I am off too.

AUBREY: No, no.

JAYNE: I must: I have to give a look to a case in Clifford Street on my way home.

AUBREY (*going to the door*): Well! (MISQUITH *and* JAYNE *exchange looks with* DRUMMLE. *Opening the door and calling.*) Morse, hats and coats! I shall write to you all next week from Genoa or Florence. Now, doctor, Frank, remember, my love to Mrs Misquith and to Mrs Jayne!

MORSE enters with hats and coats.

MISQUITH *and* JAYNE: Yes, yes – yes, yes.

AUBREY: And your young people!

As MISQUITH and JAYNE put on their coats there is the clatter of careless talk.

JAYNE: Cayley, I meet you at dinner on Sunday.

DRUMMLE: At the Stratfields'. That's very pleasant.

MISQUITH (*putting on his coat with* AUBREY's *aid*): Ah-h!

AUBREY: What's wrong?

MISQUITH: A twinge. Why didn't I go to Aix in August?

JAYNE (*shaking hands with* DRUMMLE): Good-night, Cayley.

DRUMMLE: Good-night, my dear doctor!

MISQUITH (*shaking hands with* DRUMMLE): Cayley, are you in town for long?

DRUMMLE: Dear friend, I'm nowhere for long. Good-night.

MISQUITH: Good-night.

AUBREY, JAYNE, *and* MISQUITH *go out, followed by* MORSE; *the hum of talk is continued outside.*

AUBREY: A cigar, Frank?

MISQUITH: No, thank you.

AUBREY: Going to walk, doctor?

JAYNE: If Frank will.

MISQUITH: By all means.

AUBREY: It's a cold night.

The door is closed. DRUMMLE *remains standing with his coat on his arm and his hat in his hand.*

DRUMMLE (*to himself, thoughtfully*): Now then! What the devil –!

AUBREY *returns.*

AUBREY (*eyeing* DRUMMLE *a little awkwardly*): Well, Cayley?

DRUMMLE: Well, Aubrey?

AUBREY *walks up to the fire and stands looking into it.*

AUBREY: You're not going, old chap?

DRUMMLE (*sitting*): No.

AUBREY (*after a slight pause, with a forced laugh*): Hah! Cayley, I never thought I should feel – shy – with you.

DRUMMLE: Why do you?

AUBREY: Never mind.

DRUMMLE: Now, I can quite understand a man wishing to be married in the dark, as it were.

AUBREY: You can?

DRUMMLE: In your place I should very likely adopt the same course.

AUBREY: You think so?

DRUMMLE: And if I intended marrying a lady not prominently in Society, as I presume you do – as I presume you do –

AUBREY: Well?

DRUMMLE: As I presume you do, I'm not sure that *I* should tender her for preliminary dissection at afternoon tea-tables.

AUBREY: No?

DRUMMLE: In fact, there is probably only one person – were I in your position tonight – with whom I should care to chat the matter over.

AUBREY: Who's that?

DRUMMLE: Yourself, of course. (*Going to* AUBREY *and standing beside him.*) Of course, yourself, old friend.

AUBREY (*after a pause*): I must seem a brute to you, Cayley. But there are some acts which are hard to explain, hard to defend –

DRUMMLE: To defend – ?

AUBREY: Some acts which one must trust to time to put right.

DRUMMLE *watches him for a moment, then takes up his hat and coat.*

DRUMMLE: Well, I'll be moving.

AUBREY: Cayley! Confound you and your old friendship! Do you think I forget it? Put your coat down! Why did you stay behind here? Cayley, the lady I am going to marry is the lady – who is known as – Mrs Jarman.

There is a pause.

DRUMMLE (*in a low voice*): Mrs Jarman! Are you serious?

He walks up to the fireplace, where he leans upon the mantelpiece uttering something like a groan.

AUBREY: As you've got this out of me I give you leave to say all you care to say. Come, we'll be plain with each other. You know Mrs Jarman?

DRUMMLE: I first met her at – what does it matter?

AUBREY: Yes, yes, everything! Come!

DRUMMLE: I met her at Homburg, two – three seasons ago.

AUBREY: Not as Mrs Jarman?

DRUMMLE: No.

AUBREY: She was then – ?

DRUMMLE: Mrs Dartry.

AUBREY: Yes. She has also seen you in London, she says.

DRUMMLE: Certainly.

AUBREY: In Aldford Street. Go on.

DRUMMLE: Please!

AUBREY: I insist.

DRUMMLE (*with a slight shrug of the shoulders*): Some time last year I was asked by a man to sup at his house, one night after the theatre.

AUBREY: Mr Selwyn Ethurst – a bachelor.

DRUMMLE: Yes.

AUBREY: You were surprised therefore to find Mr Ethurst aided in his cursed hospitality by a lady.

DRUMMLE: I was unprepared.

AUBREY: The lady you had known as Mrs Dartry? (DRUMMLE *inclines his head silently.*) There is something of a yachting cruise in the Mediterranean too, is there not?

DRUMMLE: I joined Peter Jarman's yacht at Marseilles, in the Spring, a month before he died.

AUBREY: Mrs Jarman was on board?

DRUMMLE: She was a kind hostess.

AUBREY: And an old acquaintance?

DRUMMLE: Yes.

AUBREY: You have told your story.

DRUMMLE: With your assistance.

AUBREY: I have put you to the pain of telling it to show you that this is not the case of a blind man entrapped by an artful woman. Let me add that Mrs Jarman has no legal right to that name, that she is simply Miss Ray – Miss Paula Ray.

DRUMMLE (*after a pause*): I should like to express my regret, Aubrey, for the way in which I spoke of George Orreyed's marriage.

AUBREY: You mean you compare Lady Orreyed with Miss Ray? (DRUMMLE *is silent*.) Oh, of course! To you, Cayley, all women who have been roughly treated, and who dare to survive by borrowing a little of our philosophy, are alike. You see in the crowd of the ill-used only one pattern; you can't detect the shades of goodness, intelligence, even nobility there. Well, how should you? The crowd is dimly lighted! And, besides, yours is the way of the world.

DRUMMLE: My dear Aubrey, I *live* in the world.

AUBREY: The name we give our little parish of St James's.

DRUMMLE (*laying a hand on* AUBREY's *shoulder*): And you are quite prepared, my friend, to forfeit the esteem of your little parish?

AUBREY: I avoid mortification by shifting from one parish to another. I give up Pall Mall for the Surrey hills; leave off varnishing my boots and double the thickness of the soles.

DRUMMLE: And your skin – do you double the thickness of that also?

AUBREY: I know you think me a fool, Cayley – you needn't infer that I'm a coward into the bargain. No! I know what I'm doing, and I do it deliberately, defiantly. I'm alone; I injure no living soul by the step I'm going to take; and so you can't urge the one argument which might restrain me. Of course, I don't expect you to think compassionately, fairly even, of the woman whom I – whom I am drawn to –

DRUMMLE: My dear Aubrey, I assure you I consider Mrs – Miss Jarman – Mrs Ray – Miss Ray – delightful. But I confess there is a form of chivalry which I gravely distrust, especially in a man of – our age.

AUBREY: Thanks. I've heard you say that from forty till fifty a man is at heart either a stoic or a satyr.

DRUMMLE (*protestingly*): Ah! now –

AUBREY: I am neither. I have a temperate, honourable affection for Mrs Jarman. She has never met a man who has treated her well – I intend to treat her well. That's all. And in a few years, Cayley, if you've not quite forsaken me, I'll prove to you that it's possible to rear a life of happiness, of good repute, on a – miserable foundation.

DRUMMLE (*offering his hand*): Do prove it!

AUBREY (*taking his hand*): We have spoken too freely of – of Mrs Jarman. I was excited – angry. Please forget it!

DRUMMLE: My dear Aubrey, when we next meet I shall remember nothing but my respect for the lady who bears your name.

MORSE *enters, closing the door behind him carefully.*

AUBREY: What is it?

MORSE (*hesitatingly*): May I speak to you, sir? (*In an undertone.*) Mrs Jarman, sir.

AUBREY (*softly to* MORSE): Mrs Jarman! Do you mean she is at the lodge in her carriage?

MORSE: No, sir – here (AUBREY *looks towards* DRUMMLE, *perplexed.*) There's a nice fire in your – in that room, sir. (*Glancing in the direction of the door leading to the bedroom.*)

AUBREY (*between his teeth, angrily*): Very well.

MORSE *retires.*

DRUMMLE (*looking at his watch*): A quarter to eleven – horrible! (*Taking up his hat and coat.*) Must get to bed – up late every night this week. (AUBREY *assists* DRUMMLE *with his coat.*) Thank you. Well, goodnight, Aubrey. I feel I've been dooced serious, quite out of keeping with myself; pray overlook it.

AUBREY (*kindly*): Ah, Cayley!

DRUMMLE (*putting on a neck-handkerchief*): And remember that, after all, I'm merely a spectator in life; nothing more than a man at a play, in fact; only, like the old-fashioned playgoer, I love to see certain characters happy and comfortable at the finish. You understand?

AUBREY: I think I do.

DRUMMLE: Then, for as long as you can, old friend, will you – keep a stall for me?

AUBREY: Yes, Cayley.

DRUMMLE (*gaily*): Ah, ha! Good-night! (*Bustling to the door.*) Don't bother! I'll let myself out! Good-night! God bless yer!

He goes out; AUBREY *follows him.* MORSE *enters by the other door, carrying some unopened letters which after a little consideration he places on the mantelpiece against the clock.* AUBREY *returns.*

AUBREY: Yes?

MORSE: You hadn't seen your letters that came by the nine o'clock post, sir; I've put 'em where they'll catch your eye by-and-by.

AUBREY: Thank you.

MORSE (*hesitatingly*): Gunter's cook and waiter have gone, sir. Would you prefer me to go to bed?

AUBREY: (*frowning*): Certainly not.

MORSE: Very well, sir. (*He goes out.*)

AUBREY (*opening the upper door*): Paula! Paula!

> PAULA *enters and throws her arms round his neck. She is a young woman of about twenty-seven: beautiful, fresh, innocent-looking. She is in superb evening dress.*

PAULA: Dearest!

AUBREY: Why have you come here?

PAULA: Angry?

AUBREY: Yes – no. But it's eleven o'clock.

PAULA (*laughing*): I know.

AUBREY: What on earth will Morse think?

PAULA: Do you trouble yourself about what servants *think?*

AUBREY: Of course.

PAULA: Goose! They're only machines made to wait upon people – and to give evidence in the Divorce Court. (*Looking round.*) Oh, indeed! A snug little dinner!

AUBREY: Three men.

PAULA (*suspiciously*): Men?

AUBREY: Men.

PAULA (*penitently*): Ah! (*Sitting at the table.*) I'm so hungry.

AUBREY: Let me get you some game pie, or some –

PAULA: No, no, hungry for this. What beautiful fruit! I love fruit when it's expensive. (*He clears a space on the table, places a plate before her, and helps her to fruit.*) I haven't dined, Aubrey dear.

AUBREY: My poor girl! Why?

PAULA: In the first place, I forgot to order any dinner, and my cook, who has always loathed me, thought he'd pay me out before he departed.

AUBREY: The beast!

PAULA: That's precisely what I –

AUBREY: No, Paula!

PAULA: What I told my maid to call him. What next will you think of me?

AUBREY: Forgive me. You must be starved.

PAULA (*eating fruit*): I didn't care. As there was nothing to eat, I sat in my best frock, with my toes on the dining-room fender, and dreamt, oh, such a lovely dinner-party.

AUBREY: Dear lonely little woman!

PAULA: It was perfect. I saw you at the end of a very long table, opposite me, and we exchanged sly glances now and again over the flowers. We were host and hostess, Aubrey, and had been married about five years.

AUBREY (*kissing her hand*): Five years.

PAULA: And on each side of us was the nicest set imaginable – you know, dearest, the sort of men and women that can't be imitated.

AUBREY: Yes, yes. Eat some more fruit.

PAULA: But I haven't told you the best part of my dream.

AUBREY: Tell me.

PAULA: Well, although we had been married only such a few years, I seemed to know by the look on their faces that none of our guests had ever heard anything – anything – anything peculiar about the fascinating hostess.

AUBREY: That's just how it will be, Paula. The world moves so quickly. That's just how it will be.

PAULA (*with a little grimace*): I wonder! (*Glancing at the fire.*) Ugh! do throw another log on.

AUBREY (*mending the fire*): There. But you mustn't be here long.

PAULA: Hospitable wretch! I've something important to tell you. No, stay where you are. (*Turning from him, her face averted.*) Look here, that was my dream, Aubrey; but the fire went out while I was dozing, and I woke up with a regular fit of the shivers. And the result of it all was that I ran upstairs and scribbled you a letter.

AUBREY: Dear baby!

PAULA: Remain where you are. (*Taking a letter from her pocket.*) This is it. I've given you an account of myself, furnished you with a list of my adventures since I – you know. (*Weighing the letter in her hand.*) I wonder if it would go for a penny. Most of it you're acquainted with; *I've* told you a good deal, haven't I?

AUBREY: Oh, Paula!

PAULA: What I haven't told you I daresay you've heard from others. But in case they've omitted anything – the dears – it's all here.

AUBREY: In Heaven's name, why must you talk like this tonight?

PAULA: It may save discussion by-and-by, don't you think? (*Holding out the letter.*) There you are.

AUBREY: No, dear, no.

PAULA: Take it. (*He takes the letter.*) Read it through after I've gone, and then – read it again, and turn the matter over in your mind finally. And if, even at the very last moment, you feel you – oughtn't to go to church with me, send a messenger to Pont Street, any time before eleven tomorrow, telling me that you're afraid, and I – I'll take the blow.

AUBREY: Why, what – what do you think I am?

PAULA: That's it. It's because I know you're such a dear good fellow that

I want to save you the chance of ever feeling sorry you married me. I really love you so much, Aubrey, that to save you that I'd rather you treated me as – as the others have done.

AUBREY (*turning from her with a cry*): Oh!

PAULA (*after a slight pause*): I suppose I've shocked you. I can't help it if I have.

> *She sits, with assumed languor and indifference. He turns to her, advances, and kneels by her.*

AUBREY: My dearest, you don't understand me. I – I can't bear to hear you always talking about – what's done with. I tell you I'll never remember it; Paula, can't you dismiss it? Try. Darling, if we promise each other to forget, to forget, we're bound to be happy. After all, it's a mechanical matter; the moment a wretched thought enters your head, you quickly think of something bright – it depends on one's will. Shall I burn this, dear? (*Referring to the letter he holds in his hand.*) Let me, let me!

PAULA (*with a shrug of the shoulders*): I don't suppose there's much that's new to you in it – just as you like. (*He goes to the fire and burns the letter.*)

AUBREY: There's an end of it. (*Returning to her.*) What's the matter?

PAULA (*rising, coldly*): Oh, nothing! I'll go and put my cloak on.

AUBREY (*detaining her*): What *is* the matter?

PAULA: Well, I think you might have said, 'You're very generous, Paula,' or at least, 'Thank you, dear,' when I offered to set you free.

AUBREY (*catching her in his arms*): Ah!

PAULA: Ah! ah! Ha, ha! It's all very well, but you don't know what it cost me to make such an offer. I do so want to be married.

AUBREY: But you never imagined – ?

PAULA: Perhaps not. And yet I *did* think of what I'd do at the end of our acquaintance if you had preferred to behave like the rest. (*Taking a flower from her bodice.*)

AUBREY: Hush!

PAULA: Oh, I forgot!

AUBREY: What would you have done when we parted?

PAULA: Why, killed myself.

AUBREY: Paula, dear!

PAULA: It's true. (*Putting the flower in his buttonhole.*) Do you know I feel certain I should make away with myself if anything serious happened to me.

AUBREY: Anything serious! What, has nothing ever been serious to you, Paula?

PAULA: Not lately; not since a long while ago. I made up my mind then to have done with taking things seriously. If I hadn't, I – However, we won't talk about that.

AUBREY: But now, now, life will be different to you, won't it – quite different? Eh, dear?

PAULA: Oh yes, now. Only, Aubrey, mind you keep me always happy.

AUBREY: I will try to.

PAULA: I know I couldn't swallow a second big dose of misery. I know that if ever I felt wretched again – truly wretched – I should take a leaf out of Connie Tirlemont's book. You remember? They found her – (*With a look of horror.*)

AUBREY: For God's sake, don't let your thoughts run on such things!

PAULA (*laughing*): Ha, ha, how scared you look! There, think of the time! Dearest, what will my coachman say! My cloak!

> *She runs off, gaily, by the upper door.* AUBREY *looks after her for a moment, then he walks up to the fire and stands warming his feet at the bars. As he does so he raises his head and observes the letters upon the mantelpiece. He takes one down quickly.*

AUBREY: Ah! Ellean! (*Opening the letter and reading.*) 'My dear father, – A great change has come over me. I believe my mother in Heaven has spoken to me, and counselled me to turn to you in your loneliness. At any rate, your words have reached my heart, and I no longer feel fitted for this solemn life. I am ready to take my place by you. Dear father, will you receive me – ELLEAN.'

> PAULA *re-enters, dressed in a handsome cloak. He stares at her as if he hardly realised her presence.*

PAULA: What are you staring at? Don't you admire my cloak?

AUBREY: Yes.

PAULA: Couldn't you wait till I'd gone before reading your letters?

AUBREY (*putting the letter away*): I beg your pardon.

PAULA: Take me downstairs to the carriage. (*Slipping her arm through his.*) How I tease you! Tomorrow! I'm so happy! (*They go out.*)

THE SECOND ACT

A morning-room in AUBREY TANQUERAY'S *house, 'Highercoombe,' near Willow-mere, Surrey — a bright and prettily furnished apartment of irregular shape, with double doors opening into a small hall at the back, another door on the left, and a large recessed window through which is obtained a view of extensive grounds. Everything about the room is charming and graceful. The fire is burning in the grate, and a small table is tastefully laid for breakfast. It is a morning in early Spring, and the sun is streaming in through the window.*

AUBREY and PAULA are seated at breakfast, and AUBREY is silently reading his letters. Two servants, a man and a woman, hand dishes and then retire. After a little while AUBREY puts his letters aside and looks across to the window.

AUBREY: Sunshine! Spring!

PAULA (*glancing at the clock*): Exactly six minutes.

AUBREY: Six minutes?

PAULA: Six minutes, Aubrey dear, since you made your last remark.

AUBREY: I beg your pardon; I was reading my letters. Have you seen Ellean, this morning?

PAULA (*coldly*): Your last observation but one was about Ellean.

AUBREY: Dearest, what shall I talk about?

PAULA: Ellean breakfasted two hours ago, Morgan tells me, and then went out walking with her dog.

AUBREY: She wraps up warmly, I hope; this sunshine is deceptive.

PAULA: I ran about the lawn last night, after dinner, in satin shoes. Were you anxious about me?

AUBREY: Certainly.

PAULA (*melting*): Really?

AUBREY: You make me wretchedly anxious; you delight in doing incautious things. You are incurable.

PAULA: Ah, what a beast I am! (*Going to him and kissing him, then glancing at the letters by his side.*) A letter from Cayley?

AUBREY: He is staying very near here, with Mrs—— Very near here.

PAULA: With the lady whose chimneys we have the honour of contemplating from our windows?

AUBREY: With Mrs Cortelyon — yes.

PAULA: Mrs Cortelyon! The woman who might have set the example of calling on me when we first threw out roots in this deadly-lively soil! Deuce take Mrs Cortelyon!

AUBREY: Hush! my dear girl!

PAULA (*returning to her seat*): Oh, I know she's an old acquaintance of yours – and of the first Mrs Tanqueray. And she joins the rest of 'em in slapping the second Mrs Tanqueray in the face. However, I have my revenge – she's six-and-forty, and I wish nothing worse to happen to any woman.

AUBREY: Well, she's going to town, Cayley says here, and his visit's at an end. He's coming over this morning to call on you. Shall we ask him to transfer himself to us? Do say yes.

PAULA: Yes.

AUBREY (*gladly*): Ah, ha! old Cayley!

PAULA (*coldly*): He'll amuse *you*.

AUBREY: And you too.

PAULA: Because you find a companion, shall I be boisterously hilarious?

AUBREY: Come, come! He talks London, and you know you like that.

PAULA: London! London or Heaven! which is farther from me!

AUBREY: Paula!

PAULA: Oh! Oh, I am so bored, Aubrey!

AUBREY (*gathering up his letters and going to her, leaning over her shoulder*): Baby, what can I do for you?

PAULA: I suppose, nothing. You have done all you can for me.

AUBREY: What do you mean?

PAULA: You have married me.

> He walks away from her thoughtfully, to the writing-table. As he places his
> letters on the table he sees an addressed letter, stamped for the post, lying on
> the blotting-book; he picks it up.

AUBREY (*in an altered tone*): You've been writing this morning before breakfast?

PAULA (*looking at him quickly, then away again*): Er – that letter.

AUBREY (*with the letter in his hand*): To Lady Orreyed. Why?

PAULA: Why not? Mabel's an old friend of mine.

AUBREY: Are you – corresponding?

PAULA: I heard from her yesterday. They've just returned from the Riviera. She seems happy.

AUBREY (*sarcastically*): That's good news.

PAULA: Why are you always so cutting about Mabel? She's a kind-hearted girl. Every thing's altered; she even thinks of letting her hair go back to brown. She's Lady Orreyed. She's married to George. What's the matter with her?

AUBREY (*turning away*): Oh!

PAULA: You drive me mad sometimes with the tone you take about things! Great goodness, if you come to that, George Orreyed's wife isn't a bit worse than yours! (*He faces her suddenly.*) I suppose I needn't have made that observation.

AUBREY: No, there was scarcely a necessity. (*He throws the letter on the table, and takes up the newspaper.*)

PAULA: I am very sorry.

AUBREY: All right, dear.

PAULA (*trifling with the letter*): I – I'd better tell you what I've written. I meant to do so, of course. I – I've asked the Orreyeds to come and stay with us. (*He looks at her and lets the paper fall to the ground in a helpless way.*) George was a great friend of Cayley's; I'm sure *he* would be delighted to meet them here.

AUBREY (*laughing mirthlessly*): Ha, ha, ha! They say Orreyed has taken to tippling at dinner. Heavens above!

PAULA: Oh! I've no patience with you! You'll kill me with this life! (*She selects some flowers from a vase on the table, cuts and arranges them, and fastens them in her bodice.*) What is my existence, Sunday to Saturday? In the morning, a drive down to the village, with the groom, to give my orders to the tradespeople. At lunch, you and Ellean. In the afternoon, a novel, the newspapers; if fine, another drive – *if* fine! Tea – you and Ellean. Then two hours of dusk; then dinner – you and Ellean. Then a game of Bésique, you and I, while Ellean reads a religious book in a dull corner. Then a yawn from me, another from you, a sigh from Ellean; three figures suddenly rise – 'Good-night, good-night, good-night!' (*Imitating a kiss.*) 'God bless you!' Ah!

AUBREY: Yes, yes, Paula – yes, dearest – that's what it is *now*. But, by-and-by, if people begin to come round us –

PAULA: Hah! That's where we've made the mistake, my friend Aubrey! (*Pointing to the window.*) Do you believe these people will *ever* come round us? Your former crony, Mrs Cortelyon? Or the grim old vicar, or that wife of his whose huge nose is positively indecent? Or the Ullathornes, or the Gollans, or Lady William Petres? I know better! And when the young ones gradually take the place of the old, there will still remain the sacred tradition that the dreadful person who lives at the top of the hill is never, under any circumstances, to be called upon! And so we shall go on here, year in and year out, until the sap is run out of our lives, and we're stale and dry and withered from sheer, solitary respectability. Upon my word, I wonder we didn't see that we should have been far happier if we'd gone in for the devil-may-care, café-living sort of life in town! After all, *I* have a set and you might have joined it. It's true I did want, dearly, dearly, to be a married woman, but where's the pride in being a married woman among married women who are – married! If – (*Seeing that* AUBREY's *head has sunk into his hands.*) Aubrey! My dear boy! You're not – crying?

> *He looks up, with a flushed face.* ELLEAN *enters, dressed very simply for walking. She is a low-voiced, grave girl of about nineteen, with a face somewhat resembling a Madonna. Towards* PAULA *her manner is cold and distant.*

AUBREY (*in an undertone*): Ellean!

ELLEAN: Good-morning, papa. Good-morning, Paula.

> PAULA *puts her arms round* ELLEAN *and kisses her.* ELLEAN *makes little response.*

PAULA: Good-morning. (*Brightly.*) We've been breakfasting this side of the house, to get the sun.

> *She sits at the piano and rattles at a gay melody. Seeing that* PAULA's *back is turned to them,* ELLEAN *goes to* AUBREY *and kisses him; he returns the kiss almost furtively. As they separate, the servants re-enter, and proceed to carry out the breakfast-table.*

AUBREY (*to* ELLEAN): I guess where you've been: there's some gorse clinging to your frock.

ELLEAN (*removing a sprig of gorse from her skirt*): Rover and I walked nearly as far as Black Moor. The poor fellow has a thorn in his pad; I am going upstairs for my tweezers.

AUBREY: Ellean! (*She returns to him.*) Paula is a little depressed – out of sorts. She complains that she has no companion.

ELLEAN: I am with Paula nearly all the day, papa.

AUBREY: Ah, but you're such a little mouse. Paula likes cheerful people about her.

ELLEAN: I'm afraid I am naturally rather silent; and it's so difficult to seem to be what one is not.

AUBREY: I don't wish that, Ellean.

ELLEAN: I will offer to go down to the village with Paula this morning – shall I?

AUBREY (*touching her hand gently*): Thank you – do.

ELLEAN: When I've looked after Rover, I'll come back to her.

> *She goes out;* PAULA *ceases playing, and turns on the music-stool looking at* AUBREY.

PAULA: Well, have you and Ellean had your little confidence?

AUBREY: Confidence?

PAULA: Do you think I couldn't feel it, like a pain between my shoulders?

AUBREY: Ellean is coming back in a few minutes to be with you. (*Bending over her.*) Paula, Paula dear, is this how you keep your promise?

PAULA: Oh! (*Rising impatiently and crossing swiftly to the settee, where she sits, moving restlessly.*) I *can't* keep my promise; I *am* jealous; it won't be smothered. I see you looking at her, watching her; your voice drops when you speak to her. I know how fond you are of that girl, Aubrey.

AUBREY: What would you have? I've no other home for her. She is my daughter.

PAULA: She is your saint. Saint Ellean!

AUBREY: You have often told me how good and sweet you think her.

PAULA: Good! – yes! Do you imagine *that* makes me less jealous? (*Going to him and clinging to his arm.*) Aubrey, there are two sorts of affection – the love for a woman you respect, and the love for a woman you – love. She gets the first from you: I never can.

AUBREY: Hush, hush! you don't realise what you say.

PAULA: If Ellean cared for me only a little, it would be different. I shouldn't be jealous then. Why doesn't she care for me?

AUBREY: She – she – she will, in time.

PAULA: You can't say that without stuttering.

AUBREY: Her disposition seems a little unresponsive; she resembles her mother in many ways; I can see it every day.

PAULA: She's marble. It's a shame. There's not the slightest excuse; for all she knows, I'm as much a saint as she – only married. Dearest, help me to win her over!

AUBREY: Help you?

PAULA: You can. Teach her that it is her duty to love me; she hangs on to every word you speak. I'm sure Aubrey, that the love of a nice woman who believed me to be like herself would do me a world of good. You'd get the benefit of it as well as I. It would soothe me; it would make me less horribly restless; it would take this – this – mischievous feeling from me. (*Coaxingly.*) Aubrey!

AUBREY: Have patience; everything will come right.

PAULA: Yes, if you help me.

AUBREY: In the meantime you will tear up your letter to Lady Orreyed, won't you?

PAULA (*kissing his hand*): Of course I will – anything!

AUBREY: Ah, thank you, dearest! (*Laughing.*) Why, good gracious! – ha, ha! – just imagine 'Saint Ellean' and that woman side by side!

PAULA (*going back with a cry*): Ah!

AUBREY: What?

PAULA (*passionately*): It's Ellean you're considering, not me? It's all Ellean with you! Ellean! Ellean!

ELLEAN *re-enters.*

ELLEAN: Did you call me, Paula? (*Clenching his hands,* AUBREY *turns away and goes out.*) Is papa angry?

PAULA: I drive him distracted sometimes. There, I confess it!

ELLEAN: Do you? Oh, why do you?

PAULA: Because I – because I'm jealous.

ELLEAN: Jealous?

PAULA: Yes – of you. (ELLEAN *is silent.*) Well, what do you think of that?

ELLEAN: I knew it; I've seen it. It hurts me dreadfully. What do you wish me to do? Go away?

PAULA: Leave us! (*Beckoning her with a motion of the head.*) Look here! (ELLEAN *goes to* PAULA *slowly and unresponsively.*) You could cure me of my jealousy very easily. Why don't you – like me?

ELLEAN: What do you mean by – like you? I don't understand.

PAULA: Love me.

ELLEAN: Love is not a feeling that is under one's control. I shall alter as time goes on, perhaps. I didn't begin to love my father deeply till a few months ago, and then I obeyed my mother.

PAULA: Ah, yes, you dream things, don't you – see them in your sleep? You fancy your mother speaks to you?

ELLEAN: When you have lost your mother it is a comfort to believe that she is dead only to this life, that she still watches over her child. I do believe that of my mother.

PAULA: Well, and so you haven't been bidden to love *me*?

ELLEAN (*after a pause, almost inaudibly*): No.

PAULA: Dreams are only a hash-up of one's day-thoughts, I suppose you know. Think intently of anything, and it's bound to come back to you at night. I don't cultivate dreams myself.

ELLEAN: Ah, I knew you would only sneer!

PAULA: I'm not sneering; I'm speaking the truth. I say that if you cared for me in the daytime I should soon make friends with those nightmares of yours. Ellean, why don't you try to look on me as your second mother? Of course there are not many years between us, but I'm ever so much older than you – in experience. I shall have no children of my own, I know that; it would be a real comfort to me if you would make me feel we belonged to each other. Won't you? Perhaps you think I'm odd – not nice. Well, the fact is I've two sides to my nature, and I've let the one almost smother the other. A few years ago I went through some trouble, and since then I haven't shed a tear. I believe if you put your arms round me just once I should run upstairs and have a good cry. There, I've talked to you as I've never talked to a woman in my life. Ellean, you seem to fear me. Don't! Kiss me!

With a cry, almost of despair, ELLEAN *turns from* PAULA *and sinks on to the settee, covering her face with her hands.*

PAULA (*indignantly*): Oh! Why is it! How dare you treat me like this? What do you mean by it? What do you mean?

A SERVANT *enters.*

SERVANT: Mr Drummle, ma'am.

CAYLEY DRUMMLE, *in riding dress, enters briskly. The* SERVANT *retires.*

PAULA (*recovering herself*): Well, Cayley!

DRUMMLE (*shaking hands with her cordially*): How are you? (*Shaking hands with* ELLEAN, *who rises.*) I saw you in the distance an hour ago, in the gorse near Stapleton's.

ELLEAN: I didn't see you, Mr Drummle.

DRUMMLE: My dear Ellean, it is my experience that no charming young lady of nineteen ever does see a man of forty-five. (*Laughing.*) Ha, ha!

ELLEAN (*going to the door*): Paula, papa wishes me to drive down to the village with you this morning. Do you care to take me?

PAULA (*coldly*): Oh, by all means. Pray tell Watts to balance the cart for three.

ELLEAN *goes out.*

DRUMMLE: How's Aubrey?

PAULA: Very well – when Ellean's about the house.

DRUMMLE: And you? I needn't ask.

PAULA (*walking away to the window*): Oh, a dog's life, my dear Cayley, mine.

DRUMMLE: Eh?

PAULA: Doesn't that define a happy marriage? I'm sleek, well-kept, well-fed, never without a bone to gnaw and fresh straw to lie upon. (*Gazing out of the window.*) Oh, dear me!

DRUMMLE: H'm! Well, I heartily congratulate you on your kennel. The view from the terrace here is superb.

PAULA: Yes, I can see London.

DRUMMLE: London! Not quite so far, surely?

PAULA: *I* can. Also the Mediterranean, on a fine day. I wonder what Algiers looks like this morning from the sea! (*Impulsively.*) Oh, Cayley, do you remember those jolly times on board Peter Jarman's yacht when we lay off – ? (*Stopping suddenly, seeing* DRUMMLE *staring at her.*) Good gracious! What are we talking about!

AUBREY *enters*.

AUBREY (*to* DRUMMLE): Dear old chap! Has Paula asked you?

PAULA: Not yet.

AUBREY: We want you to come to us, now that you're leaving Mrs Cortelyon – at once, today. Stay a month, as long as you please – eh, Paula?

PAULA: As long as you can possibly endure it – do, Cayley.

DRUMMLE (*looking at* AUBREY): Delighted. (*To* PAULA.) Charming of you to have me.

PAULA: My dear man, you're a blessing. I must telegraph to London for more fish! A strange appetite to cater for! Something to do, to do, to do! (*She goes out in a mood of almost childish delight.*)

DRUMMLE (*eyeing* AUBREY): Well?

AUBREY (*with a wearied, anxious look*): Well, Cayley?

DRUMMLE: How are you getting on?

AUBREY: My position doesn't grow less difficult. I told you, when I met you last week, of this feverish, jealous attachment of Paula's for Ellean?

DRUMMLE: Yes. I hardly know why, but I came to the conclusion that you don't consider it an altogether fortunate attachment.

AUBREY: Ellean doesn't respond to it.

DRUMMLE: These are early days. Ellean will warm towards your wife by-and-by.

AUBREY: Ah, but there's the question, Cayley!

DRUMMLE: What question?

AUBREY: The question which positively distracts me. Ellean is so different from – most women; I don't believe a purer creature exists out of heaven. And I – I ask myself, am I doing right in exposing her to the influence of poor Paula's light, careless nature?

DRUMMLE: My dear Aubrey!

AUBREY: That shocks you! So it does me. I assure you I long to urge my girl to break down the reserve which keeps her apart from Paula, but somehow I can't do it – well, I don't do it. How can I make you understand? But when you come to us you'll understand quickly enough. Cayley, there's hardly a subject you can broach on which poor Paula hasn't some strange, out-of-the-way thought to give utterance to; some curious, warped notion. They are not mere worldly thoughts – unless, good God! they belong to the little hellish world which our black-guardism has created: no, her ideas have too little calculation in them to be called worldly. But it makes it the more dreadful that such thoughts should be ready, spontaneous; that expressing them has become a perfectly natural process; that her words, acts even, have almost lost their proper significance for her, and seem beyond her control. Ah, and the pain of listening to it all from the woman one loves, the woman one hoped to make happy and contented, who is really and truly a good woman, as it were, maimed! Well, this is my burden, and I shouldn't speak to you of it but for my anxiety about Ellean. Ellean! What is to be her future? It is in my hands; what am I to do? Cayley, when I remember how Ellean comes to me, from another world I always think, when I realise the charge that's laid on me, I find myself wishing, in a sort of terror, that my child were safe under the ground!

DRUMMLE: My dear Aubrey, aren't you making a mistake?

AUBREY: Very likely. What is it?

DRUMMLE: A mistake, not in regarding your Ellean as an angel, but in believing that, under any circumstances, it would be possible for her to go through life without getting her white robe – shall we say, a little dusty at the hem? Don't take me for a cynic. I am sure there are many women upon earth who are almost divinely innocent; but being on earth, they must send their robes to the laundry occasionally. Ah, and it's right that they should have to do so, for what can they learn from the checking of their little washing-bills but lessons of charity? Now I see but two courses open to you for the disposal of your angel.

AUBREY: Yes?

DRUMMLE: You must either restrict her to a paradise which is, like every earthly paradise, necessarily somewhat imperfect, or treat her as an ordinary flesh-and-blood young woman, and give her the advantages of that society to which she properly belongs.

AUBREY: Advantages?

DRUMMLE: My dear Aubrey, of all forms of innocence mere ignorance is the least admirable. Take my advice, let her walk and talk and suffer and be healed with the great crowd. Do it, and hope that she'll some day meet a good, honest fellow who'll make her life complete, happy, secure. Now you see what I'm driving at.

AUBREY: A sanguine programme, my dear Cayley! Oh, I'm not pooh-poohing it. Putting sentiment aside, of course I know that a fortunate marriage for Ellean would be the best – perhaps the only – solution of my difficulty. But you forget the danger of the course you suggest.

DRUMMLE: Danger?

AUBREY: If Ellean goes among men and women, how can she escape from learning, sooner or later, the history of – poor Paula's – old life?

DRUMMLE: H'm! You remember the episode of the Jeweller's Son in the Arabian Nights? Of course you don't. Well, if your daughter lives, she *can't* escape – what you're afraid of. (AUBREY *gives a half stifled exclamation of pain.*) And when she does hear the story, surely it would be better that she should have some knowledge of the world to help her to understand it.

AUBREY: To understand!

DRUMMLE: To understand, to – to philosophise.

AUBREY: To philosophise?

DRUMMLE: Philosophy is toleration, and it is only one step from toleration to forgiveness.

AUBREY: You're right, Cayley; I believe you always are. Yes, yes. But, even if I had the courage to attempt to solve the problem of Ellean's future in this way, I – I'm helpless.

DRUMMLE: How?

AUBREY: What means have I now of placing my daughter in the world I've left?

DRUMMLE: Oh, some friend – some woman friend.

AUBREY: I have none; they're gone.

DRUMMLE: You're wrong there; I know one –

AUBREY (listening): That's Paula's cart. Let's discuss this again.

DRUMMLE (going up to the window and looking out): It isn't the dog-cart. (Turning to AUBREY.) I hope you'll forgive me, old chap.

AUBREY: What for?

DRUMMLE: Whose wheels do you think have been cutting ruts in your immaculate drive?

    A SERVANT enters.

SERVANT (to AUBREY): Mrs Cortelyon, sir.

AUBREY: Mrs Cortelyon! (After a short pause.) Very well. (The SERVANT withdraws.) What on earth is the meaning of this?

DRUMMLE: Ahem! While I've been our old friend's guest, Aubrey, we have very naturally talked a good deal about you and yours.

AUBREY: Indeed, have you?

DRUMMLE: Yes, and Alice Cortelyon has arrived at the conclusion that it would have been far kinder had she called on Mrs Tanqueray long ago. She's going abroad for Easter before settling down in London for the season, and I believe she has come over this morning to ask for Ellean's companionship.

AUBREY: Oh, I see! (Frowning.) Quite a friendly little conspiracy, my dear Cayley!

DRUMMLE: Conspiracy! Not at all, I assure you. (Laughing.) Ha, ha!

    ELLEAN enters from the hall with MRS CORTELYON, a handsome, good-humoured, spirited woman of about forty-five.

ELLEAN: Papa –

MRS CORTELYON (to AUBREY, shaking hands with him heartily): Well, Aubrey, how are you? I've just been telling this great girl of yours that I knew her when she was a sad-faced, pale baby. How is Mrs Tanqueray? I have been a bad neighbour, and I'm here to beg forgiveness. Is she indoors?

AUBREY: She's upstairs putting on a hat, I believe.

MRS CORTELYON (*sitting comfortably*): Ah! (*She looks round:* DRUMMLE *and* ELLEAN *are talking together in the hall.*) We used to be very frank with each other, Aubrey. I suppose the old footing is no longer possible, eh?

AUBREY: If so, I'm not entirely to blame, Mrs Cortelyon.

MRS CORTELYON: Mrs Cortelyon? H'm! No, I admit it. But you must make some little allowance for me, *Mr Tanqueray*. Your first wife and I, as girls, were like two cherries on one stalk, and then I was the confidential friend of your married life. That post, perhaps, wasn't altogether a sinecure. And now − well, when a woman gets to my age I suppose she's a stupid, prejudiced, conventional creature. However, I've got over it and − (*Giving him her hand.*) − I hope you'll be enormously happy and let me be a friend once more.

AUBREY: Thank you, Alice.

MRS CORTELYON: That's right. I feel more cheerful than I've done for weeks. But I suppose it would serve me right if the second Mrs Tanqueray showed me the door. Do you think she will?

AUBREY (*listening*): Here is my wife. (MRS CORTELYON *rises, and* PAULA *enters, dressed for driving; she stops abruptly on seeing* MRS CORTELYON.) Paula dear, Mrs Cortelyon has called to see you.

PAULA *starts, looks at* MRS CORTELYON *irresolutely, then after a slight pause barely touches* MRS CORTELYON'*s extended hand.*

PAULA (*whose manner now alternates between deliberate insolence and assumed sweetness*): Mrs − ? What name, Aubrey?

AUBREY: Mrs Cortelyon.

PAULA: Cortelyon? Oh, yes. Cortelyon.

MRS CORTELYON (*carefully guarding herself throughout against any expression of resentment*): Aubrey ought to have told you that Alice Cortelyon and he are very old friends.

PAULA: Oh, very likely he has mentioned the circumstance. I have quite a wretched memory.

MRS CORTELYON: You know we are neighbours, Mrs Tanqueray.

PAULA: Neighbours? Are we really? Won't you sit down? (*They both sit.*) Neighbours! That's most interesting!

MRS CORTELYON: Very near neighbours. You can see my roof from your windows.

PAULA: I fancy I *have* observed a roof. But you have been away from home; you have only just returned.

MRS CORTELYON: I? What makes you think that?

PAULA: Why, because it is two months since we came to Highercoombe, and I don't remember your having called.

MRS CORTELYON: Your memory is now terribly accurate. No, I've not been away from home, and it is to explain my neglect that I am here, rather unceremoniously, this morning.

PAULA: Oh, to explain – quite so. (*With mock solicitude*.) Ah, you've been very ill; I ought to have seen that before.

MRS CORTELYON: Ill!

PAULA: You look dreadfully pulled down. We poor women show illness so plainly in our faces, don't we?

AUBREY (*anxiously*): Paula dear, Mrs Cortelyon is the picture of health.

MRS CORTELYON (*with some asperity*): I have never *felt* better in my life.

PAULA (*looking round innocently*): Have I said anything awkward? Aubrey, tell Mrs Cortelyon how stupid and thoughtless I always am!

MRS CORTELYON (*to* DRUMMLE *who is now standing close to her*): Really, Cayley – ! (*He soothes her with a nod and smile and a motion of his finger to his lip*.) Mrs Tanqueray, I am afraid my explanation will not be quite so satisfactory as either of those you have just helped me to. You may have heard – but, if you have heard, you have doubtless forgotten – that twenty years ago, when your husband first lived here, I was a constant visitor at Highercoombe.

PAULA: Twenty years ago – fancy! I was a naughty little child then.

MRS CORTELYON: Possibly. Well, at that time, and till the end of her life, my affections were centred upon the lady of this house.

PAULA: Were they? That was very sweet of you.

ELLEAN *approaches* MRS CORTELYON, *listening intently to her*.

MRS CORTELYON: I will say no more on that score, but I must add this: when, two months ago, you came here, I realised, perhaps for the first time, that I was a middle-aged woman, and that it had become impossible for me to accept without some effort a breaking-in upon many tender associations. There, Mrs Tanqueray, that is my confession. Will you try to understand it and pardon me?

PAULA (*watching* ELLEAN, – *sneeringly*): Ellean dear, you appear to be very interested in Mrs Cortelyon's reminiscences; I don't think I can do better than make you my mouthpiece – there is such sympathy between us. What do you say – can we bring ourselves to forgive Mrs Cortelyon for neglecting us for two weary months?

MRS CORTELYON (*to* ELLEAN, *pleasantly*): Well, Ellean? (*With a little cry of tenderness* ELLEAN *impulsively sits beside* MRS CORTELYON *and takes her hand*.) My dear child!

PAULA (*in an undertone to* AUBREY): Ellean isn't so very slow in taking to Mrs Cortelyon!

MRS CORTELYON (*to* PAULA *and* AUBREY): Come, this encourages me to broach my scheme. Mrs Tanqueray, it strikes me that you two good people are just now excellent company for each other, while Ellean would perhaps be glad of a little peep into the world you are anxious to avoid. Now, I'm going to Paris tomorrow for a week or two before settling down in Chester Square, so – don't gasp, both of you! – if this girl is willing, will you let her come with me to Paris, and afterwards remain with me in town during the Season? (ELLEAN *utters an exclamation of surprise.* PAULA *is silent.*) What do you say?

AUBREY: Paula – Paula dear. (*Hesitatingly.*) My dear Mrs Cortelyon, this is wonderfully kind of you; I am really at a loss to – eh, Cayley?

DRUMMLE (*watching* PAULA *apprehensively*): Kind! Now I must say I don't think so! I begged Alice to take *me* to Paris, and she declined. I am thrown over for Ellean! Ha! ha!

MRS CORTELYON (*laughing*): What nonsense you talk, Cayley!

The laughter dies out. PAULA *remains quite still.*

AUBREY: Paula dear.

PAULA (*slowly collecting herself*): One moment. I – I don't quite – (*To* MRS CORTELYON.) You propose that Ellean leaves Highercoombe almost at once and remains with you some months?

MRS CORTELYON: It would be a mercy to me. You can afford to be generous to a desolate old widow. Come, Mrs Tanqueray, won't you spare her?

PAULA: Won't *I* spare her. (*Suspiciously.*) Have you mentioned your plan to Aubrey – before I came in?

MRS CORTELYON: No, I had no opportunity.

PAULA: Nor to Ellean?

MRS CORTELYON: Oh, no.

PAULA (*looking about her, in suppressed excitement*): This hasn't been discussed at all, behind my back?

MRS CORTELYON: My dear Mrs Tanqueray!

PAULA: Ellean, let us hear your voice in the matter!

ELLEAN: I should like to go with Mrs Cortelyon –

PAULA: Ah!

ELLEAN: That is, if – if –

PAULA: If – if what?

ELLEAN (*looking towards* AUBREY, *appealingly*): Papa!

PAULA (*in a hard voice*): Oh, of course – I forgot. (*To* AUBREY.) My dear Aubrey, it rests with you, naturally, whether I am – to lose – Ellean.

AUBREY: Lose Ellean! (*Advancing to* PAULA.) There is no question of losing Ellean. You would see Ellean in town constantly when she returned from Paris; isn't that so, Mrs Cortelyon?

MRS CORTELYON: Certainly.

PAULA (*laughing softly*): Oh, I didn't know I should be allowed that privilege.

MRS CORTELYON: Privilege, my dear Mrs Tanqueray!

PAULA: Ha, ha! that makes all the difference, doesn't it?

AUBREY (*with assumed gaiety*): All the difference? I should think so! (*To* ELLEAN, *laying his hand upon her head, tenderly.*) And are you quite certain you wish to see what the world is like on the other side of Black Moor?

ELLEAN: If you are willing, papa, I am quite certain.

AUBREY (*looking at* PAULA *irresolutely, then speaking with an effort*): Then I – I am willing.

PAULA (*rising and striking the table lightly with her clenched hand*) That decides it! (*There is a general movement. Excitedly to* MRS CORTELYON, *who advances towards her.*) When do you want her?

MRS CORTELYON: We go to town this afternoon at five o'clock, and sleep tonight at Bayliss's. There is barely time for her to make her preparations.

PAULA: I will undertake that she is ready.

MRS CORTELYON: I've a great deal to scramble through at home too, as you may guess. Good-bye!

PAULA (*turning away*): Mrs Cortelyon is going.

PAULA *stands looking out of the window, with her back to those in the room.*

MRS CORTELYON (*to* DRUMMLE): Cayley –

DRUMMLE (*to her*): Eh?

MRS CORTELYON: I've gone through it, for the sake of Aubrey and his child, but I – I feel a hundred. Is that a mad-woman?

DRUMMLE: Of course; all jealous women are mad. (*He goes out with* AUBREY.)

MRS CORTELYON (*hesitatingly, to* PAULA): Good-bye, Mrs Tanqueray.

PAULA *inclines her head with the slightest possible movement, then resumes her former position.* ELLEAN *comes from the hall and takes* MRS CORTELYON *out of the room. After a brief silence,* PAULA *turns with a fierce cry, and hurriedly takes off her coat and hat, and tosses them upon the settee.*

PAULA: Oh! Oh! Oh! (*She drops into the chair as* AUBREY *returns; he stands looking at her.*) Who's that?

AUBREY: I. You have altered your mind about going out?

PAULA: Yes. Please to ring the bell.

AUBREY (*touching the bell*): You are angry about Mrs Cortelyon and Ellean. Let me try to explain my reasons –

PAULA: Be careful what you say to me just now! I have never felt like this – except once – in my life. Be careful what you say to me!

A SERVANT *enters.*

PAULA (*rising*): Is Watts at the door with the cart?

SERVANT: Yes, ma'am.

PAULA: Tell him to drive down to the post-office directly, with this. (*Picking up the letter which has been lying upon the table.*)

AUBREY: With that?

PAULA: Yes. My letter to Lady Orreyed. (*Giving the letter to the* SERVANT, *who goes out.*)

AUBREY: Surely you don't wish me to countermand any orders of yours to a servant? Call the man back – take the letter from him!

PAULA: I have not the slightest intention of doing so.

AUBREY: I must, then. (*Going to the door. She snatches up her hat and coat and follows him.*) What are you going to do?

PAULA: If you stop that letter, walk out of the house.

He hesitates, then leaves the door.

AUBREY: I am right in believing that to be the letter inviting George Orreyed and his wife to stay here, am I not?

PAULA: Oh yes – quite right.

AUBREY: Let it go; I'll write to him by-and-by.

PAULA (*facing him*): You dare!

AUBREY: Hush, Paula!

PAULA: Insult me again and, upon my word, I'll go straight out of the house!

AUBREY: Insult you?

PAULA: Insult me! What else is it? My God! what else is it? What do you mean by taking Ellean from me?

AUBREY: Listen –

PAULA: Listen to *me!* And how do you take her? You pack her off in the care of a woman who has deliberately held aloof from me, who's thrown mud at me! Yet this Cortelyon creature has only to put foot here once to be entrusted with the charge of the girl you know I dearly want to keep near me!

AUBREY: Paula dear! hear me – !

PAULA: Ah! of course, of course! I can't be so useful to your daughter as such people as this; and so I'm to be given the go-by for any town friend of yours who turns up and chooses to patronise us! Hah! Very well, at any rate, as you take Ellean from me you justify my looking for companions where I can most readily find 'em.

AUBREY: You wish me to fully appreciate your reason for sending that letter to Lady Orreyed?

PAULA: Precisely — I do.

AUBREY: And could you, after all, go back to associates of that order? It's not possible!

PAULA (*mockingly*): What, not after the refining influence of these intensely respectable surroundings? (*Going to the door.*) We'll see!

AUBREY: Paula!

PAULA (*violently*): We'll see!

She goes out. He stands still looking after her.

THE THIRD ACT

The drawing-room at 'Highercoombe'. Facing the spectator are two large French windows, sheltered by a verandah, leading into the garden; on the right is a door opening into a small hall. The fireplace, with a large mirror above it, is on the left-hand side of the room, and higher up in the same wall are double doors recessed. The room is richly furnished, and everything betokens taste and luxury. The windows are open, and there is moonlight in the garden.

LADY ORREYED, a pretty, affected doll of a woman with a mincing voice and flaxen hair, is sitting on the ottoman, her head resting against the drum, and her eyes closed. PAULA, looking pale, worn, and thoroughly unhappy, is sitting at a table. Both are in sumptuous dinner-gowns.

LADY ORREYED (*opening her eyes*): Well, I never! I dropped off! (*Feeling her hair.*) Just fancy! Where are the men?

PAULA (*icily*): Outside, smoking.

> *A SERVANT enters with coffee, which he hands to LADY ORREYED. SIR GEORGE ORREYED comes in by the window. He is a man of about thirty-five, with a low forehead, a receding chin, a vacuous expression, and an ominous redness about the nose.*

LADY ORREYED (*taking coffee*): Here's Dodo.

SIR GEORGE: I say, the flies under the verandah make you swear. (*The SERVANT hands coffee to PAULA, who declines it, then to SIR GEORGE, who takes a cup.*) Hi! wait a bit! (*He looks at the tray searchingly, then puts back his cup.*) Never mind. (*Quietly to LADY ORREYED.*) I say, they're dooced sparin' with their liqueur, ain't they?

> *The SERVANT goes out at window.*

PAULA (*to SIR GEORGE*): Won't you take coffee, George?

SIR GEORGE: No thanks. It's gettin' near time for a whisky and potass. (*Approaching PAULA, regarding LADY ORREYED admiringly.*) I say, Birdie looks rippin' tonight, don't she?

PAULA: Your wife?

SIR GEORGE: Yaas — Birdie.

PAULA: Rippin'?

SIR GEORGE: Yaas.

PAULA: Quite — quite rippin'.

He moves round to the settee. PAULA *watches him with distaste, then rises and walks away.* SIR GEORGE *falls asleep on the settee.*

LADY ORREYED: Paula love, I fancied you and Aubrey were a little more friendly at dinner. You haven't made it up, have you?

PAULA: We? Oh, no. We speak before others, that's all.

LADY ORREYED: And how long do you intend to carry on this game, dear?

PAULA (*turning away impatiently*): I really can't tell you.

LADY ORREYED: Sit down, old girl; don't be so fidgety. (PAULA *sits on the upper seat of the ottoman with her back to* LADY ORREYED.) Of course, it's my duty, as an old friend, to give you a good talking-to – (PAULA *glares at her suddenly and fiercely.*) – but really I've found one gets so many smacks in the face through interfering in matrimonial squabbles that I've determined to drop it.

PAULA: I think you're wise.

LADY ORREYED: However, I must say that I do wish you'd look at marriage in a more solemn light – just as I do, in fact. It is such a beautiful thing – marriage, and if people in our position don't respect it, and set a good example by living happily with their husbands, what can you expect from the middle classes? When did this sad state of affairs between you and Aubrey actually begin?

PAULA: Actually, a fortnight and three days ago; I haven't calculated the minutes.

LADY ORREYED: A day or two before Dodo and I turned up – arrived.

PAULA: Yes. One always remembers one thing by another; we left off speaking to each other the morning I wrote asking you to visit us.

LADY ORREYED: Lucky for you I was able to pop down, wasn't it, dear?

PAULA (*glaring at her again*): Most fortunate.

LADY ORREYED: A serious split with your husband without a pal on the premises – I should say, without a friend in the house – would be most unpleasant.

PAULA (*turning to her abruptly*): This place must be horribly doleful for you and George just now. At least you ought to consider him before me. Why don't you leave me to my difficulties?

LADY ORREYED: Oh, we're quite comfortable, dear, thank you – both of us. George and me are so wrapped up in each other, it doesn't matter where we are. I don't want to crow over you, old girl, but I've got a perfect husband.

SIR GEORGE *is now fast asleep, his head thrown back and his mouth open, looking hideous.*

PAULA (*glancing at* SIR GEORGE): So you've given me to understand.

LADY ORREYED: Not that we don't have our little differences. Why, we fell out only this very morning. You remember the diamond and ruby tiara Charley Prestwick gave poor dear Connie Tirlemont years ago, don't you?

PAULA: No, I do not.

LADY ORREYED: No? Well, it's in the market. Benjamin of Piccadilly has got it in his shop-window, and I've set my heart on it.

PAULA: You consider it quite necessary?

LADY ORREYED: Yes, because what I say to Dodo is this – a lady of my station must smother herself with hair ornaments. It's different with you, love – people don't look for so much blaze from you, but I've got rank to keep up; haven't I?

PAULA: Yes.

LADY ORREYED: Well, that was the cause of the little set-to between I and Dodo this morning. He broke two chairs, he was in such a rage. I forgot, they're your chairs; do you mind?

PAULA: No.

LADY ORREYED: You know, poor Dodo can't lose his temper without smashing something; if it isn't a chair, it's a mirror; if it isn't that, it's china – a bit of Dresden for choice. Dear old pet! he loves a bit of Dresden when he's furious. He doesn't really throw things *at* me, dear; he simply lifts them up and drops them, like a gentleman. I expect our room upstairs will look rather wrecky before I get that tiara.

PAULA: Excuse the suggestion, perhaps your husband can't afford it.

LADY ORREYED: Oh, how dreadfully changed you are, Paula! Dodo can always mortgage something, or borrow of his ma. What *is* coming to you!

PAULA: Ah! (*She sits at the piano and touches the keys.*)

LADY ORREYED: Oh, yes, do play! That's the one thing I envy you for.

PAULA: What shall I play?

LADY ORREYED: What was that heavenly piece you gave us last night, dear?

PAULA: A bit of Schubert. Would you like to hear it again?

LADY ORREYED: You don't know any comic songs, do you?

PAULA: I'm afraid not.

LADY ORREYED: I leave it to you, then.

      PAULA *plays.* AUBREY *and* CAYLEY DRUMMLE *appear outside the window; they look into the room.*

AUBREY (*to* DRUMMLE): You can see her face in that mirror. Poor girl, how ill and wretched she looks.

DRUMMLE: When are the Orreyeds going?

AUBREY: Heaven knows! (*Entering the room.*)

DRUMMLE: But *you're* entertaining them; what's it to do with Heaven? (*Following* AUBREY.)

AUBREY: Do you know, Cayley, that even the Orreyeds serve a useful purpose? My wife actually speaks to me before our guests – think of that! I've come to rejoice at the presence of the Orreyeds!

DRUMMLE: I daresay; we're taught that beetles are sent for a benign end.

AUBREY: Cayley, talk to Paula again tonight.

DRUMMLE: Certainly, if I get the chance.

AUBREY: Let's contrive it. George is asleep; perhaps I can get that doll out of the way. (*As they advance into the room,* PAULA *abruptly ceases playing and finds interest in a volume of music.* SIR GEORGE *is now nodding and snoring apoplectically*.) Lady Orreyed, whenever you feel inclined for a game of billiards I'm at your service.

LADY ORREYED (*jumping up*): Charmed, I'm sure! I really thought you'd forgotten poor little me. Oh, look at Dodo!

AUBREY: No, no, don't wake him; he's tired.

LADY ORREYED: I must, he looks so plain. (*Rousing* SIR GEORGE.) Dodo! Dodo!

SIR GEORGE (*stupidly*): 'Ullo!

LADY ORREYED: Dodo, dear, you were snoring.

SIR GEORGE: Oh, I say, you could 'a told me that by-and-by.

AUBREY: You want a cigar, George; come into the billiard-room. (*Giving his arm to* LADY ORREYED.) Cayley, bring Paula.

AUBREY *and* LADY ORREYED *go out.*

SIR GEORGE (*rising*): Hey, what! Billiard-room! (*Looking at his watch.*) How goes the – ? Phew! 'Ullo, 'Ullo! Whisky and potass!

He goes rapidly after AUBREY *and* LADY ORREYED. PAULA *resumes playing.*

PAULA (*after a pause*): Don't moon about after me, Cayley; follow the others.

DRUMMLE: Thanks, by-and-by. (*Sitting.*) That's pretty.

PAULA (*after another pause, still playing*): I wish you wouldn't stare so.

DRUMMLE: Was I staring? I'm sorry. (*She plays a little longer, then stops suddenly, rises, and goes to the window, where she stands looking out.* DRUMMLE *moves from the ottoman to the settee.*) A lovely night.

PAULA (*startled*): Oh! (*Without turning to him.*) Why do you hop about like a monkey?

DRUMMLE: Hot rooms play the deuce with the nerves. Now, it would have done you good to have walked in the garden with us after dinner and made merry. Why didn't you?

PAULA: You know why.

DRUMMLE: Ah, you're thinking of the – difference between you and Aubrey?

PAULA: Yes, I *am* thinking of it.

DRUMMLE: Well, so am I. How long – ?

PAULA: Getting on for three weeks.

DRUMMLE: Bless me, it must be! And this would have been such a night to have healed it! Moonlight, the stars, the scent of flowers; and yet enough darkness to enable a kind woman to rest her hand for an instant on the arm of a good fellow who loves her. Ah, ha! it's a wonderful power, dear Mrs Aubrey, the power of an offended woman! Only realise it! Just that one touch – the mere tips of her fingers – and, for herself and another, she changes the colour of the whole world!

PAULA (*turning to him, calmly*): Cayley, my dear man, you talk exactly like a very romantic old lady. (*She leaves the window and sits playing with the knick-knacks on the table.*)

DRUMMLE (*to himself*): H'm, that hasn't done it! Well – ha, ha! – I accept the suggestion. An old woman, eh?

PAULA: Oh, I didn't intend –

DRUMMLE: But why not? I've every qualification – well, almost. And I confess it would have given this withered bosom a throb of grandmotherly satisfaction if I could have seen you and Aubrey at peace before I take my leave tomorrow.

PAULA: Tomorrow, Cayley!

DRUMMLE: I must.

PAULA: Oh, this house is becoming unendurable.

DRUMMLE: You're very kind. But you've got the Orreyeds.

PAULA (*fiercely*): The Orreyeds! I – I hate the Orreyeds! I lie awake at night, hating them!

DRUMMLE: Pardon me, I've understood that their visit is, in some degree, owing to – hem! – your suggestion.

PAULA: Heavens! that doesn't make me like them better. Somehow or another, I – I've outgrown these people. This woman – I used to think her 'jolly!' – sickens me. I can't breathe when she's near me: the whiff of her handkerchief turns me faint! And she patronises me by the hour, until I – I feel my nails growing longer with every word she speaks!

DRUMMLE: My dear lady, why on earth don't you say all this to Aubrey?

PAULA: Oh, I've been such an utter fool, Cayley!

DRUMMLE (*soothingly*): Well, well, mention it to Aubrey!

PAULA: No, no, you don't understand. What do you think I've done?

DRUMMLE: Done! What, *since* you invited the Orreyeds!

PAULA: Yes; I must tell you –

DRUMMLE: Perhaps you'd better not.

PAULA: Look here! I've intercepted some letters from Mrs Cortelyon and Ellean to – him. (*Producing three unopened letters from the bodice of her dress.*) There are the accursed things! From Paris – two from the Cortelyon woman, the other from Ellean!

DRUMMLE: But why – why?

PAULA: I don't know. Yes, I do! I saw letters coming from Ellean to her father; not a line to me – not a line. And one morning it happened I was downstairs before he was, and I spied this one lying with his heap on the breakfast-table, and I slipped it into my pocket – out of malice, Cayley, pure devilry! And a day or two afterwards I met Elwes the postman at the Lodge, and took the letters from him, and found these others amongst 'em. I felt simply fiendish when I saw them – fiendish! (*Returning the letters to her bodice.*) And now I carry them about with me, and they're scorching me like a mustard plaster!

DRUMMLE: Oh, this accounts for Aubrey not hearing from Paris lately!

PAULA: That's an ingenious conclusion to arrive at! Of course it does! (*With an hysterical laugh.*) Ha, ha!

DRUMMLE: Well, well! (*Laughing.*) Ha, ha, ha!

PAULA (*turning upon him*): I suppose it *is* amusing!

DRUMMLE: I beg pardon.

PAULA: Heaven knows I've little enough to brag about! I'm a bad lot, but not in mean tricks of this sort. In all my life this is the most caddish thing I've done. How am I to get rid of these letters – that's what I want to know? How am I to get rid of them?

DRUMMLE: If I were you I should take Aubrey aside and put them into his hands as soon as possible.

PAULA: What! and tell him to his face that I – ! No, thank you. I suppose *you* wouldn't like to –

DRUMMLE: No, no; I won't touch 'em!

PAULA: And you call yourself my friend?

DRUMMLE (*good-humouredly*): No, I don't!

PAULA: Perhaps I'll tie them together and give them to his man in the morning.

DRUMMLE: That won't avoid an explanation.

PAULA (*recklessly*): Oh, then he must miss them –

DRUMMLE: And trace them.

PAULA (*throwing herself upon the ottoman*): I don't care!

DRUMMLE: I know you don't; but let me send him to you now, may I?

PAULA: Now! What do you think a woman's made of? I couldn't stand it, Cayley. I haven't slept for nights; and last night there was thunder, too! I believe I've got the horrors.

DRUMMLE (*taking the little hand-mirror from the table*): You'll sleep well enough when you deliver those letters. Come, come, Mrs Aubrey – a good night's rest! (*Holding the mirror before her face.*) It's quite time.

She looks at herself for a moment, then snatches the mirror from him.

PAULA: You brute, Cayley, to show me that!

DRUMMLE: Then – may I? Be guided by a fr – a poor old woman! May I?

PAULA: You'll kill me, amongst you!

DRUMMLE: What do you say?

PAULA (*after a pause*): Very well. (*He nods his head and goes out rapidly. She looks after him for a moment, and calls 'Cayley! Cayley!' Then she again produces the letters, deliberately, one by one, fingering them with aversion. Suddenly she starts, turning her head towards the door.*) Ah!

AUBREY *enters quickly.*

AUBREY: Paula!

PAULA (*handing him the letters, her face averted*): There! (*He examines the letters, puzzled, and looks at her inquiringly.*) They are many days old. I stole them, I suppose to make you anxious and unhappy.

He looks at the letters again, then lays them aside on the table.

AUBREY (*gently*): Paula, dear, it doesn't matter.

PAULA (*after a short pause*): Why – why do you take it like this?

AUBREY: What did you expect?

PAULA: Oh, but I suppose silent reproaches are really the severest. And then, naturally, you are itching to open your letters. (*She crosses the room as if to go.*)

AUBREY: Paula! (*She pauses.*) Surely, surely it's all over now?

PAULA: All over! (*Mockingly.*) Has my step-daughter returned then? When did she arrive? I haven't heard of it!

AUBREY: You can be very cruel.

PAULA: That word's always on a man's lips; he uses it if his soup's cold. (*With another movement as if to go.*) Need we –

AUBREY: I know I've wounded you, Paula. But isn't there any way out of this?

PAULA: When does Ellean return? Tomorrow? Next week?

AUBREY (*wearily*): Oh! Why should we grudge Ellean the little pleasure she is likely to find in Paris and in London.

PAULA: I grudge her nothing, if that's a hit at me. But with that woman –

AUBREY: It must be that woman or another. You know that at present we are unable to give Ellean the opportunity of – of –

PAULA: Of mixing with respectable people.

AUBREY: The opportunity of gaining friends, experience, ordinary knowledge of the world. If you are interested in Ellean, can't you see how useful Mrs Cortelyon's good offices are?

PAULA: May I put one question? At the end of the London season, when Mrs Cortelyon has done with Ellean, is it quite understood that the girl comes back to us? (AUBREY *is silent*.) Is it? Is it?

AUBREY: Let us wait till the end of the season –

PAULA: Oh! I knew it. You're only fooling me; you put me off with any trash. I believe you've sent Ellean away, not for the reasons you give, but because you don't consider me a decent companion for her, because you're afraid she might get a little of her innocence rubbed off in my company? Come, isn't that the truth? Be honest! Isn't that it?

AUBREY: Yes. (*There is a moment's silence on both sides*.)

PAULA (*with uplifted hands as if to strike him*): Oh!

AUBREY (*taking her by the wrists*): Sit down. Sit down. (*He puts her into a chair; she shakes herself free with a cry*.) Now listen to me. Fond as you are, Paula, of harking back to your past, there's one chapter of it, you always let alone. I've never asked you to speak of it; you've never offered to speak of it. I mean the chapter that relates to the time when you were – like Ellean. (*She attempts to rise; he restrains her*.) No, no.

PAULA: I don't choose to talk about that time. I won't satisfy your curiosity.

AUBREY: My dear Paula, I have no curiosity – I know what you were at Ellean's age. I'll tell you. You hadn't a thought that wasn't a wholesome one, you hadn't an impulse that didn't tend towards good, you never harboured a notion you couldn't have gossiped about to a parcel of children. (*She makes another effort to rise: he lays his hand lightly on her shoulder*.) And this was a very few years back – there are days now when you look like a schoolgirl – but think of the difference between the two Paulas. You'll have to think hard, because after a cruel life one's perceptions grow a thick skin. But, for God's sake, do think till you get these two images clearly in your mind, and then ask yourself what sort of a friend such a woman as you are today would have been for a girl of seven or eight years ago.

PAULA (*rising*): How dare you? I could be almost as good a friend to Ellean as her own mother would have been had she lived. I know what you mean. How dare you?

AUBREY: You say that; very likely you believe it. But you're blind, Paula; you're blind. You! Every belief that a young, pure-minded girl holds sacred – that you once held sacred – you now make a target for a jest, a sneer, a paltry cynicism. I tell you, you're not mistress any longer of your thoughts or your tongue. Why, how often, sitting between you and Ellean, have I seen her cheeks turn scarlet as you've rattled off some tale that belongs by right to the club or the smoking-room! Have you noticed the blush? If you have, has the cause of it ever struck you? And this is the girl you say you love, I admit that you *do* love, whose love you expect in return! Oh, Paula, I make the best, the only, excuse for you when I tell you you're blind!

PAULA: Ellean – Ellean blushes easily.

AUBREY: You blushed as easily a few years ago.

PAULA (*after a short pause*): Well! Have you finished your sermon?

AUBREY (*with a gesture of despair*): Oh, Paula!

Going up to the window and standing with his back to the room.

PAULA (*to herself*): A few – years ago! (*She walks slowly towards the door, then suddenly drops upon the ottoman in a paroxysm of weeping.*) O God! A few years ago!

AUBREY (*going to her*): Paula!

PAULA (*sobbing*): Oh, don't touch me!

AUBREY: Paula!

PAULA: Oh, go away from me! (*He goes back a few steps, and after a little while she becomes calmer and rises unsteadily; then in an altered tone.*) Look here – ! (*He advances a step; she checks him with a quick gesture.*) Look here! Get rid of these people – Mabel and her husband – as soon as possible! I – I've done with them!

AUBREY (*in a whisper*): Paula!

PAULA: And then – then – when the time comes for Ellean to leave Mrs Cortelyon, give me – give me another chance! (*He advances again, but she shrinks away.*) No, no!

She goes out by the door on the right. He sinks on to the settee, covering his eyes with his hands. There is a brief silence, then a SERVANT *enters.*

SERVANT: Mrs Cortelyon, sir, with Miss Ellean.

AUBREY *rises to meet* MRS CORTELYON, *who enters, followed by* ELLEAN, *both being in travelling dresses. The* SERVANT *withdraws.*

MRS CORTELYON (*shaking hands with* AUBREY): Oh, my dear Aubrey!

AUBREY: Mrs Cortelyon! (*Kissing* ELLEAN.) Ellean dear!

ELLEAN: Papa, is all well at home?

MRS CORTELYON: We're shockingly anxious.

AUBREY: Yes, yes, all's well. This is quite unexpected. (*To* MRS CORTELYON.) You've found Paris insufferably hot?

MRS CORTELYON: Insufferably hot! Paris is pleasant enough. We've had no letter from you!

AUBREY: I wrote to Ellean a week ago.

MRS CORTELYON: Without alluding to the subject I had written to you upon.

AUBREY (*thinking*): Ah, of course –

MRS CORTELYON: And since then we've both written and you've been absolutely silent. Oh, it's too bad!

AUBREY (*picking up the letters from the table*): It isn't altogether my fault. Here are the letters –

ELLEAN: Papa!

MRS CORTELYON: They're unopened.

AUBREY: An accident delayed their reaching me till this evening. I'm afraid this has upset you very much.

MRS CORTELYON: Upset me!

ELLEAN (*in an undertone to* MRS CORTELYON): Never mind. Not now, dear – not tonight.

AUBREY: Eh?

MRS CORTELYON (*to* ELLEAN *aloud*): Child, run away and take your things off. She doesn't look as if she'd journeyed from Paris today.

AUBREY: I've never seen her with such a colour. (*Taking* ELLEAN'*s hands*.)

ELLEAN (*to* AUBREY, *in a faint voice*): Papa, Mrs Cortelyon has been so very, very kind to me, but I – I have come home. (*She goes out*.)

AUBREY: Come home! (*To* MRS CORTELYON.) Ellean returns to us, then?

MRS CORTELYON: That's the very point I put to you in my letters, and you oblige me to travel from Paris to Willowmere on a warm day to settle it. I think perhaps it's right that Ellean should be with you just now, although I – My dear friend, circumstances are a little altered.

AUBREY: Alice, you're in some trouble.

MRS CORTELYON: Well – yes, I *am* in trouble. You remember pretty little Mrs Brereton who was once Caroline Ardale?

AUBREY: Quite well.

MRS CORTELYON: She's a widow now, poor thing. She has the *entresol* of the house where we've been lodging in the Avenue de Friedland. Caroline's a dear chum of mine; she formed a great liking for Ellean.

AUBREY: I'm very glad.

MRS CORTELYON: Yes, it's nice for her to meet her mother's friends. Er – that young Hugh Ardale the papers were full of some time ago – he's Caroline Brereton's brother, you know.

AUBREY: No, I didn't know. What did he do? I forget.

MRS CORTELYON: Checked one of those horrid mutinies at some far-away station in India, marched down with a handful of his men and a few faithful natives, and held the place until he was relieved. They gave him his company and a V.C. for it.

AUBREY: And he's Mrs Brereton's brother?

MRS CORTELYON: Yes. He's with his sister – *was*, rather – in Paris. He's home – invalided. Good gracious, Aubrey, why don't you help me out? Can't you guess what has occurred?

AUBREY: Alice.

MRS CORTELYON: Young Ardale – Ellean!

AUBREY: An attachment?

MRS CORTELYON: Yes, Aubrey. (*After a little pause.*) Well, I suppose I've got myself into sad disgrace. But really I didn't forsee anything of this kind. A serious, reserved child like Ellean, and a boyish, high-spirited soldier – it never struck me as being likely. (AUBREY *paces to and fro thoughtfully.*) I did all I could directly Captain Ardale spoke – wrote to you at once. Why on earth don't you receive your letters promptly, and when you do get them why can't you open them? I endured the anxiety till last night, and then made up my mind – home! Of course, it has worried me terribly. My head's bursting. Are there any salts about? (AUBREY *fetches a bottle from the cabinet and hands it to her.*) We've had one of those hateful smooth crossings that won't let you be properly indisposed.

AUBREY: My dear Alice, I assure you I've no thought of blaming you.

MRS CORTELYON: That statement always precedes a quarrel.

AUBREY: I don't know whether this is the worst or the best luck. How will my wife regard it? Is Captain Ardale a good fellow?

MRS CORTELYON: My dear Aubrey, you'd better read up the accounts of his wonderful heroism. Face to face with death for a whole week; always with a smile and a cheering word for the poor helpless souls depending on him! Of course, it's that that has stirred the depths of your child's nature. I've watched her while we've been dragging the story out of him, and if angels look different from Ellean at that moment, I don't desire to meet any, that's all!

AUBREY: If you were in my position – ? But you can't judge.

MRS CORTELYON: Why, if I had a marriageable daughter of my own and Captain Ardale proposed for her, naturally I should cry my eyes out all night – but I should thank Heaven in the morning.

AUBREY: You believe so thoroughly in him?

MRS CORTELYON: Do you think I should have only a headache at this minute if I didn't! Look here, you've got to see me down the lane; that's the least you can do, my friend. Come into my house for a moment and shake hands with Hugh.

AUBREY: What, is he here?

MRS CORTELYON: He came through with us, to present himself formally tomorrow. Where are my gloves? (AUBREY *fetches them from the ottoman.*) Make my apologies to Mrs Tanqueray, please. She's well, I hope? (*Going towards the door.*) I can't feel sorry she hasn't seen me in this condition.

ELLEAN *enters.*

ELLEAN (*to* MRS CORTELYON): I've been waiting to wish you good-night. I was afraid I'd missed you.

MRS CORTELYON: Good-night, Ellean.

ELLEAN (*in a low voice, embracing* MRS CORTELYON): I can't thank you. Dear Mrs Cortelyon!

MRS CORTELYON (*her arms round* ELLEAN, *in a whisper to* AUBREY): Speak a word to her. (MRS CORTELYON *goes out.*)

AUBREY (*to* ELLEAN): Ellean, I'm going to see Mrs Cortelyon home. Tell Paula where I am; explain, dear. (*Going to door.*)

ELLEAN (*her head drooping*): Yes. (*Quickly.*) Father! You are angry with me – disappointed?

AUBREY: Angry? – no.

ELLEAN: Disappointed?

AUBREY (*smiling and going to her and taking her hand*): If so, it's only because you've shaken my belief in my discernment. I thought you took after your poor mother a little, Ellean; but there's a look on your face tonight, dear, that I never saw on hers – never, never.

ELLEAN (*leaning her head on his shoulder*): Perhaps I ought not to have gone away?

AUBREY: Hush! You're quite happy?

AUBREY: Yes.

AUBREY: That's right. Then, as you are quite happy there is something I particularly want you to do for me Ellean.

ELLEAN: What is that?

AUBREY: Be very gentle with Paula. Will you?

ELLEAN: You think I have been unkind.

AUBREY (*kissing her upon the forehead*): Be very gentle with Paula.

He goes out and she stands looking after him, then, as she turns thoughtfully from the door, a rose is thrown through the window and falls at her feet. She picks up the flower wonderingly and goes to the window.

ELLEAN (*starting back*): Hugh!

HUGH ARDALE, *a handsome young man of about seven-and-twenty, with a boyish face and manner, appears outside the window.*

HUGH: Nelly! Nelly dear!

ELLEAN: What's the matter?

HUGH: Hush! Nothing. It's only fun. (*Laughing.*) Ha, ha, ha! I've found out that Mrs Cortelyon's meadow runs up to your father's plantation; I've come through a gap in the hedge.

ELLEAN: Why, Hugh?

HUGH: I'm miserable at The Warren; it's so different from the Avenue de

Friedland. Don't look like that! Upon my word I meant just to peep at your home and go back, but I saw figures moving about here, and came nearer, hoping to get a glimpse of you. Was that your father? (*Entering the room.*)

ELLEAN: Yes.

HUGH: Isn't this fun! A rabbit ran across my foot while I was hiding behind that old yew.

ELLEAN: You must go away; it's not right for you to be here like this.

HUGH: But it's only fun, I tell you. You take everything so seriously. Do wish me good-night.

ELLEAN: We have said good-night.

HUGH: In the hall at The Warren before Mrs Cortelyon and a man-servant. Oh, it's so different from the Avenue de Friedland!

ELLEAN (*giving him her hand hastily*): Good-night, Hugh.

HUGH: Is that all? We might be the merest acquaintances.

He momentarily embraces her, but she releases herself.

ELLEAN: It's when you're like this that you make me feel utterly miserable. (*Throwing the rose from her angrily.*) Oh!

HUGH: I've offended you now, I suppose?

ELLEAN: Yes.

HUGH: Forgive me, Nelly. Come into the garden for five minutes; we'll stroll down to the plantation.

ELLEAN: No, no.

HUGH: For two minutes – to tell me you forgive me.

ELLEAN: I forgive you.

HUGH: Evidently. I sha'n't sleep a wink tonight after this. What a fool I am! Come down to the plantation. Make it up with me.

ELLEAN: There is somebody coming into this room. Do you wish to be seen here?

HUGH: I shall wait for you behind that yew-tree. You must speak to me. Nelly!

He disappears. PAULA *enters.*

PAULA: Ellean!

ELLEAN: You – you are very surprised to see me, Paula, of course.

PAULA: Why are you here? Why aren't you with – your friend?

ELLEAN: I've come home – if you'll have me. We left Paris this morning; Mrs Cortelyon brought me back. She was here a minute or two ago; papa has just gone with her to The Warren. He asked me to tell you.

PAULA: There are some people staying with us that I'd rather you didn't meet. It was hardly worth your while to return for a few hours.

ELLEAN: A few hours?

PAULA: Well, when do you go to London?

ELLEAN: I don't think I go to London, after all.

PAULA (*eagerly*): You — you've quarrelled with her?

ELLEAN: No, no, no, not that; but — Paula! (*In an altered tone.*) Paula.

PAULA (*startled*): Eh? (ELLEAN *goes deliberately to* PAULA *and kisses her.*) Ellean!

ELLEAN: Kiss me.

PAULA: What — what's come to you?

ELLEAN: I want to behave differently to you in the future. Is it too late?

PAULA: Too — late! (*Impulsively kissing* ELLEAN *and crying.*) No — no — no! No — no!

ELLEAN: Paula, don't cry.

PAULA (*wiping her eyes*): I'm a little shaky; I haven't been sleeping. It's all right, — talk to me.

ELLEAN: There is something I want to tell you —

PAULA: Is there — is there?

They sit together on the ottoman, PAULA *taking* ELLEAN'*s hand.*

ELLEAN: Paula, in our house in the Avenue de Friedland, on the floor below us, there was a Mrs Brereton. She used to be a friend of my mother's. Mrs Cortelyon and I spent a great deal of our time with her.

PAULA (*suspiciously*): Oh! (*Letting* ELLEAN'*s hand fall.*) Is this lady going to take you up in place of Mrs Cortelyon?

ELLEAN: No, no. Her brother is staying with her — *was* staying with her. Her brother — (*Breaking off in confusion.*)

PAULA: Well?

ELLEAN (*almost inaudibly*): Paula —

She rises and walks away, PAULA *following her.*

PAULA: Ellean! (*Taking hold of her.*) You're not in love!

ELLEAN *looks at* PAULA *appealingly.*

PAULA: Oh! *You* in love! You! Oh, this is why you've come home! Of course, you can make friends with me now! You'll leave us for good soon, I suppose; so it doesn't much matter being civil to me for a little while!

ELLEAN: Oh, Paula!

PAULA: Why, how you have deceived us — all of us! We've taken you for a cold-blooded little saint. The fools you've made of us! Saint Ellean! Saint Ellean!

ELLEAN: Ah, I might have known you'd only mock me!

PAULA (*her tone changing*): Eh?

ELLEAN: I — I can't talk to you. (*Sitting on the settee.*) You do nothing else but mock and sneer, nothing else.

PAULA: Ellean dear! Ellean! I didn't mean it. I'm so horribly jealous, it's a sort of curse on me. (*Kneeling beside* ELLEAN *and embracing her.*) My tongue

386 The Second Mrs Tanqueray

runs away with me. I'm going to alter, I swear I am. I've made some good resolutions, and, as God's above me, I'll keep them! If you are in love, if you do ever marry, that's no reason why we shouldn't be fond of each other. Come, you've kissed me of your own accord – you can't take it back. Now we're friends again, aren't we? Ellean dear! I want to know everything, everything. Ellean dear, Ellean!

ELLEAN: Paula, Hugh has done something that makes me very angry. He came with us from Paris today, to see papa. He is staying with Mrs Cortelyon and – I ought to tell you –

PAULA: Yes, yes. What?

ELLEAN: He has found his way by The Warren meadow through the plantation up to this house. He is waiting to bid me good-night. (*Glancing towards the garden.*) He is – out there.

PAULA: Oh!

ELLEAN: What shall I do?

PAULA: Bring him in to see me! Will you?

ELLEAN: No, no.

PAULA: But I'm dying to know him. Oh, yes, you must. I shall meet him before Aubrey does. (*Excitedly running her hands over her hair.*) I'm so glad. (ELLEAN *goes out by the window.*) The mirror – mirror. What a fright I must look! (*Not finding the hand-glass on the table, she jumps on to the settee, and surveys herself in the mirror over the mantelpiece, then sits quietly down and waits.*) Ellean! Just fancy! Ellean!

After a pause ELLEAN *enters by the window with* HUGH.

ELLEAN: Paula, this is Captain Ardale – Mrs Tanqueray.

PAULA *rises and turns, and she and* HUGH *stand staring blankly at each other for a moment or two; then* PAULA *advances and gives him her hand.*

PAULA (*in a strange voice, but calmly*): How do you do?

HUGH: How do you do?

PAULA (*to* ELLEAN): Mr Ardale and I have met in London, Ellean. Er – Captain Ardale, now?

HUGH: Yes.

ELLEAN: In London?

PAULA: They say the world's very small, don't they?

HUGH: Yes.

PAULA: Ellean, dear, I want to have a little talk about you to Mr Ardale – Captain Ardale – alone. (*Putting her arms round* ELLEAN, *and leading her to the door.*) Come back in a little while. (ELLEAN *nods to* PAULA *with a smile and goes out, while* PAULA *stands watching her at the open door.*) In a little while – in a little – (*Closing the door and then taking a seat facing* HUGH.) Be quick! Mr

Tanqueray has only gone down to The Warren with Mrs Cortelyon. What is to be done?

HUGH (*blankly*): Done?

PAULA: Done — done. Something must be done.

HUGH: I understand that Mr Tanqueray had married a Mrs — Mrs —

PAULA: Jarman?

HUGH: Yes.

PAULA: I'd been going by that name. You didn't follow my doings after we separated.

HUGH: No.

PAULA (*sneeringly*): No.

HUGH: I went out to India.

PAULA: What's to be done?

HUGH: Damn this chance!

PAULA: Oh, my God!

HUGH: Your husband doesn't know, does he?

PAULA: That you and I — ?

HUGH: Yes.

PAULA: No. He knows about others.

HUGH: Not about me. How long were we — ?

PAULA: I don't remember, exactly.

HUGH: Do you — do you think it matters?

PAULA: His — his daughter. (*With a muttered exclamation he turns away and sits with his head in his hands.*) What's to be done?

HUGH: I wish I could think.

PAULA: Oh! Oh! What happened to that flat of ours in Ethelbert Street?

HUGH: I let it.

PAULA: All that pretty furniture?

HUGH: Sold it.

PAULA: I came across the key of the escritoire the other day in an old purse! (*Suddenly realising the horror and hopelessness of her position, and starting to her feet with an hysterical cry of rage.*) What am I maundering about?

HUGH: For God's sake, be quiet! Do let me think.

PAULA: This will send me mad! (*Suddenly turning and standing over him.*) You — you beast, to crop up in my life again like this!

HUGH: I always treated you fairly.

PAULA (*weakly*): Oh! I beg your pardon — I know you did — I — (*She sinks on to the settee, crying hysterically.*)

HUGH: Hush!

PAULA: She kissed me tonight! I'd won her over! I've had such a fight to make her love me! And now – just as she's beginning to love me, to bring this on her!

HUGH: Hush, hush! Don't break down!

PAULA (*sobbing*): You don't know! I – I haven't been getting on well in my marriage. It's been my fault. The life I used to lead spoilt me completely. But I'd made up my mind to turn over a new life from tonight. From tonight!

HUGH: Paula –

PAULA: Don't you call me that!

HUGH: Mrs Tanqueray, there is no cause for you to despair in this way. It's all right, I tell you – it *shall* be all right.

PAULA (*shivering*): What are we to do?

HUGH: Hold our tongues.

PAULA: Eh? (*Staring vacantly.*)

HUGH: The chances are a hundred to one against any one ever turning up who knew us when we were together. Besides, no one would be such a brute as to split on us. If anybody did do such a thing we should have to lie! What are we upsetting ourselves like this for, when we've simply got to hold our tongues?

PAULA: You're as mad as I am!

HUGH: Can you think of a better plan?

PAULA: There's only one plan possible – let's come to our senses! – Mr Tanqueray must be told.

HUGH: Your husband! What, and I lose Ellean! I lose Ellean!

PAULA: You've got to lose her.

HUGH: I won't lose her! I can't lose her!

PAULA: Didn't I read of your doing any number of brave things in India? Why, you seem to be an awful coward!

HUGH: That's another sort of pluck altogether; I haven't this sort of pluck.

PAULA: Oh, I don't ask *you* to tell Mr Tanqueray. That's my job.

HUGH (*standing over her*): You – you – you'd better! You –!

PAULA (*rising*): Don't bully me! I intend to.

HUGH (*taking hold of her; she wrenches herself free*): Look here, Paula! I never treated you badly – you've owned it. Why should you want to pay me out like this? You don't know how I love Ellean!

PAULA: Yes, that's just what I *do* know.

HUGH: I say you don't! She's as good as my own mother. I've been downright honest with her too. I told her, in Paris, that I'd been a bit wild at one time, and, after a damned wretched day, she promised to forgive me because of what I'd done since in India. She's behaved like an angel to me!

Surely I oughtn't to lose her, after all, just because I've been like other fellows! No; I haven't been half as rackety as a hundred men we could think of. Paula, don't pay me out for nothing; be fair to me, there's a good girl – be fair to me!

PAULA: Oh, I'm not considering you at all! I advise you not to stay here any longer; Mr Tanqueray is sure to be back soon.

HUGH (*taking up his hat*): What's the understanding between us then? What have we arranged to do?

PAULA: I don't know what you're going to do; I've got to tell Mr Tanqueray.

HUGH: By God, you shall do nothing of the sort! (*Approaching her fiercely.*)

PAULA: You shocking coward!

HUGH: If you dare! (*Going up to the window.*) Mind! If you dare!

PAULA (*following him*): Why, what would you do?

HUGH (*after a short pause, sullenly*): Nothing. I'd shoot myself – that's nothing. Good-night.

PAULA: Good-night.

>*He disappears. She walks unsteadily to the ottoman, and sits; and as she does so her hand falls upon the little silver mirror, which she takes up, staring at her own reflection.*

THE FOURTH ACT

The Drawing-room at 'Highercoombe', the same evening.

PAULA *is still seated on the ottoman, looking vacantly before her, with the little mirror in her hand.* LADY ORREYED *enters.*

LADY ORREYED: There you are! You never came into the billiard-room. Isn't it maddening – Cayley Drummle gives me sixty out of a hundred and beats me. I must be out of form, because I know I play remarkably well for a lady. Only last month – (PAULA *rises.*) Whatever is the matter with you, old girl?

PAULA: Why?

LADY ORREYED (*staring*): It's the light, I suppose. (PAULA *replaces the mirror on the table.*) By Aubrey's bolting from the billiard-table in that fashion I thought perhaps –

PAULA: Yes; it's all right.

LADY ORREYED: You've patched it up? (PAULA *nods.*) Oh, I am jolly glad –! I mean –

PAULA: Yes, I know what you mean. Thanks, Mabel.

LADY ORREYED (*kissing* PAULA): Now take my advice; for the future –

PAULA: Mabel, if I've been disagreeable to you while you've been staying here, I – I beg your pardon. (*Walking away and sitting down.*)

LADY ORREYED: You disagreeable, my dear? I haven't noticed it. Dodo and me both consider you make a first-class hostess, but then you've had such practice, haven't you? (*Dropping on to the ottoman and gaping.*) Oh, talk about being sleepy –!

PAULA: Why don't you –!

LADY ORREYED: Why, dear, I must hang about for Dodo. You may as well know it; he's in one of his moods.

PAULA (*under her breath*): Oh –!

LADY ORREYED: Now, it's not his fault; it was deadly dull for him while we were playing billiards. Cayley Drummle did ask him to mark, but I stopped that; it's so easy to make a gentleman look like a billiard-marker. This is just how it always is; if poor old Dodo has nothing to do, he loses count, as you may say.

PAULA: Hark!

SIR GEORGE ORREYED *enters, walking slowly and deliberately; he looks pale and watery-eyed.*

SIR GEORGE (*with mournful indistinctness*): I'm 'fraid we've lef' you a grea' deal to yourself tonight, Mrs Tanqueray. Attra'tions of billiards. I apol'gise. I say, where's ol' Aubrey?

PAULA: My husband has been obliged to go out to a neighbour's house.

SIR GEORGE: I want his advice on a rather pressing matter connected with my family – my family. (*Sitting.*) Tomorrow will do just as well.

LADY ORREYED (*to* PAULA): This is the mood I hate so – drivelling about his precious family.

SIR GEORGE: The fact is, Mrs Tanqueray, I am not easy in my min' 'bout the way I am treatin' my poor ol' mother.

LADY ORREYED (*to* PAULA): Do you hear that? That's *his* mother, but *my* mother he won't so much as look at!

SIR GEORGE: I shall write to Bruton Street firs' thing in the morning.

LADY ORREYED (*to* PAULA): Mamma has stuck to me through everything – well, you know!

SIR GEORGE: I'll get ol' Aubrey to figure out a letter. I'll drop line to Uncle Fitz too – dooced shame of the ol' feller to chuck me over in this manner. (*Wiping his eyes.*) All my family have chucked me over.

LADY ORREYED (*rising*): Dodo!

SIR GEORGE: Jus' because I've married beneath me, to be chucked over! Aunt Lydia, the General, Hooky Whitgrave, Lady Sugnall – my own dear sister! – all turn their backs on me. It's more than I can stan'!

LADY ORREYED (*approaching him with dignity*): Sir George, wish Mrs Tanqueray good-night at once and come upstairs. Do you hear me?

SIR GEORGE (*rising angrily*): Wha' –

LADY ORREYED: Be quiet!

SIR GEORGE: You presoom to order me about!

LADY ORREYED: You're making an exhibition of yourself!

SIR GEORGE: Look 'ere – !

LADY ORREYED: Come along, I tell you!

He hesitates, utters a few inarticulate sounds, then snatches up a fragile ornament from the table, and is about to dash it on to the ground. LADY ORREYED *retreats, and* PAULA *goes to him.*

PAULA: George!

He replaces the ornament.

SIR GEORGE (*shaking* PAULA'S *hand*): Good ni', Mrs Tanqueray.

LADY ORREYED (*to* PAULA): Good-night, darling. Wish Aubrey good-night for me. Now, Dodo? (*She goes out.*)

SIR GEORGE (*to* PAULA): I say, are you goin' to sit up for ol' Aubrey?

PAULA: Yes.

SIR GEORGE: Shall I keep you company?

PAULA: No, thank you, George.

SIR GEORGE: Sure?

PAULA: Yes, sure.

SIR GEORGE (*shaking hands*): Good-night again.

PAULA: Good-night.

> *She turns away. He goes out, steadying himself carefully.* DRUMMLE *appears outside the window, smoking.*

DRUMMLE (*looking into the room, and seeing* PAULA): My last cigar. Where's Aubrey?

PAULA: Gone down to The Warren, to see Mrs Cortelyon home.

DRUMMLE (*entering the room*): Eh? Did you say Mrs Cortelyon?

PAULA: Yes. She has brought Ellean back.

DRUMMLE: Bless my soul! Why?

PAULA: I – I'm too tired to tell you, Cayley. If you stroll along the lane you'll meet Aubrey. Get the news from him.

DRUMMLE (*going up to the window*): Yes, yes. (*Returning to* PAULA.) I don't want to bother you, only – the anxious old woman, you know. Are you and Aubrey – ?

PAULA: Good friends again?

DRUMMLE (*nodding*): Um.

PAULA (*giving him her hand*): Quite, Cayley, quite.

DRUMMLE (*retaining her hand*): That's capital. As I'm off so early tomorrow morning, let me say now – thank you for your hospitality. (*He bends over her hand gallantly, then goes out by the window.*)

PAULA (*to herself*): 'Are you and Aubrey – ?' 'Good friends again?' 'Yes.' 'Quite, Cayley, quite.'

> *There is a brief pause, then* AUBREY *enters hurriedly, wearing a light overcoat and carrying a cap.*

AUBREY: Paula dear! Have you seen Ellean?

PAULA: I found her here when I came down.

AUBREY: She – she's told you?

PAULA: Yes, Aubrey.

AUBREY: It's extraordinary, isn't it! Not that somebody should fall in love with Ellean or that Ellean herself should fall in love. All that's natural enough and was bound to happen, I suppose, sooner or later. But this young fellow! You know his history?

PAULA: His history?

AUBREY: You remember the papers were full of his name a few months ago?

PAULA: Oh, yes.

AUBREY: The man's as brave as a lion, there's no doubt about that; and, at the same time, he's like a big good-natured schoolboy, Mrs Cortelyon says. Have you ever pictured the kind of man Ellean would marry some day?

PAULA: I can't say that I have.

AUBREY: A grave, sedate fellow I've thought about – hah! She has fallen in love with the way in which Ardale practically laid down his life to save those poor people shut up in the Residency. (*Taking of his coat.*) Well, I suppose if a man can do that sort of thing, one ought to be content. And yet – (*Throwing his coat on the settee.*) I should have met him tonight, but he'd gone out. Paula dear, tell me how you look upon this business.

PAULA: Yes, I will – I must. To begin with, I – I've seen Mr Ardale.

AUBREY: Captain Ardale?

PAULA: Captain Ardale.

AUBREY: Seen him?

PAULA: While you were away he came up here, through our grounds, to try to get a word with Ellean. I made her fetch him in and present him to me.

AUBREY (*frowning*): Doesn't Captain Ardale know there's a lodge and a front door to this place? Never mind! What is your impression of him?

PAULA: Aubrey, do you recollect my bringing you a letter – a letter giving you an account of myself – to the Albany late one night – the night before we got married?

AUBREY: A letter?

PAULA: You burnt it; don't you know?

AUBREY: Yes; I know.

PAULA: His name was in that letter.

AUBREY (*going back from her slowly, and staring at her*): I don't understand.

PAULA: Well – Ardale and I once kept house together. (*He remains silent, not moving.*) Why don't you strike me? Hit me in the face – I'd rather you did! Hurt me! hurt me!

AUBREY (*after a pause*): What did you – and this man – say to each other – just now?

PAULA: I – hardly – know.

AUBREY: Think!

PAULA: The end of it all was that I – I told him I must inform you of – what had happened . . . he didn't want me to do that . . . I declared that I would . . . he dared me to. (*Breaking down.*) Let me alone! – oh!

AUBREY: Where was my daughter while this went on?

PAULA: I – I had sent her out of the room . . . that is all right.

AUBREY: Yes, yes – yes, yes. (*He turns his head towards the door.*)

PAULA: Who's that?

A SERVANT *enters with a letter.*

SERVANT: The coachman has just run up with this from The Warren, sir. (AUBREY *takes the letter.*) It's for Mrs Tanqueray, sir; there's no answer.

The SERVANT *withdraws.* AUBREY *goes to* PAULA *and drops the letter into her lap; she opens it with uncertain hands.*

PAULA (*reading it to herself*): It's from – him. He's going away – or gone – I think. (*Rising in a weak way.*) What does it say? I never could make out his writing.

She gives the letter to AUBREY *and stands near him, looking at the letter over his shoulder as he reads.*

AUBREY (*reading*): 'I shall be in Paris by tomorrow evening. Shall wait there, at Meurice's, for a week, ready to receive any communication you or your husband may address to me. Please invent some explanation to Ellean. Mrs Tanqueray, for God's sake, do what you can for me.'

PAULA *and* AUBREY *speak in low voices, both still looking at the letter.*

PAULA: Has he left The Warren, I wonder, already?

AUBREY: That doesn't matter.

PAULA: No, but I can picture him going quietly off. Very likely he's walking on to Bridgeford or Cottering tonight, to get the first train in the morning. A pleasant stroll for him.

AUBREY: We'll reckon he's gone, that's enough.

PAULA: That isn't to be answered in any way?

AUBREY: Silence will answer that.

PAULA: He'll soon recover his spirits, I know.

AUBREY: You know. (*Offering her the letter.*) You don't want this, I suppose?

PAULA: No.

AUBREY: It's done with – done with.

He tears the letter into small pieces. She has dropped the envelope; she searches for it, finds it, and gives it to him.

PAULA: Here!

AUBREY (*looking at the remnants of the letter*): This is no good; I must burn it.

PAULA: Burn it in your room.

AUBREY: Yes.

PAULA: Put it in your pocket for now.

AUBREY: Yes.

He does so. ELLEAN *enters and they both turn, guiltily, and stare at her.*

ELLEAN (*after a short silence, wonderingly*): Papa –

AUBREY: What do you want, Ellean?

ELLEAN: I heard from Willis that you had come in; I only want to wish you good-night. (PAULA *steals away, without looking back.*) What's the matter? Ah! Of course, Paula has told you about Captain Ardale?

AUBREY: Well?

ELLEAN: Have you and he met?

AUBREY: No.

ELLEAN: You are angry with him; so was I. But tomorrow when he calls and expresses his regret — tomorrow —

AUBREY: Ellean — Ellean!

ELLEAN: Yes, papa?

AUBREY: I — I can't let you see this man again. (*He walks away from her in a paroxysm of distress, then, after a moment or two, he returns to her and takes her to his arms.*) Ellean! my child!

ELLEAN (*releasing herself*): What has happened, papa? What is it?

AUBREY (*thinking out his words deliberately*): Something has occurred, something has come to my knowledge, in relation to Captain Ardale, which puts any further acquaintanceship between you two out of the question.

ELLEAN: Any further acquaintanceship . . . out of the question?

AUBREY: Yes.

Advancing to her quickly, but she shrinks from him.

ELLEAN: No, no — I am quite well. (*After a short pause.*) It's not an hour ago since Mrs Cortelyon left you and me together here; you had nothing to urge against Captain Ardale then.

AUBREY: No.

ELLEAN: You don't know each other; you haven't even seen him this evening. Father!

AUBREY: I have told you he and I have not met.

ELLEAN: Mrs Cortelyon couldn't have spoken against him to you just now. No, no, no; she's too good a friend to both of us. Aren't you going to give me some explanation? You can't take this position towards me — towards Captain Ardale — without affording me the fullest explanation.

AUBREY: Ellean, there are circumstances connected with Captain Ardale's career which you had better remain ignorant of. It must be sufficient for you that I consider these circumstances render him unfit to be your husband.

ELLEAN: Father!

AUBREY: You must trust me, Ellean; you must try to understand the depth of my love for you and the — the agony it gives me to hurt you. You must trust me.

ELLEAN: I will, father; but you must trust me a little too. Circumstances connected with Captain Ardale's career?

AUBREY: Yes.

ELLEAN: When he presents himself here tomorrow of course you will see him and let him defend himself?

AUBREY: Captain Ardale will not be here tomorrow.

ELLEAN: Not! You have stopped his coming here?

AUBREY: Indirectly – yes.

ELLEAN: But just now he was talking to me at that window! Nothing had taken place then! And since then nothing can have – ! Oh! Why – you have heard something against him from Paula.

AUBREY: From – Paula!

ELLEAN: She knows him.

AUBREY: She has told you so?

ELLEAN: When I introduced Captain Ardale to her she said she had met him in London. Of course! It is Paula who has done this!

AUBREY (*in a hard voice*): I – I hope you – you'll refrain from rushing at conclusions. There's nothing to be gained by trying to avoid the main point, which is that you must drive Captain Ardale out of your thoughts. Understand that! You're able to obtain comfort from your religion, aren't you? I'm glad to think that's so. I talk to you in a harsh way, Ellean, but I feel your pain almost as acutely as you do. (*Going to the door.*) I – I can't say anything more to you tonight.

ELLEAN: Father! (*He pauses at the door.*) Father, I'm obliged to ask you this; there's no help for it – I've no mother to go to. Does what you have heard about Captain Ardale concern the time when he led a wild, a dissolute life in London?

AUBREY (*returning to her slowly and staring at her*): Explain yourself!

ELLEAN: He has been quite honest with me. One day – in Paris – he confessed to me – what a man's life is – what his life had been.

AUBREY (*under his breath*): Oh!

ELLEAN: He offered to go away, not to approach me again.

AUBREY: And you – you accepted his view of what a man's life is!

ELLEAN: As far as *I* could forgive him, I forgave him.

AUBREY (*with a groan*): Why, when was it you left us? It hasn't taken you long to get your robe 'just a little dusty at the hem!'

ELLEAN: What do you mean?

AUBREY: Hah! A few weeks ago my one great desire was to keep you ignorant of evil.

ELLEAN: Father, it is impossible to be ignorant of evil. Instinct, common instinct, teaches us what is good and bad. Surely I am none the worse for knowing what is wicked and detesting it!

AUBREY: Detesting it! Why, you love this fellow!

ELLEAN: Ah, you don't understand! I have simply judged Captain Ardale as we all pray to be judged. I have lived in imagination through that one week in India when he deliberately offered his life back to God to save those wretched, desperate people. In his whole career I see now nothing but that one week; those few hours bring him nearer the Saints, I believe, than fifty uneventful years of mere blamelessness would have done! And so, father, if Paula has reported anything to Captain Ardale's discredit –

AUBREY: Paula – !

ELLEAN: It must be Paula; it can't be anybody else.

AUBREY: You – you'll please keep Paula out of the question. Finally, Ellean, understand me – I have made up my mind. (*Again going to the door.*)

ELLEAN: But wait – listen! I have made up my mind also.

AUBREY: Ah! I recognise your mother in you now!

ELLEAN: You need not speak against my mother because you are angry with me!

AUBREY: I – I hardly know what I'm saying to you. In the morning – in the morning –

He goes out. She remains standing, and turns her head to listen. Then, after a moment's hesitation she goes softly to the window, and looks out under the verandah.

ELLEAN (*in a whisper*): Paula! Paula!

PAULA *appears outside the window and steps into the room; her face is white and drawn, her hair is a little disordered.*

PAULA (*huskily*): Well?

ELLEAN: Have you been under the verandah all the while – listening?

PAULA: N – no.

ELLEAN: You *have* overheard us – I see you have. And it *is* you who have been speaking to my father against Captain Ardale. Isn't it? Paula, why don't you own it or deny it?

PAULA: Oh, I – I don't mind owning it; why should I?

ELLEAN: Ah! You seem to have been very very eager to tell your tale.

PAULA: No, I wasn't eager, Ellean. I'd have given something not to have had to do it. I wasn't eager.

ELLEAN: Not! Oh, I think you might safely have spared us all for a little while.

PAULA: But, Ellean, you forget I – I am your step-mother. It was my – my duty – to tell your father what I – what I knew –

ELLEAN: What you knew! Why, after all, what can you know! You can only speak from gossip, report, hearsay! How is it possible that you – ! (*She stops abruptly. The two women stand staring at each other for a moment; then ELLEAN backs away from PAULA slowly.*) Paula!

PAULA: What – what's the matter?

ELLEAN: You – you knew Captain Ardale in London!

PAULA: Why – what do you mean?

ELLEAN: Oh!

She makes for the door, but PAULA *catches her by the wrist.*

PAULA: You shall tell me what you mean!

ELLEAN: Ah! (*Suddenly, looking fixedly in* PAULA*'s face.*) You know what I mean.

PAULA: You accuse me!

ELLEAN: It's in your face!

PAULA (*hoarsely*): You – you think I'm – that sort of creature, do you?

ELLEAN: Let me go!

PAULA: Answer me! You've always hated me! (*Shaking her.*) Out with it!

ELLEAN: You hurt me!

PAULA: You've always hated me! You shall answer me!

ELLEAN: Well, then, I have always – always –

PAULA: What?

ELLEAN: I have always known what you were!

PAULA: Ah! Who – who told you?

ELLEAN: Nobody but yourself. From the first moment I saw you I knew you were altogether unlike the good women I'd left; directly I saw you I knew what my father had done. You've wondered why I've turned from you! There – that's the reason! Oh, but this is a horrible way for the truth to come home to every one! Oh!

PAULA: It's a lie! It's all a lie! (*Forcing* ELLEAN *down upon her knees.*) You shall beg my pardon for it. (ELLEAN *utters a loud shriek of terror.*) Ellean, I'm a good woman! I swear I am! I've always been a good woman! You dare to say I've ever been anything else! It's a lie! (*Throwing her off violently.*)

AUBREY *re-enters.*

AUBREY: Paula! (PAULA *staggers back as* AUBREY *advances. Raising* ELLEAN.) What's this? What's this?

ELLEAN (*faintly*): Nothing. It – it's my fault. Father, I – I don't wish to see Captain Ardale again.

She goes out, AUBREY *slowly following her to the door.*

PAULA: Aubrey, she – she guesses.

AUBREY: Guesses?

PAULA: About me – and Ardale.

AUBREY: About you – and Ardale?

PAULA: She says she suspected my character from the beginning . . . that's why she's always kept me at a distance . . . and now she sees through – (*She falters; he helps her to the ottoman, where she sits.*)

AUBREY (*bending over her*): Paula, you must have said something — admitted something —

PAULA: I don't think so. It — it's in my face.

AUBREY: What?

PAULA: She tells me so. She's right! I'm tainted through and through; anybody can see it, anybody can find it out. You said much the same to me tonight.

AUBREY: If she has got this idea into her head we must drive it out, that's all. We must take steps to — What shall we do? We had better — better — What — what? (*Sitting and staring before him.*)

PAULA: Ellean! So meek, so demure! You've often said she reminded you of her mother. Yes, I know now what your first marriage was like.

AUBREY: We must drive this idea out of her head. We'll do something. What shall we do?

PAULA: She's a regular woman too. She could forgive *him* easily enough — but *me!* That's just a woman!

AUBREY: What *can* we do?

PAULA: Why, nothing! She'd have no difficulty in following up her suspicions. Suspicions! You should have seen how she looked at me! (*He buries his head in his hands. There is silence for a time, then she rises slowly, and goes and sits beside him.*) Aubrey!

AUBREY: Yes.

PAULA: I'm very sorry.

Without meeting her eyes, he lays his hand on her arm for a moment.

AUBREY: Well, we must look things straight in the face. (*Glancing round.*) At any rate, we've done with this.

PAULA: I suppose so. (*After a brief pause.*) Of course, she and I can't live under the same roof any more. You know she kissed me tonight, of her own accord.

AUBREY: I asked her to alter towards you.

PAULA: That was it, then.

AUBREY: I — I'm sorry I sent her away.

PAULA: It was my fault; I made it necessary.

AUBREY: Perhaps now she'll propose to return to the convent, — well, she must.

PAULA: Would you like to keep her with you and — and leave me?

AUBREY: Paula — !

PAULA: You needn't be afraid I'd go back to — what I was. I couldn't.

AUBREY: Sssh, for God's sake! We — you and I — we'll get out of this place . . . what a fool I was to come here again!

PAULA: You lived here with your first wife!

AUBREY: We'll get out of this place and go abroad again, and begin afresh.

PAULA: Begin afresh?

AUBREY: There's no reason why the future shouldn't be happy for us – no reason that I can see –

PAULA: Aubrey!

AUBREY: Yes?

PAULA: You'll never forget this, you know.

AUBREY: This?

PAULA: Tonight, and everything that's led up to it. Our coming here, Ellean, our quarrels – cat and dog! – Mrs Cortelyon, the Orreyeds, this man! What an everlasting nightmare for you!

AUBREY: Oh, we can forget it, if we choose.

PAULA: That was always your cry. How *can* one do it!

AUBREY: We'll make our calculations solely for the future, talk about the future, think about the future.

PAULA: I believe the future is only the past again, entered through another gate.

AUBREY: That's an awful belief.

PAULA: Tonight proves it. You must see now that, do what we will, go where we will, you'll be continually reminded of – what I was. I see it.

AUBREY: You're frightened tonight; meeting this man has frightened you. But that sort of thing isn't likely to recur. The world isn't quite so small as all that.

PAULA: Isn't it! The only great distances it contains are those we carry within ourselves – the distances that separate husbands and wives, for instance. And so it'll be with us. You'll do your best – oh, I know that – you're a good fellow. But circumstances will be too strong for you in the end, mark my words.

AUBREY: Paula –!

PAULA: Of course I'm pretty now – I'm pretty still – and a pretty woman, whatever else she may be, is always – well, endurable. But even now I notice that the lines of my face are getting deeper; so are the hollows about my eyes. Yes, my face is covered with little shadows that usen't to be there. Oh, I know I'm 'going off'. I hate paint and dye and those messes, but, by-and-by, I shall drift the way of the others; I sha'n't be able to help myself. And then, some day – perhaps very suddenly, under a queer, fantastic light at night or in the glare of the morning – that horrid, irresistible truth that physical repulsion forces on men and women will come to you, and you'll sicken at me.

AUBREY: I –!

PAULA: You'll see me then, at last, with other people's eyes; you'll see me just as your daughter does now, as all wholesome folks see women like me. And I shall have no weapon to fight with – not one serviceable little bit of prettiness left me to defend myself with! A worn-out creature – broken up, very likely, some time before I ought to be – my hair bright, my eyes dull, my body too thin or too stout, my cheeks raddled and ruddled – a ghost, a wreck, a caricature, a candle that gutters, call such an end what you like! Oh, Aubrey, what shall I be able to say to you then? And this is the future you talk about! I know it – I know it! (*He is still sitting staring forward; she rocks herself to and fro as if in pain.*) Oh, Aubrey! Oh! Oh!

AUBREY: Paula –! (*Trying to comfort her.*)

PAULA: Oh, and I wanted so much to sleep tonight! (*Laying her head upon his shoulder. From the distance, in the garden, there comes the sound of DRUMMLE's voice; he is singing as he approaches the house.*) That's Cayley, coming back from The Warren. (*Starting up.*) He doesn't know, evidently. I – I won't see him!

> *She goes out quickly. DRUMMLE's voice comes nearer. AUBREY rouses himself and snatches up a book from the table, making a pretence of reading. After a moment or two, DRUMMLE appears at the window and looks in.*

DRUMMLE: Aha! my dear chap!

AUBREY: Cayley?

DRUMMLE (*coming into the room*): I went down to The Warren after you?

AUBREY: Yes?

DRUMMLE: Missed you. Well? I've been gossiping with Mrs Cortelyon. Confound you, I've heard the news!

AUBREY: What have you heard?

DRUMMLE: What have I heard! Why – Ellean and young Ardale! (*Looking at AUBREY keenly.*) My dear Aubrey! Alice is under the impression that you are inclined to look on the affair favourably.

AUBREY (*rising and advancing to DRUMMLE*): You've not – met – Captain Ardale?

DRUMMLE: No. Why do you ask? By-the-bye, I don't know that I need tell you – but it's rather strange. He's not at The Warren tonight.

AUBREY: No?

DRUMMLE: He left the house half-an-hour ago, to stroll about the lanes; just now a note came from him, a scribble in pencil, simply telling Alice that she would receive a letter from him tomorrow. What's the matter? There's nothing very wrong, is there! My dear chap, pray forgive me if I'm asking too much.

AUBREY: Cayley, you – you urged me to send her away!

DRUMMLE: Ellean! Yes, yes. But – but – by all accounts this is quite an eligible young fellow. Alice has been giving me the history –

AUBREY: Curse him! (*Hurling his book to the floor.*) Curse him! Yes, I do curse him – him and his class! Perhaps I curse myself too in doing it. He has only led 'a man's life' – just as I, how many of us, have done! The misery he has brought on me and mine it's likely enough we, in our time, have helped to bring on others by this leading 'a man's life'! But I do curse him for all that. My God, *I've* nothing more to fear – I've paid *my* fine! And so I can curse him in safety. Curse him! Curse him!

DRUMMLE: In Heaven's name, tell me what's happened?

AUBREY (*gripping* DRUMMLE's *arm*): Paula! Paula!

DRUMMLE: What?

AUBREY: They met to-night here. They – they – they're not strangers to each other.

DRUMMLE: Aubrey!

AUBREY: Curse him! My poor, wretched wife! My poor, wretched wife!

The door opens and ELLEAN *appears. The two men turn to her. There is a moment's silence.*

ELLEAN: Father . . . father . . .

AUBREY: Ellean?

ELLEAN: I – I want you. (*He goes to her.*) Father . . . go to Paula! (*He looks into her face, startled.*) Quickly – quickly! (*He passes her to go out, she seizes his arm, with a cry.*) No, no; don't go!

He shakes her off and goes. ELLEAN *staggers back towards* DRUMMLE.

DRUMMLE (*to* ELLEAN): What do you mean? What do you mean?

ELLEAN: I – I went to her room – to tell her I was sorry for something I had said to her. And I *was* sorry – I *was* sorry. I heard the fall. I – I've seen her. It's horrible.

DRUMMLE: She – she has – !

ELLEAN: Killed – herself? Yes – yes. So everybody will say. But I know – I helped to kill her. If I had only been merciful!

She faints upon the ottoman. He pauses for a moment irresolutely – then he goes to the door, opens it, and stands looking out.

Further Reading

Squire and Marie Bancroft, *On and Off the Stage* (Richard Bentley, 1888).

Daniel Barrett, *T.W. Robertson and the Prince of Wales's Theatre* (Peter Lang Publishing, 1995).

Ian Bradley, *The Complete Annotated Gilbert and Sullivan*, (Oxford University Press, 1996).

Kellow Chesney, *The Victorian Underworld* (Penguin, 1972). Fascinating historical background. Section on prize fighters and the underworld inhabited by the Smiffel Lamb.

Sidney Dark and Roland Grey, *W.S. Gilbert, his Life And Letters* (Methuen, 1923). Old-style biography.

John Dawick, *Pinero, a theatrical life* (University of Colorado Press, 1993).

Tracy C. Davis, *Actresses as Working Women: their Social Identity in Victorian Culture* (Routledge, 1991).

Maurice Willson Disher, *Blood and Thunder: Mid-Victorian Melodrama and its Origins* (Frederick Muller, 1949).

Viv Gardner and Susan Rutherford (eds) *The New Woman and Her Sisters. Feminism and Theatre 1850–1914* (Harvester Wheatsheaf, 1992).

Augustine Godwin, *Gilbert and Sullivan: a critical appreciation of the Savoy Operas* (J.M. Dent, 1926). Foreword by G.K. Chesterton.

Eric Griffiths, *The Printed Voice of Victorian Poetry* (Oxford University Press, 1989).

Henry Arthur Jones, Introduction to *The English Stage: Being an Account of the Victorian Drama* by Augustin Filon (John Milne, 1897).

T.W. Robertson, *Collected Works* (Samuel French, 1889). Includes a memoir by his son.

Jane Stedman, *W.S. Gilbert, A Classic Victorian and his Theatre* (Oxford University Press, 1996).

John Stokes, *In The Nineties* (Harvester Wheatsheaf, 1985).

Stephen Wyatt (ed.), *Pinero: Three Plays* (Methuen, 1985). Includes *The Magistrate, The Second Mrs Tanqueray, Trewlany of the Wells.*

NOTES ON THE TEXTS

MANSFIELD PARK

'. . . there is something so *maternal* in her manner'. Maria's
character Agatha was the mother of Crawford's Frederick. *Lovers'
Vows* was adapted from Kotzebue's German play *Das Kind der Liebe*
by Mrs Inchbald and first acted in 1798. The plot turns on Agatha
who, in her youth, was seduced by Baron Wildenhaim (Mr Yates).
The Baron deserts her and Agatha is left destitute. Frederick, the son
of this unhappy union, learns the story of his birth and goes out
begging, where he chances upon his unknown father and tries to rob
him. After his arrest his identity is revealed and with the aid of the
pastor Anhalt (Edmund Bertram) he persuades the Baron to marry
Agatha. The Baron also agrees to let his daughter Amelia (Mary
Crawford) marry Anhalt instead of the rich Count Cassell (Mr
Rushworth).

VANITY FAIR

'and ladies wore gigots' Leg of mutton sleeves.
Bedwin Sands The Orient was in vogue in the later eighteenth
century and early nineteenth century. Byron visited the Levant and
there was a crop of novels and poems with exotic, Middle or Far
Eastern settings. Sands is obviously a composite of the aristocratic
traveller and his oriental tales are likely to be bogus. He has a black
slave; note that slavery was not abolished in Britain until 1833 and it
would have been possible for Sands to buy the man in England –
perhaps in Bristol, the chief port for 'the Africa trade'. The oriental
theme of the first charade is self-consciously fashionable with its
excessive use of 'oriental' words.
Brian de Bois Guilbert The charming baddie of Sir Walter Scott's
Ivanhoe (1819), de Bois Guilbert was a good character turned evil, a
Templar knight.
Janizaries Turkish infantry constituting the Sultan's guard first

organised in the fourteenth century from children of Christians, abolished 1826.

Tarboosh A cap of cloth, usually red, with a tassel, worn by Muslims.

Narghile A tobacco pipe where the smoke passes through water, a hookah.

Yataghan A sword with a double-curved blade.

Maraschino Cherry liqueur. Not a likely exchange, but a good story.

Odalisque A female slave or concubine in a harem.

Piastres Small Turkish coins.

Zuleikah A common name in Persian poetry, also Potiphar's wife. Potiphar was an Old Testament Egyptian captain and master of Joseph. His wife, who is unnamed in the Bible, tried to seduce Joseph and then when she failed, tore her clothes and pretended that he had raped her.

Firman An edict or order. Presumably in this case a death warrant. The bow-string will be used to strangle Hassan. This part of the charade represents the first two syllables, Aga.

'it is sunrise in the desert' This part of the charade represents Memnon, the demi-god whose statue at Thebes in Egypt was said to give forth a musical sound when touched by the dawn.

'the last act opens' This part represents the whole word, Agamemnon. The story chosen by Becky is the murder of Agamemnon, commander in chief of the Greek expedition against Troy, by his wife Clytemnestra, sister of Helen of Troy. Ægisthus was Clytemnestra's lover. Iphigenia was Agamemnon's daughter who he killed as a sacrifice to appease Artemis. The theme of female treachery is spectacularly crass given Becky's antics with Lord Steyne.

Anax andrôn King of men.

'as Calypso did . . .' One of the delays on Ulysses' voyage home from Troy was due to the attractions of the nymph Calypso whose charms kept him on her island.

Montessu and Noblet Parisian dancers. Mr Wagg is thought to be Theodore Hook (1788–1841) who may also be the original of Lucian Gay in Disraeli's novel *Coningsby* (1844).

Philomèle Latin authors have it that Philomela was turned into a nightingale after being raped by Tereus.

Stephens, Caradoni, Ronzi de Begnis All professional female singers who retired respectably. Catherine Stevens married the Earl of Essex, Maria Caradoni retired from the stage to sing in oratorios and concerts, de Begnis retired while still young. Becky obviously has similar ambitions.

Vestris Madame Vestris (1797–1856), famous manager of the Olympic and later the Lyceum.

Taglioni Marie Taglione (1809–1884), a famous dancer.

ACTING PROVERBS

'fatal day at Worcester' Battle of Worcester (1651) when Cromwell's forces crushed Prince Charles' attempt to recover the throne. In the aftermath of battle, Charles managed to escape to France.

Old Noll Nickname for Oliver Cromwell (1599–1658), leader of the Parliamentarians and later Lord Protector.

Zounds An attempt at historical language. Contraction of 'God's wounds', popularly considered to be an 'olden days' royal oath.

The Young Man Code for Charles II, a pun.

Wilmot First Earl of Rochester. Father of the Restoration wit John Wilmot who was known for his obscene verse.

Amalek Amalek, grandson of Esau, established the Armalekites, an ancient group of nomadic marauders.

'the men of Moab' Genuinely seventeenth-century term for Roman Catholics, taken from the people of Moab in the Bible.

'Nell's teeth' An anachronism. Charles is supposedly referring to Nell Gwyn (1650–87), but she didn't become his mistress until after the Restoration in 1660.

Jahaleel Killjoy Cromwell's men's names are parodies of the Puritan likng for unwieldy Old Testament Christian names combined with virtues.

'by the Dutch –' Cromwell instigated action against the Dutch merchant navy in 1651 which led to war the following year.

Midianites Nomads living in the desert south of Moab. Allied with the Amalekites to oppress Israelites. Among the first to domesticate camels.

THE SORROWS OF SATAN

'Russia!' Refers to the tyranny of the Tsars before the revolutions. **Silenus** A satyr. **Sic transit gloria mundi! Vale!** Bid farewell to this world's transitory glory.

NICHOLAS NICKLEBY

'Many and many is the circuit this pony has gone.' Crummles is making a joke. Regional theatres were divided up by area into circuits usually worked by one or two theatrical families who travelled between the theatres in their territory. T.W. Robertson's family were in control of the theatres on the Lincoln circuit.

'. . . the infant phenomenon' Crummles and his daughter are thought to be based on T.D. Davenport and his eight-year-old daughter Jean who leased the Portsmouth Theatre in 1837. According to the playbill, 'the most celebrated Juvenile Actress of the day' danced a hornpipe, played Shylock and sang songs while wearing various national costumes.

'a part of twelve lengths' A length was forty lines. Mr Lenville has quite a bit to learn.

'at her benefit' A special performance when the profits went to a particular company member who also got to choose the play.

'Mortal Struggle . . . Ways and Means' Play titles. *Mortal Struggle* has not been identified, perhaps Dickens made it up to parody the Crummles company's struggles for subsistence. *Intrigue* was by John Poole, and George Colman the younger wrote *Ways and Means; or, A Trip to Dover.*

'just turn that into English, and put your name on the title-page' Lots of plays at this time were straight translations from French originals. T.W. Robertson adapted plays for his family troupe.

'Rover too . . . and Cassio and Jeremy Diddler' Jack Rover was the hero of the hugely popular *Wild Oats; or, The Strolling Gentleman* (1791) by John O'Keeffe. Cassio is presumably from Shakespeare's *Julius Caesar* and Jeremy Diddler was the hero of James Kenney's farce *Raising the Wind* (1803). Diddler's habit of borrowing money without repaying was the source of the slang term 'to diddle'.

FAR FROM THE MADDING CROWD

Nijni Novgorod Russian city, now Gorky, known for its fairs.

Vermiculated Hardy seems to intend a double sense, meaning both that the horns themselves had a worm-like, sinuous twist and also that the natural grooves in the surface of the horn were like the tracks worms eat in wood.

The Royal Hippodrome The Hippodrome in Leicester Square opened in 1800. Famous for its naval dramas staged in a huge tank of water, it later became a music hall.

Cheesewring Jan Coggan means he is being squeezed in a press of people like milk curds in a wring when cheese is made.

jumping-jack A Jack-in-the-box which folds flat before springing up again.

'The brig . . . Troy read the articles' Troy was picked up by a sailing ship and joined the Navy. To do this he had to agree to abide by the Articles of War, the governing regulations.

Tom King Turpin's side-kick.

Shutter An improvised stretcher board.

AN EVENING AT A WHITECHAPEL GAFF

gaff An improvised theatre to be found in the rougher parts of London and other cities where entry usually cost one penny. The lowest types were nicknamed 'blood tubs' because of the violence of the melodrama staged there. Not to be confused with private theatres where stage-struck youths paid to act.

'the Game of High Toby' High toby is slang for the highway as a place for robbery. A high toby man is a superior highwayman, one well-armed and well-mounted. The term is sixteenth-century in origin.

'it is against the law' Not true generally. Perhaps there was a specific regulation restricting this area of Whitechapel, or maybe the theatre lacked the necessary magistrate's licence.

Hammercloth Cloth covering the driver's seat in a state or family coach.

THE ENCHANTED ISLE

Scene directions These present Prospero as a Victorian showman in an example of ironical Victorian self-referentiality.

'pleases . . . "the cheese" is' As with the closely related extravaganza form, burlesque favoured rhyming couplets which raised a laugh by their ludicrous rhymes and punning use of language rather than actual dramatic action. Much of the wit is verbal.

'boxes . . . tears' Terrible pun on boxing ears typical of this form. See the next two lines for equally excruciating examples. Unlikely that modern audiences would have the patience to untangle all these puns, let alone relish them as the Victorians did.

et cetera From *Childe Harold's Pilgrimage* (1812–18) by Byron. The lines are:

> 'Hereditary bondsman! Know ye not
> Who would be free themselves must strike the blow?'

fairy special train The elaborate staging of this must have been one of the highlights of any performance.

'Who am dat knocking at de door?' Booth's edition cites a minstrel song of the early 1840s 'Who Dat Knocking at My Door?'

uncle's Pawnbroker.

Richelieu See Act III scene i of Bulwer-Lytton's *Richelieu* (1839).

'Rappel was beating' A rappel is drum roll calling men to arms.

'to work six ottomans in Berlin wool' An ottoman was a blackless, armless sofa-seat often upholstered in tapestry. Berlin wool is a type of tapestry wool.

JASON IN COLCHIS

Jason and the Argonauts enter Jason, son of Aeson, was brought up in exile by the centaur Chiron after his father was usurped. On reaching manhood Jason returned to Iolcus to claim his throne but was induced to go on a voyage in search of the Golden Fleece which King Aeetes had stolen from Jason's cousin. Jason set sail in the Argo and after many adventures he and his crew arrived in Colchis. King Aeetes set them the task of yoking a pair of fire-breathing bulls to plough a field, sow it with teeth from the dragon guarding the fleece and kill the warriors who would spring up from the field. Jason did

this with help from the king's daughter Medea who was in love with Jason. Jason retrieved the fleece and fled with Medea back to Iolcus.
'He's partial to an ardent spirit' Obviously gin, which is flavoured with juniper berries. See Medea's 'gin-cantation'.
Sally Lunn A type of bun or cake.

THE COLLEEN BAWN

Colleen Bawn Literally, the fair-haired girl, or the pretty girl. Boucicault adapted the play from a novel, *The Collegians*, (1829) by Irish writer Gerald Griffin (1803–40). In Griffin's novel young Cregan is lured by wealth and beauty into allowing the murder of his humble wife. The novel was based on a real murder in Limerick. Griffin attended the trial as a young reporter in 1819. *The Colleen Bawn* was also made into an opera, *The Lily of Killarney* (1862). Boucicault collaborated on the libretto.
'I'm free trade – coppleens, mules and biddys' Coppleen: corruption of coppaleen, a pony. A biddy is more usually a maidservant but may also be a donkey.
'deep in the chest as a pool-a-dhoil' The Devil's Pool within the water cave where Danny later tries to drown Eily.
Myles na Coppaleen Miles of the ponies.
Nebuckadezzar Nebuchadnezzar, king of Babylon whose power was legendary.
'Thurra mon dhoil, what's that?' Your soul to the devil, what's that?
spalpeen Slang for a tramp.
'acushla agrah asthore machree! . . . avourneen!' My pulse, my love, my treasure, my heart . . . my darling.
'Eily a suilish machree!' Eily, light of my heart.
poteen Strong spirit distilled illicitly.
cruiskeen Little jug.
'Eily, aroon' Eily, my darling.
'Gramchree, mavourneen, slanta gal avourneen,/ Gramachree ma Cruiskeen Lawn, Lawn, Lawn,' Love of my heart, my darling, bright health of my darling/ Love of my heart my little full jug, full, full.
shebeen House where distilled liquor is sold illicitly without a licence.

Eily utters a cry and falls – Tableau Ending acts with a tableau or picture was a convention of the Victorian stage. Actors would group into an arresting 'picture' to show the moment of high emotional drama, in this case Eily's faint, and then stand motionless in their attitudes for a few moments before the curtain came down. See also the end of Act III Scene ii, the end of *The Factory Lad* and glossary of stage terms.

'after going Leandering' Anne is referring to the myth of Leander, who swam the Hellespont to be with Hero.

'Shule, shule, agrah!' Walk, walk, my love!

'she'll get the ring itself in that helpin' of kale-canon' Kale-canon, more usually colcannon, is Irish mashed potato with vegetables.

alaina My dear.

'Mavourneen a sweelish machree' My darling, light of my heart.

Colleen Ruaidh Red-haired girl.

'Eily astoir' Eily my treasure.

'avick . . . Oh! hone' My son . . . Alas!

asthore My treasure.

THE FACTORY LAD

'the poor man's friend!' There may be an allusion here to The Poor Man's Friend, a famous cure-all patent remedy invented at the end of the eighteenth century by Dr Giles Roberts (1766–1834), a Methodist preacher and chemist from Bridport in Dorset. By 1830 the remedy was being sold in America. The remedy's commercial success continued after Dr Roberts' death. The distinctive bottles are relatively common finds in old china middens. More gruesomely, 'poor man's friend' was also a nickname for the hangman's rope.

'the Game Laws' Legislation protecting animals and birds regarded as game, e.g. hares, rabbits and partridges, from being killed by anyone but the landowner. Fiercely applied, the punishment could be transportation or even death.

'parish charity' *The Factory Lad* is set in a time of social turmoil. Charitable relief for the poor was based on the Speenhamland System which geared the size of relief payments to the price of bread and the number of family dependents. *The Factory Lad* played at The

Surrey in 1832 when post-war deflation and increased unemployment meant taxpayers were paying high rates of relief for the poor. Ratepaper resistance and public criticism of the system led to a Royal Commission being established to inquire into the poor relief system. In 1832 the Royal Commission on Poor Laws made its report. In 1834 the Poor Law Amendment Act was passed creating a central Poor Law Board. The same year a group of farmworkers from Tolpuddle in Dorset were transported for attempting to form a trade union. The intervening year of 1833 saw the first Factory Act passed, making it illegal to employ children aged less than nine years old in a factory.

'the Harriers' The village pub. Its name is symbolic, harriers are hounds and huntsmen who chase the hare, one of the tastiest and most protected of quarries. The secondary meaning of harrying in the sense of laying waste also lurks behind the name, given the fact that the plan to burn the factory is hatched there.

SOCIETY

'lucifer seller' Match seller.

'In place of the clock' The clock on the masthead of *The Times*.

'honour, love, obedience, troops of friends' From *Macbeth* Act V scene iii. Sidney quotes accurately for once.

Jemmy Masseys Jem Mace (1831–1910) English heavyweight prizefighting champion.

the Fancy The prizefighting fraternity.

'tin on the mill' Wager money on the fight.

'a cross' The fight's fixed.

Big Ben A topical reference. Big Ben first struck the hour in 1859.

canaille Vile herd, plebs.

esclandre Unpleasant notoriety, a scene which might give rise to such.

Fra Poco *Ere Long*, a popular aria from Donizetti's opera *Lucia di Lammermoor* (1835), H.J. Byron's burlesque of the opera accompanied *Society*'s London premiere at The Prince of Wales on 11 November 1865.

'in suffering everything, has suffered nothing.' A misquote from *Hamlet* Act III scene ii, should be 'in suff'ring all, that suffers nothing'.

MacUsquebaugh Usquebaugh is Gaelic for water of life, i.e. whisky.

portmonnaie Rather euphemistic term for wallet. Its use suggests that Sidney is too financially embarrassed, in a gentlemanly sort of way, to speak plainly.

'Cock-a-doodle' The song originally had a journalistic verse which was cut in performance and replaced with the commercial variant because it was considered too offensive for the critics. The omitted verse was:

> When papers speak with puff and praise
> Of things and people nowadays
> Of kings, quack-medicines, railways – plays –
>   Old laws, inventions new
> Alliterative words and fuss
> Big adjectives, terms curious,
> Sounds fury – what's all this to us
>   But cock-a-doodle-doo!

In his 'Memoir' prefacing the original *Collected Works*, Robertson's son says the tune was adopted from a familiar song called 'As Mars and Bellona', a burlesque of which was sung at The Savage Club when Robertson was a member. The amatory stanza is also different in the Lord Chamberlain's copy; for more detail on this and other changes which were not performed see editorial note in *Plays by Tom Robertson*, edited by William Tydeman (Cambridge University Press, 1982).

'Send in some whiskey – Irish – and the devil.' The punchline of a protracted pun. A printer's devil was the errand boy for a printer.

copperas Ferrous sulphate, an ingredient in printing ink.

'on the tapis' On the table cloth, under discussion. Current newspaper slang; *OED* cites its use in a report in the *York Herald* from 1865. Its use in the theatre was much older, Henry Mayhew's short farce *The Wandering Minstrel* used the phrase in 1834.

the lines between inverted commas can be omitted Cost considerations means that these lines were left out in the premiere and the Bancrofts' revivals so that the action could all be set at Lord Ptarmigant's.

Mr Si–len–us Lady Ptarmigant insults Tom by calling him after the satyr who made King Midas drunk, i.e. a drunken old coward. Tom later says he'd like to return the taunt by calling her Ariadne.

'He'll do for dummy' He'll make up the numbers, also has the sense of 'fool'.

'What's that?' The pipe joke is reworked by W.S. Gilbert in Act II of *Princess Ida* when Lady Blanche finds cigars in the discarded handbag of one of the men disguised as women.

'bramah-locked' Joseph Bramah (1748–1814) inventor. His lock was patented in 1784. See Asa Briggs' *Victorian Things* (Penguin Books, 1990) p.42, on the importance of locks and the Victorians' desire to make things impregnable.

regalia Another pun, a regalia was a present of choice food, drink or entertainment. It was also the name of a large and expensive cigar.

'Thou art mated to a clown' Sidney misquotes Tennyson's 'Locksley Hall' (1842) lines 47 to 50. The lines should be:

As the husband is, the wife is: thou art mated with a clown,
And the grossness of his nature will have weight to drag thee
    down.

He will hold thee, when his passion shall have spent its novel
    force,
Something better than his dog, a little dearer than his horse.

'Bradshaw' Train timetable, still exists.

'A tumbler of the waters No. 2' Possibly a childish joke. Spa water was usually very smelly.

'Dutch-metalled' An alloy of copper and zinc used in cheap imitation of gold.

bonnets To crush down his hat over his eyes.

'pin money' Money settled on wife at marriage.

pur sang from the French, 'pure blood'. Well brought up.

'who galloped to death in the service of his country' The implication is that Charles died a hero in the Charge of the Light Brigade (1854) at Balaclava.

THE MIKADO

'A thing of shreds and patches,' See *Hamlet* Act III scene iv line

103 'A king of shreds and patches'. Nanki-Poo is a prince disguised. Medieval mystery plays used to dress the figure of Vice in motley as a mimic king. Hard to tell whether Gilbert extends his pun to include this older meaning, but if he did then it makes the satire all the sharper.

'Oh, willow, willow!' Later editions of the libretto replace 'willow' with 'sorrow'.

'And if you call for a song of the sea' The immense popularity of nautical themes can be traced back to Douglas Jerrold's nautical melodrama *Black Ey'd Susan* (1829) which gave rise to a whole genre of plays featuring jolly jack tars singing sea-shanties. Gilbert and Sullivan had already made two successful voyages into these waters with *H.M.S. Pinafore* (1878) and *The Pirates of Penzance* (1879).

'Don't mention it . . . all their posts at once' This speech of Pooh-Bah's yearns to become a classic 'patter' song.

'dine with middle class people' This particular service is often squeamishly omitted in modern performances.

'a dignified and potent officer' A phallic pun. Feminists might interpret Ko-Ko as a classic study of phallic impotence; he fails to marry the virgin Yum-Yum, is too incompetent to wield his executioner's sword effectively and ends up with the castrating virago Katisha. Ko-Ko is the only character apart from the Mikado whose name actually means something in Japanese. In fact it has numerous meanings including 'pickles' and 'trussed girder'.

'the pestilential nuisances who write for autographs' Gilbert liked fame but was famously tetchy.

'All children who are up in dates' Evidently one of Gilbert's pet annoyances. In *Princess Ida* (1884) Hilarion accuses Lady Psyche of being:

> 'that learned little Psyche, who
> At dinner parties, brought into dessert,
> Would tackle visitors with 'You don't know
> Who first determined longitude – I do –
> Hipparchus 'twas – BC one sixty-three!'

'All persons who in shaking hands' Probably a reference to limp handshakes rather than Masonic ones. Gilbert joined the Masons in

1871. Gilbert varied the items of annoyance to keep them topical. There is a children's version of this song which refers to a nursemaid.

'nigger serenader, and the others of his race' Rendered as 'banjo serenader' in modern performances.

'dresses like a guy' Dresses like a tramp, unfashionable or ludicrous attire. Does not mean dresses as a man.

'Nisi Prius' Unless before; a legal term. Refers to assize judges who heard cases 'nisi prius'. Gilbert engaged in several lawsuits.

Lucius Junius Brutus Founder of the Roman Republic and Tanginer.

'con fuoco' Passionately. 'Gioco' means joke, and 'toco' is schoolboy slang for a punishment diet of bread and water.

'perform the Happy Dispatch with this dagger' A visual pun on 'Bridport dagger', i.e. a hangman's rope. The slang term arose because most hangman's ropes were made in Bridport, Dorset, a centre of the net- and rope-making industry. The preceding stage direction 'enter Nanki-Poo *with a rope in his hands*', Ko-Ko's question, 'what are you going to do with that rope?' and Nanki-Poo's actual preparation of the rope make it clear that Gilbert intended this pun. Productions which show Nanki-Poo threatening to stab himself with a knife are mistaken. 'Happy dispatch' means suicide and may refer to the Japanese custom of committing suicide to atone for a mistake. Admittedly, this was done by disembowelling using a sword, but in this case the meaning is less specific and 'happy dispatch' is merely a slang term for suicide in general.

'O ni! bikkuri shakkuri to!' These are geniune Japanese words but they don't make much sense. The nearest translation is something like 'she devil, surprise, shock, oh!'.

gambado Fantastic movement or caper.

'Yes I am indeed beautiful' Yum-Yum's complacent appreciation of her own charms is similar to Maggie's in Gilbert's comedy *Engaged* (1877).

tocsin Alarm bell.

'Miya sama . . . na!' A Japanese war song of the 1870s, the Tokotonyare. The first verse says: 'Your majesty, your majesty, what is it that flutters in front of the stallion?' The chorus is legendary for containing an obscure but obscene Japanese joke playing on the meaning of 'finish'. Sadly, I have been unable to find an unexpurgated translation.

'is blacked like a nigger' Rendered as 'is painted with vigour' in modern performances.

'Parliamentary trains' Cheapest and slowest form of rail travel. It was a condition of the 1844 Act that all train companies should run at least one train a day which stopped at every station and charged fares at a penny a mile.

'Monday pops' Popular concerts held on a Monday.

'The criminal cried . . .' There is an odd divergence between the scansion of this song when read aloud, as Gilbert wrote it, and the way it is sung to Sullivan's music. Sullivan scans it on a rigid tum-ti-tum, which fits, but the true rhythm of the original is closer to Coleridge's ballad 'The Rime of the Ancient Mariner' (1798). If Gilbert was alluding to Coleridge the reference was lost on Sullivan. Ironically, Sullivan often complained that Gilbert's lyrics were too 'tum-ti-tum' to give scope for his composing genius. Was Sullivan being obtuse or was he merely reading the lines according to contemporary notions about metre and rhythm? Gerard Manley Hopkins' sprung rhythm was unintelligible to some of his contemporaries. See Ted Hughes' essay 'Myths, Metres, Rhythms' in *Winter Pollen, Occasional Prose* (Faber and Faber, 1994) for a discussion of the 'unsayable' in poetry which may also be the 'unhearable'.

persiflage Banter.

'On a tree by a river . . .' Gilbert's burlesque version of Desdemona's willow song in *Othello* Act IV scene ii. The effect is bathetic. The verses are also similar to verses by the poet Nicholas Rowe (1674–1718).

THE SECOND MRS TANQUERAY

bésique Bezique, a game of cards.

'tell Watts to balance the cart for three' Carriages with two wheels required balancing to make the weight sit over the axle so that the shafts would float against the horse's sides without exerting downward pressure on the harness. By 'cart' Paula probably means a governess cart, a vehicle of the type nowadays often referred to as a trap.

ottoman A cushioned seat, strictly speaking without back or arms, although Lady Orreyed has her head resting against the drum, this circular one must have a central pillar.

mustard plaster A hot poultice.

Residency Presumably the residence of the district controller or commissioner of the hill station in this part of India.

ruddled Ruddle or reddle was a type of red dye commonly used to mark sheep. See the reddleman in Hardy's *Return of the Native* (1878). Paula is comparing rouge to this coarse dye.

GLOSSARY OF VICTORIAN STAGE TERMS

The nineteenth century developed its own argot of stage terms. Usually these were abbreviated to the point of incomprehensibility to anyone outside the theatre.

act–drop a late eighteenth-century term for the painted cloth lowered between acts for scene shifting. Distinct from the front curtain, lowering of which signalled the end of the play.

backing an early type of scenery. Painted canvas was hung at the back of the stage and behind windows or doors to make the illusion of background, hence the term 'backed'. Largely replaced by the all-in-one box set of flats, first used in 1832 by Madame Vestris at the Olympic.

batten a row of lights above the stage.

C centre.

change a change of scenery done in full audience view.

check reduce light power.

close in conceal by sliding on stage scenery flats in grooves. (See below for explanation of grooves and flats.)

down can mean two things; moving downstage towards the audience and reducing the power of lights.

drop canvas-painted scene lowered from above.

flat came in pairs and formed the back scene, sliding apart to the side wings. They form the three walls of a box set.

grooves these were the slots in the floor of the stage and above which held the scenery. 1st grooves were those nearest the audience, 2nd grooves the next upstage. Often mentioned to indicate where actors enter, the grooves established entrance positions. Hence **L. 1E.**

L the actor's left. **R** is right.

L.C. left, centre for the actor. **R.C.** is right centre.

L.1E. first entrance (first grooves) on the actor's left. The entrance nearest the audience. **R.1E.** is the first entrance on the right.

L.2E the second entrance (second grooves) on the actor's left. **R.2E.** is the second entrance on the right.

L.U.E. the entrance farthest upstage on the actor's left, the backstage. **R.U.E.** is the entrance farthest upstage on the right.

picture or tableau acts which ended on a particularly melodramatic scene often closed with a picture when the actors would freeze into a living picture or tableau illustrative of the dramatic moment. The pose would be held for a short while before the drop or curtain came down.

practical real, can be used – as opposed to a painted illusion. Robertson insisted on real stage props.

set set scene. Scenery arrangement set up in advance of curtain or drop lifting. Pantomimes and extravaganzas sometimes featured a carpenter's scene played in front of a backcloth masking the elaborate scenery being erected behind.

up upstage, away from audience. Also to brighten the light.

SOURCES

The aim of this edition is to reproduce authentic texts that are as close as possible to those available to the original mass audiences. The editions prepared from the sources below have, however, been lightly regularised and corrected against later editions where it makes sense to do so.

Mansfield Park by Jane Austen is taken from the second edition of 1816 which was corrected by Austen. (Chapman and Hall). It has been checked against Dr R.W. Chapman's edition of 1923 (Oxford University Press).

Vanity Fair by William Makepeace Thackeray is taken from the first edition of 1848 (Bradbury and Evans).

Acting Proverbs, author anonymous (Routledge & Co, 1858).

The Sorrows of Satan by Marie Corelli is from the first edition (Methuen, 1895).

Nicholas Nickleby by Charles Dickens is from the Cheap Edition of 1848 (Chapman and Hall).

Far from the Madding Crowd by Thomas Hardy is from the Wessex Edition of 1912 (Macmillan).

'An Evening at a Whitechapel Gaff' is from *The Wilds of London* by James Greenwood (Chatto and Windus, 1874).

The Enchanted Isle by William and Robert Brough (National Acting Drama, 1848). First performed at the Royal Ampitheatre, Liverpool, 7 August 1848, and Adelphi Theatre, London, 20 November 1848.

Jason in Colchis by James Robinson Planché (S.G. Fairbrother, 1845). First performed at the Theatre Royal, Haymarket, Easter Monday 24 March 1845.

The Colleen Bawn by Dion Boucicault (Thomas Hailes Lacy, 1860). First performed at Laura Keene's Theatre, New York, 27 March 1860 and the Adelphi Theatre, London, 10 September 1860.

The Factory Lad by John Walker (Duncombe's British Theatre vol 11, 1825). Performance history unclear.

Society by Thomas William Robertson from *The Principal Dramatic Works of T.W. Robertson* (Samuel French, 1889). First performed at the Prince of Wales Theatre, Liverpool, 8 May 1865 and the Prince of Wales Theatre, London, 11 November 1865.

The Mikado by William Schwenck Gilbert (Chappell and Co, 1885). First performed at the Savoy Theatre, 14 March 1885. This is the original version of the libretto.

The Second Mrs Tanqueray by Arthur Wing Pinero (William Heinemann, 1895) by kind permission of Methuen Publishing Ltd, 215 Vauxhall Bridge Road, London. First performed at the St James's Theatre, London, 27 May 1893.

CHRONOLOGY

1800   Emma Hamilton performs her poses at William Beckford's Christmas party at Fonthill Abbey.

1803   Astley's Amphitheatre near Westminster Bridge burnt down and rebuilt.

1804   Child prodigy William Betty, 'The Infant Roscius', causes a sensation on the London stage. Napoleonic Wars: Britain joins coalition with Austria, Russia and Sweden.

1805   Battle of Trafalgar. Nelson defeats French and Spanish fleets.

1806   Royal Circus rebuilt in Blackfriars Road, London, becomes the Surrey Theatre under Robert Elliston with a ballet in every production, including Shakespeare, to evade Patent laws.

1808   Covent Garden theatre burns down, 23 firemen are killed, Handel's organ is destroyed along with manuscripts of several of his operas.

1809   Drury Lane destroyed by fire 15 years after installing the first 'iron' safety curtain. Charles Darwin and Alfred Tennyson born.

1811   Jane Austen begins writing *Mansfield Park*. William Makepeace Thackeray born in India. Prince of Wales becomes Regent due to George III's madness.

1812   Drury Lane rebuilt with money from the brewer, Samuel Whitbread. Charles Dickens born. War breaks out between Britain and America. Luddite riots in Nottinghamshire, Lancashire and Yorkshire.

1814   Edmund Kean's Drury Lane debut as Shylock. *Mansfield Park* published. Philip Astley dies. Robert Elliston leaves the Surrey and it becomes a circus again.

1815   Battle of Waterloo. Emma Hamilton dies in Calais.

1816   William Macready makes Covent Garden debut. Surrey re-opens as a theatre. Coleridge publishes *Christabel* and *Kubla Khan*. Gaslight widely used in London.

1817   Gas lighting in use at Drury Lane and Covent Garden theatres. Jane Austen dies in Winchester. Keats' *Poems* published.

1818   James Planché's first play *Amoroso, King of Little Britain*. Mary Shelley publishes *Frankenstein*. Karl Marx born in Prussia.

1819   Adelphi opens on the Strand. Peterloo massacre in Manchester. George Eliot born in Warwickshire.

1820   Planché's *The Vampire; or, The Bride of the Isles* introduces the vampire trap to the English stage. Dion Boucicault born in Dublin. George III dies, George IV accedes to the throne. Cato Street Conspiracy fails to murder government members and take over London.

1821   Death of Napoleon on exile in St Helena, and of Keats in Rome.

1822   Shelley drowns in Gulf of Spezia in Italy.

1823   Charles Kemble revives *King John* at Drury Lane with Planché's costumes.

1824   George Stephenson's *Locomotion* pulls the first passenger train on the Stockton to Darlington line.

1826   Lancashire Power Loom Riots.

1829   Jerrold's *Black-Ey'd Susan* revives reputation of the Surrey. Thomas William Robertson born. Daguerre and Niepce develop their photographic inventions in partnership.

1830   Madame Vestris takes on management of the Olympic and opens with Planché's *Olympic Revels*. William IV accedes to the throne. Swing Riots, agricultural risings in the South, are savagely suppressed.

1831   Michael Faraday demonstrates electromagnetic current.

1832   Goethe dies. First Reform Bill becomes law.

1833   Dramatic Copyright Act passed securing playwrights' control of work. Edmund Kean collapses while playing *Othello* and dies a week later. Charles Dickens produces private theatricals at his parents' home. Slavery abolished in British Empire. Factory Act bans labour of children aged under nine.

1834   H.J. Byron born. Robert Peel Prime Minister. Poor Law Amendment Act. Transportation of Tolpuddle Martyrs for forming a union.

1835   Charles Mathews appears for the first time at the Olympic in his own play *The Humpbacked Lover*.

1836   Dickens' *Pickwick Papers* begins. W.S. Gilbert born.

1837   Macready becomes manager of Covent Garden. Victoria accedes to the throne.

1838   Boucicault premieres *A Legend of the Devil's Dyke* at Theatre Royal in Brighton. Madame Vestris gives up the Olympic and marries Charles Mathews. Henry Irving born in Somerset. Dickens' *Nicholas Nickleby* begins. Chartists draw up their Six Points in The People's Charter, launched in Birmingham and endorsed all over country. Anti-Corn Law Association formed in Manchester. Paddington Station opened.

1839   Vestris and Charles Mathews take over Covent Garden from Macready. Marie Wilton born. Limelight used in the theatre for the first time. Chartists riot after first petition rejected.

1840   Queen Victoria marries Prince Albert. Thomas Hardy born in Dorset.

1841   Macready takes over Drury Lane. Boucicault's *London Assurance*. William Batty rebuilds Astley's and renames it after himself.

1842   Chartists present second petition to Parliament. Riots in the North.

1843   Theatre Regulation Act ends monopoly of patent theatres to present serious drama. Macready leaves Drury Lane. Henry James born in New York.

1844 Phelps takes over management of Sadler's Wells. Sarah Bernhardt born in Paris. Thackeray's *The Luck of Barry Lyndon*. Factory Act limits working hours for women and children.

1845 Irish famine begins.

1846 Repeal of the Corn Laws.

1847 Vestris and Mathews take over the Lyceum. Covent Garden re-opens as the Royal Italian Opera House. Ellen Terry born. Thackeray's *Vanity Fair* begins serial publication.

1848 Richard Shepherd takes over at the Surrey and establishes its reputation for melodrama. First Windsor Castle command performances. Electrical carbon-arc used in theatre. Chartists' third petition fails. Public Health Act passes. Waterloo Station opened. Karl Marx publishes *The Communist Manifesto*.

1849 Strindberg born.

1850 Ibsen completes *Catilina*. Wordsworth dies. Tennyson succeeds as Poet Laureate. Chartism finally collapses.

1851 Macready retires after playing Macbeth at Drury Lane. The Great Exhibition.

1852 Canterbury Hall opens in Lambeth as the first purpose-built music hall.

1853 Boucicault goes to USA.

1854 Madame Vestris retires. Oscar Wilde born in Dublin. Britain invades the Crimea – Charge of the Light Brigade – Tennyson's poem published.

1855 Arthur Wing Pinero and Marie Corelli born.

1856 Henry Irving makes debut at the Lyceum, Sunderland. Marie Wilton (later Mrs Bancroft) makes London debut.

George Bernard Shaw born in Dublin. Madame Vestris dies. Matrimonial Causes Act.

1857 Boucicault's *The Poor of New York* premieres. Indian Mutiny.

1858 New Covent Garden Opera opens.

1859 US premiere of Boucicault's *The Octoroon*. Charles Kean retires. Darwin publishes *On the Origin of the Species*.

1860 Boucicault returns to Britain and premieres *The Colleen Bawn*.

1861 Prince Albert dies. US Civil War breaks out.

1862 Sarah Bernhardt's first appearance at the Comédie Francaise, Paris. Ellen Terry makes her London debut at the Haymarket. Phelps ends Sadler's Wells management. Boucicault makes disastrous attempt at managing the former Astley's, attempting to turn it into the Theatre Royal, Westminster; theatre reverts to old name.

1863 W.M. Thackeray dies. London's first Underground line opened between Paddington and Farringdon by the Metropolitan Railway Company.

1864 Boucicault's *Arran-na-Pogue; or the Wicklow Wedding* at the Princess's Theatre, London. Adah Isaacs Menken plays the lead in the equestrian drama adapted from Byron's poem *Mazeppa* at Astley's. Robertson achieves first success with *David Garrick* at the Haymarket.

1865 Marie Wilton renovates the tumbledown Scala Theatre and reopens it as the Prince of Wales. Premiere of Robertson's *Society*. The Surrey burns down and is rebuilt to seat 2,161. Mrs Patrick Campbell born Beatrice Tanner. US Civil War ends.

1866 Robertson's *Ours* at the Prince of Wales. Gilbert's first dramatic work, the extravaganza *Dulcamara; or, the Little Duck and the Great Quack*. House of Commons Select Committee investigates theatrical licences and regulations. Women's suffrage movement is formed in Manchester.

1867 Robertson's *Caste*. Second Reform Act.

1868 Robertson's *Play*. Charles Kean dies.——

1869 Robertson's *School*. J.S. Mill's *The Subjection of Women*.

1870 Gilbert's first successful serious play *The Palace of Truth*. Dickens dies. Elementary Education Act. Franco-Prussian war breaks out.

1871 Gilbert and Sullivan first collaborate on *Thespis; or The Gods Grown Old* which opens at the Gaiety on Boxing Day. George and John Sanger, circus proprietors, take over Astley's. Irving stars in *The Bells* at the Lyceum. Robertson dies. Hardy publishes *Desperate Remedies*, George Eliot *Middlemarch*, Darwin *The Descent of Man*.

1872 Boucicault returns to US.

1874 Irving plays Hamlet at the Lyceum. Hardy publishes *Far from the Madding Crowd*.

1875 Boucicault premieres *The Shaughraun* in New York (written 1874). Ellen Terry plays Portia at the Prince of Wales.

1876 Queen Victoria proclaimed Empress of India.

1877 Gilbert's *Engaged*. Gilbert and Sullivan's *The Sorcerer* at the Opera Comique. Pinero's *£200 A Year* at the Globe Theatre. Electric street lighting introduced in London.

1878 Gilbert and Sullivan's *HMS Pinafore*. Irving takes control of the Lyceum with Terry as leading lady. Shakespeare Memorial Theatre opens in Stratford. *Daisy Miller* by Henry James published. First telephone exchange.

1879 Bancrofts takes over management of the Haymarket. Gilbert and Sullivan's *The Pirates of Penzance* opens in Paignton, transfers to New York and opens in London in 1880. Planché and Eliot die. Gladstone Prime Minister. First Boer War breaks out.

1881 Gilbert and Sullivan's anti-aesthete opera *Patience* transfers to the new Savoy Theatre, the first London theatre with electric light. Married Women's Property Act.

1882   Henry Arthur Jones' *The Silver King* premieres. Gilbert and Sullivan's *Iolanthe* opens at The Savoy and uses electric haloes for fairies.

1883   Irving first tours US.

1884   Gladstone's Reform Act enfranchises more male workers.

1885   Gilbert and Sullivan's *The Mikado*, Pinero's *The Magistrate*. Bancrofts retire from the Haymarket.

1886   Marie Corelli's first novel *A Romance of Two Worlds* published.

1887   Queen Victoria's Golden Jubilee.

1888   T.S. Eliot born in St Louis, Missouri. Box camera invented.

1889   Ibsen's *A Doll's House* performed in London for the first time.

1890   Mrs Patrick Campbell makes debut on London stage. Boucicault dies.

1891   Hardy's *Tess of the D'Urbervilles*. Free elementary education.

1892   Shaw's *Widowers' Houses*. Wilde's *Lady Windermere's Fan*.

1893   Premiere of Pinero's *The Second Mrs Tanqueray* with Mrs Patrick Campbell as Paula. Astley's declared unsafe.

1894   Shaw's *Arms and the Man* at the Avenue Theatre.

1895   Wilde imprisoned, Irving knighted. Shaw becomes drama critic for *The Saturday Review* and pleads for a less artificial drama. Astley's demolished. Marie Corelli publishes *The Sorrows of Satan*.

1896   Prince of Wales' Derby winner's victory shown on film at the Empire music hall Leicester Square. *The Grand Duke*, Gilbert and Sullivan's last opera at the Savoy.

ACKNOWLEDGEMENTS

The publishers gratefully acknowledge permission to reproduce all previously published material included in this volume.

Deborah Vlock, *Dickens, Novel Reading and the Victorian Popular Theatre* (Cambridge University Press) 1998
Eric Griffiths, *The Printed Voice of Victorian Poetry* (Oxford University Press) 1989
Marilyn Butler, *Jane Austen and the War of Ideas* (Oxford University Press) 1975
Michael Booth, *Victorian Spectacular Theatre* (Routledge) 1981
Harriet Ritvo, *The Animal Estate, The English and Other Creatures* (Havard University Press) 1987
Richard Altick, *The Shows of London* (Havard University Press) 1978
Goethe, trans. W. H. Auden & Elizabeth Mayer, *Italian Journey* (Harper Collins) 1962
Angus Wilson, *The Naughty Nineties* (Eyre Methuen) 1976, courtesy of Curtis Brown
Arthur Wing Pinero, *The Second Mrs Tanqueray* (Methuen) 1985

All attempts have been made to trace the copyright holders of all previously published material.